SHONEN JUMP MANGA

Vol. 20

DB: 36 of 42

STORY AND ART BY
AKIRA TORIYAMA

THE MAIN CHARACTERS

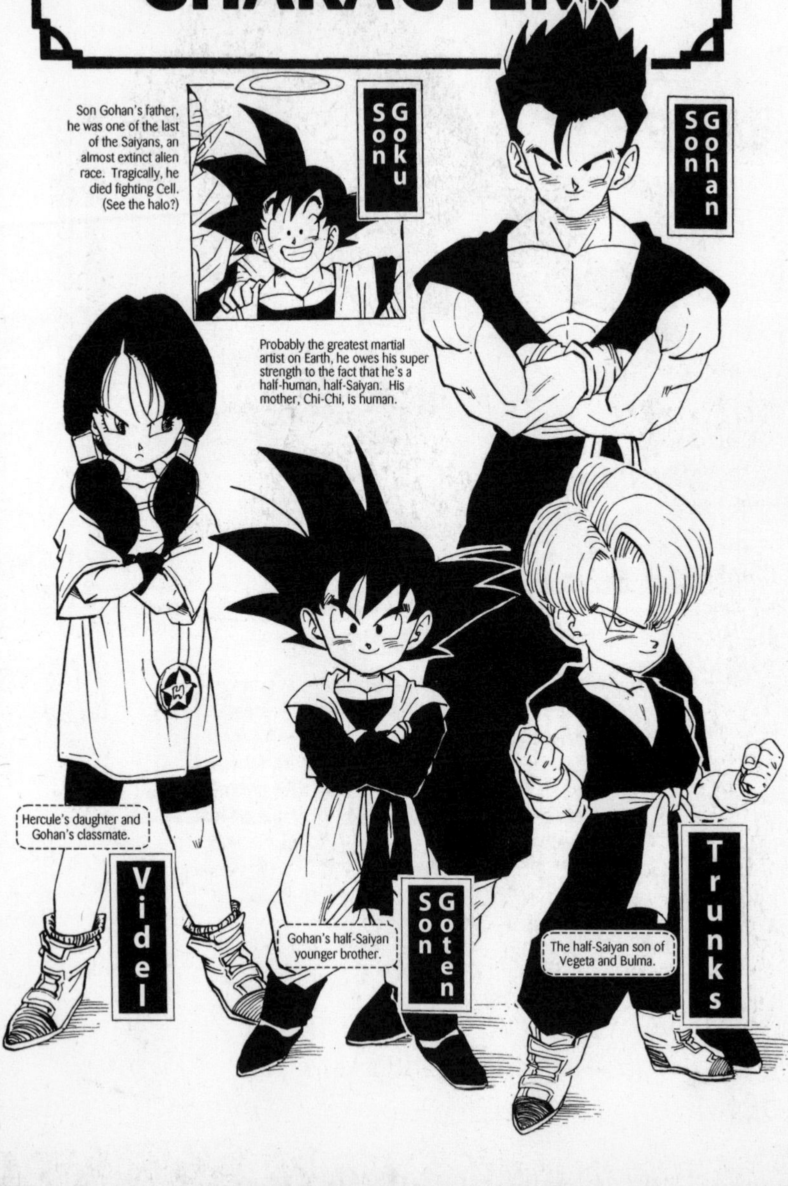

Son Gohan
Probably the greatest martial artist on Earth, he owes his super strength to the fact that he's a half-human, half-Saiyan. His mother, Chi-Chi, is human.
Son Goku
Son Gohan's father, he was one of the last of the Saiyans, an almost extinct alien race. Tragically, he died fighting Cell. (See the halo?)
Trunks
The half-Saiyan son of Vegeta and Bulma.
Son Goten
Gohan's half-Saiyan younger brother.
Videl
Hercule's daughter and Gohan's classmate.

鳥 山 明

I got on a bike for the first time in a while…and my legs turned into rubber from just a short ride. I went to Disneyland with my kids, ran around the park with them…and the next day I was in bed with a fever. Then we went to the beach. I'd always had a good arm, so I showed off by skipping stones against the water…and my arm got so sore I couldn't even draw. I'm so out of shape. Forget work, I have to go out and play more!
        —Akira Toriyama, 1993

Widely known all over the world for his playful, innovative storytelling and humorous, distinctive art style, **Dragon Ball** creator Akira Toriyama is also known in his native Japan for the wildly popular **Dr. Slump**, his previous manga series about the adventures of a mad scientist and his android "daughter." His hit series **Dragon Ball** ran from 1984 to 1995 in Shueisha's **Weekly Shonen Jump** magazine. He is also known for his design work on video games such as **Dragon Warrior**, **Chrono Trigger** and **Tobal No. 1**. His recent manga works include **Cowa!**, **Kajika**, **Sand Land**, **Neko Majin**, and a children's book, **Toccio the Angel**. He lives with his family in Japan.

DRAGON BALL Z VOL.20
SHONEN JUMP Manga Edition

STORY AND ART BY
AKIRA TORIYAMA

English Adaptation/Gerard Jones
Translation/Lillian Olsen
Touch-up Art & Lettering/Wayne Truman
Design/Sean Lee
Editor/Jason Thompson

In the original Japanese edition, DRAGON BALL and DRAGON BALL Z are known collectively as the 42-volume series DRAGON BALL. The English DRAGON BALL Z was originally volumes 17–42 of the Japanese DRAGON BALL.

Printed in the U.S.A.

Published by VIZ Media, LLC
P.O. Box 77010
San Francisco, CA 94107

10 9 8 7
First printing, May 2005
Seventh printing, October 2012

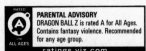

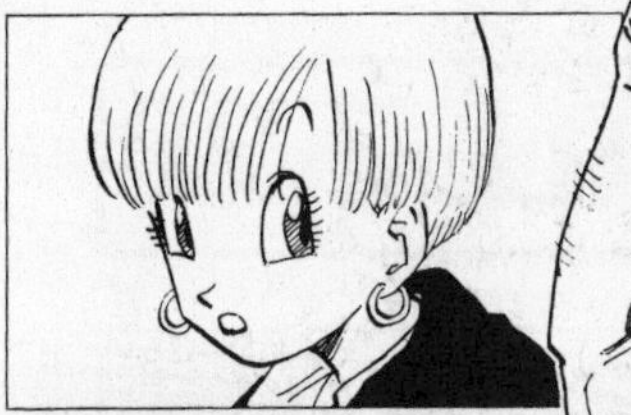

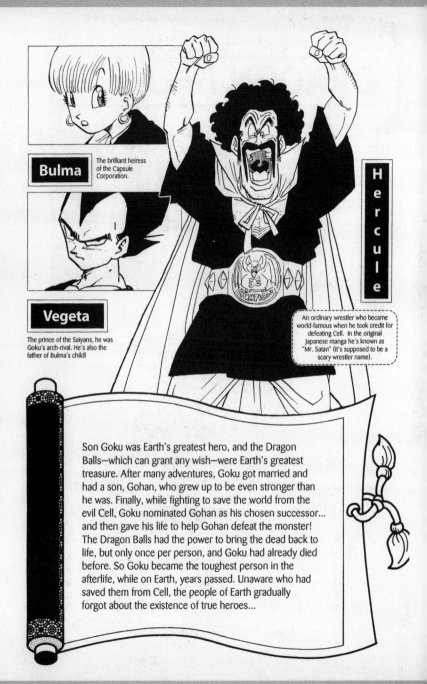

Bulma

The brilliant heiress of the Capsule Corporation.

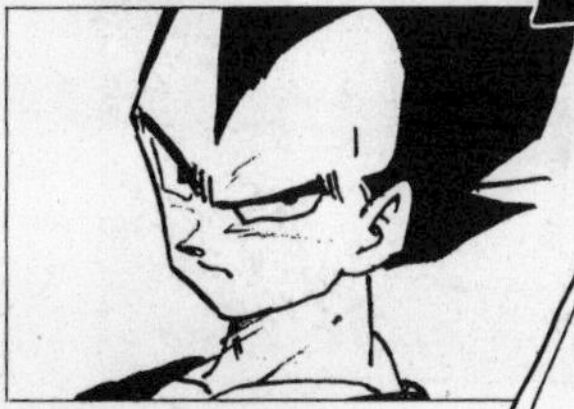

Vegeta

The prince of the Saiyans, he was Goku's arch-rival. He's also the father of Bulma's child!

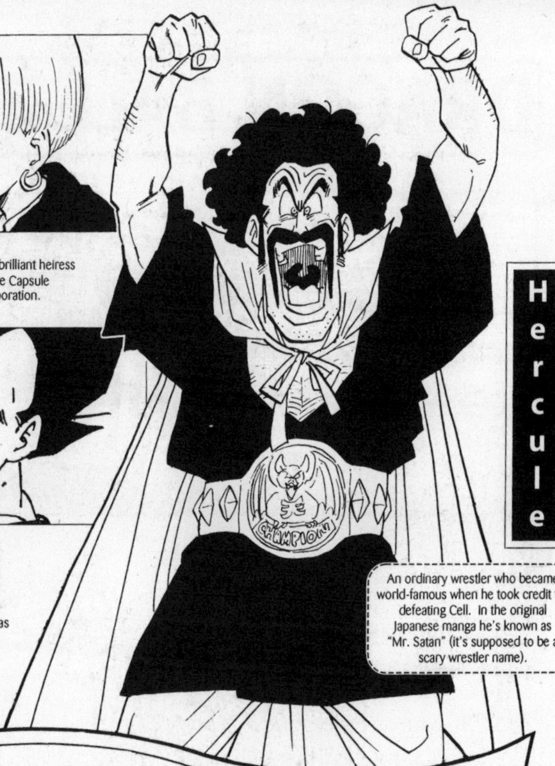
CHAMPION

Hercule

An ordinary wrestler who became world-famous when he took credit for defeating Cell. In the original Japanese manga he's known as "Mr. Satan" (it's supposed to be a scary wrestler name).

Son Goku was Earth's greatest hero, and the Dragon Balls—which can grant any wish—were Earth's greatest treasure. After many adventures, Goku got married and had a son, Gohan, who grew up to be even stronger than he was. Finally, while fighting to save the world from the evil Cell, Goku nominated Gohan as his chosen successor... and then gave his life to help Gohan defeat the monster! The Dragon Balls had the power to bring the dead back to life, but only once per person, and Goku had already died before. So Goku became the toughest person in the afterlife, while on Earth, years passed. Unaware who had saved them from Cell, the people of Earth gradually forgot about the existence of true heroes...

DRAGON BALL Z 20

WA HA HA HA! WHO DARES READ HERCULE'S CONTENTS?

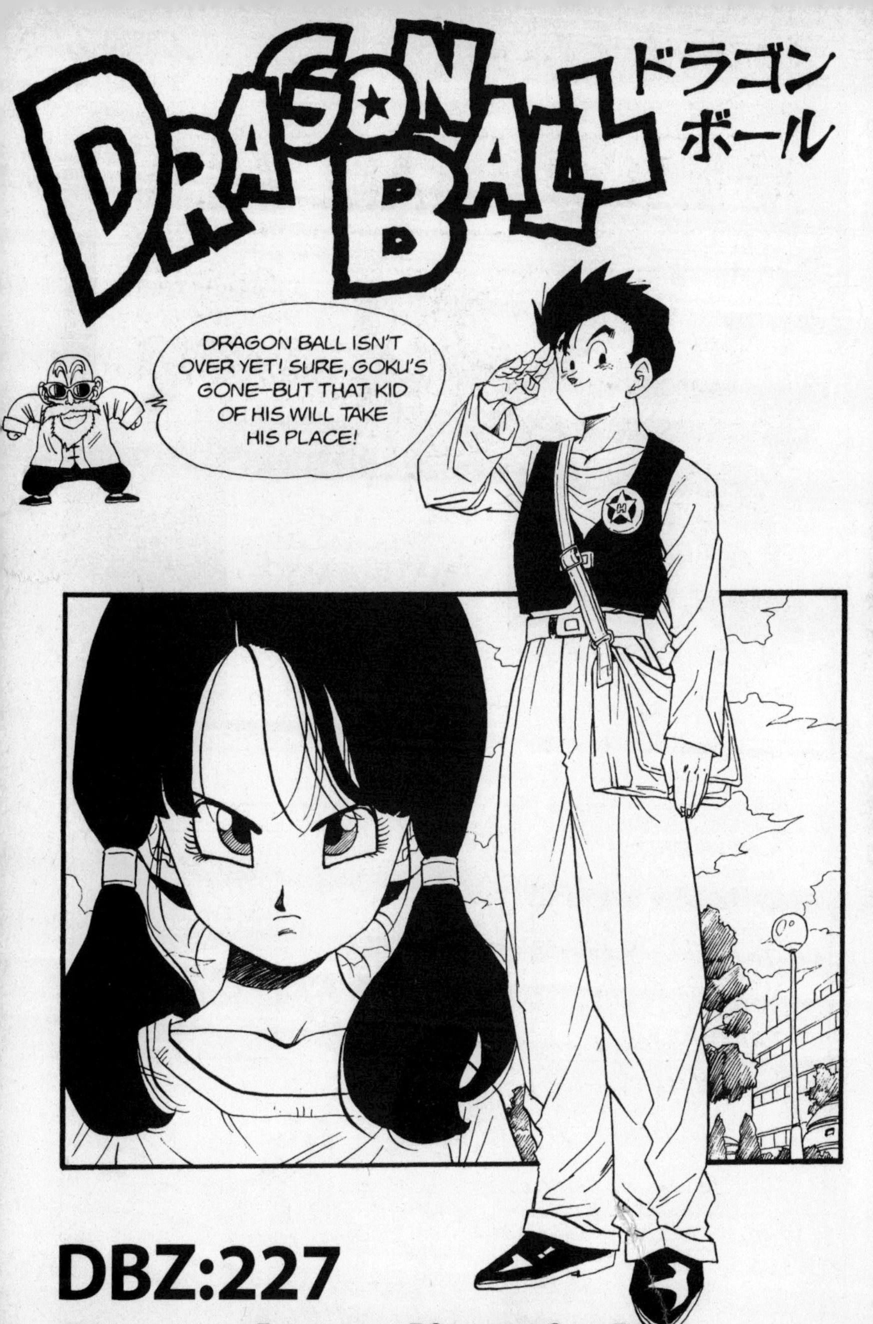
DRAGON BALL ISN'T OVER YET! SURE, GOKU'S GONE—BUT THAT KID OF HIS WILL TAKE HIS PLACE!

DBZ:227

Herculopolis High

READ THIS WAY

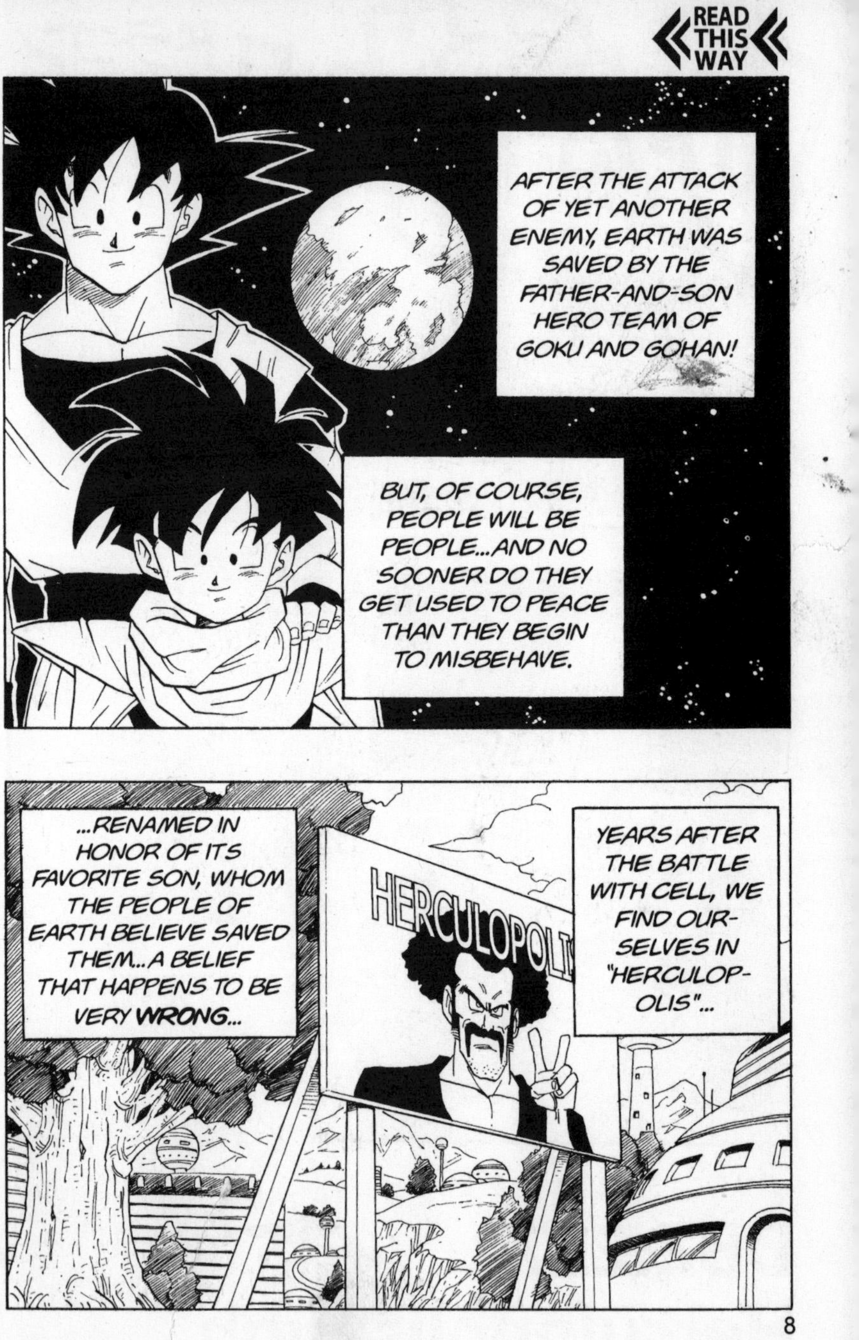

AFTER THE ATTACK OF YET ANOTHER ENEMY, EARTH WAS SAVED BY THE FATHER-AND-SON HERO TEAM OF GOKU AND GOHAN!
BUT, OF COURSE, PEOPLE WILL BE PEOPLE...AND NO SOONER DO THEY GET USED TO PEACE THAN THEY BEGIN TO MISBEHAVE.
YEARS AFTER THE BATTLE WITH CELL, WE FIND OUR-SELVES IN "HERCULOP-OLIS"...
HERCULOPOLI
...RENAMED IN HONOR OF ITS FAVORITE SON, WHOM THE PEOPLE OF EARTH BELIEVE SAVED THEM...A BELIEF THAT HAPPENS TO BE VERY **WRONG**...

READ THIS WAY

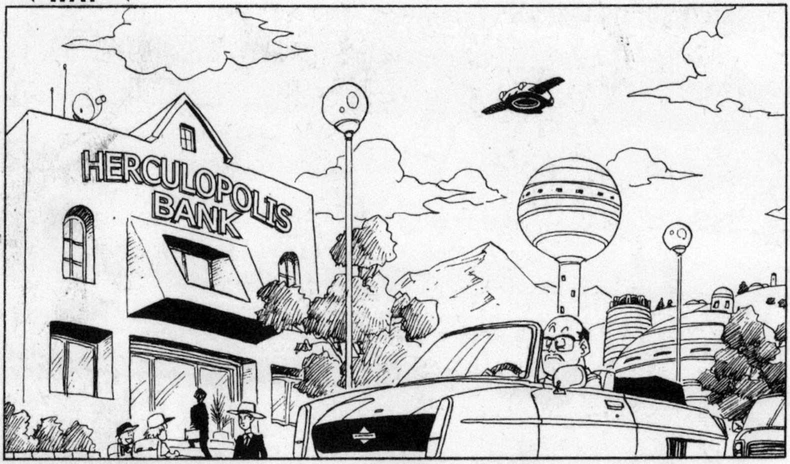
HERCULOPOLIS BANK

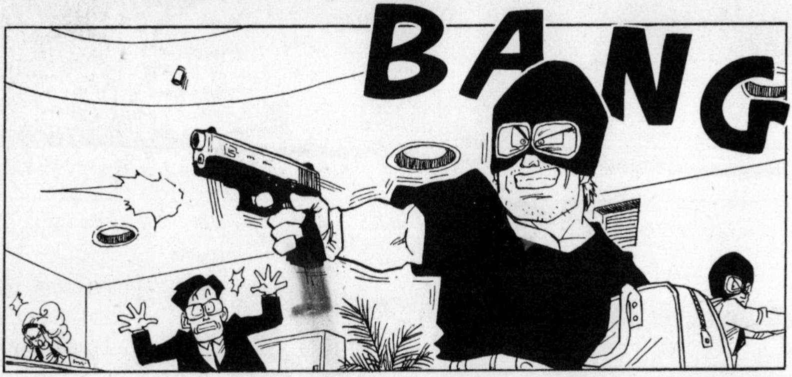
BANG

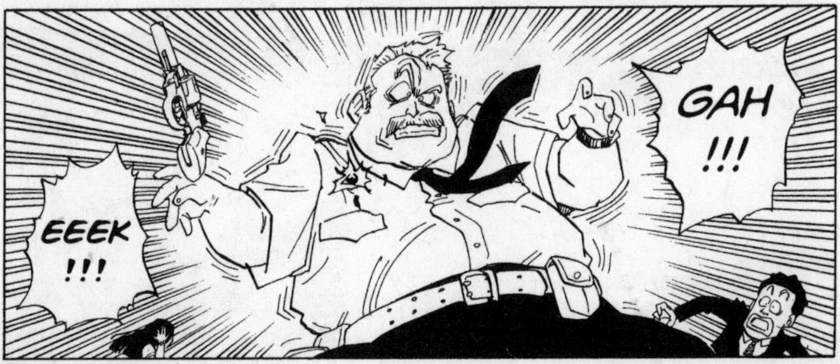
GAH !!!
EEEK !!!

READ THIS WAY

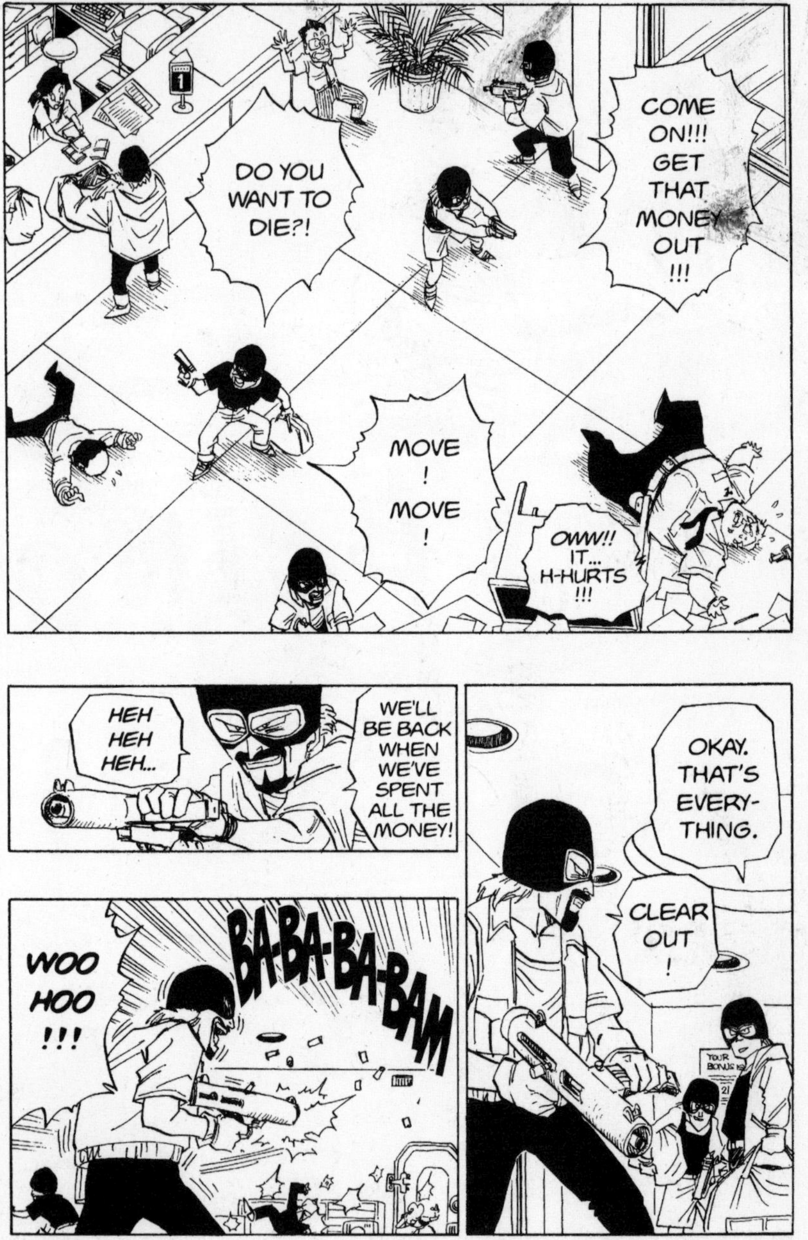
COME ON!!! GET THAT MONEY OUT !!!
DO YOU WANT TO DIE?!
MOVE ! MOVE !
OWW!! IT... H-HURTS !!!
OKAY. THAT'S EVERY-THING.
CLEAR OUT !
WE'LL BE BACK WHEN WE'VE SPENT ALL THE MONEY!
HEH HEH HEH...
BA-BA-BA-BAM
WOO HOO !!!

READ THIS WAY

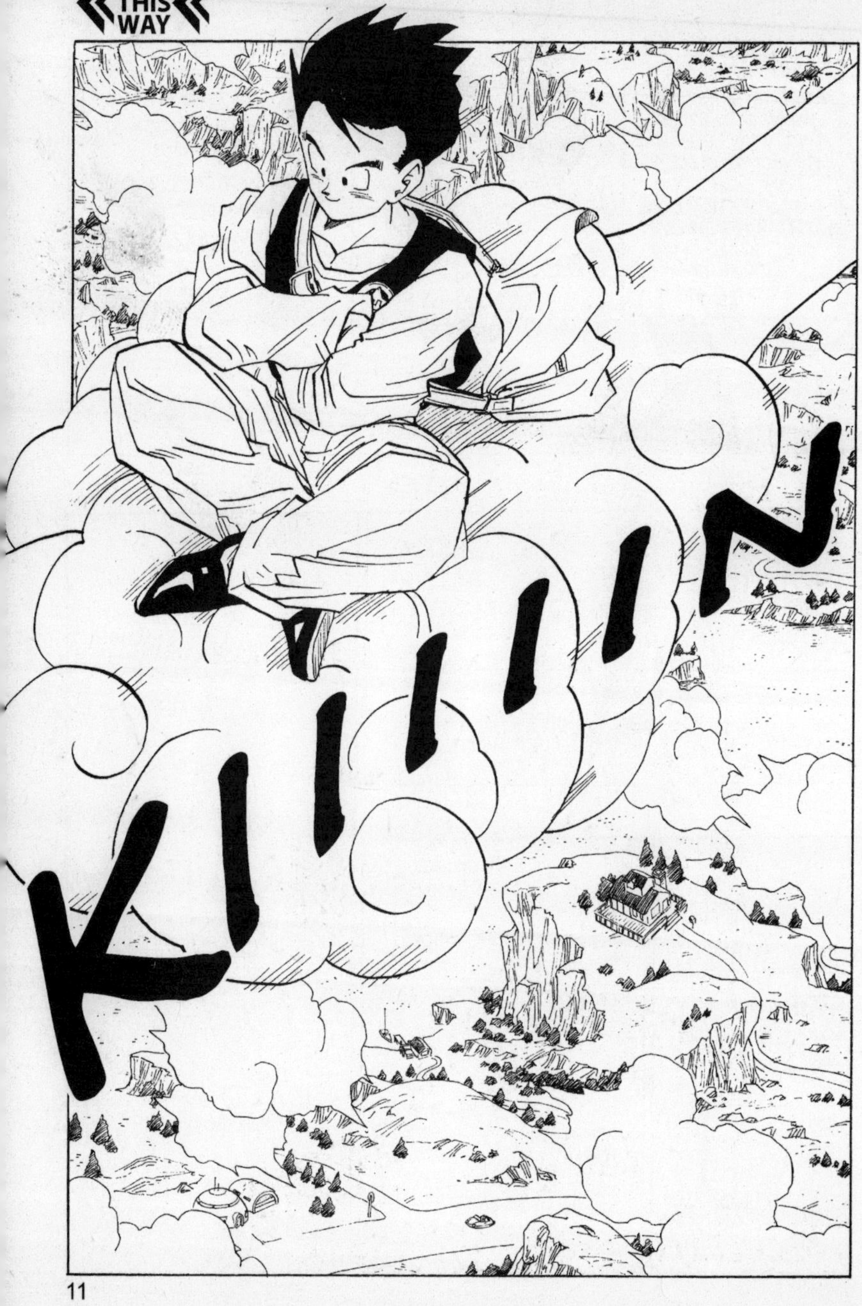
KIIIIIN

READ THIS WAY

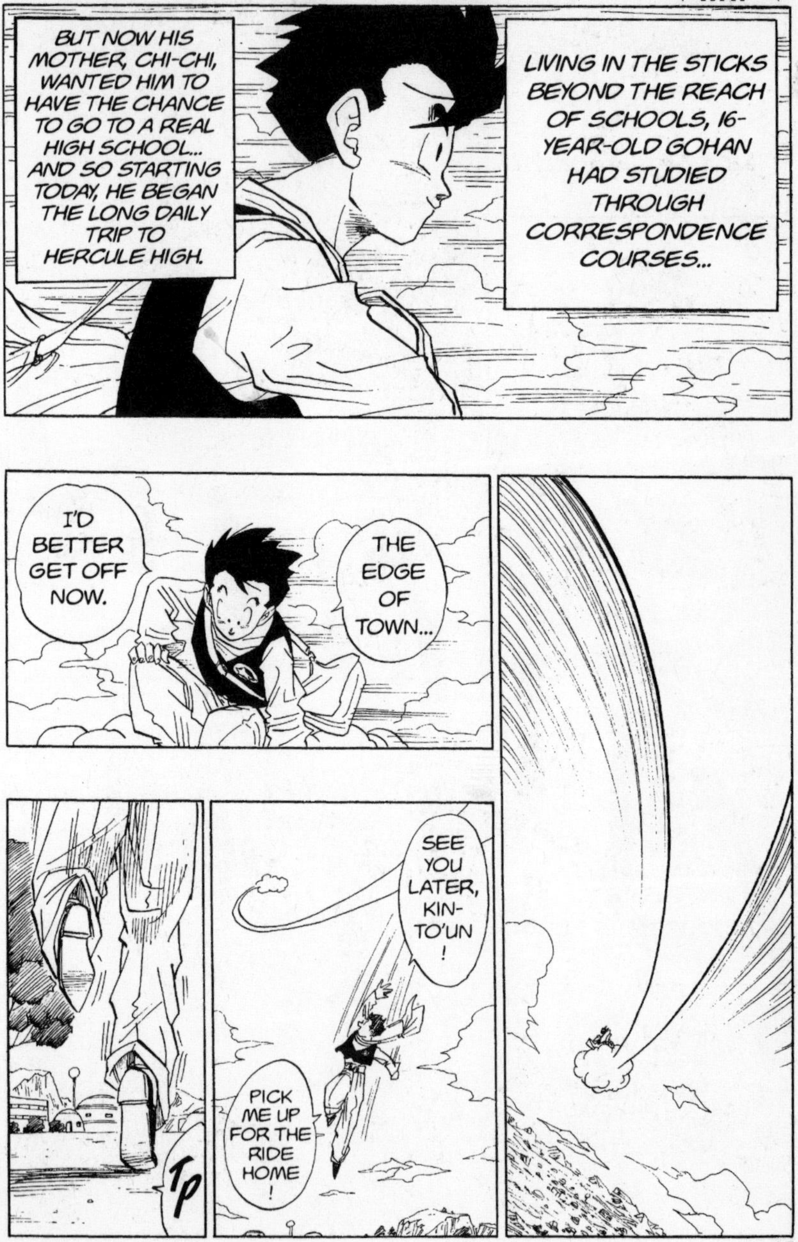

LIVING IN THE STICKS BEYOND THE REACH OF SCHOOLS, 16-YEAR-OLD GOHAN HAD STUDIED THROUGH CORRESPONDENCE COURSES...
BUT NOW HIS MOTHER, CHI-CHI, WANTED HIM TO HAVE THE CHANCE TO GO TO A REAL HIGH SCHOOL... AND SO STARTING TODAY, HE BEGAN THE LONG DAILY TRIP TO HERCULE HIGH.
THE EDGE OF TOWN...
I'D BETTER GET OFF NOW.
SEE YOU LATER, KIN-TO'UN!
PICK ME UP FOR THE RIDE HOME!
TP

READ THIS WAY

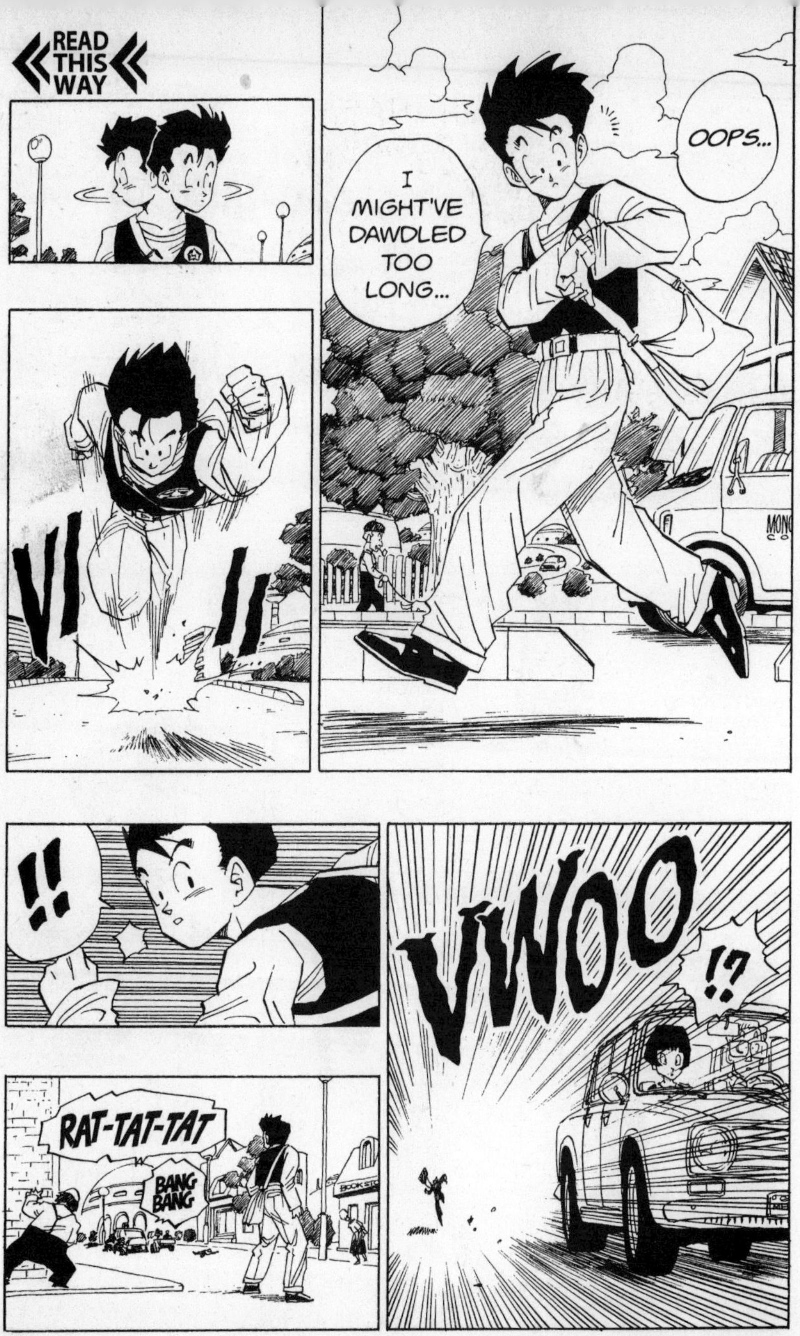
OOPS...
I MIGHT'VE DAWDLED TOO LONG...
VWOO
!?
!!
RAT-TAT-TAT
BANG BANG

READ THIS WAY

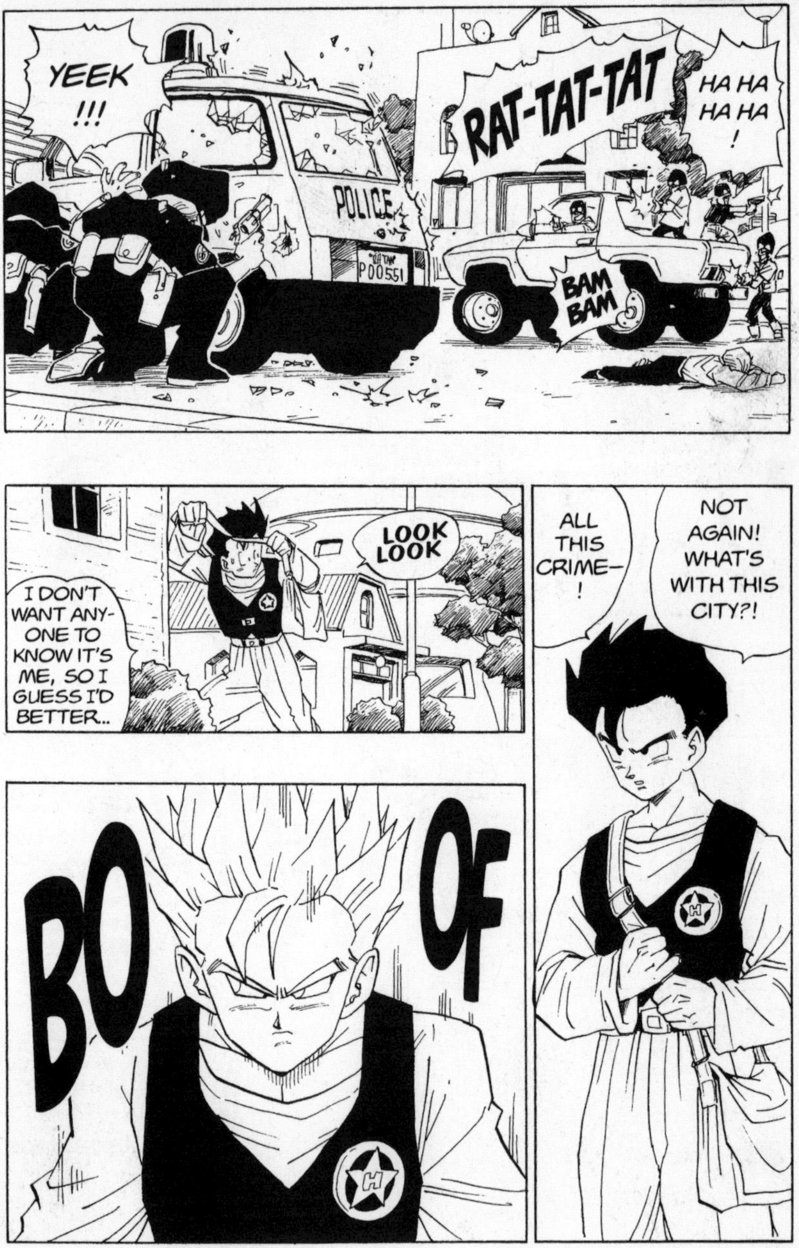
HA HA HA HA!
RAT-TAT-TAT
YEEK!!!
BAM BAM
NOT AGAIN! WHAT'S WITH THIS CITY?!
ALL THIS CRIME—!
LOOK LOOK
I DON'T WANT ANY-ONE TO KNOW IT'S ME, SO I GUESS I'D BETTER...
BOOF

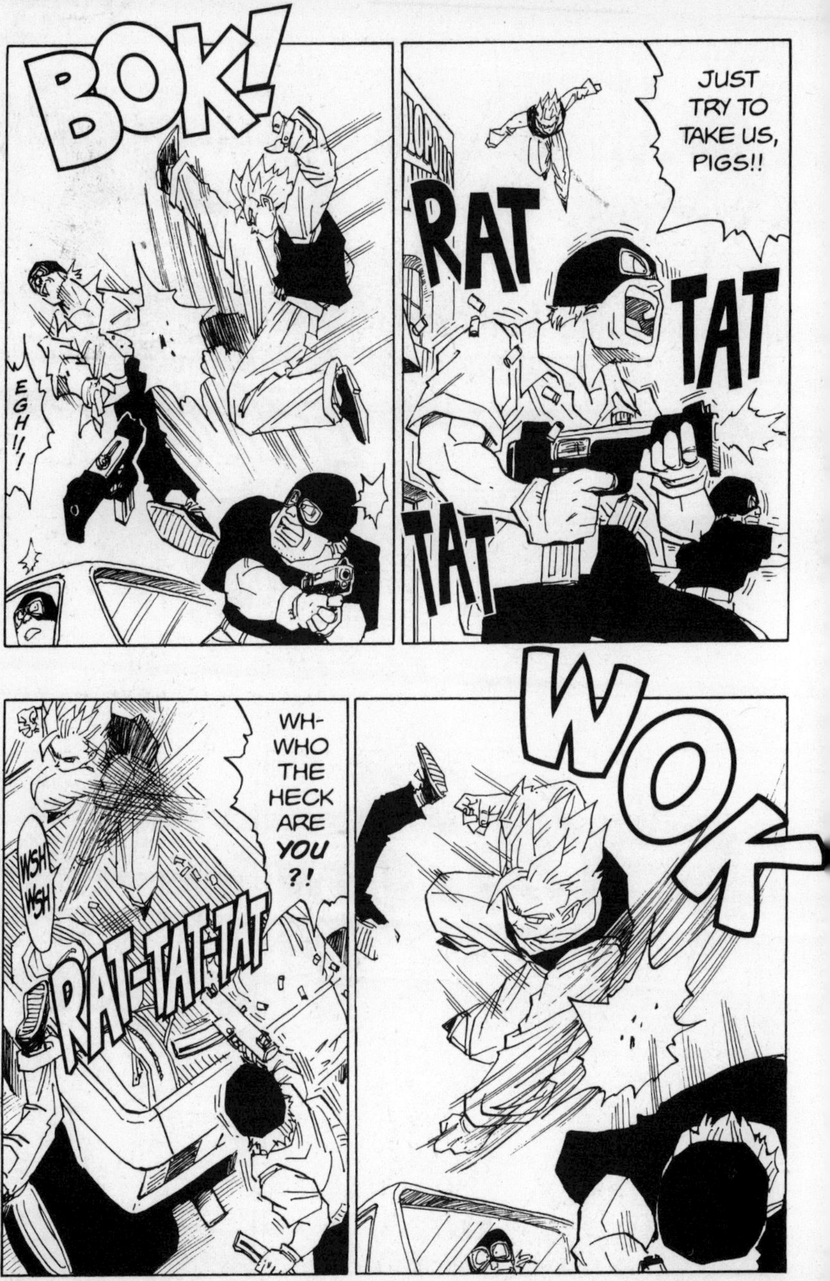
JUST TRY TO TAKE US, PIGS!!
RAT
TAT
TAT
BOK!
EGH!!!
WOK
WH- WHO THE HECK ARE *YOU* ?!
WSH WSH
RAT-TAT-TAT

READ THIS WAY

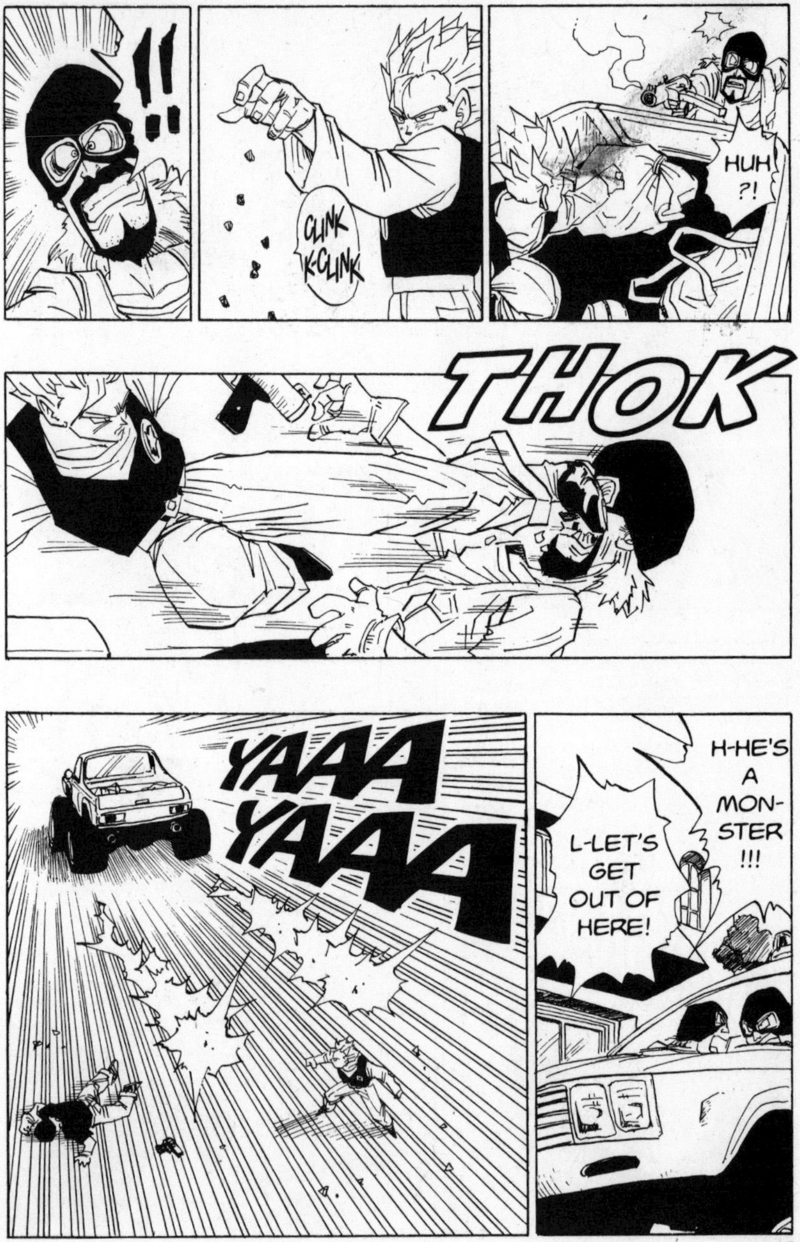
HUH ?!
CLINK K-CLINK
!!
THOK
H-HE'S A MONSTER !!!
L-LET'S GET OUT OF HERE!
YAAA YAAA

READ THIS WAY

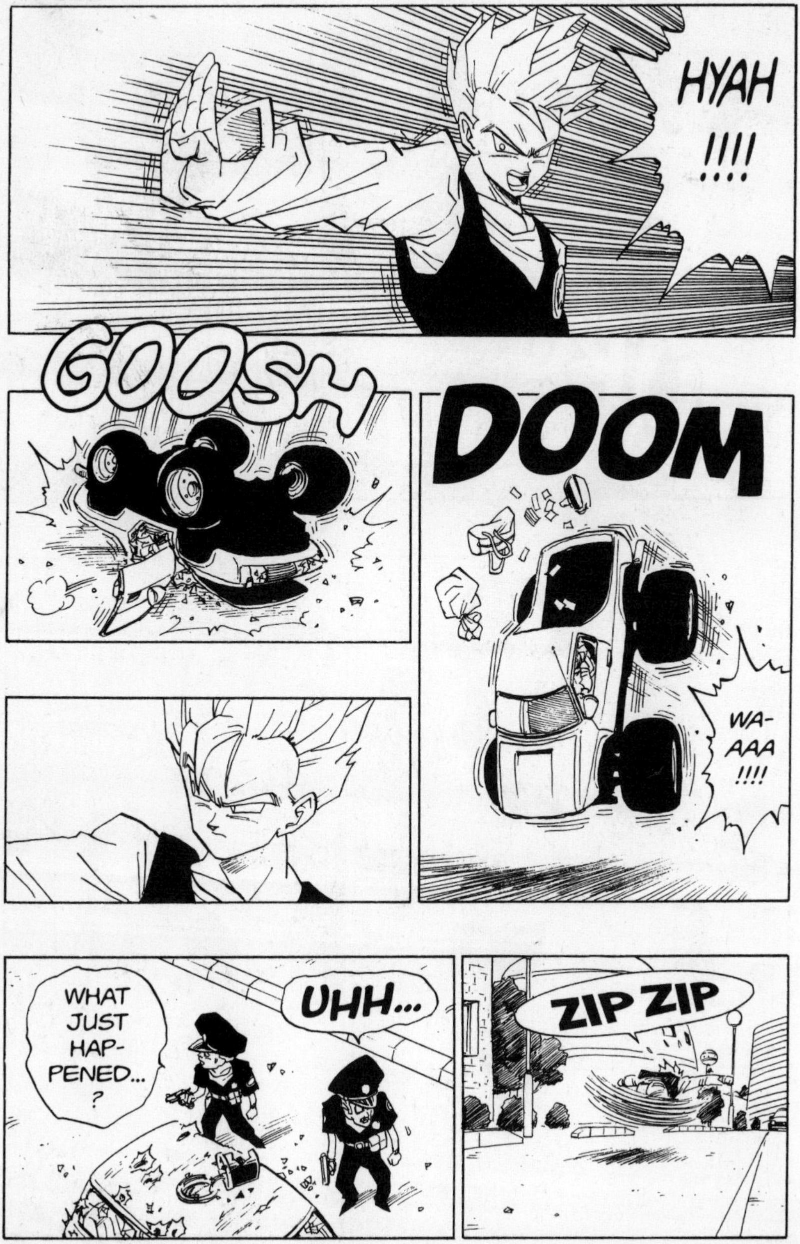
HYAH !!!!
DOOM
WA-AAA !!!!
GOOSH
ZIP ZIP
UHH...
WHAT JUST HAP-PENED... ?

READ THIS WAY

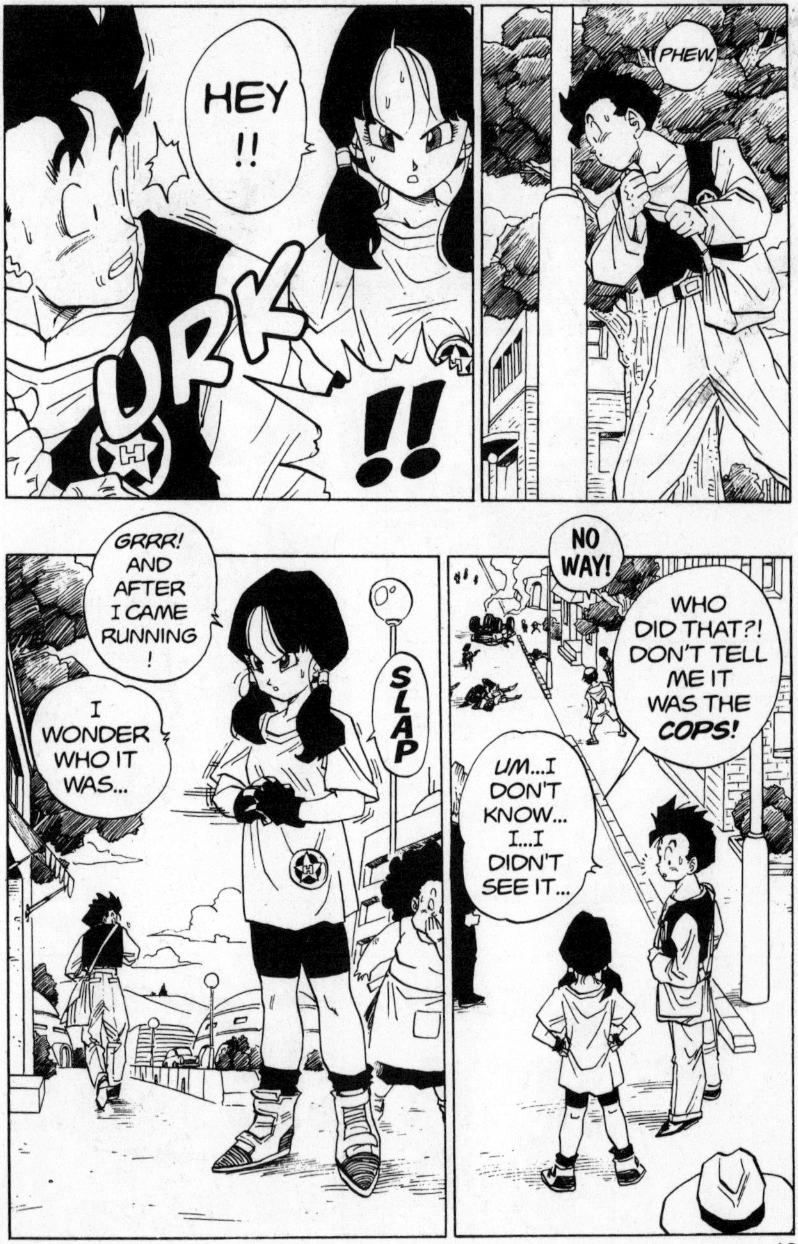
PHEW.
HEY !!
URK
!!
NO WAY!
WHO DID THAT?! DON'T TELL ME IT WAS THE COPS!
UM...I DON'T KNOW... I...I DIDN'T SEE IT...
GRRR! AND AFTER I CAME RUNNING!
SLAP
I WONDER WHO IT WAS...

READ THIS WAY

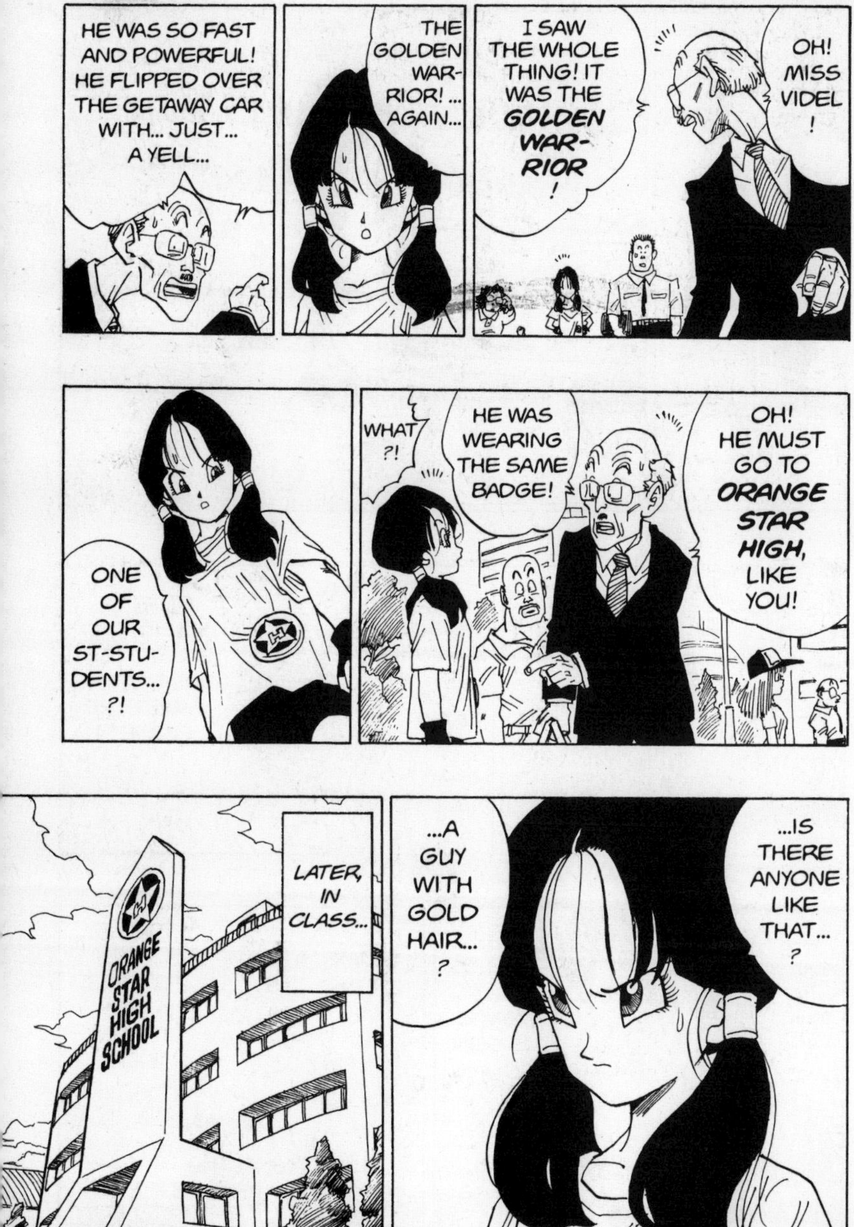

OH! MISS VIDEL!
I SAW THE WHOLE THING! IT WAS THE GOLDEN WAR-RIOR!
THE GOLDEN WAR-RIOR! ... AGAIN...
HE WAS SO FAST AND POWERFUL! HE FLIPPED OVER THE GETAWAY CAR WITH... JUST... A YELL...
OH! HE MUST GO TO ORANGE STAR HIGH, LIKE YOU!
HE WAS WEARING THE SAME BADGE!
WHAT ?!
ONE OF OUR ST-STU-DENTS... ?!
...IS THERE ANYONE LIKE THAT... ?
...A GUY WITH GOLD HAIR... ?
LATER, IN CLASS...
ORANGE STAR HIGH SCHOOL

READ THIS WAY

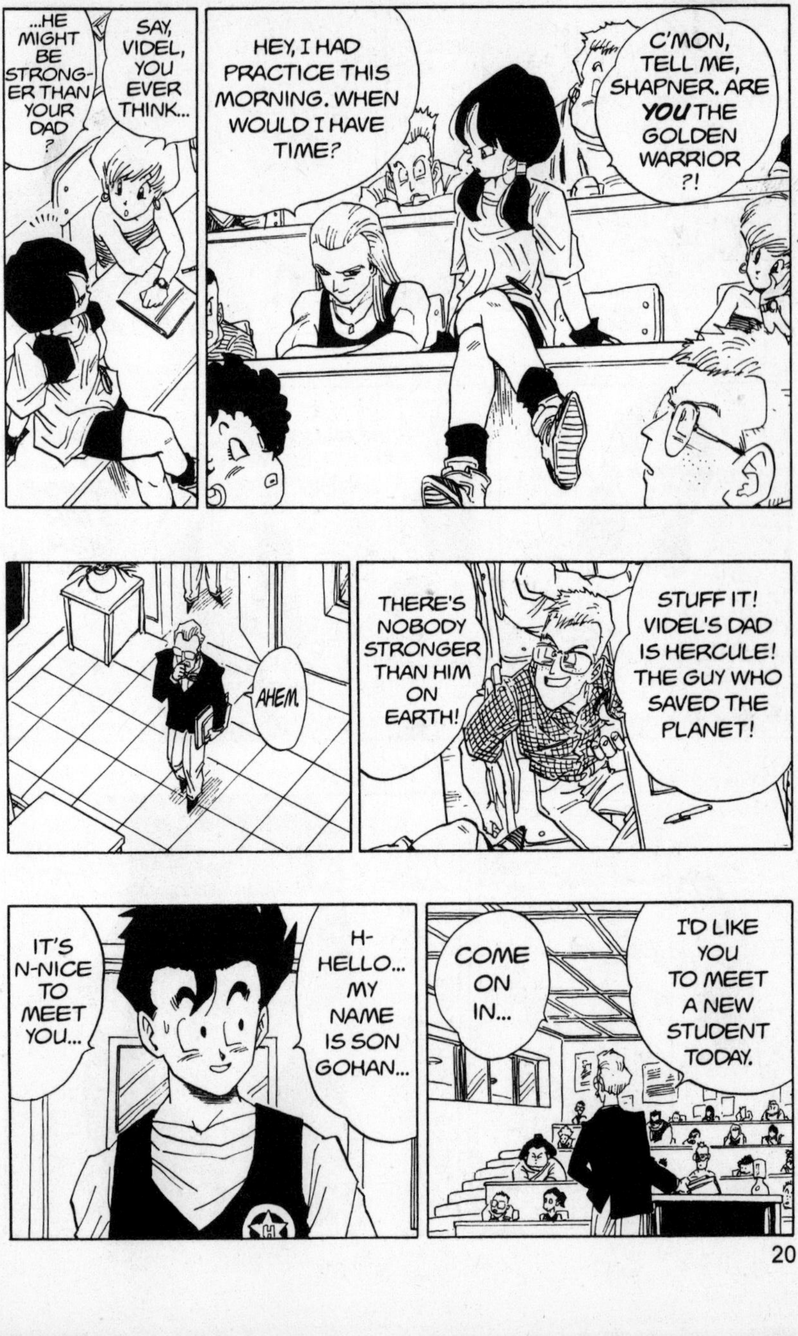
C'MON, TELL ME, SHAPNER. ARE **YOU** THE GOLDEN WARRIOR?!
HEY, I HAD PRACTICE THIS MORNING. WHEN WOULD I HAVE TIME?
SAY, VIDEL, YOU EVER THINK...
...HE MIGHT BE STRONGER THAN YOUR DAD?
STUFF IT! VIDEL'S DAD IS HERCULE! THE GUY WHO SAVED THE PLANET!
THERE'S NOBODY STRONGER THAN HIM ON EARTH!
AHEM.
I'D LIKE YOU TO MEET A NEW STUDENT TODAY.
COME ON IN...
H-HELLO... MY NAME IS SON GOHAN...
IT'S N-NICE TO MEET YOU...

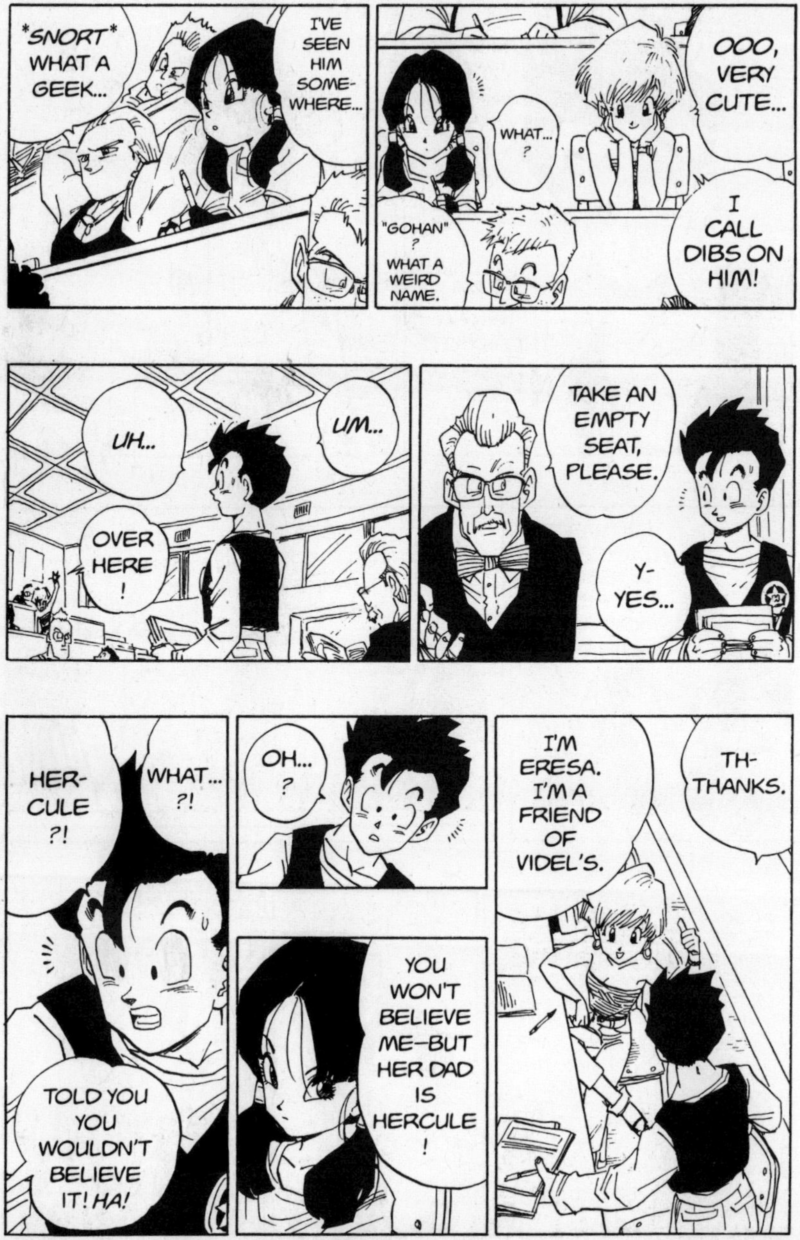

OOO, VERY CUTE...
I CALL DIBS ON HIM!
WHAT...?
"GOHAN"? WHAT A WEIRD NAME.
I'VE SEEN HIM SOME-WHERE...
SNORT WHAT A GEEK...
TAKE AN EMPTY SEAT, PLEASE.
Y-YES...
UM...
UH...
OVER HERE!
TH-THANKS.
I'M ERESA. I'M A FRIEND OF VIDEL'S.
OH...?
YOU WON'T BELIEVE ME—BUT HER DAD IS HERCULE!
WHAT...?!
HER-CULE?!
TOLD YOU YOU WOULDN'T BELIEVE IT! HA!

NEXT: *One Tired Gohan*

DBZ:228 • Undercover

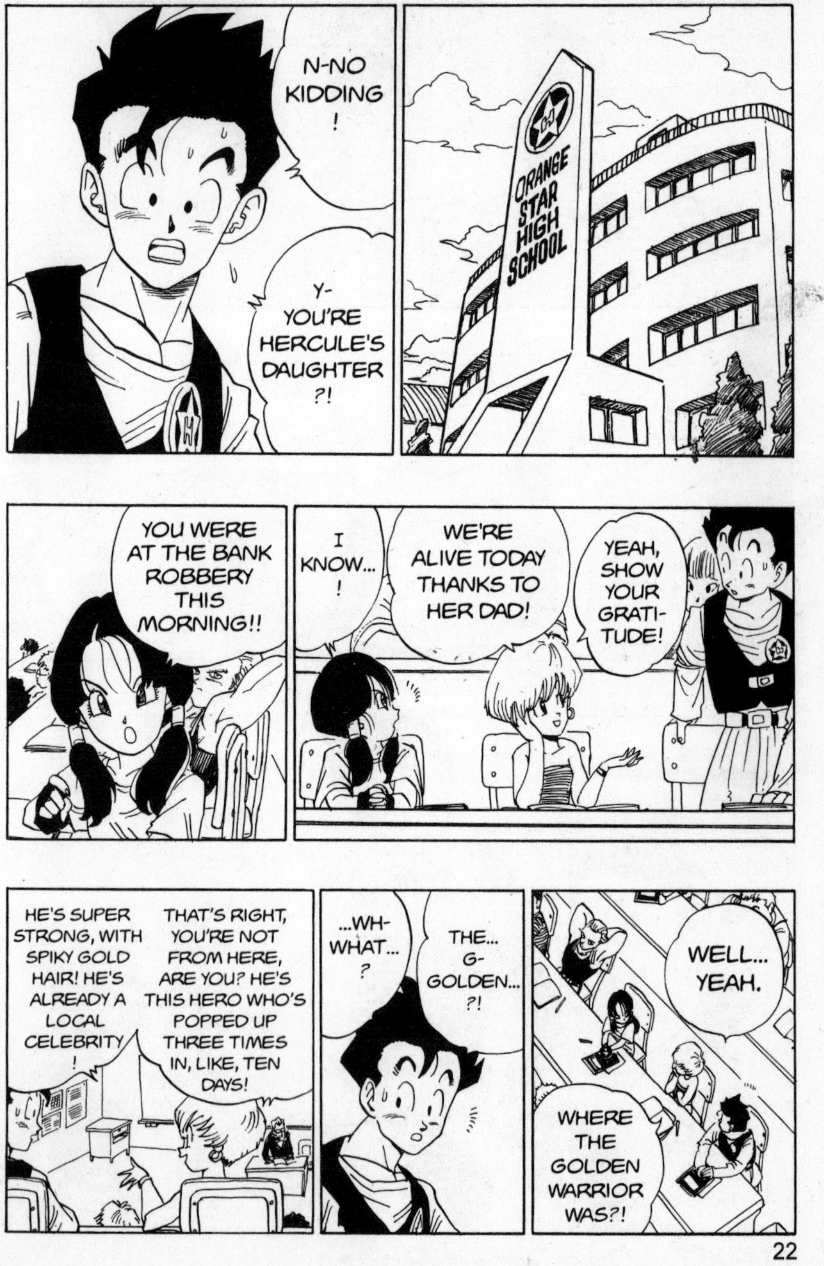
ORANGE STAR HIGH SCHOOL
N-NO KIDDING !
Y-YOU'RE HERCULE'S DAUGHTER ?!
YEAH, SHOW YOUR GRATITUDE!
WE'RE ALIVE TODAY THANKS TO HER DAD!
I KNOW... !
YOU WERE AT THE BANK ROBBERY THIS MORNING!!
WELL... YEAH.
WHERE THE GOLDEN WARRIOR WAS?!
THE... G-GOLDEN... ?!
...WH-WHAT... ?
THAT'S RIGHT, YOU'RE NOT FROM HERE, ARE YOU? HE'S THIS HERO WHO'S POPPED UP THREE TIMES IN, LIKE, TEN DAYS!
HE'S SUPER STRONG, WITH SPIKY GOLD HAIR! HE'S ALREADY A LOCAL CELEBRITY !

READ THIS WAY

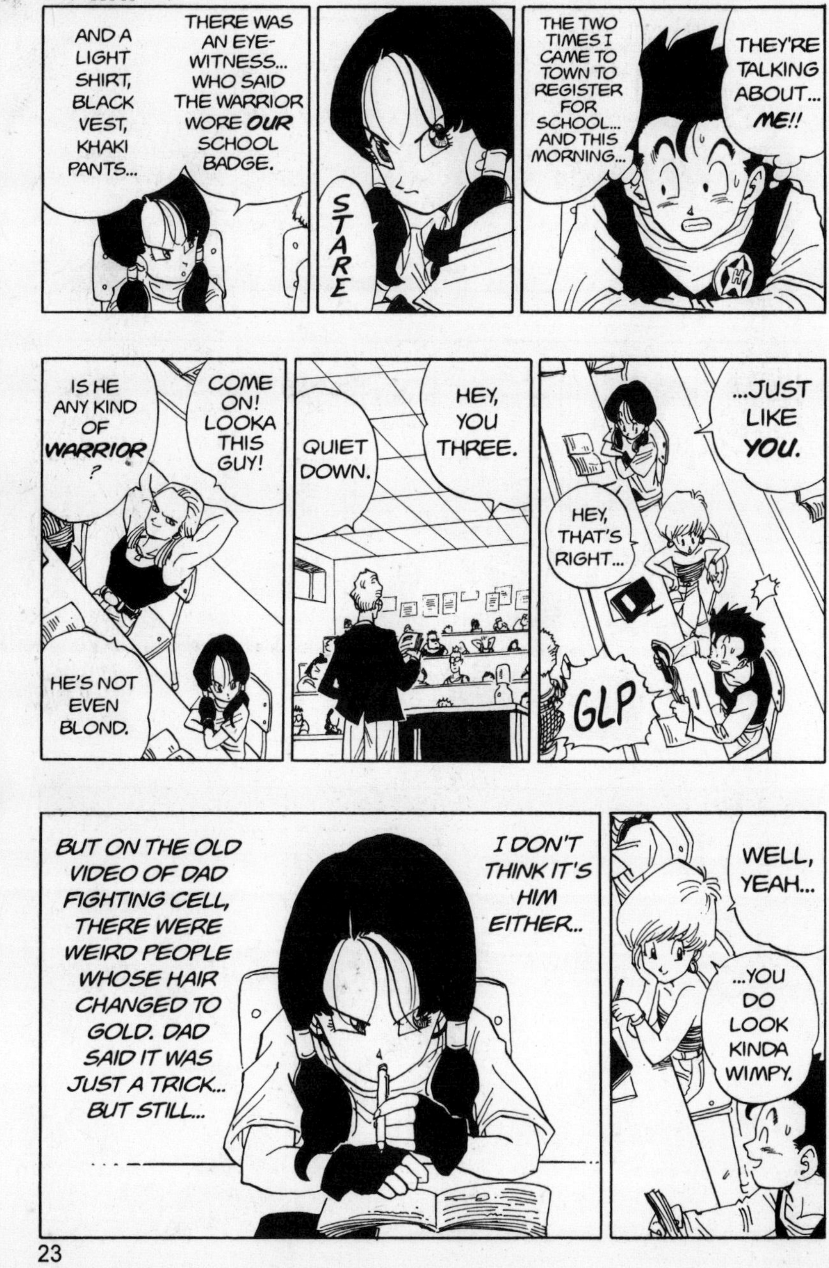
THEY'RE TALKING ABOUT... ME!!
THE TWO TIMES I CAME TO TOWN TO REGISTER FOR SCHOOL... AND THIS MORNING...
STARE
THERE WAS AN EYE-WITNESS... WHO SAID THE WARRIOR WORE OUR SCHOOL BADGE.
AND A LIGHT SHIRT, BLACK VEST, KHAKI PANTS...
...JUST LIKE YOU.
HEY, THAT'S RIGHT...
GLP
HEY, YOU THREE.
QUIET DOWN.
COME ON! LOOKA THIS GUY!
IS HE ANY KIND OF WARRIOR?
HE'S NOT EVEN BLOND.
WELL, YEAH...
...YOU DO LOOK KINDA WIMPY.
I DON'T THINK IT'S HIM EITHER...
BUT ON THE OLD VIDEO OF DAD FIGHTING CELL, THERE WERE WEIRD PEOPLE WHOSE HAIR CHANGED TO GOLD. DAD SAID IT WAS JUST A TRICK... BUT STILL...
...

READ THIS WAY

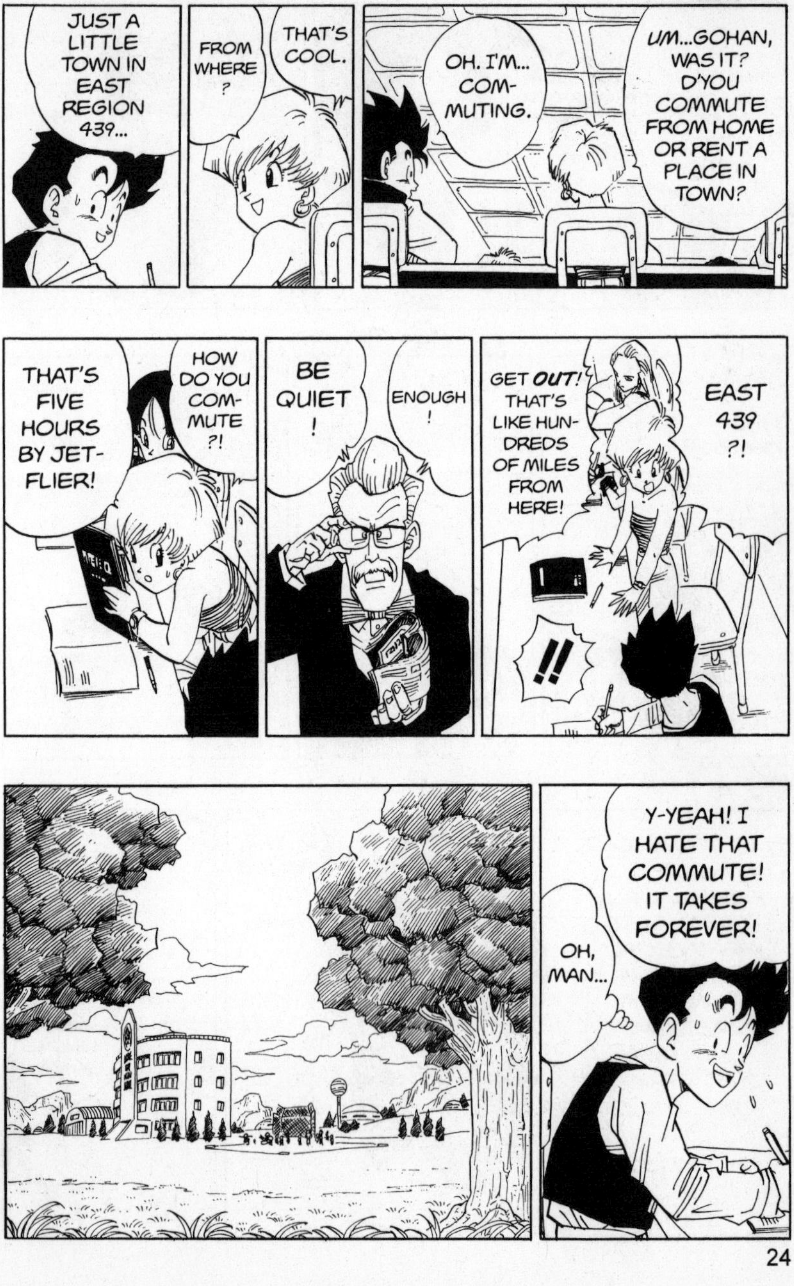
UM...GOHAN, WAS IT? D'YOU COMMUTE FROM HOME OR RENT A PLACE IN TOWN?
OH. I'M... COM-MUTING.
THAT'S COOL.
FROM WHERE?
JUST A LITTLE TOWN IN EAST REGION 439...
EAST 439?!
GET OUT! THAT'S LIKE HUN-DREDS OF MILES FROM HERE!
!!
ENOUGH!
BE QUIET!
HOW DO YOU COM-MUTE?!
THAT'S FIVE HOURS BY JET-FLIER!
Y-YEAH! I HATE THAT COMMUTE! IT TAKES FOREVER!
OH, MAN...

READ THIS WAY

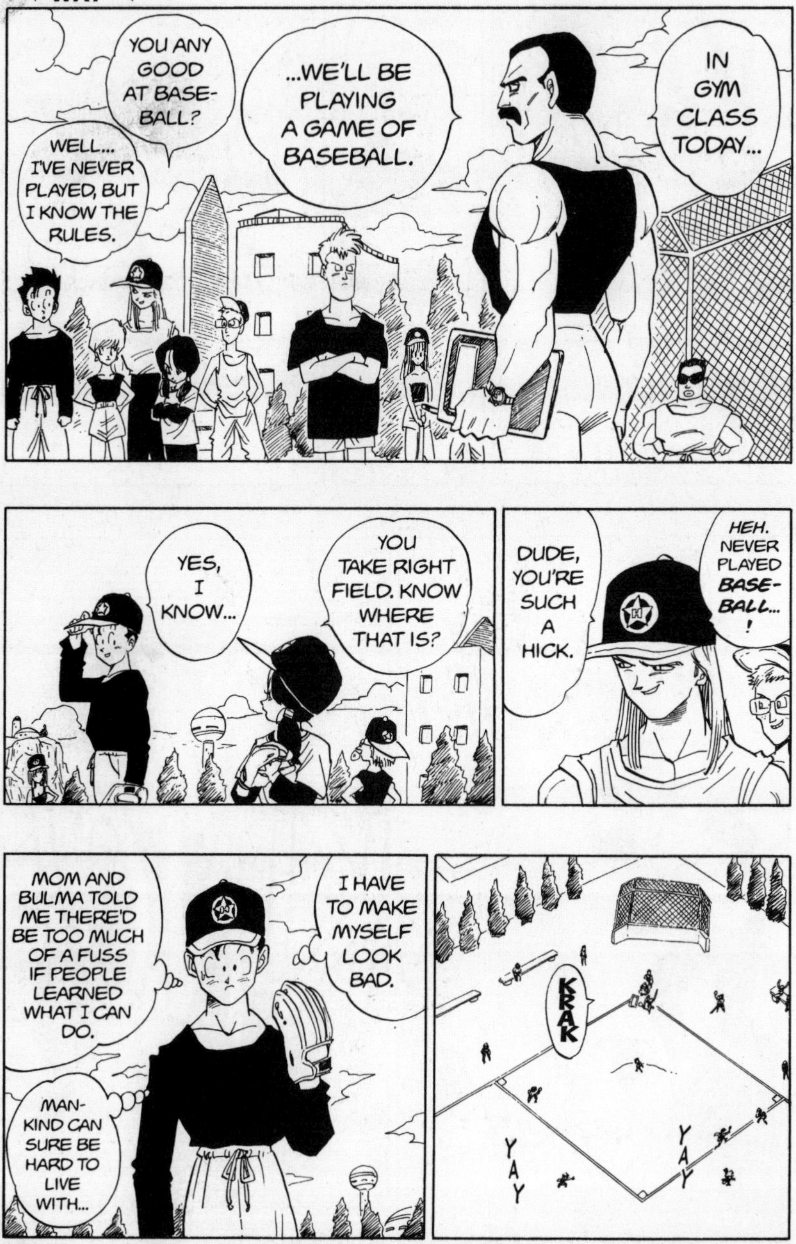
IN GYM CLASS TODAY...
...WE'LL BE PLAYING A GAME OF BASEBALL.
YOU ANY GOOD AT BASE-BALL?
WELL... I'VE NEVER PLAYED, BUT I KNOW THE RULES.
HEH. NEVER PLAYED BASE-BALL...!
DUDE, YOU'RE SUCH A HICK.
YOU TAKE RIGHT FIELD. KNOW WHERE THAT IS?
YES, I KNOW...
KRAK
YAY
YAY
I HAVE TO MAKE MYSELF LOOK BAD.
MOM AND BULMA TOLD ME THERE'D BE TOO MUCH OF A FUSS IF PEOPLE LEARNED WHAT I CAN DO.
MAN-KIND CAN SURE BE HARD TO LIVE WITH...

READ THIS WAY

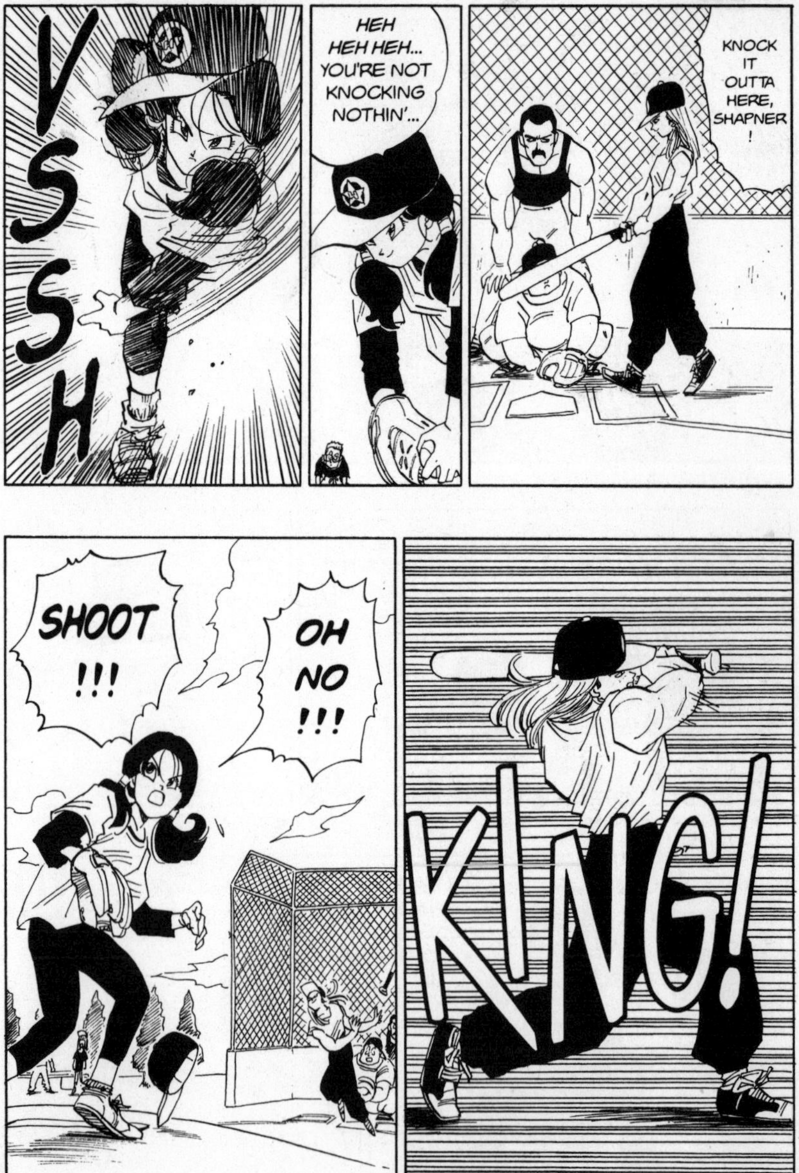

KNOCK IT OUTTA HERE, SHAPNER!
HEH HEH HEH... YOU'RE NOT KNOCKING NOTHIN'...
VSSH
KING!
OH NO!!!
SHOOT!!!

READ THIS WAY

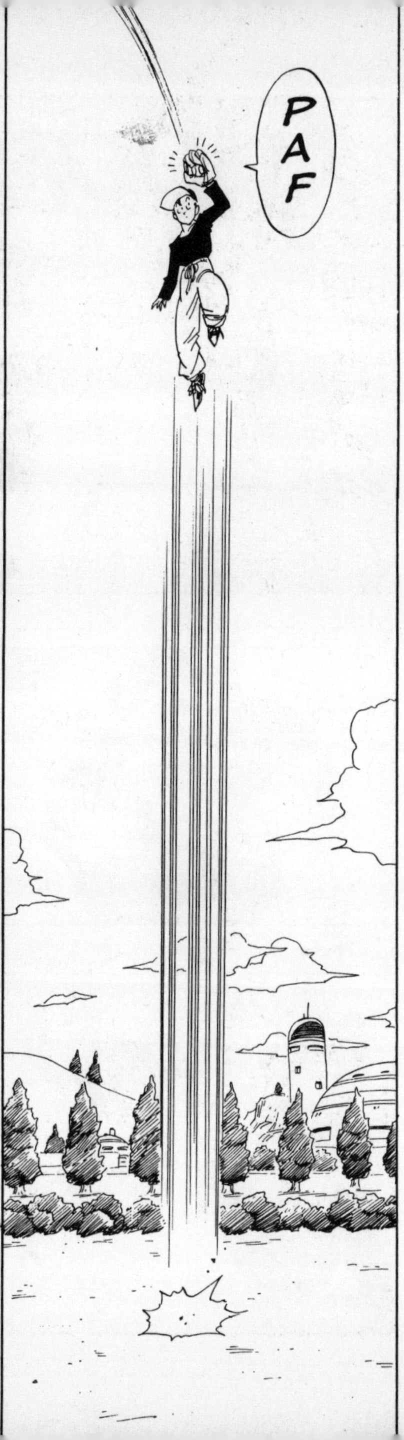
PAF

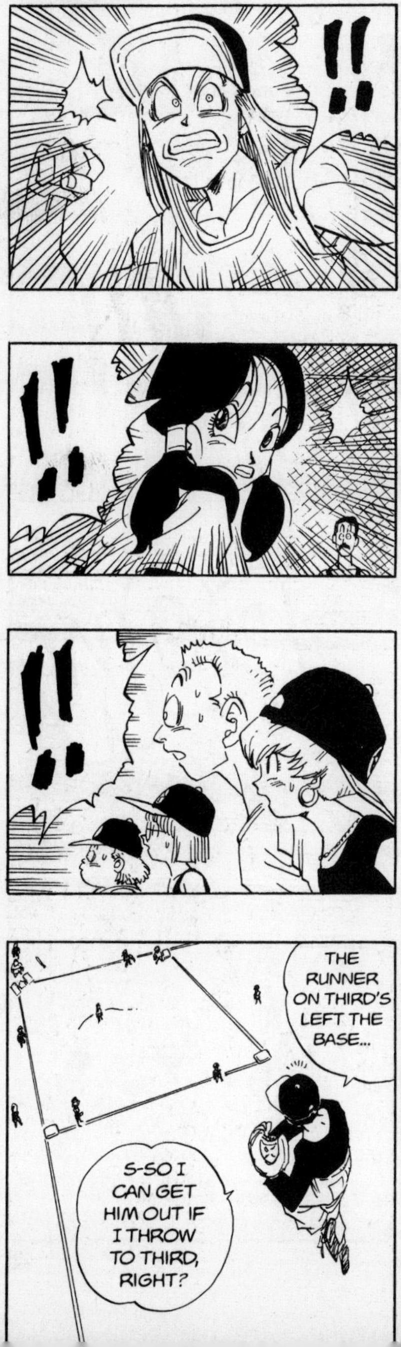
!!
!!
!!
THE RUNNER ON THIRD'S LEFT THE BASE...
S-SO I CAN GET HIM OUT IF I THROW TO THIRD, RIGHT?

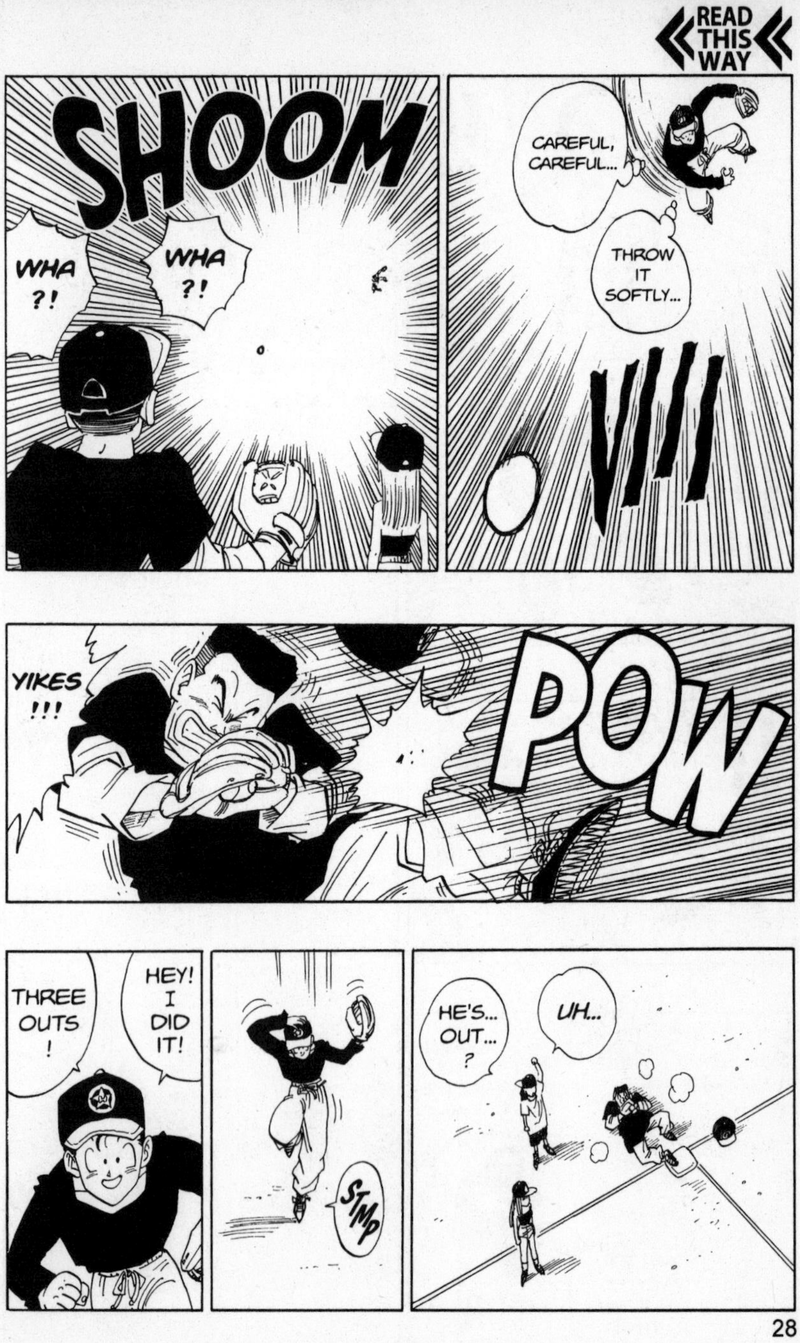
CAREFUL, CAREFUL...
THROW IT SOFTLY...
VIII
SHOOM
WHA ?!
WHA ?!
POW
YIKES !!!
UH...
HE'S... OUT... ?
STMP
HEY! I DID IT!
THREE OUTS !

READ THIS WAY

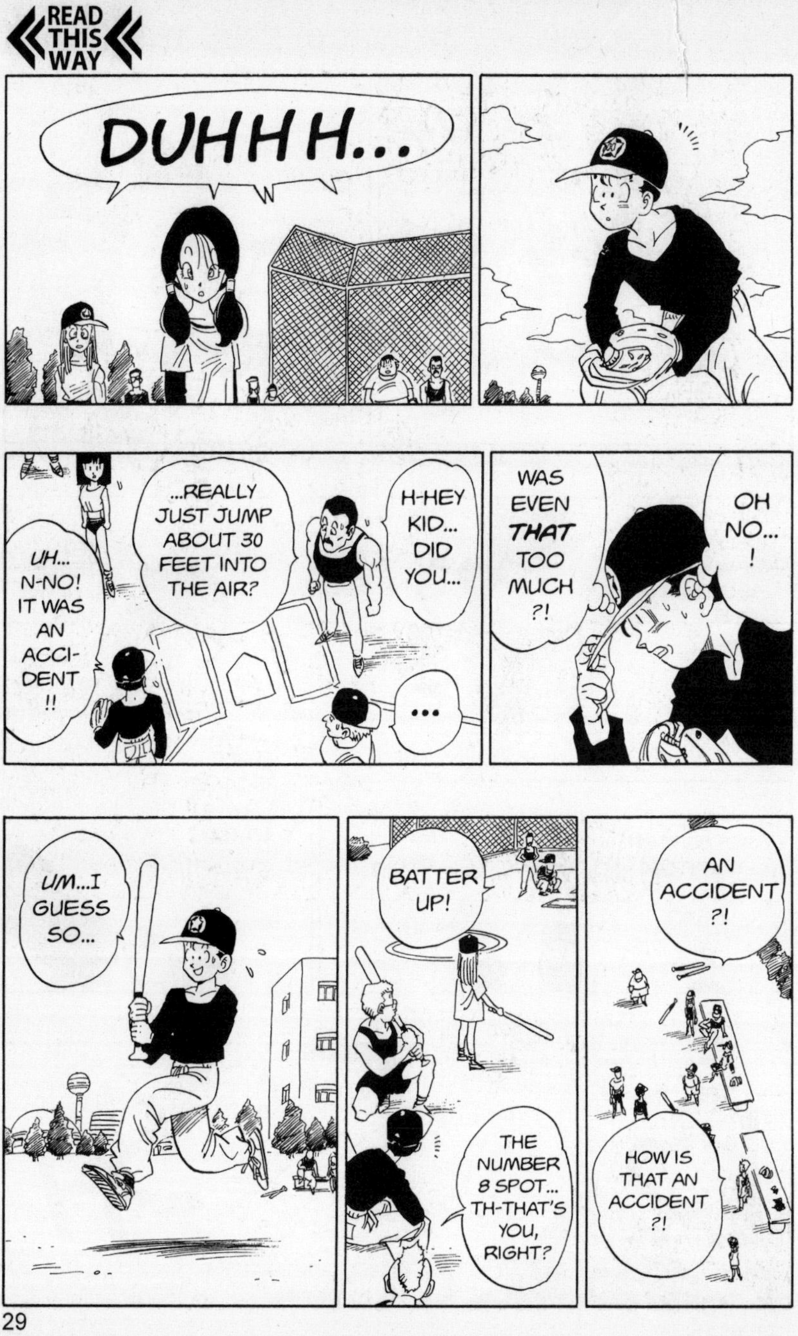
DUHHH...
OH NO...!
WAS EVEN *THAT* TOO MUCH?!
H-HEY KID... DID YOU...
...REALLY JUST JUMP ABOUT 30 FEET INTO THE AIR?
UH... N-NO! IT WAS AN ACCIDENT!!
...
AN ACCIDENT?!
HOW IS THAT AN ACCIDENT?!
BATTER UP!
THE NUMBER 8 SPOT... TH-THAT'S YOU, RIGHT?
UM...I GUESS SO...

READ THIS WAY

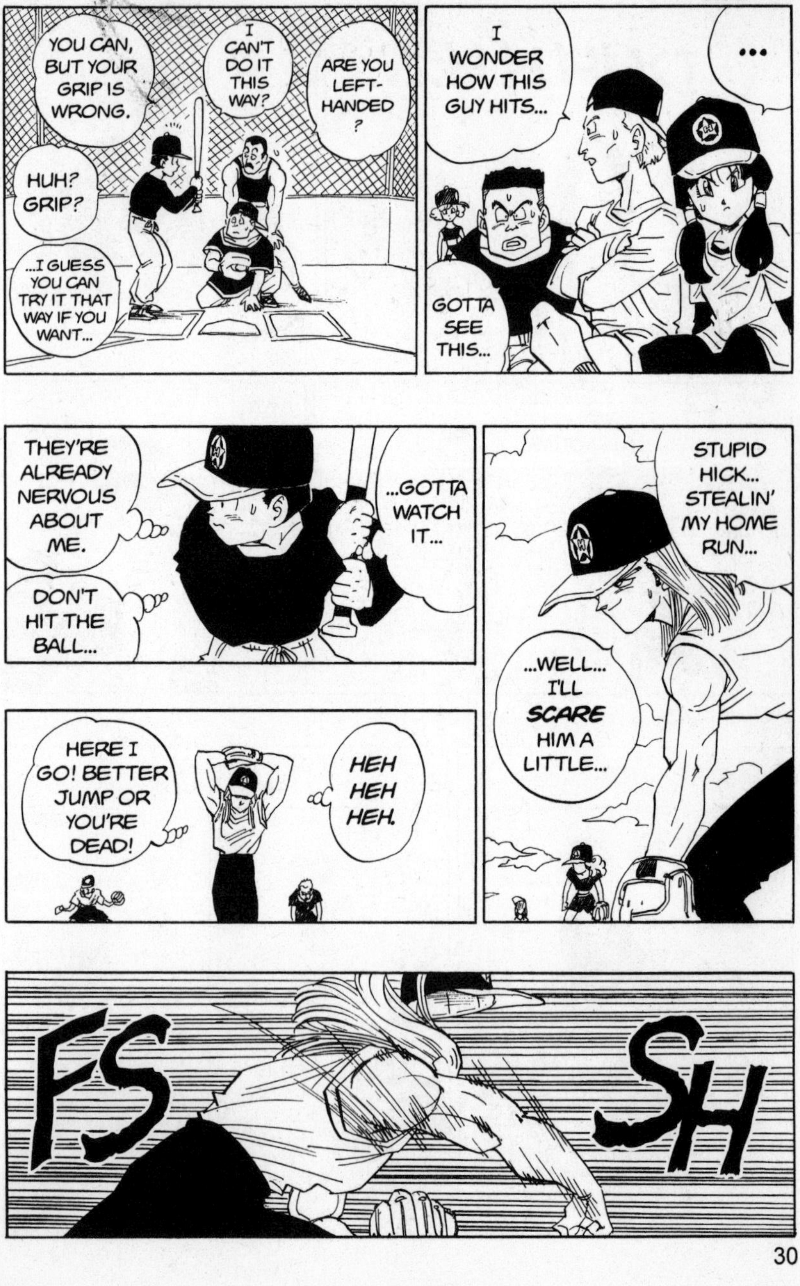

...
I WONDER HOW THIS GUY HITS...
GOTTA SEE THIS...
ARE YOU LEFT-HANDED?
I CAN'T DO IT THIS WAY?
YOU CAN, BUT YOUR GRIP IS WRONG.
HUH? GRIP?
...I GUESS YOU CAN TRY IT THAT WAY IF YOU WANT...
STUPID HICK... STEALIN' MY HOME RUN...
...WELL... I'LL SCARE HIM A LITTLE...
...GOTTA WATCH IT...
THEY'RE ALREADY NERVOUS ABOUT ME.
DON'T HIT THE BALL...
HEH HEH HEH.
HERE I GO! BETTER JUMP OR YOU'RE DEAD!
FSSH

READ THIS WAY

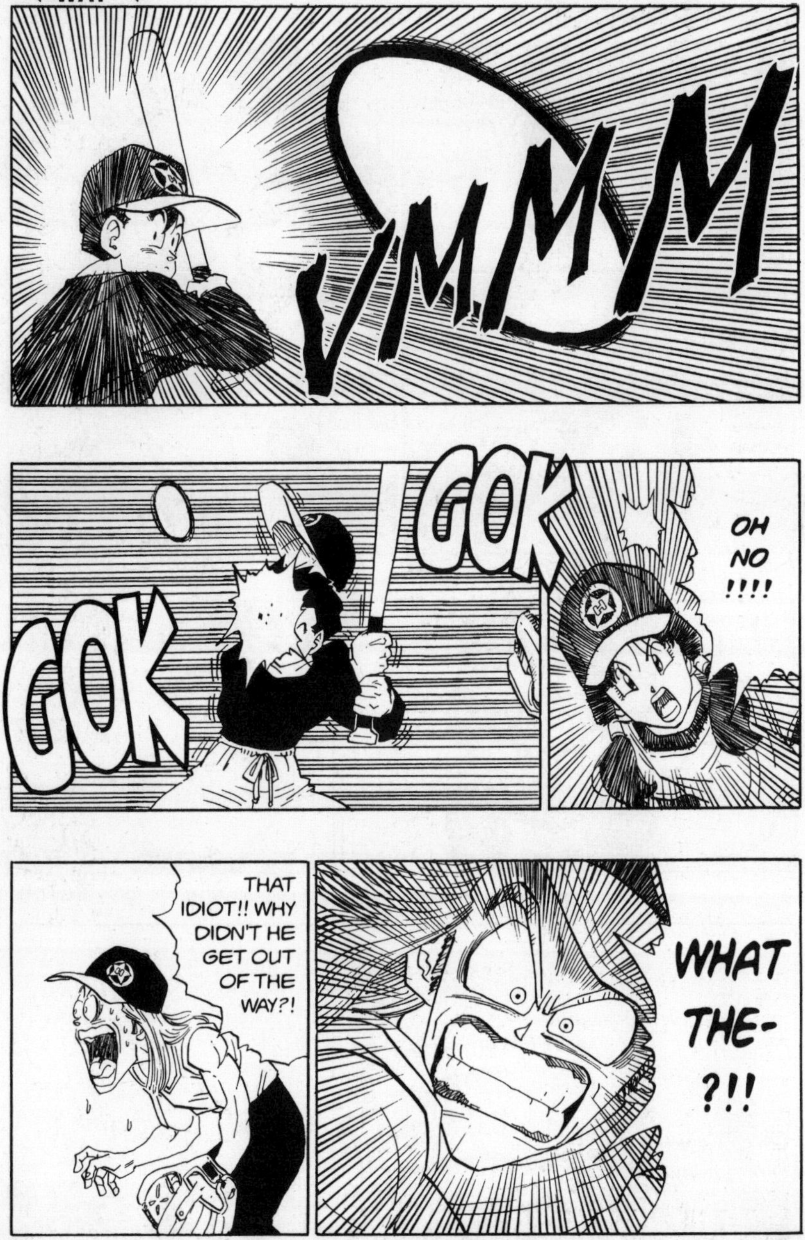
VMMM
OH NO !!!!
GOK
GOK
WHAT THE-?!!
THAT IDIOT!! WHY DIDN'T HE GET OUT OF THE WAY?!

READ THIS WAY

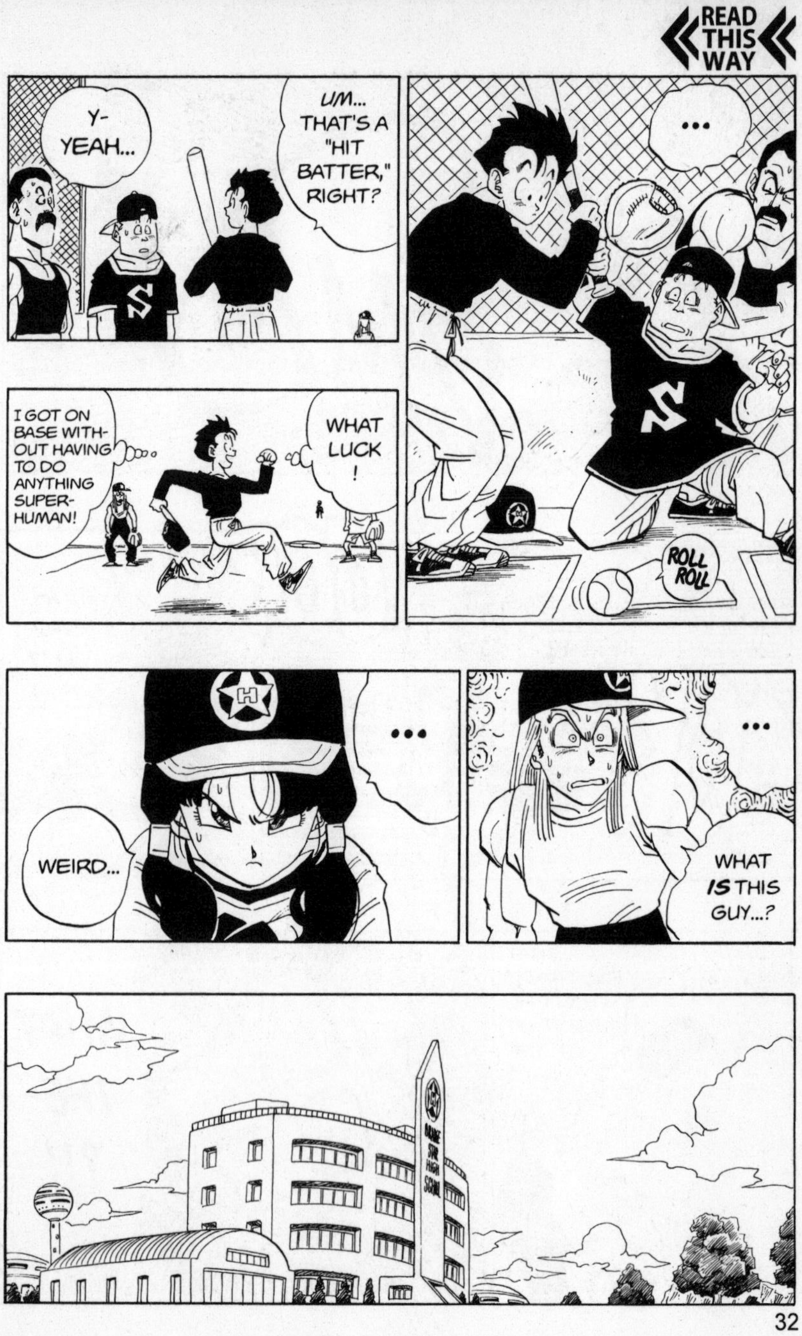

...
ROLL ROLL
UM... THAT'S A "HIT BATTER," RIGHT?
Y- YEAH...
WHAT LUCK!
I GOT ON BASE WITHOUT HAVING TO DO ANYTHING SUPERHUMAN!
...
WHAT *IS* THIS GUY...?
...
WEIRD...
ORANGE STAR HIGH SCHOOL

READ THIS WAY

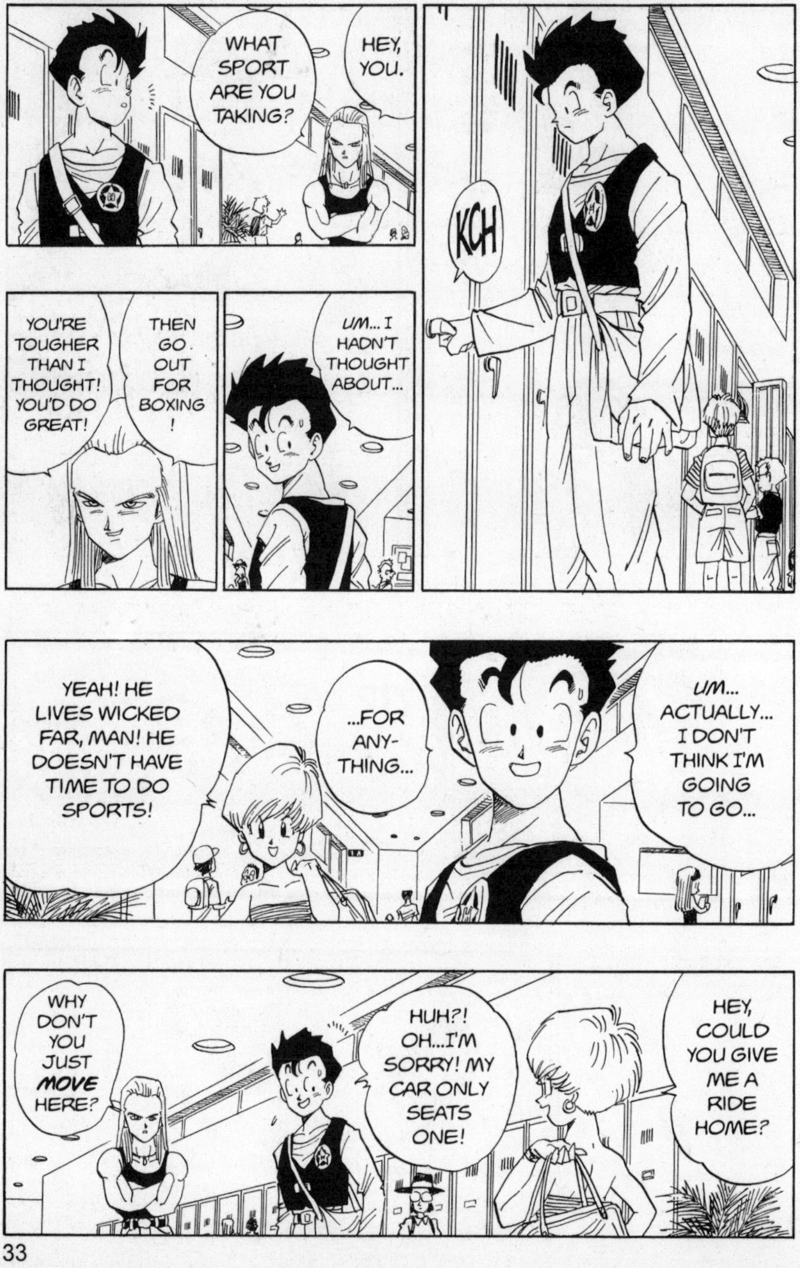
KCH
HEY, YOU.
WHAT SPORT ARE YOU TAKING?
UM... I HADN'T THOUGHT ABOUT...
THEN GO OUT FOR BOXING!
YOU'RE TOUGHER THAN I THOUGHT! YOU'D DO GREAT!
UM... ACTUALLY... I DON'T THINK I'M GOING TO GO...
...FOR ANYTHING...
YEAH! HE LIVES WICKED FAR, MAN! HE DOESN'T HAVE TIME TO DO SPORTS!
HEY, COULD YOU GIVE ME A RIDE HOME?
HUH?! OH...I'M SORRY! MY CAR ONLY SEATS ONE!
WHY DON'T YOU JUST *MOVE* HERE?

READ THIS WAY

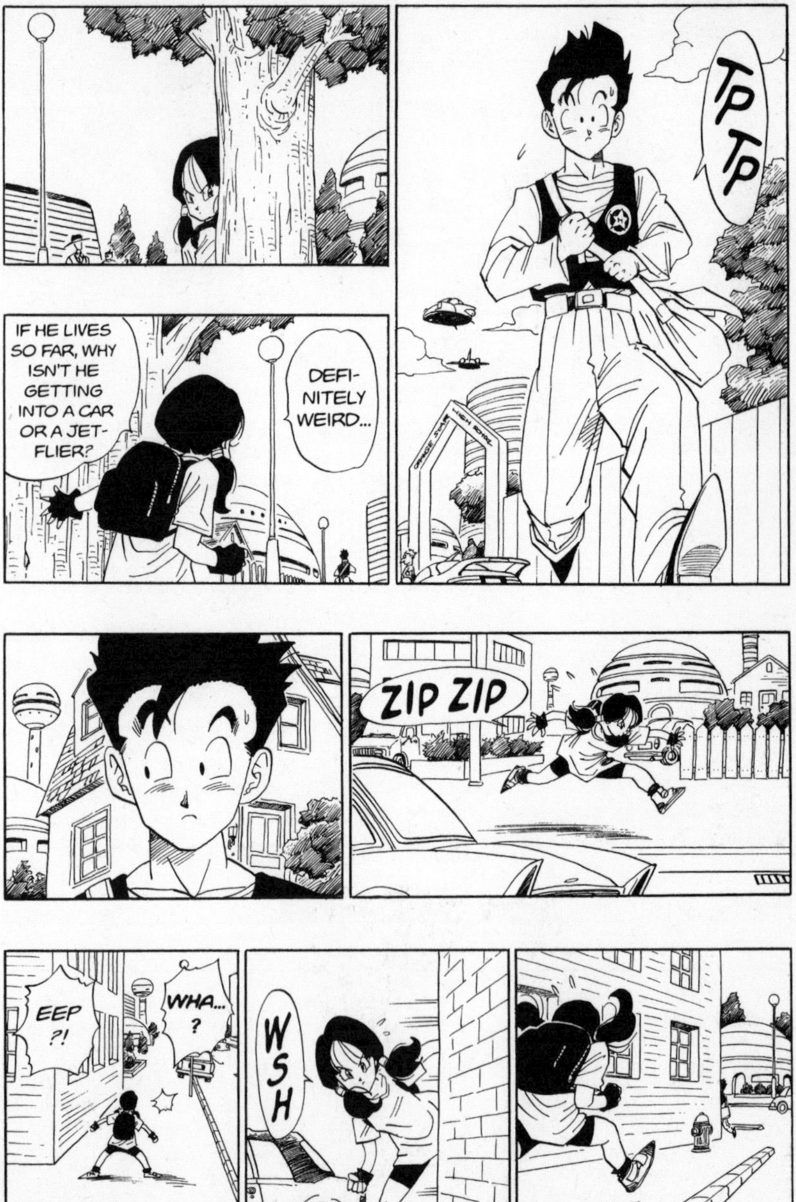

TP TP
IF HE LIVES SO FAR, WHY ISN'T HE GETTING INTO A CAR OR A JET-FLIER?
DEFI-NITELY WEIRD...
ZIP ZIP
WSH
WHA... ?
EEP ?!

READ THIS WAY

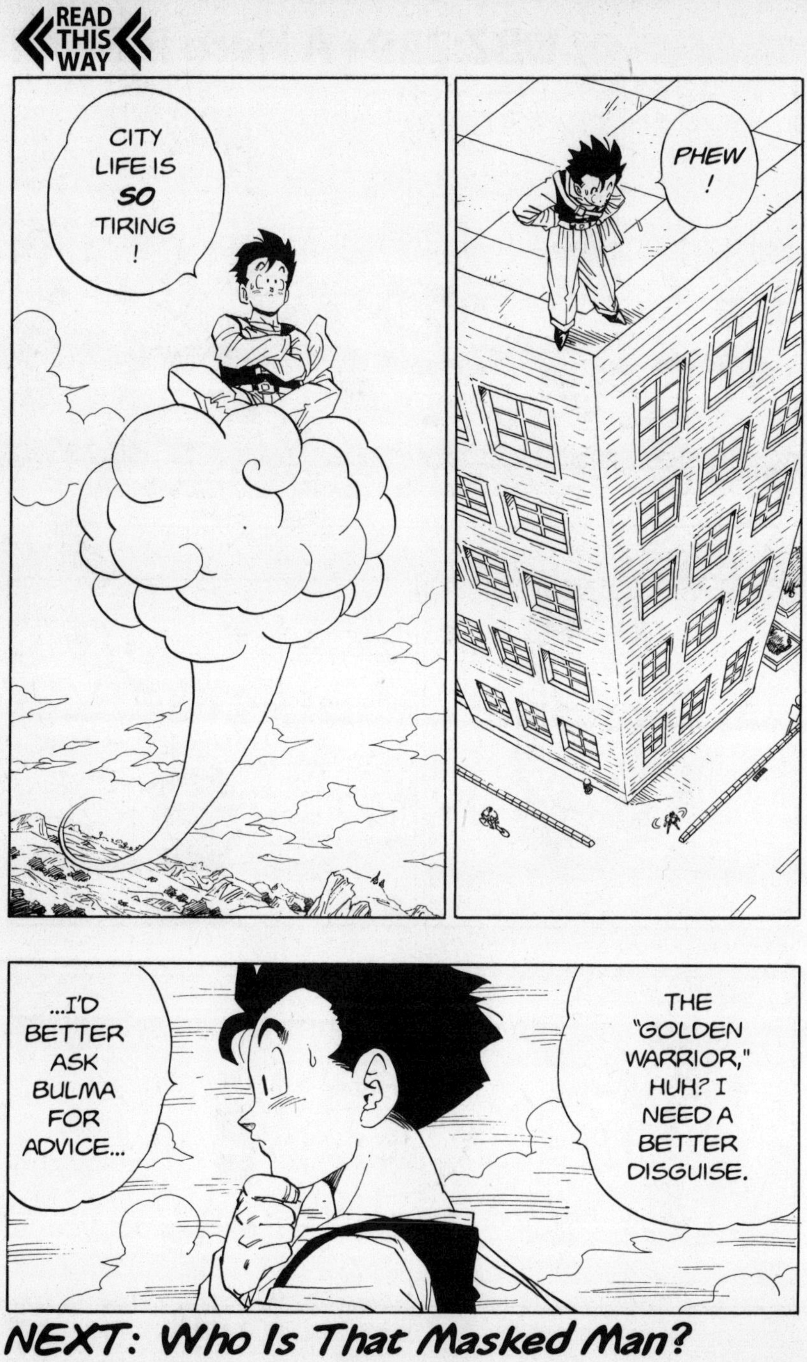
PHEW!
CITY LIFE IS SO TIRING!
THE "GOLDEN WARRIOR," HUH? I NEED A BETTER DISGUISE.
...I'D BETTER ASK BULMA FOR ADVICE...

NEXT: Who Is That Masked Man?

DBZ:229 • A Hero is Born!

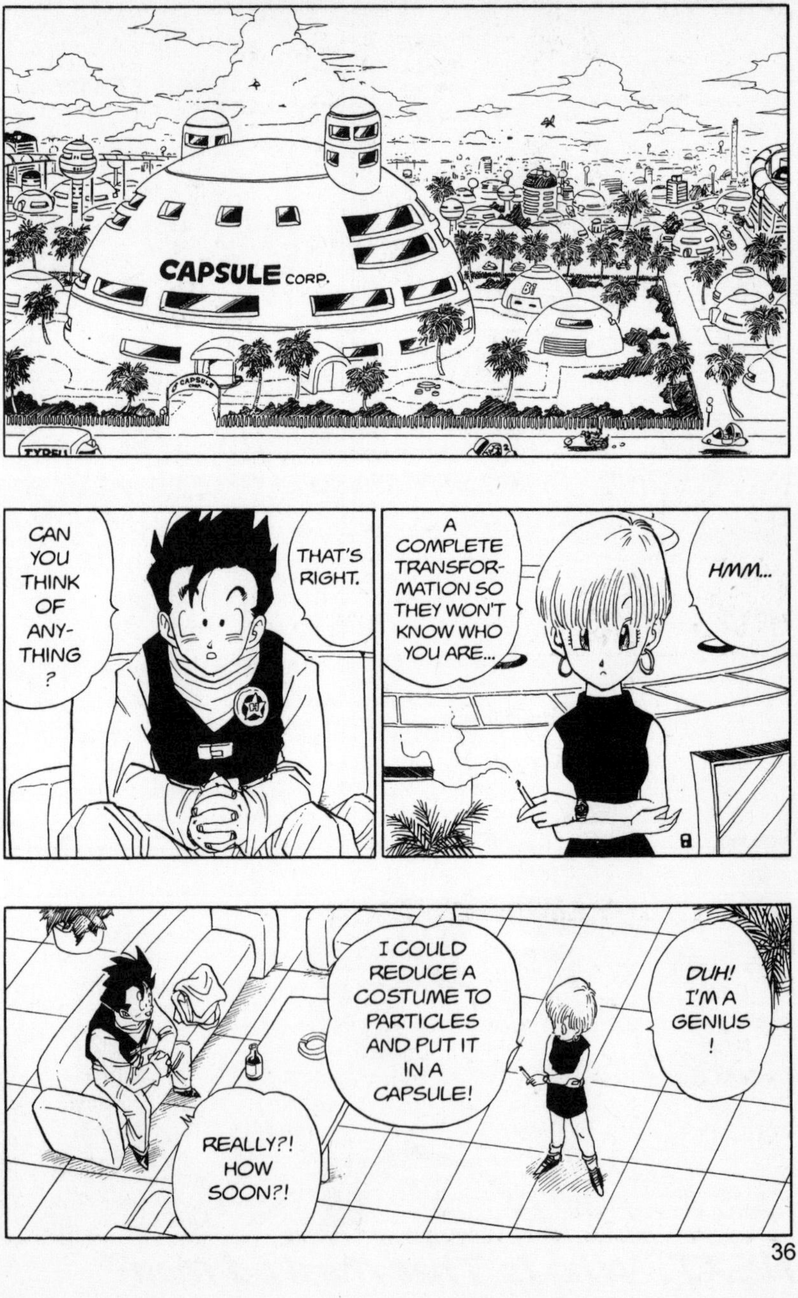
CAPSULE CORP.
HMM...
A COMPLETE TRANSFORMATION SO THEY WON'T KNOW WHO YOU ARE...
THAT'S RIGHT.
CAN YOU THINK OF ANYTHING?
DUH! I'M A GENIUS!
I COULD REDUCE A COSTUME TO PARTICLES AND PUT IT IN A CAPSULE!
REALLY?! HOW SOON?!

READ THIS WAY

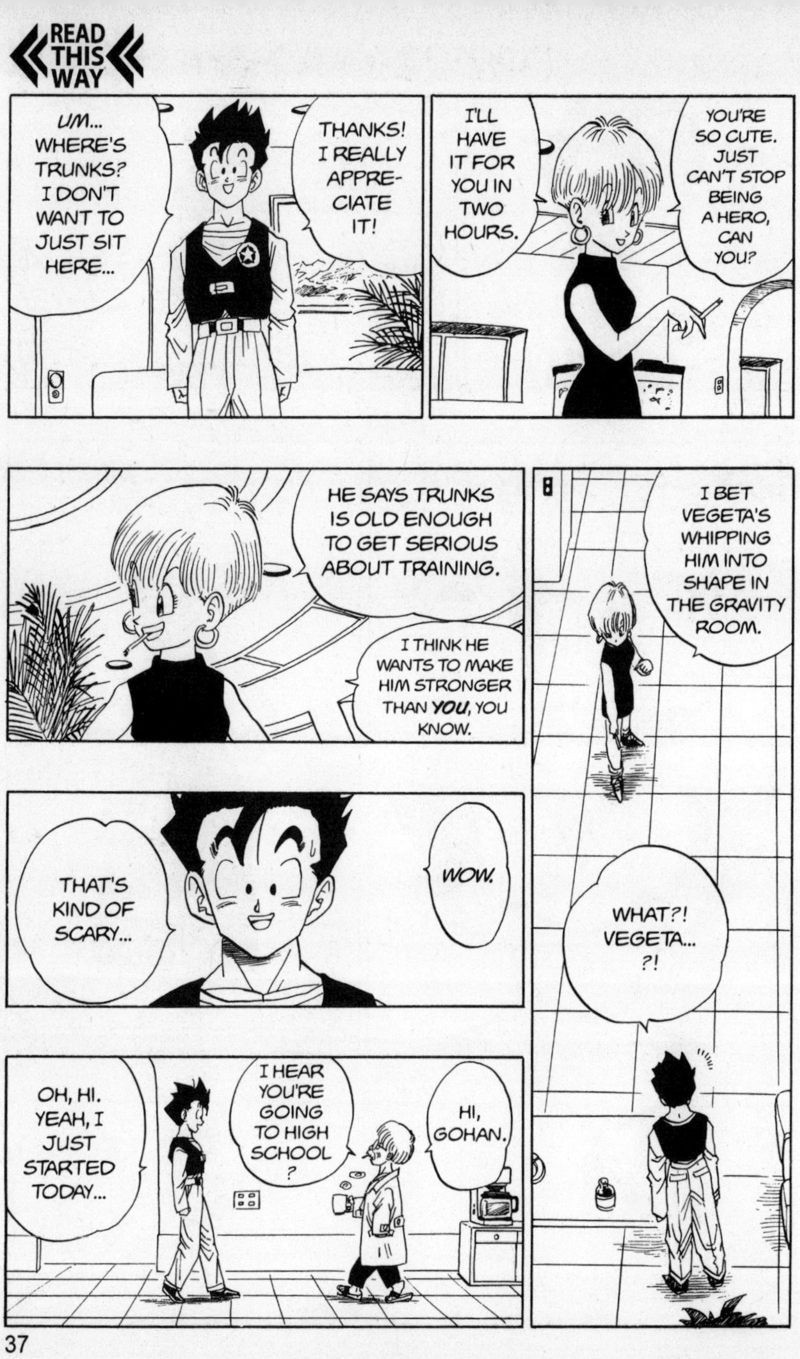
YOU'RE SO CUTE. JUST CAN'T STOP BEING A HERO, CAN YOU?
I'LL HAVE IT FOR YOU IN TWO HOURS.
THANKS! I REALLY APPRE-CIATE IT!
UM... WHERE'S TRUNKS? I DON'T WANT TO JUST SIT HERE...
I BET VEGETA'S WHIPPING HIM INTO SHAPE IN THE GRAVITY ROOM.
WHAT?! VEGETA...?!
HE SAYS TRUNKS IS OLD ENOUGH TO GET SERIOUS ABOUT TRAINING.
I THINK HE WANTS TO MAKE HIM STRONGER THAN YOU, YOU KNOW.
WOW.
THAT'S KIND OF SCARY...
HI, GOHAN.
I HEAR YOU'RE GOING TO HIGH SCHOOL?
OH, HI. YEAH, I JUST STARTED TODAY...

READ THIS WAY

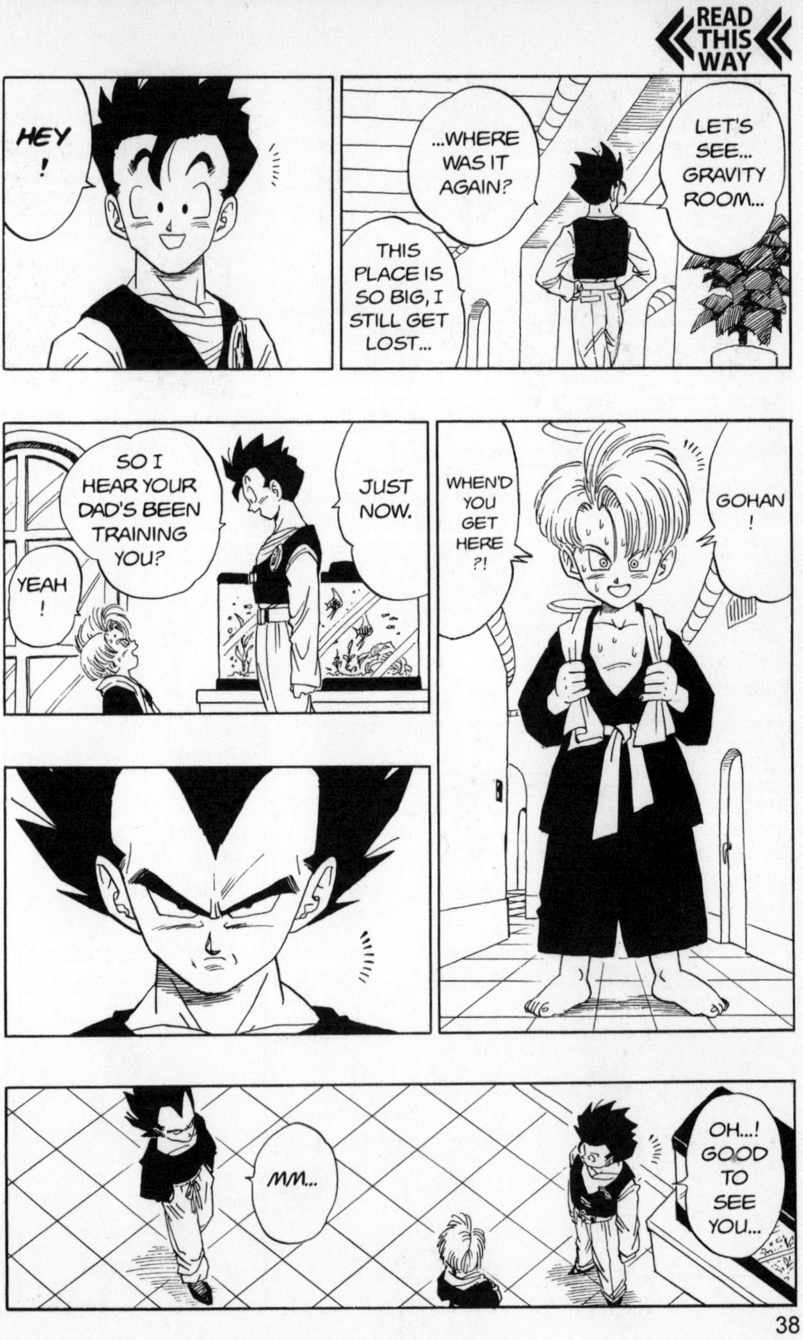
LET'S SEE... GRAVITY ROOM...
...WHERE WAS IT AGAIN?
THIS PLACE IS SO BIG, I STILL GET LOST...
HEY!
GOHAN!
WHEN'D YOU GET HERE?!
JUST NOW.
SO I HEAR YOUR DAD'S BEEN TRAINING YOU?
YEAH!
OH...! GOOD TO SEE YOU...
MM...

READ THIS WAY

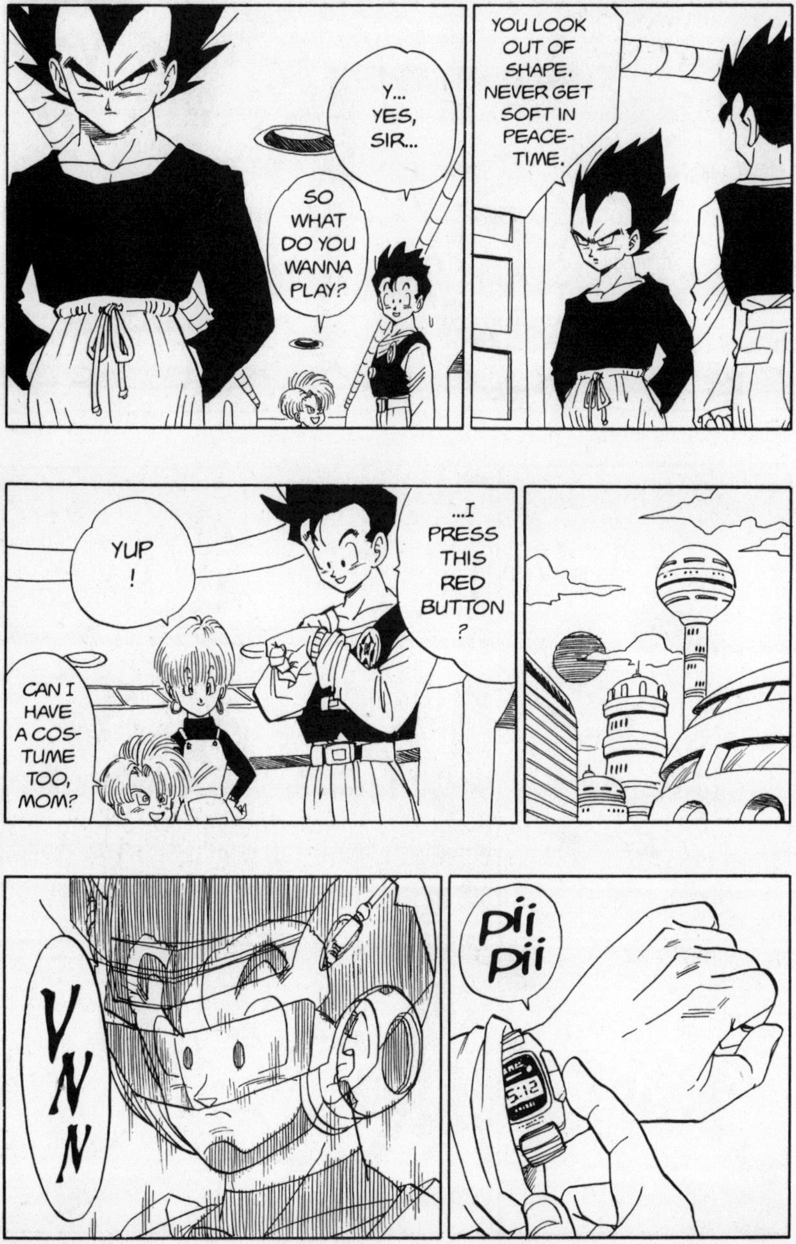
YOU LOOK OUT OF SHAPE. NEVER GET SOFT IN PEACE-TIME.
Y... YES, SIR...
SO WHAT DO YOU WANNA PLAY?
...I PRESS THIS RED BUTTON?
YUP!
CAN I HAVE A COSTUME TOO, MOM?
Pii Pii
VNN

READ THIS WAY

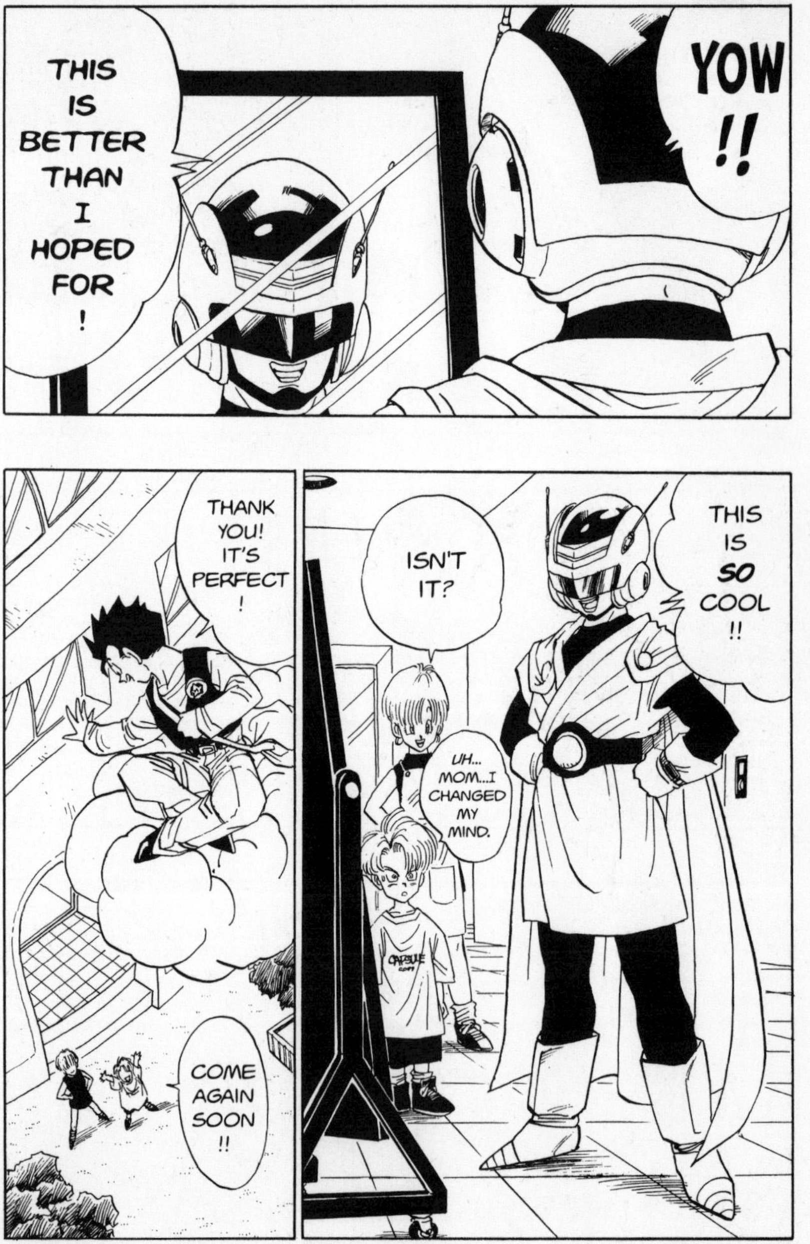
YOW !!
THIS IS BETTER THAN I HOPED FOR !
THIS IS SO COOL !!
ISN'T IT?
UH... MOM...I CHANGED MY MIND.
THANK YOU! IT'S PERFECT !
COME AGAIN SOON !!

READ THIS WAY

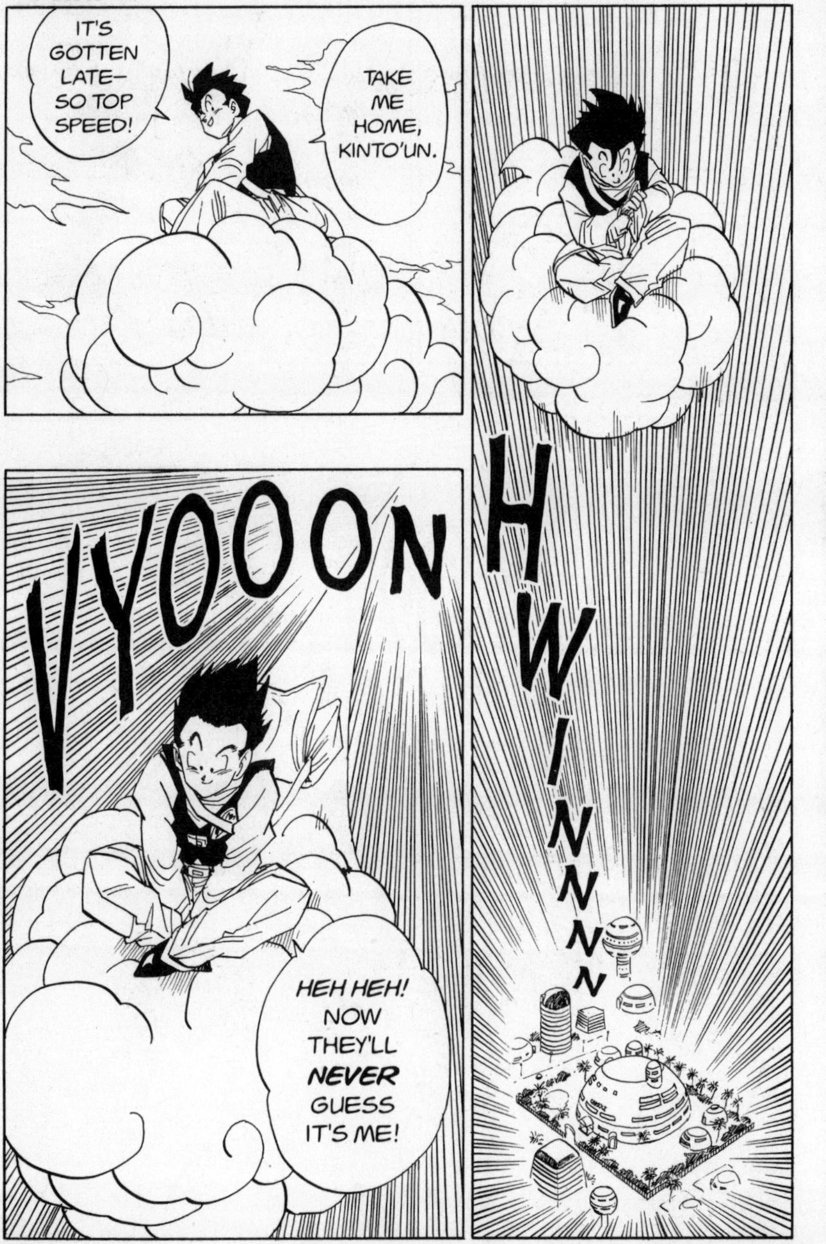
HWINNNN
TAKE ME HOME, KINTO'UN.
IT'S GOTTEN LATE—SO TOP SPEED!
VYOOON
HEH HEH! NOW THEY'LL *NEVER* GUESS IT'S ME!

READ THIS WAY

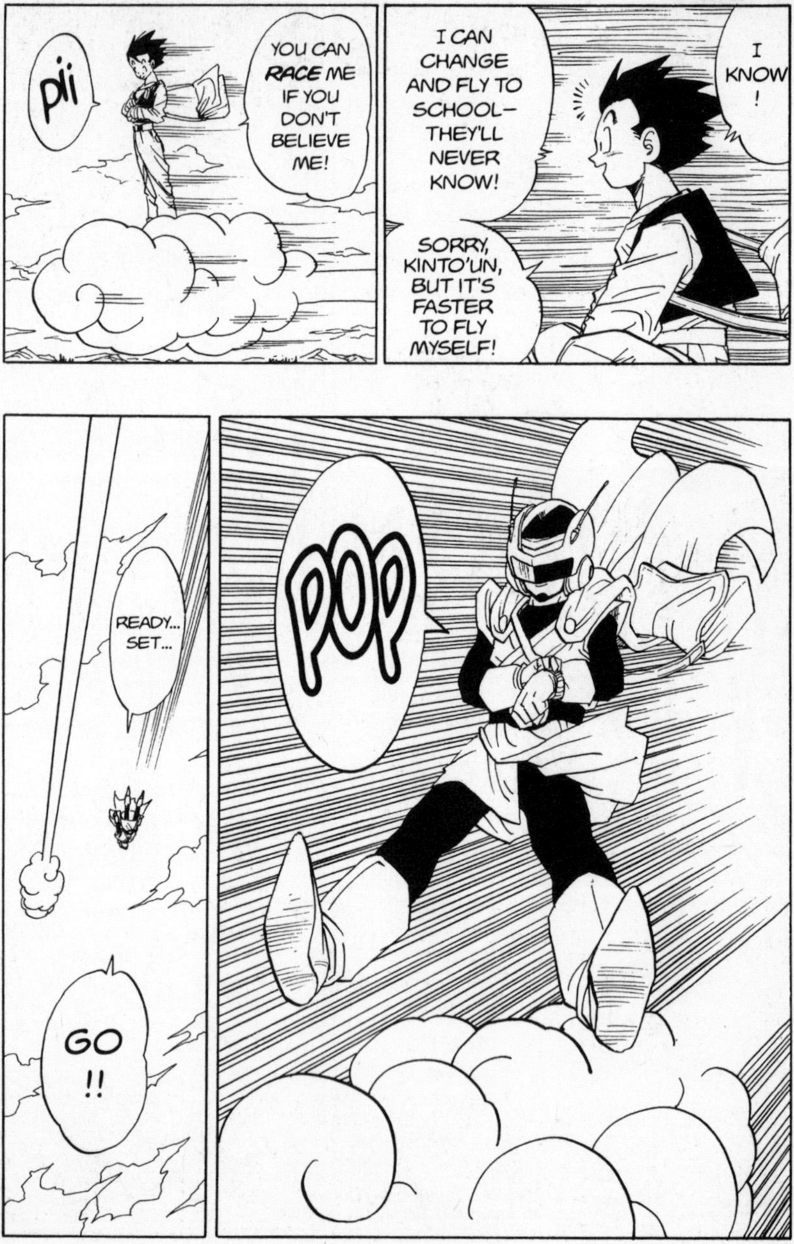
I KNOW!
I CAN CHANGE AND FLY TO SCHOOL— THEY'LL NEVER KNOW!
SORRY, KINTO'UN, BUT IT'S FASTER TO FLY MYSELF!
YOU CAN RACE ME IF YOU DON'T BELIEVE ME!
pii
POP
READY... SET...
GO !!

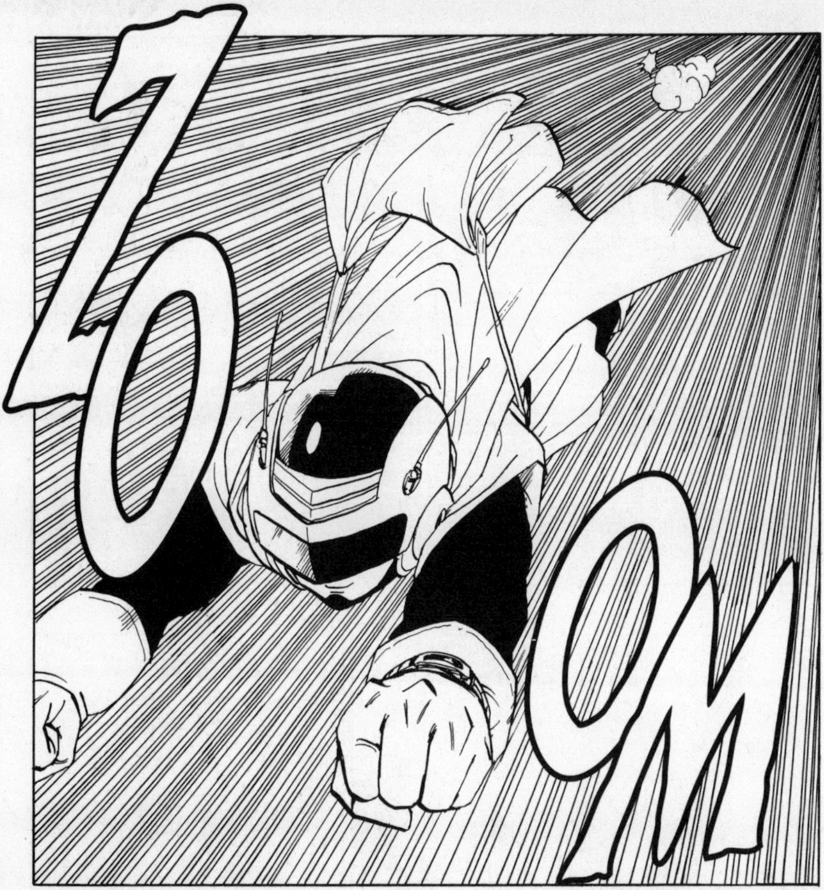
ZOOM

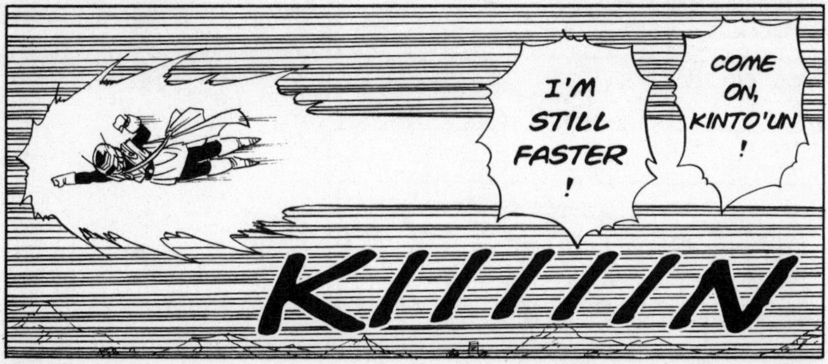
COME ON, KINTO'UN!
I'M STILL FASTER!
KIIIIIN

READ THIS WAY

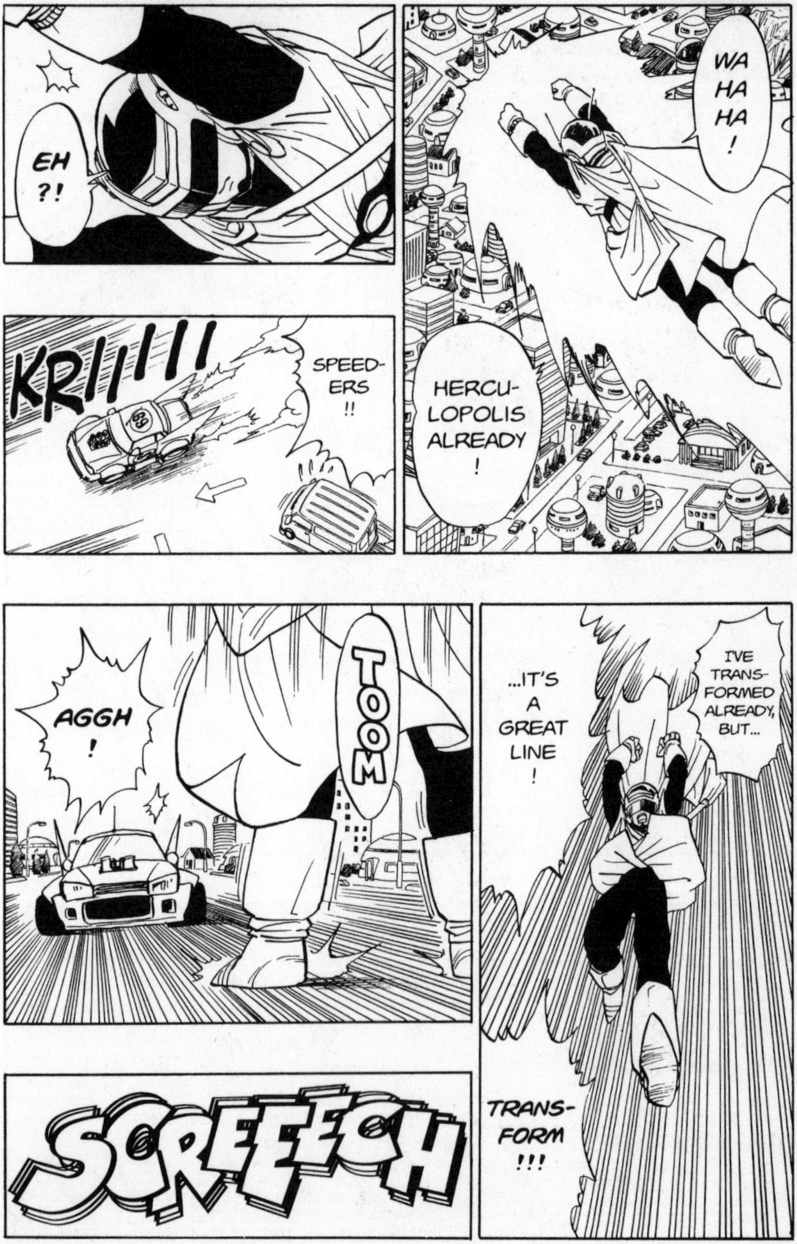
WA HA HA!
HERCULOPOLIS ALREADY!
EH?!
SPEEDERS!!
KRIIIII
I'VE TRANSFORMED ALREADY, BUT...
...IT'S A GREAT LINE!
TRANSFORM!!!
TOOM
AGGH!
SCREEECH

READ THIS WAY

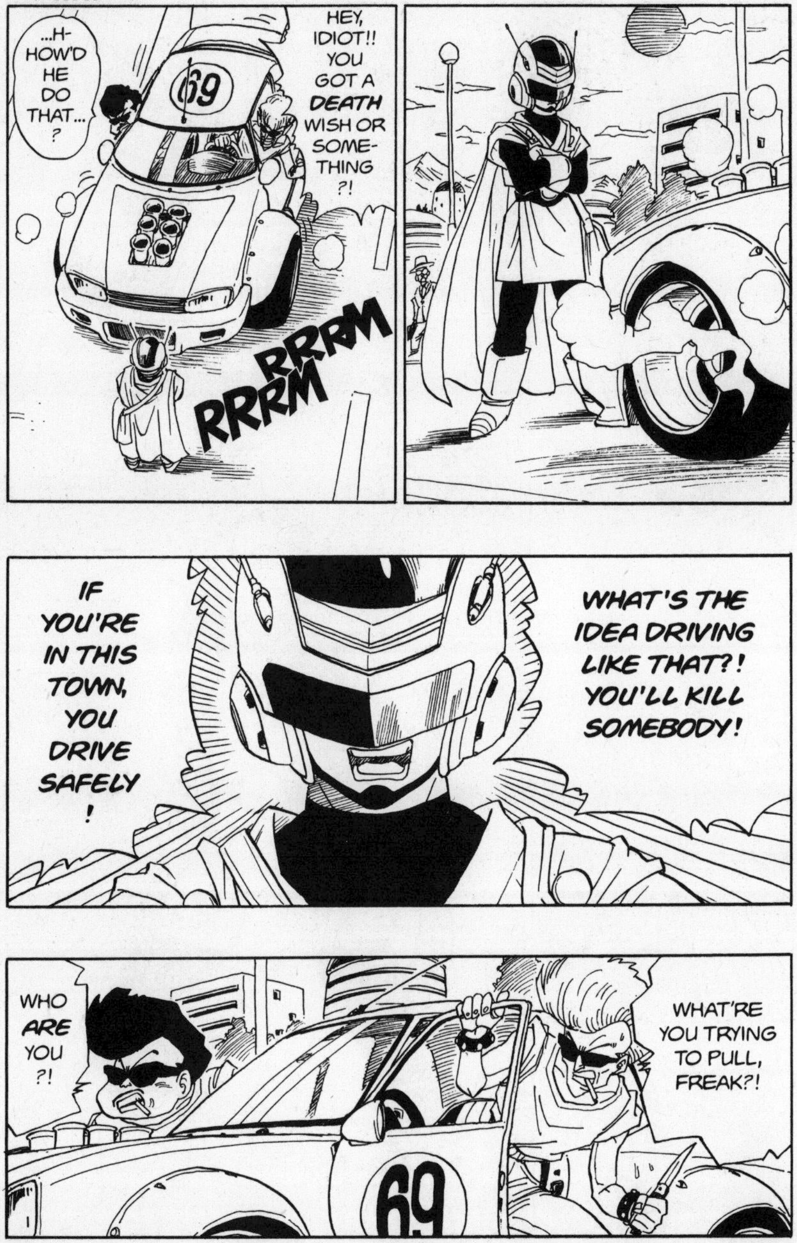
HEY, IDIOT!! YOU GOT A DEATH WISH OR SOMETHING?!
...H-HOW'D HE DO THAT...?
RRRM RRRM
WHAT'S THE IDEA DRIVING LIKE THAT?! YOU'LL KILL SOMEBODY!
IF YOU'RE IN THIS TOWN, YOU DRIVE SAFELY!
WHAT'RE YOU TRYING TO PULL, FREAK?!
WHO ARE YOU?!

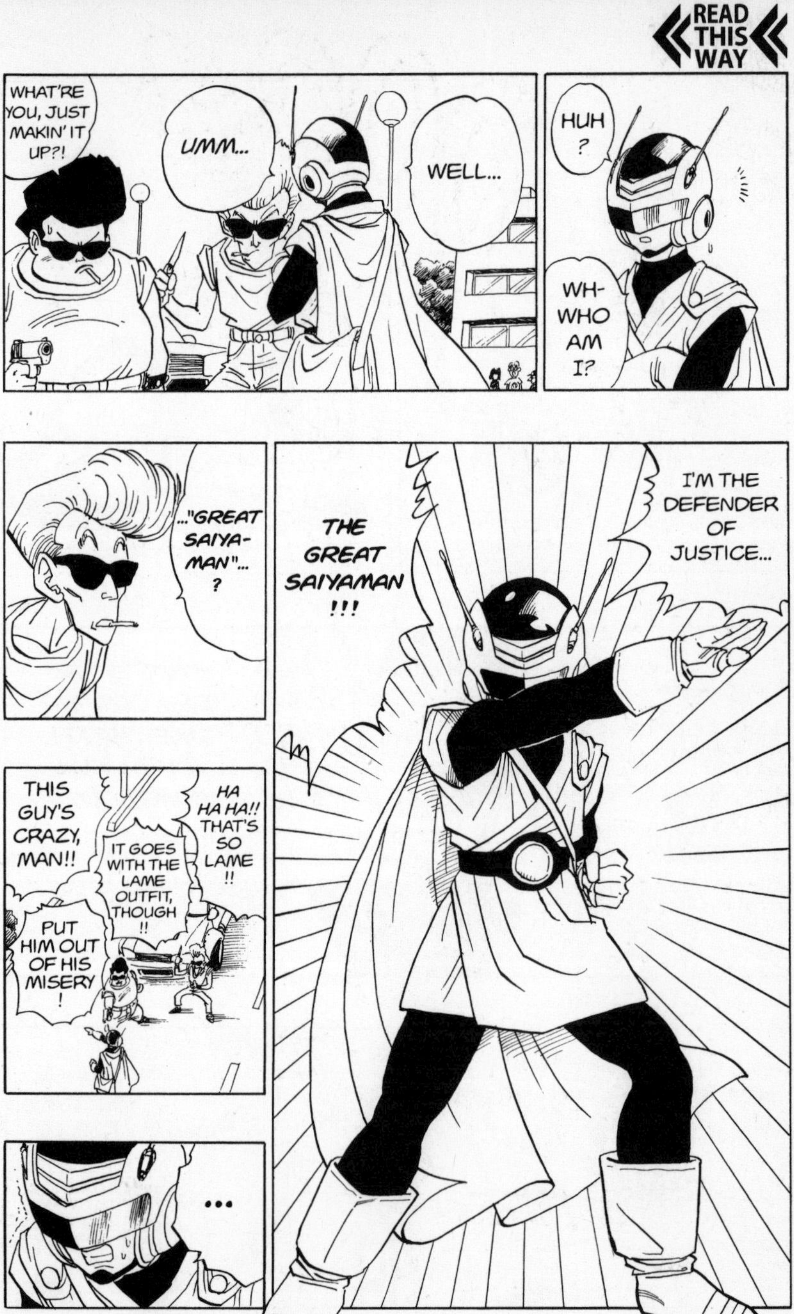
READ THIS WAY
HUH ?
WH- WHO AM I?
WELL...
UMM...
WHAT'RE YOU, JUST MAKIN' IT UP?!
I'M THE DEFENDER OF JUSTICE...
THE GREAT SAIYAMAN !!!
..."GREAT SAIYA-MAN"... ?
HA HA HA!! THAT'S SO LAME !!
IT GOES WITH THE LAME OUTFIT, THOUGH !!
THIS GUY'S CRAZY, MAN!!
PUT HIM OUT OF HIS MISERY !
...

READ THIS WAY

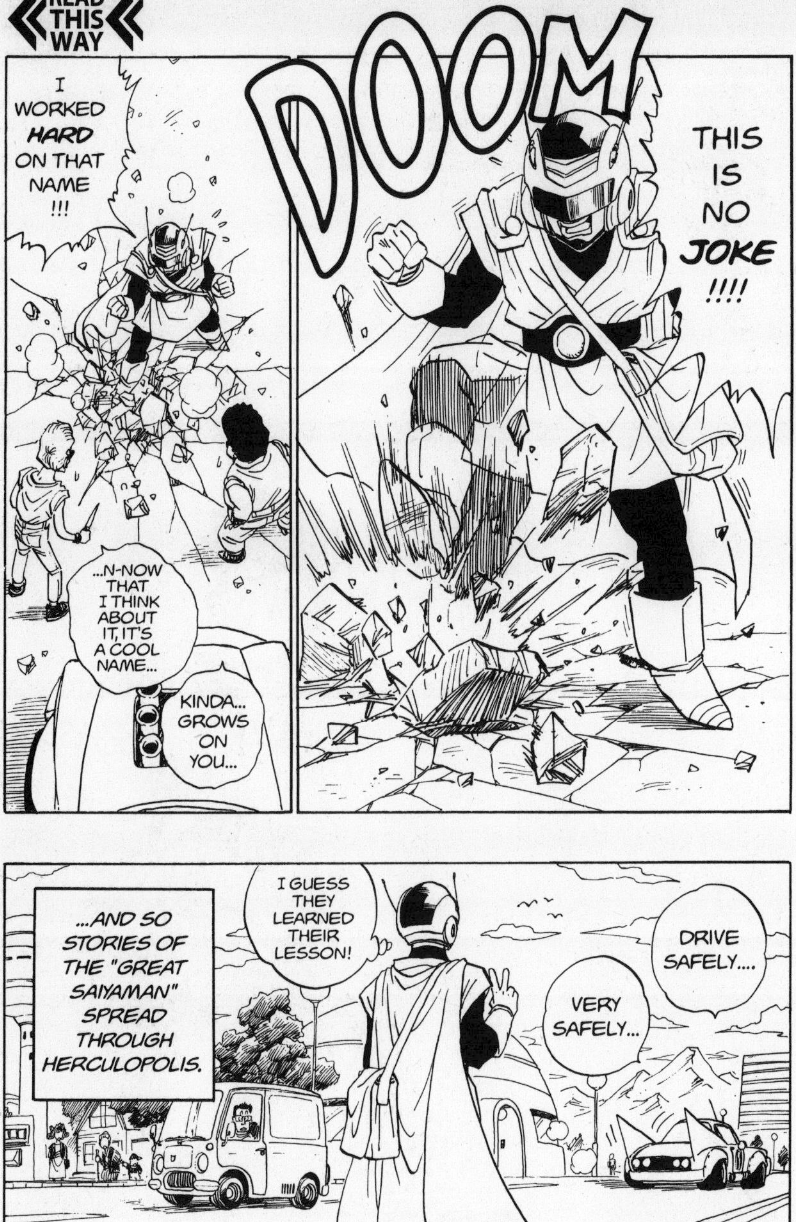
DOOM
THIS IS NO JOKE!!!!
I WORKED HARD ON THAT NAME!!!
...N-NOW THAT I THINK ABOUT IT, IT'S A COOL NAME...
KINDA... GROWS ON YOU...
DRIVE SAFELY....
VERY SAFELY...
I GUESS THEY LEARNED THEIR LESSON!
...AND SO STORIES OF THE "GREAT SAIYAMAN" SPREAD THROUGH HERCULOPOLIS.

DBZ:230
Videl's Emergency!!

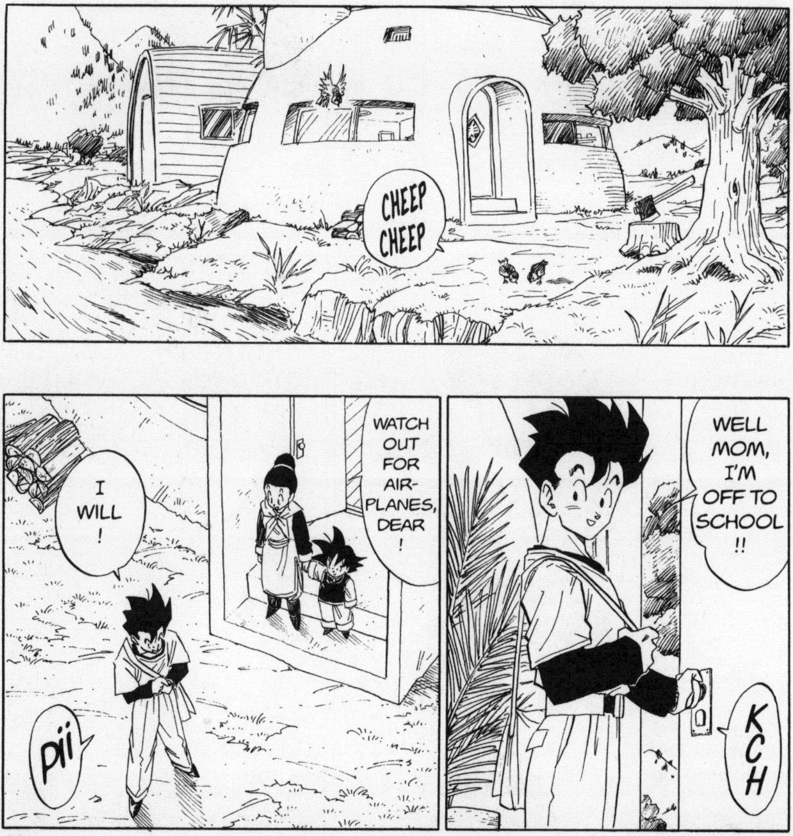
CHEEP CHEEP
WELL MOM, I'M OFF TO SCHOOL!!
KCH
WATCH OUT FOR AIR-PLANES, DEAR!
I WILL!
Pii

READ THIS WAY

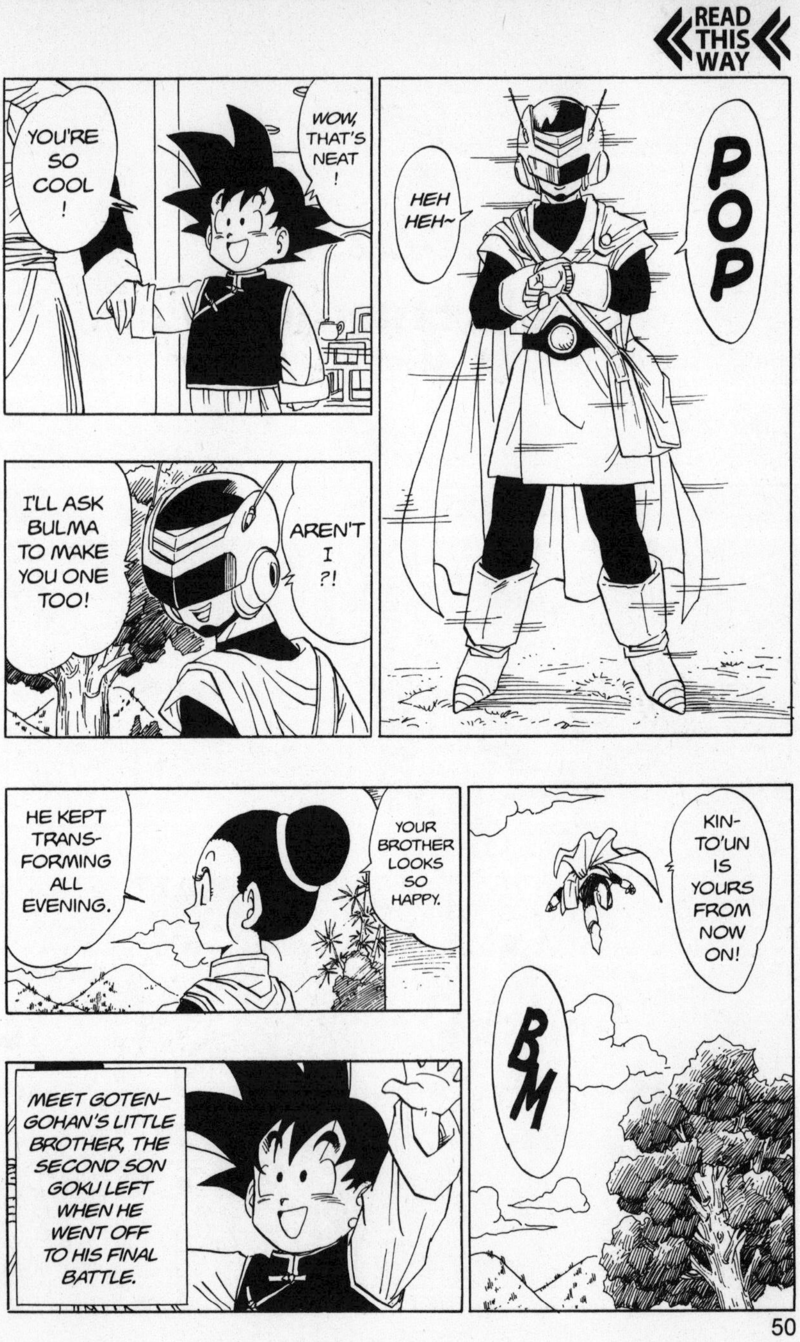

POP
HEH HEH~
WOW, THAT'S NEAT!
YOU'RE SO COOL!
AREN'T I ?!
I'LL ASK BULMA TO MAKE YOU ONE TOO!
KIN-TO'UN IS YOURS FROM NOW ON!
BM
YOUR BROTHER LOOKS SO HAPPY.
HE KEPT TRANS-FORMING ALL EVENING.
MEET GOTEN—GOHAN'S LITTLE BROTHER, THE SECOND SON GOKU LEFT WHEN HE WENT OFF TO HIS FINAL BATTLE.

READ THIS WAY

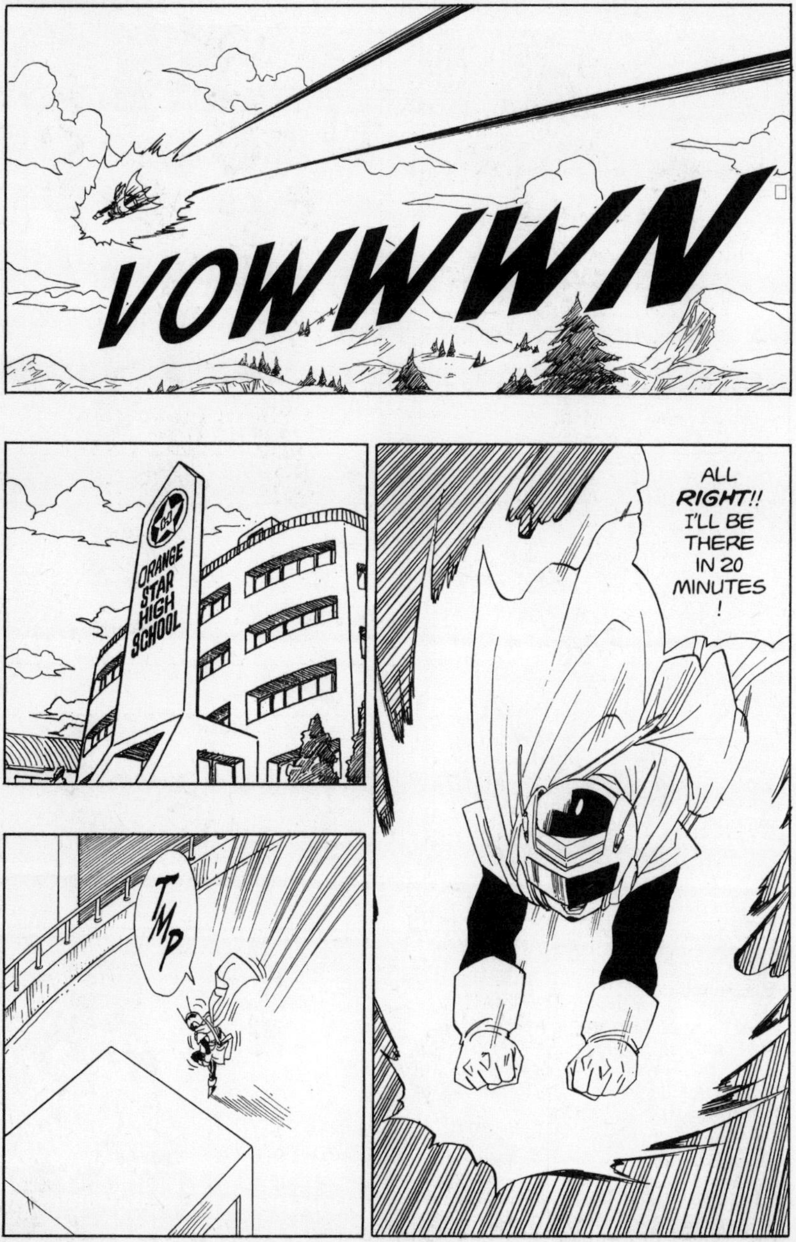
VOWWWN
ALL **RIGHT**!! I'LL BE THERE IN 20 MINUTES!
ORANGE STAR HIGH SCHOOL
TMP

READ THIS WAY

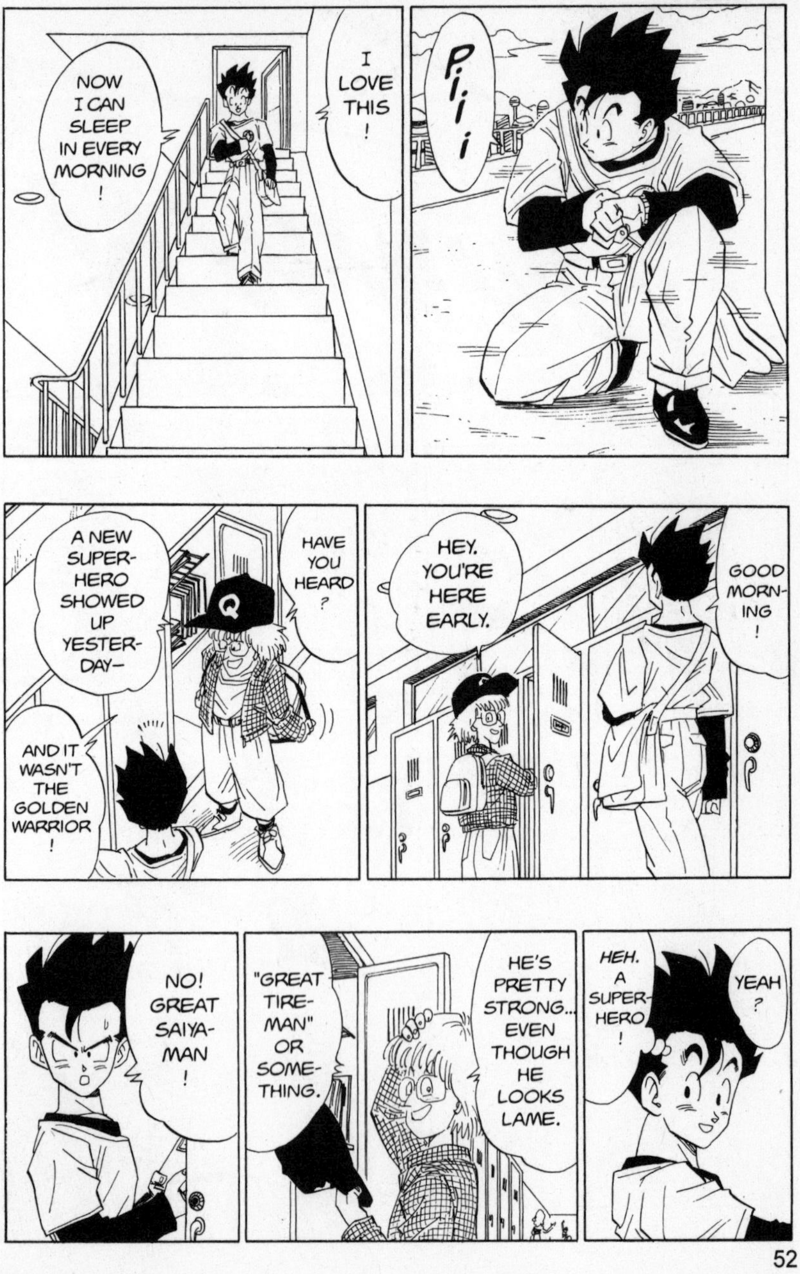
Piii
I LOVE THIS!
NOW I CAN SLEEP IN EVERY MORNING!
GOOD MORNING!
HEY. YOU'RE HERE EARLY.
HAVE YOU HEARD?
A NEW SUPER-HERO SHOWED UP YESTERDAY—
AND IT WASN'T THE GOLDEN WARRIOR!
YEAH?
HEH. A SUPER-HERO!
HE'S PRETTY STRONG... EVEN THOUGH HE LOOKS LAME.
"GREAT TIRE-MAN" OR SOMETHING.
NO! GREAT SAIYA-MAN!

READ THIS WAY

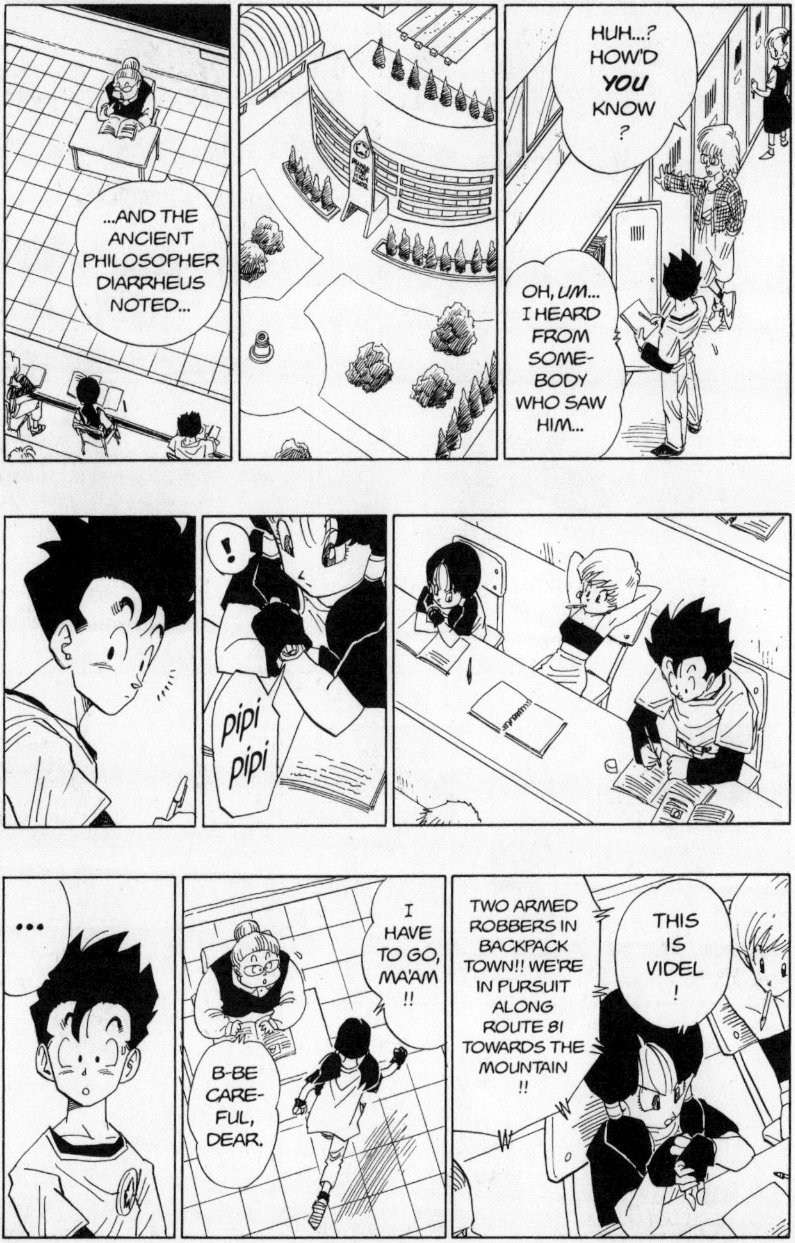
HUH...? HOW'D YOU KNOW?
OH, UM... I HEARD FROM SOME-BODY WHO SAW HIM...
...AND THE ANCIENT PHILOSOPHER DIARRHEUS NOTED...
!
pipi pipi
THIS IS VIDEL!
TWO ARMED ROBBERS IN BACKPACK TOWN!! WE'RE IN PURSUIT ALONG ROUTE 81 TOWARDS THE MOUNTAIN!!
I HAVE TO GO, MA'AM!!
B-BE CARE-FUL, DEAR.
...

READ THIS WAY

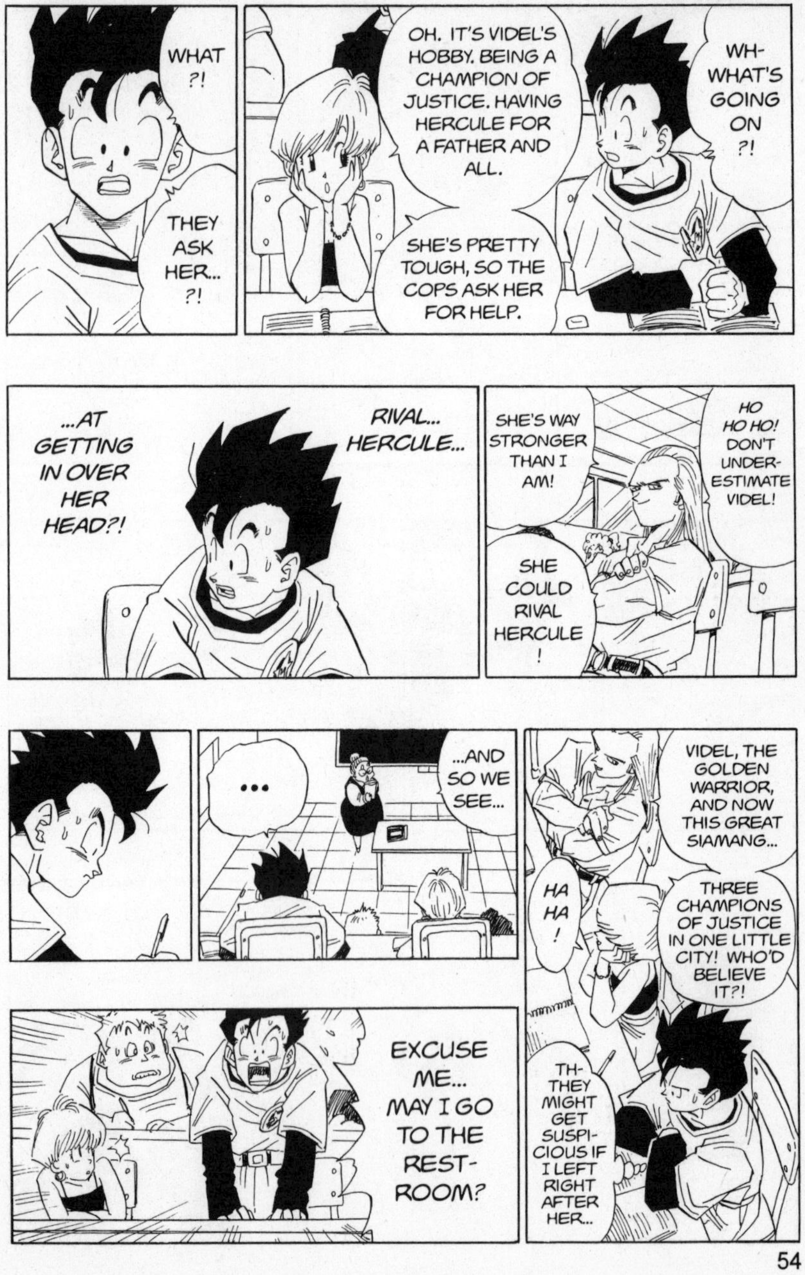
WH- WHAT'S GOING ON ?!
OH. IT'S VIDEL'S HOBBY. BEING A CHAMPION OF JUSTICE. HAVING HERCULE FOR A FATHER AND ALL.
SHE'S PRETTY TOUGH, SO THE COPS ASK HER FOR HELP.
WHAT ?!
THEY ASK HER... ?!
HO HO HO! DON'T UNDER-ESTIMATE VIDEL!
SHE'S WAY STRONGER THAN I AM!
SHE COULD RIVAL HERCULE!
RIVAL... HERCULE...
...AT GETTING IN OVER HER HEAD?!
VIDEL, THE GOLDEN WARRIOR, AND NOW THIS GREAT SIAMANG...
HA HA!
THREE CHAMPIONS OF JUSTICE IN ONE LITTLE CITY! WHO'D BELIEVE IT?!
TH-THEY MIGHT GET SUSPICIOUS IF I LEFT RIGHT AFTER HER...
...AND SO WE SEE...
...
EXCUSE ME... MAY I GO TO THE REST-ROOM?

READ THIS WAY

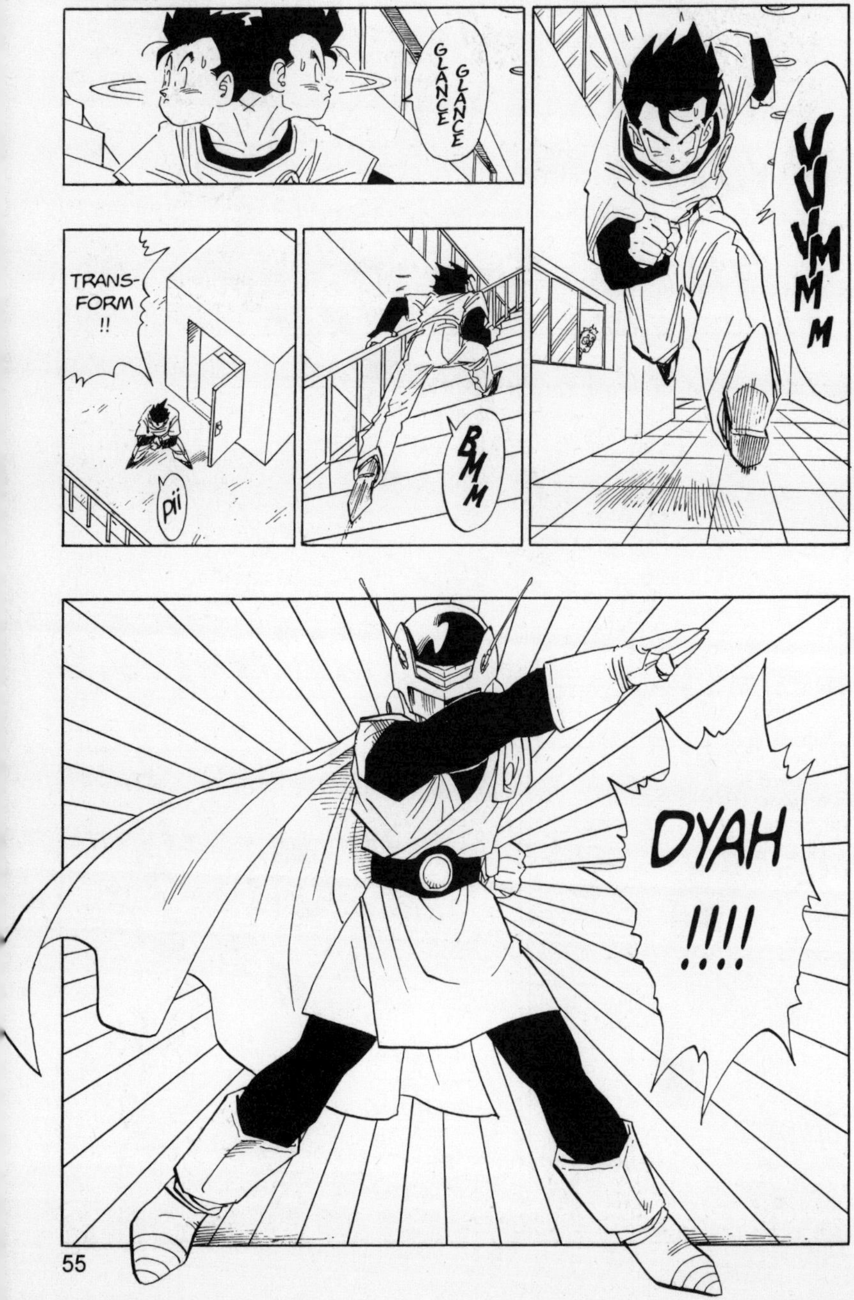
VUMMM
GLANCE GLANCE
BMM
TRANS-FORM !!
pii
DYAH !!!!

READ THIS WAY

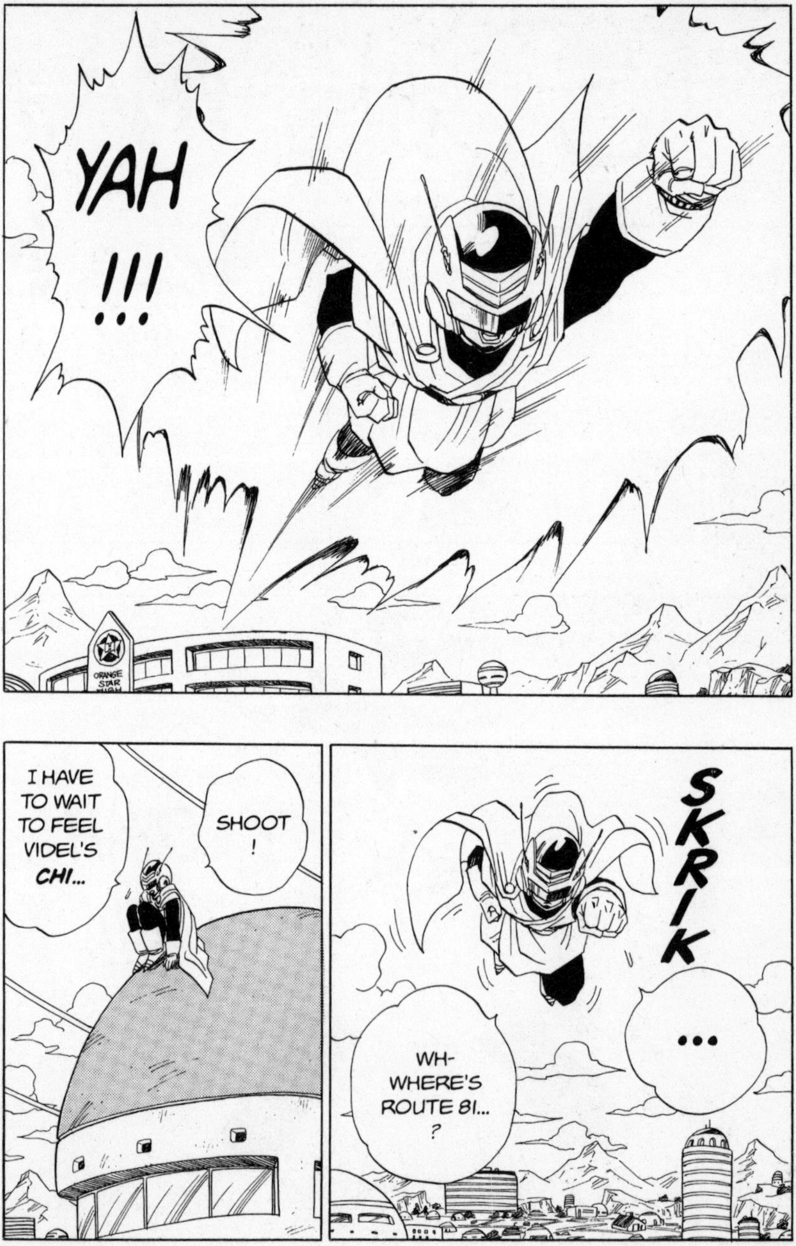

YAH!!!
ORANGE STAR
SKRIK
...
WH- WHERE'S ROUTE 81...?
SHOOT!
I HAVE TO WAIT TO FEEL VIDEL'S **CHI**...

READ THIS WAY

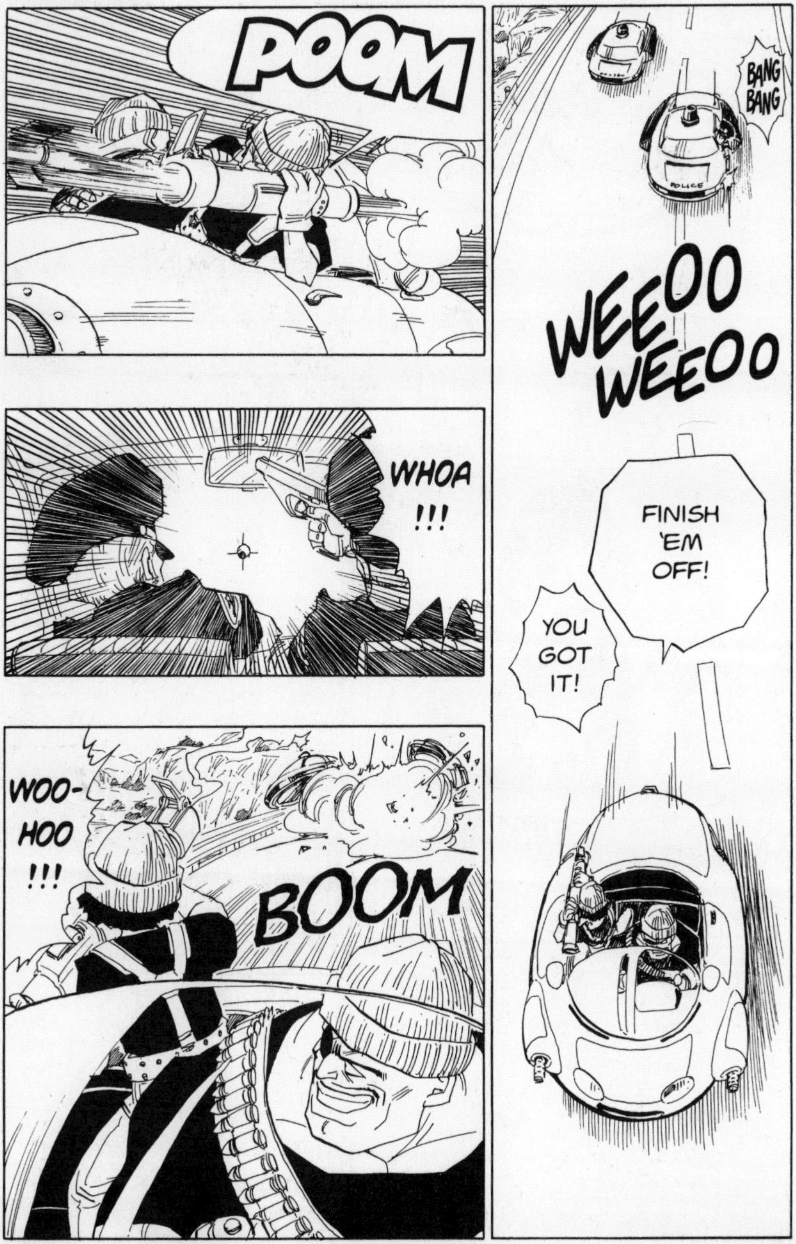
BANG BANG
WEEOO WEEOO
FINISH 'EM OFF!
YOU GOT IT!
POOM
WHOA !!!
BOOM
WOO-HOO !!!

READ THIS WAY

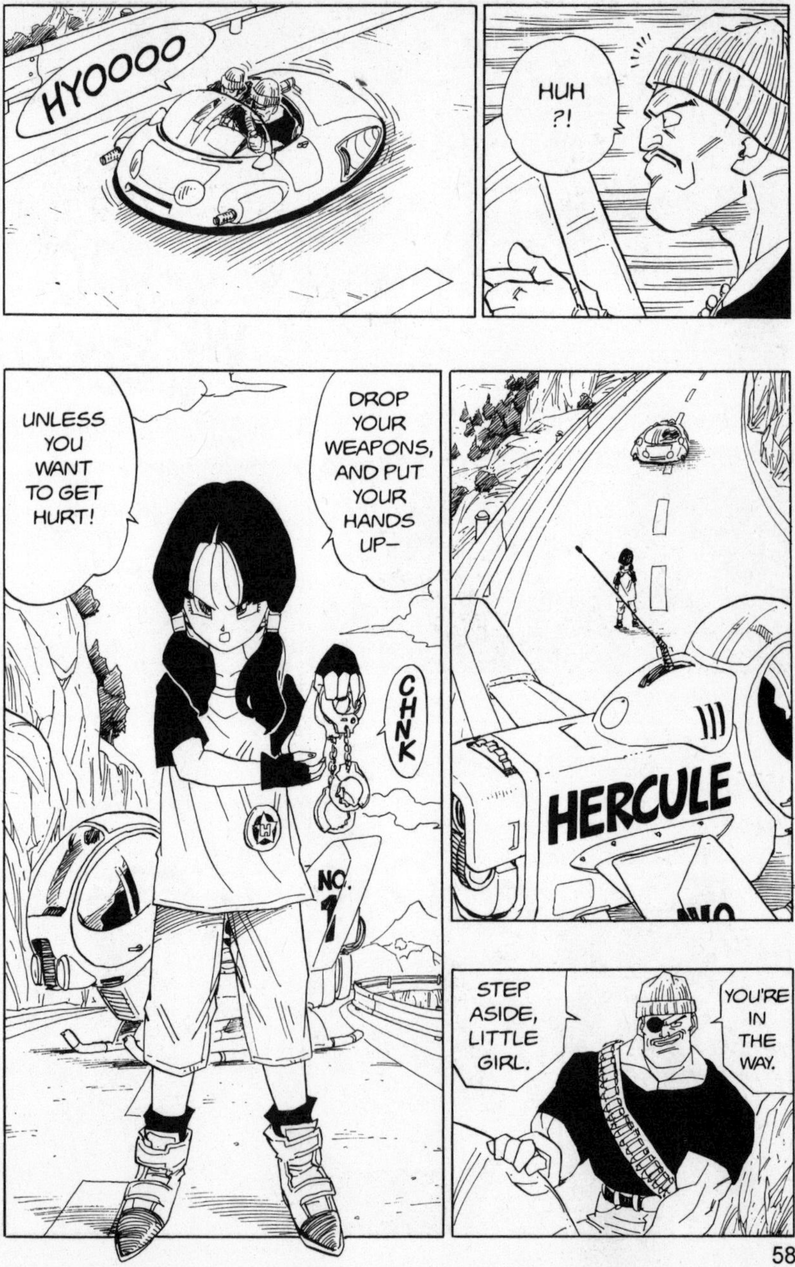

HUH ?!
HYOOOO
HERCULE
STEP ASIDE, LITTLE GIRL.
YOU'RE IN THE WAY.
DROP YOUR WEAPONS, AND PUT YOUR HANDS UP—
UNLESS YOU WANT TO GET HURT!
CHNK
NO. 1

READ THIS WAY

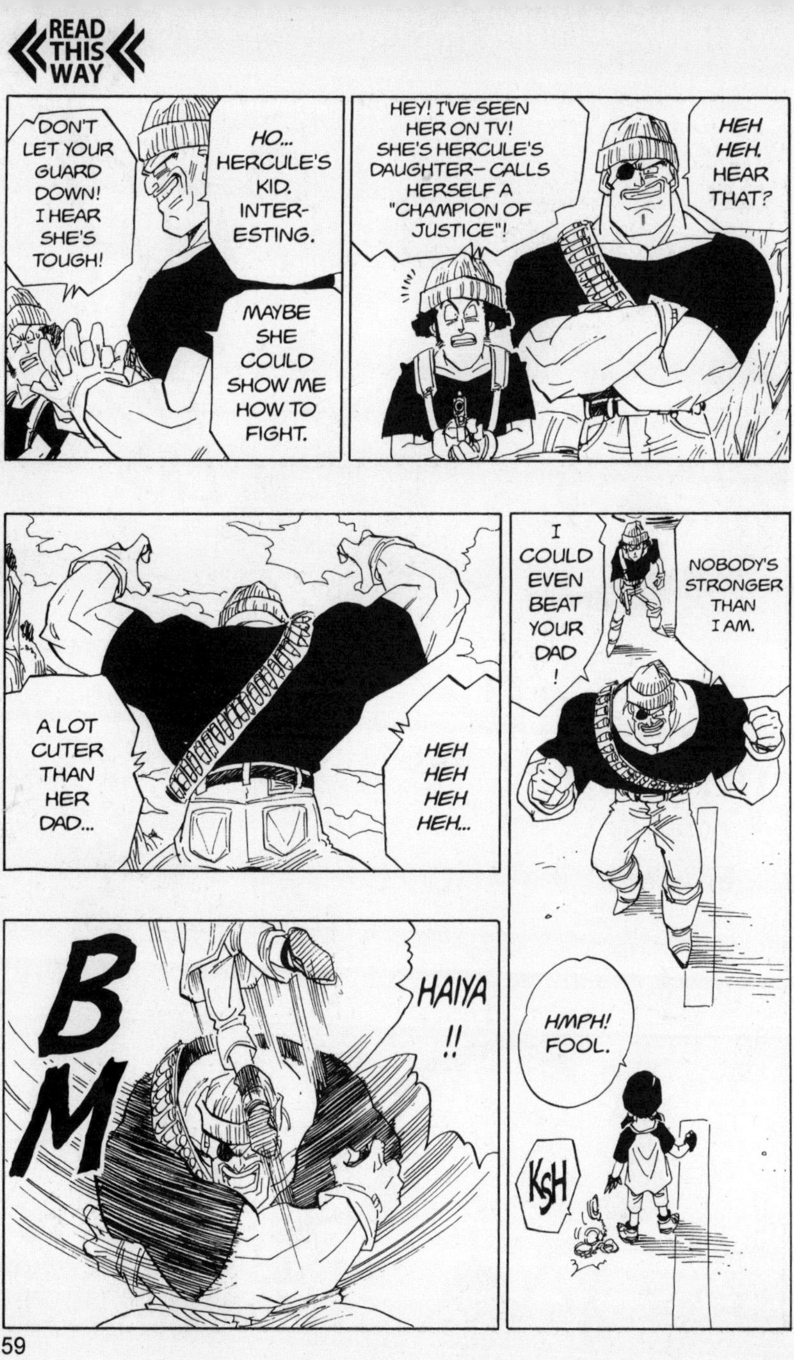
HEH HEH. HEAR THAT?
HEY! I'VE SEEN HER ON TV! SHE'S HERCULE'S DAUGHTER— CALLS HERSELF A "CHAMPION OF JUSTICE"!
HO... HERCULE'S KID. INTER-ESTING.
DON'T LET YOUR GUARD DOWN! I HEAR SHE'S TOUGH!
MAYBE SHE COULD SHOW ME HOW TO FIGHT.
NOBODY'S STRONGER THAN I AM.
I COULD EVEN BEAT YOUR DAD!
HMPH! FOOL.
KSH
HEH HEH HEH HEH...
A LOT CUTER THAN HER DAD...
HAIYA!!
BM

READ THIS WAY

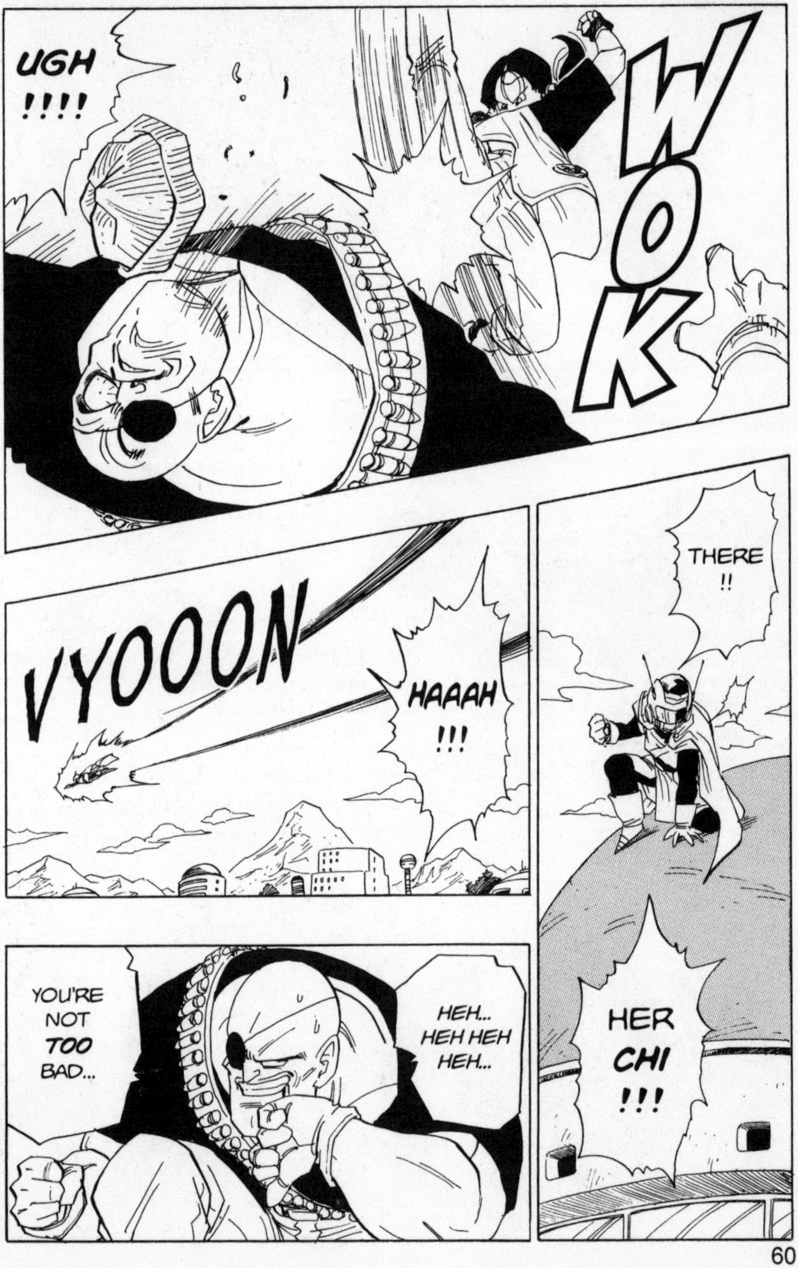
WOK
UGH !!!!
THERE !!
HER CHI !!!
HAAAH !!!
VYOOON
HEH... HEH HEH HEH...
YOU'RE NOT TOO BAD...

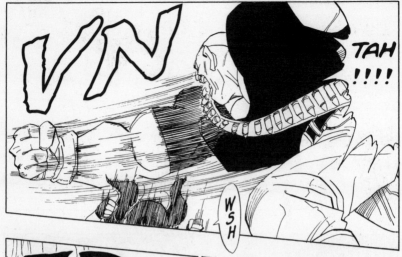

VN

TAH!!!!

WSH

ZDD

WOK

A-ARE YOU OK?!

OF COURSE I AM!!!

AND I'M THROUGH PLAYING AROUND!!

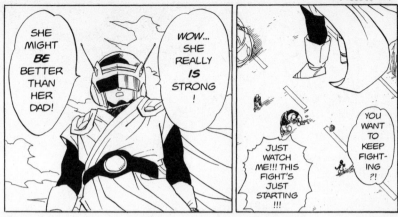

READ THIS WAY

YOU WANT TO KEEP FIGHTING?!
JUST WATCH ME!!! THIS FIGHT'S JUST STARTING!!!
WOW... SHE REALLY IS STRONG!
SHE MIGHT BE BETTER THAN HER DAD!
WOK
ZUD
GOK
!!
DOP
WELL?! HAS IT STARTED YET?!
TAKE THIS...!
RRG
OH NO!

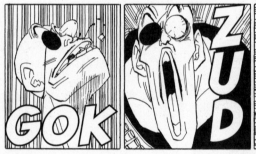

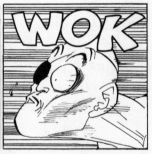

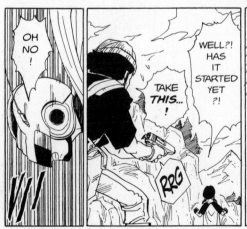

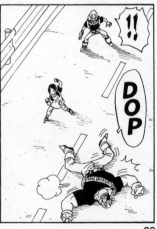

READ THIS WAY

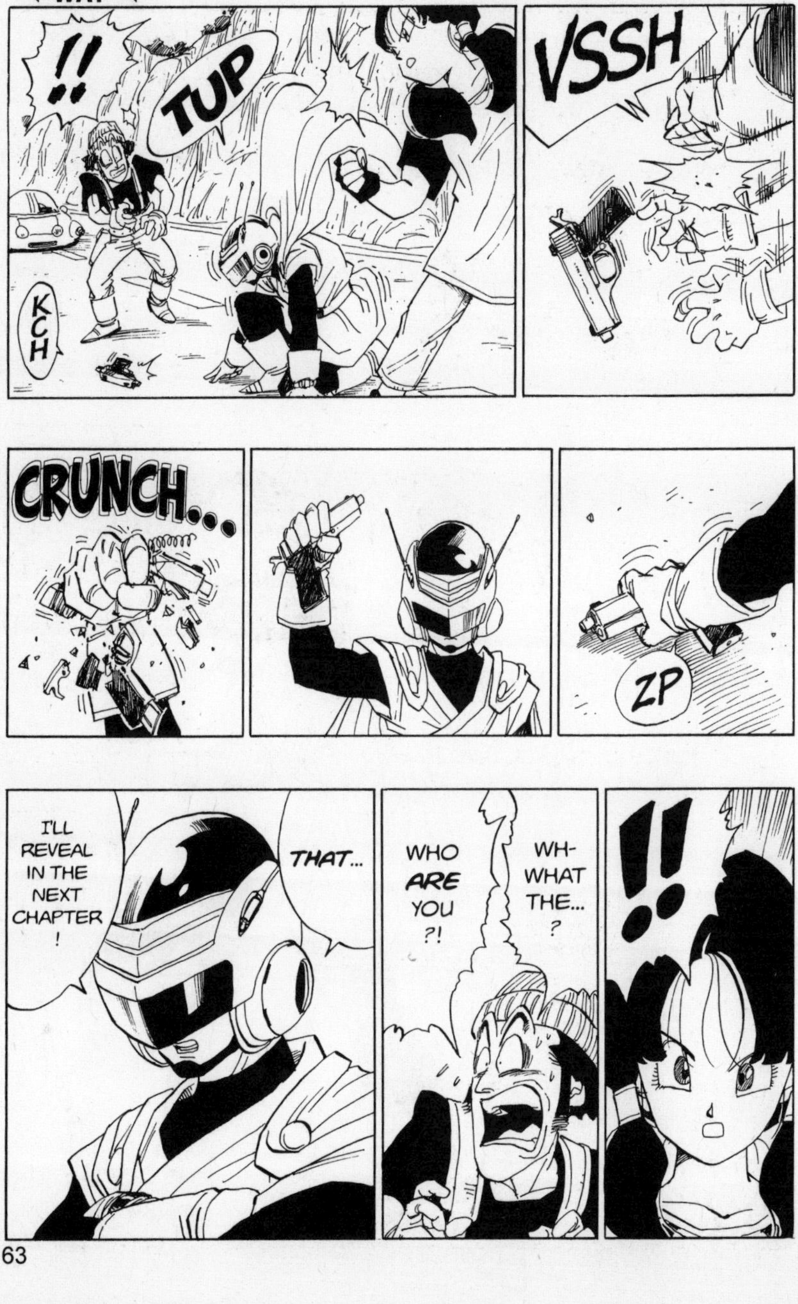

VSSH
TUP
!!
KCH
ZP
CRUNCH...
!!
WH- WHAT THE...?
WHO ARE YOU?!
THAT...
I'LL REVEAL IN THE NEXT CHAPTER!

DBZ:231 • Revealed!!!

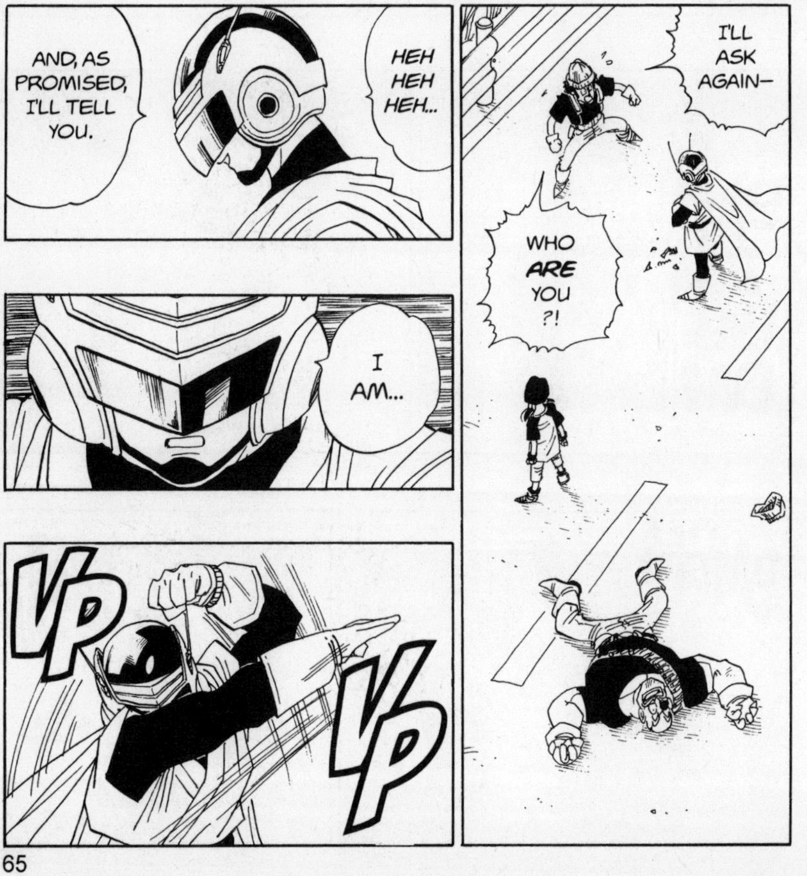
I'LL ASK AGAIN—
WHO **ARE** YOU ?!
HEH HEH HEH...
AND, AS PROMISED, I'LL TELL YOU.
I AM...
VP
VP

READ THIS WAY

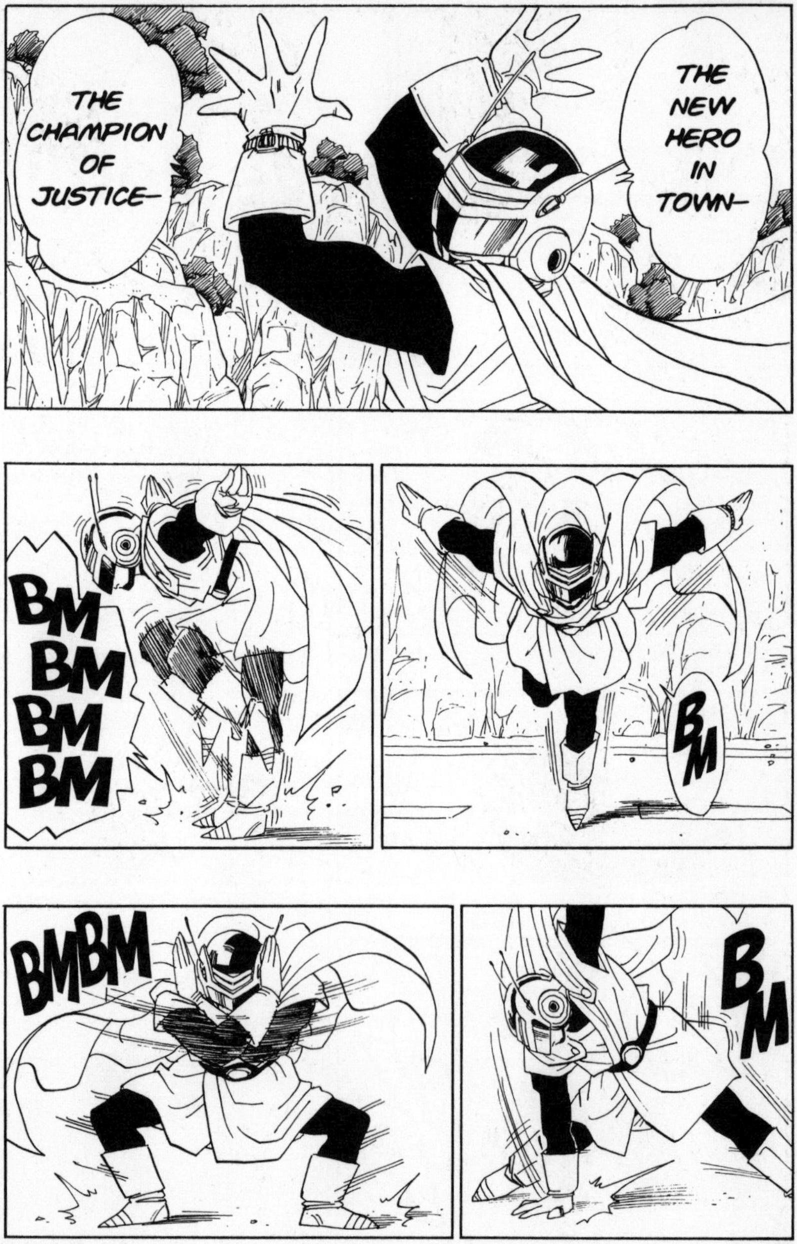
THE NEW HERO IN TOWN—
THE CHAMPION OF JUSTICE—
BM
BM BM BM BM
BM
BMBM

READ THIS WAY

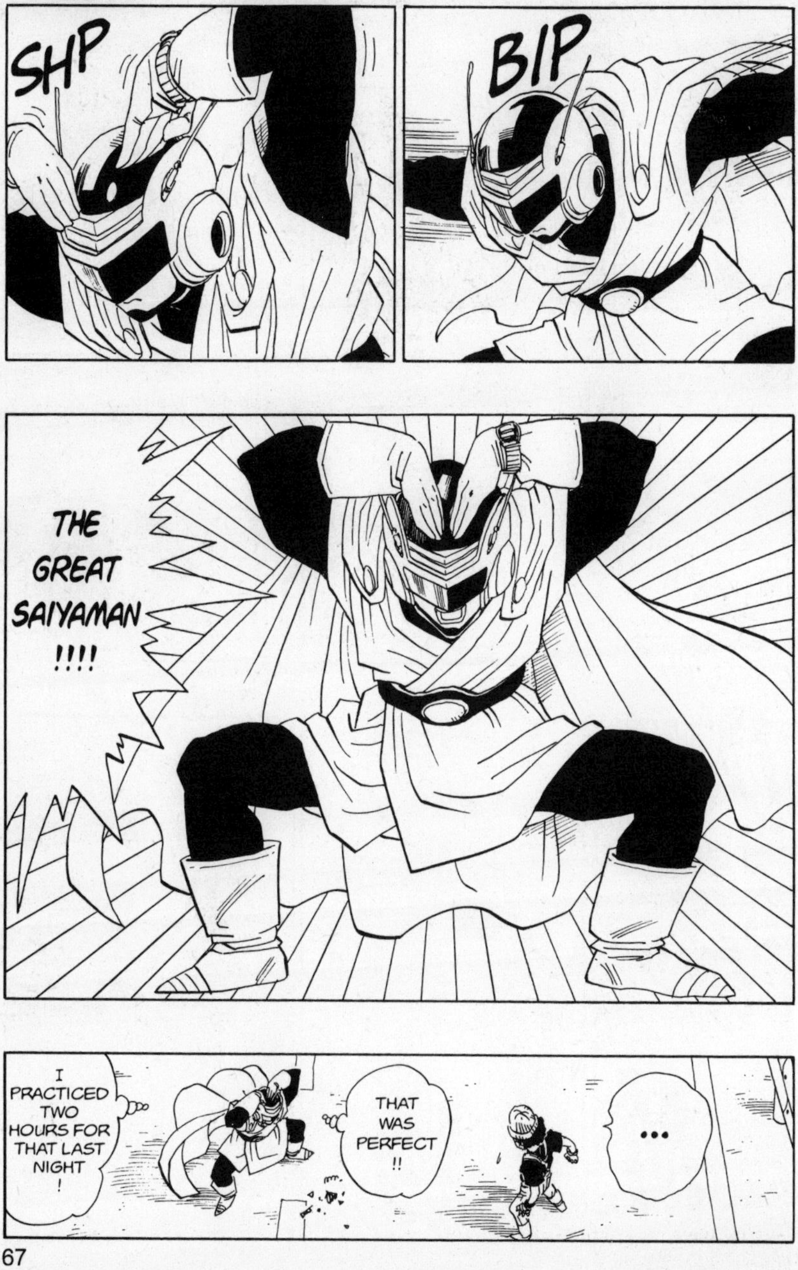
BIP
SHP
THE GREAT SAIYAMAN!!!!
...
THAT WAS PERFECT!!
I PRACTICED TWO HOURS FOR THAT LAST NIGHT!

READ THIS WAY

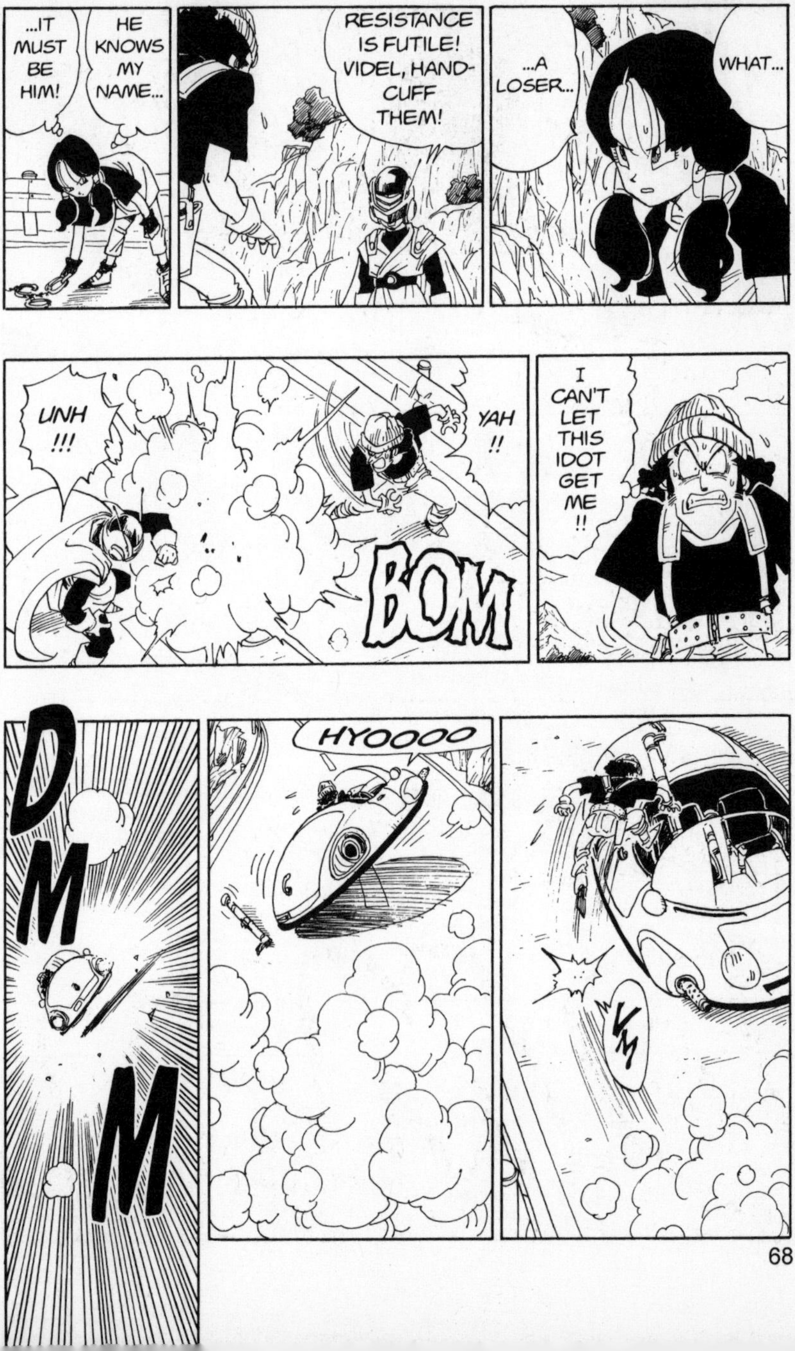

WHAT...
...A LOSER...
RESISTANCE IS FUTILE! VIDEL, HAND-CUFF THEM!
HE KNOWS MY NAME...
...IT MUST BE HIM!
I CAN'T LET THIS IDOT GET ME !!
YAH !!
BOM
UNH !!!
VM
HYOOOO
DMMM

READ THIS WAY

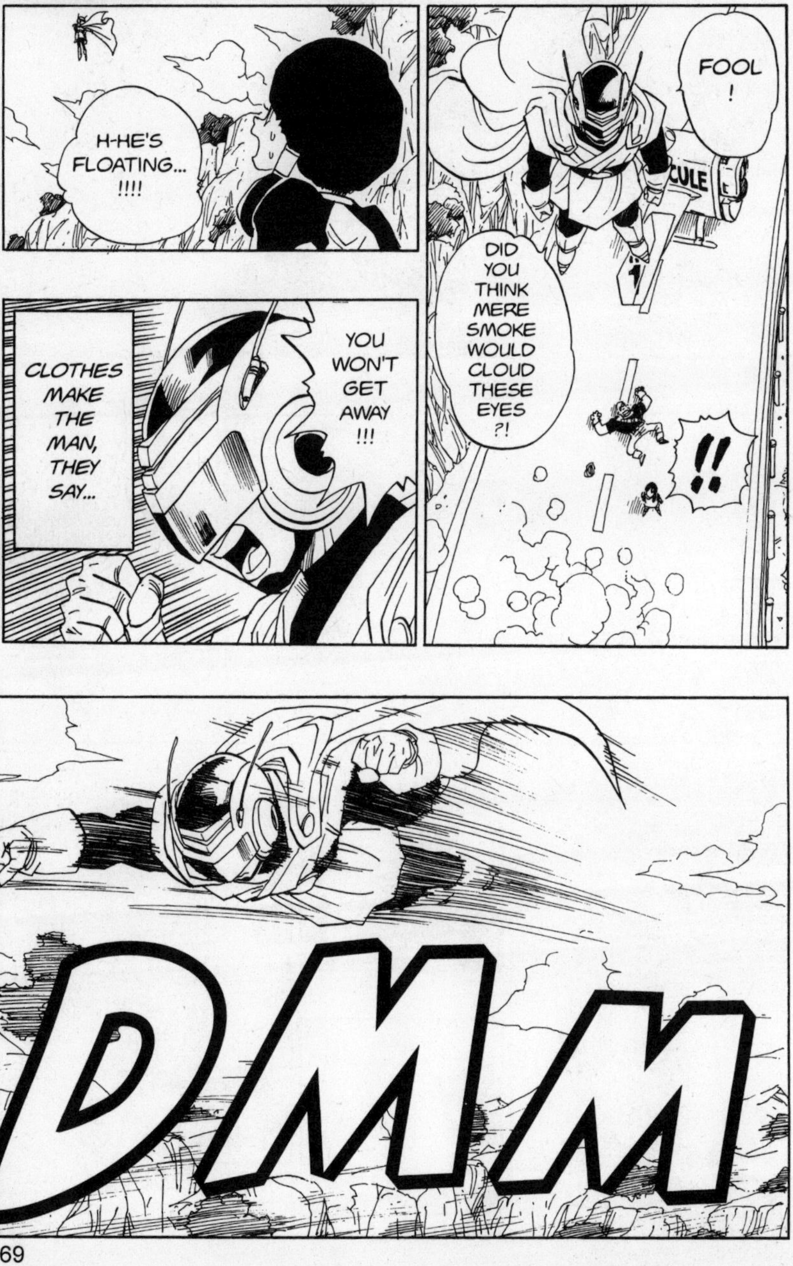
FOOL !
DID YOU THINK MERE SMOKE WOULD CLOUD THESE EYES ?!
!!
H-HE'S FLOATING... !!!!
YOU WON'T GET AWAY !!!
CLOTHES MAKE THE MAN, THEY SAY...
DMM

READ THIS WAY

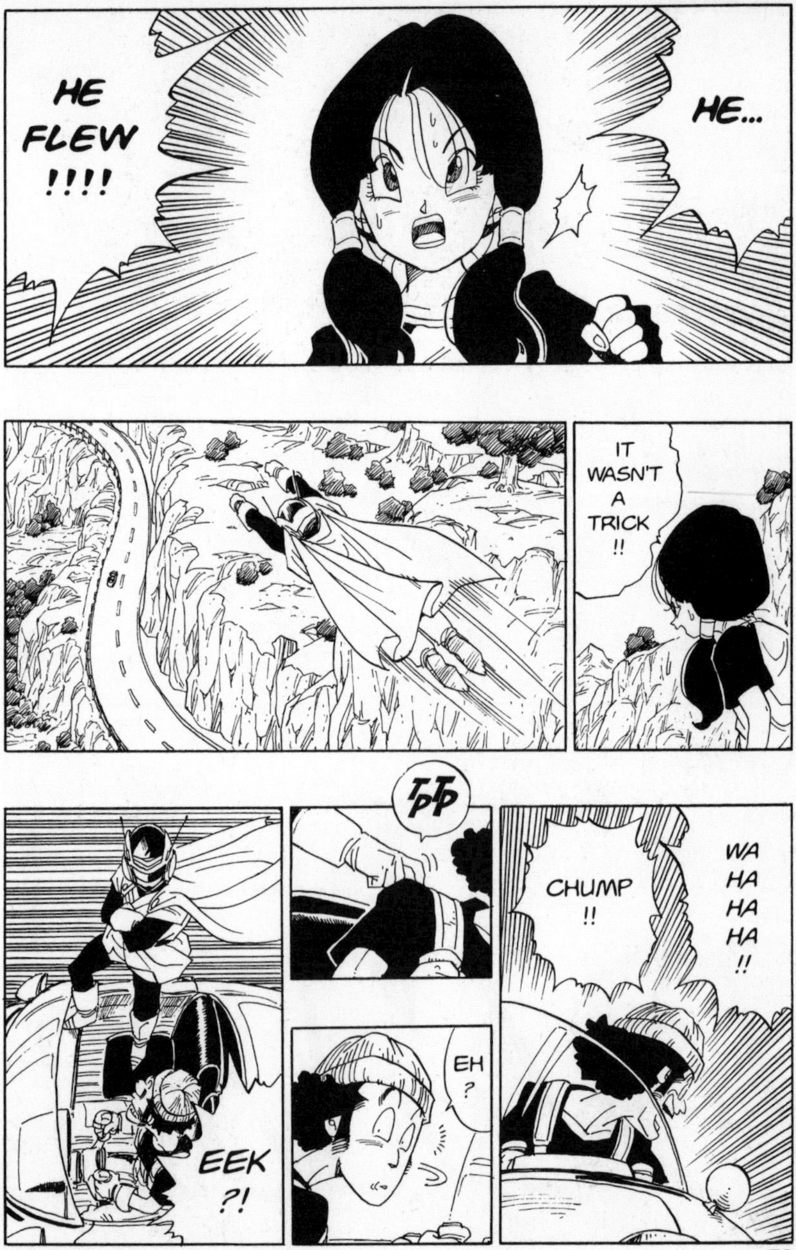
HE...
HE FLEW !!!!
IT WASN'T A TRICK !!
WA HA HA HA !!
CHUMP !!
TPTP
EH ?
EEK ?!

READ THIS WAY

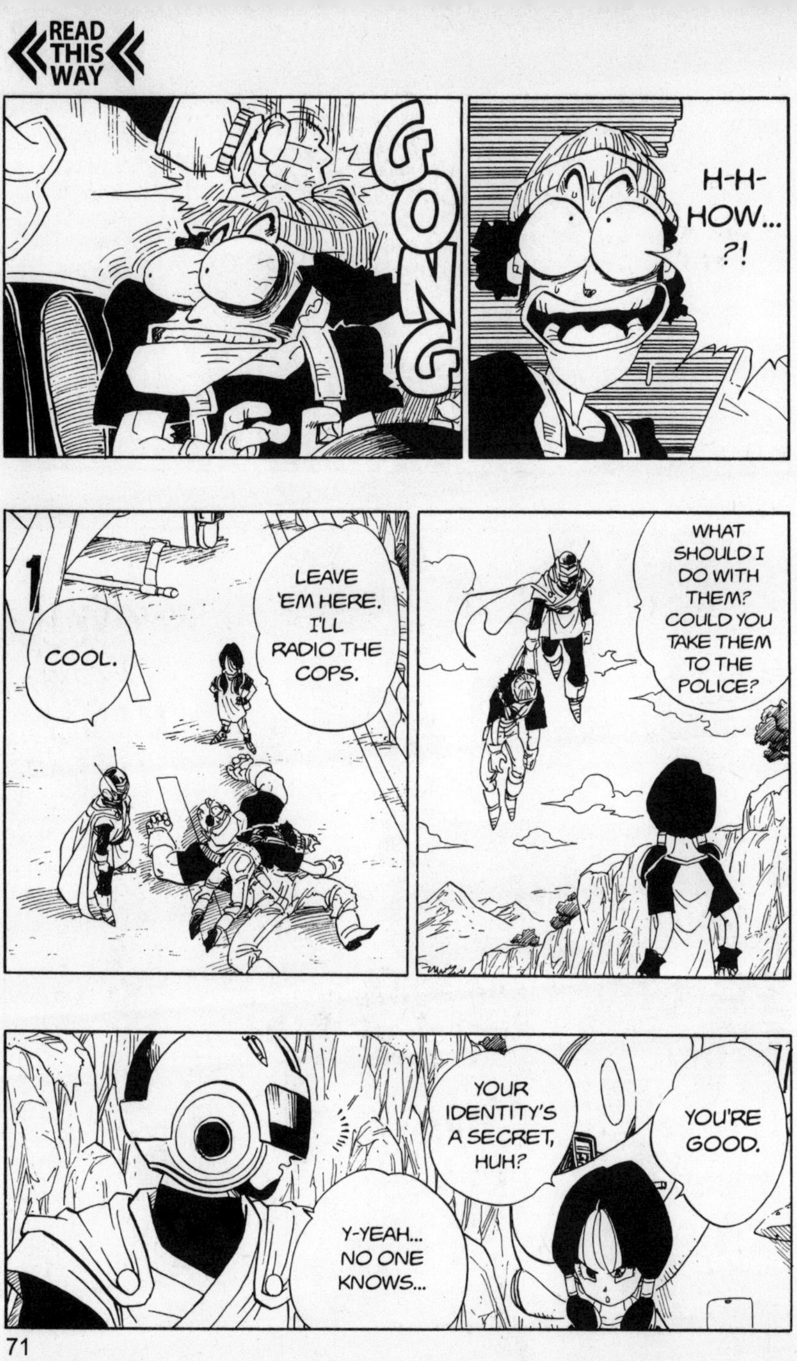

H-H-HOW...?!
GONG
WHAT SHOULD I DO WITH THEM? COULD YOU TAKE THEM TO THE POLICE?
LEAVE 'EM HERE. I'LL RADIO THE COPS.
COOL.
YOU'RE GOOD.
YOUR IDENTITY'S A SECRET, HUH?
Y-YEAH... NO ONE KNOWS...

READ THIS WAY

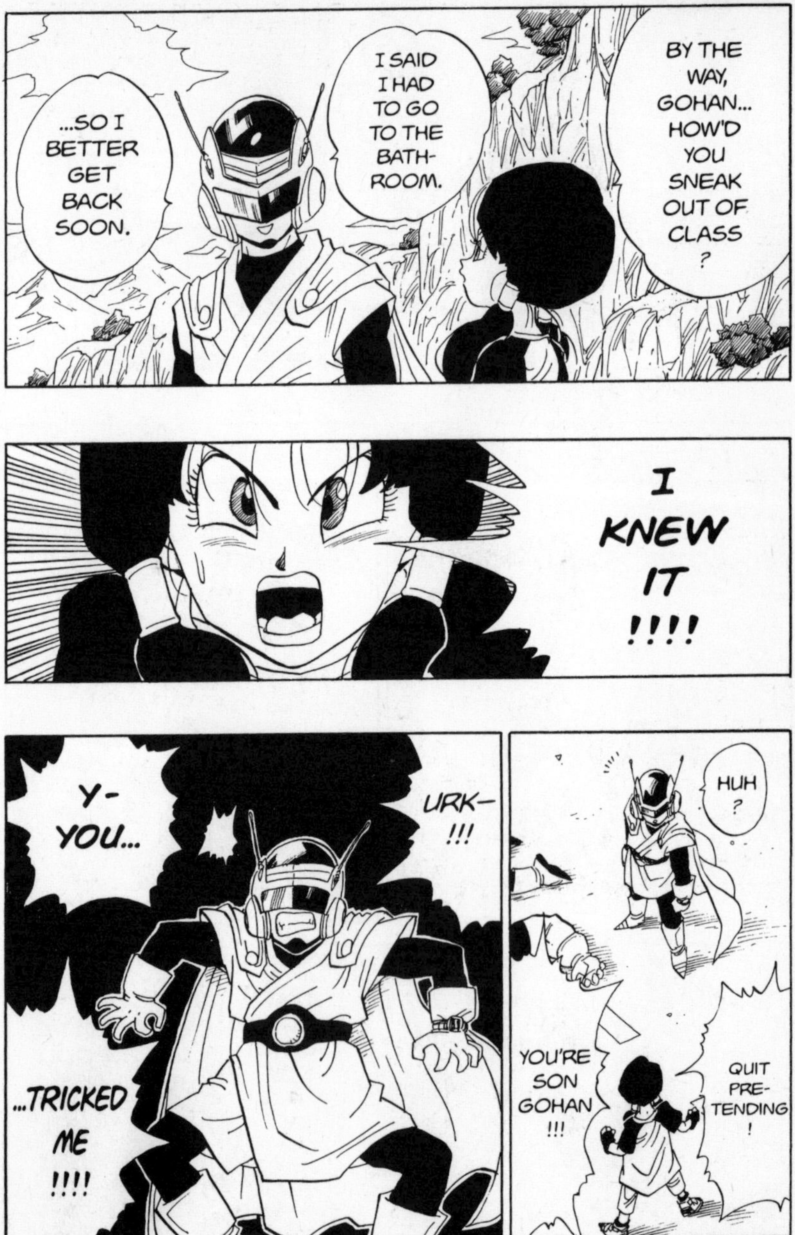

BY THE WAY, GOHAN... HOW'D YOU SNEAK OUT OF CLASS?
I SAID I HAD TO GO TO THE BATHROOM.
...SO I BETTER GET BACK SOON.
I KNEW IT !!!!
HUH?
QUIT PRETENDING!
YOU'RE SON GOHAN !!!
URK- !!!
Y-YOU...
...TRICKED ME !!!!

READ THIS WAY

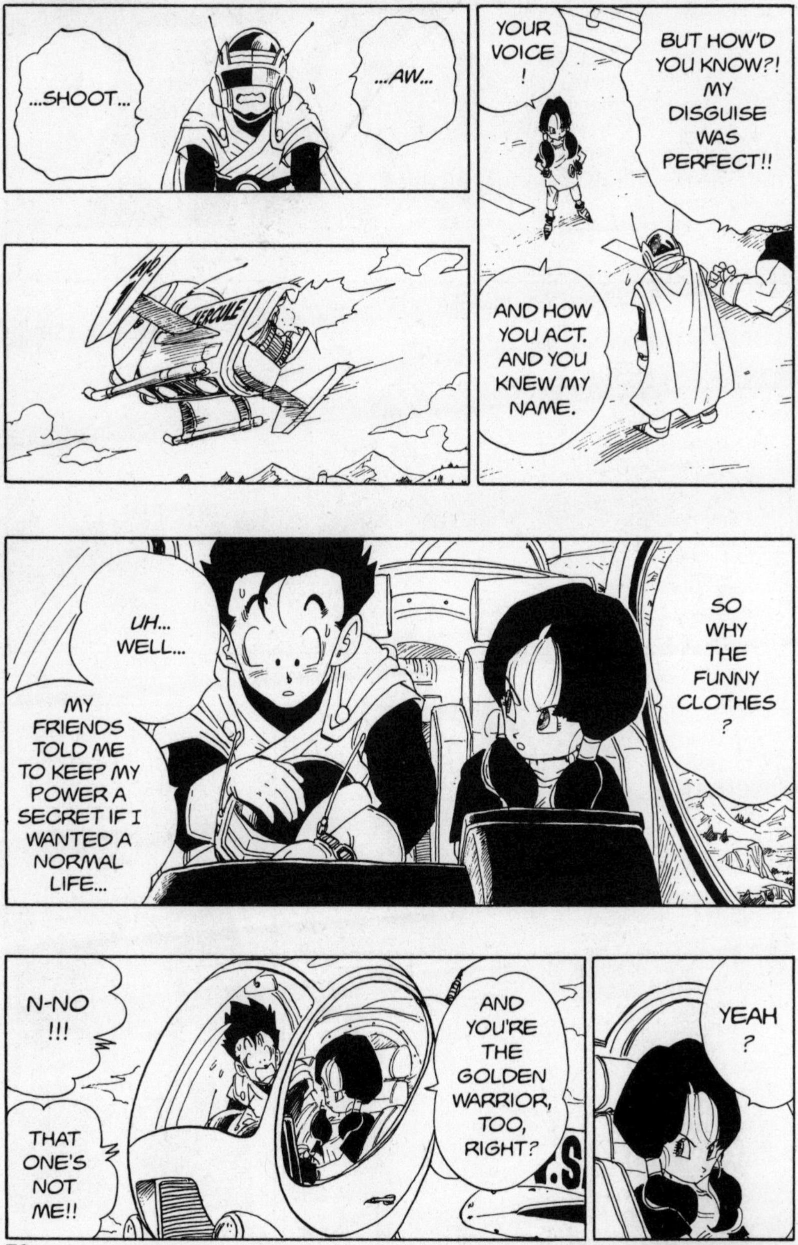
BUT HOW'D YOU KNOW?! MY DISGUISE WAS PERFECT!!
YOUR VOICE !
AND HOW YOU ACT. AND YOU KNEW MY NAME.
...AW...
...SHOOT...
HERCULE
SO WHY THE FUNNY CLOTHES ?
UH... WELL...
MY FRIENDS TOLD ME TO KEEP MY POWER A SECRET IF I WANTED A NORMAL LIFE...
YEAH ?
AND YOU'RE THE GOLDEN WARRIOR, TOO, RIGHT?
N-NO !!!
THAT ONE'S NOT ME!!

READ THIS WAY

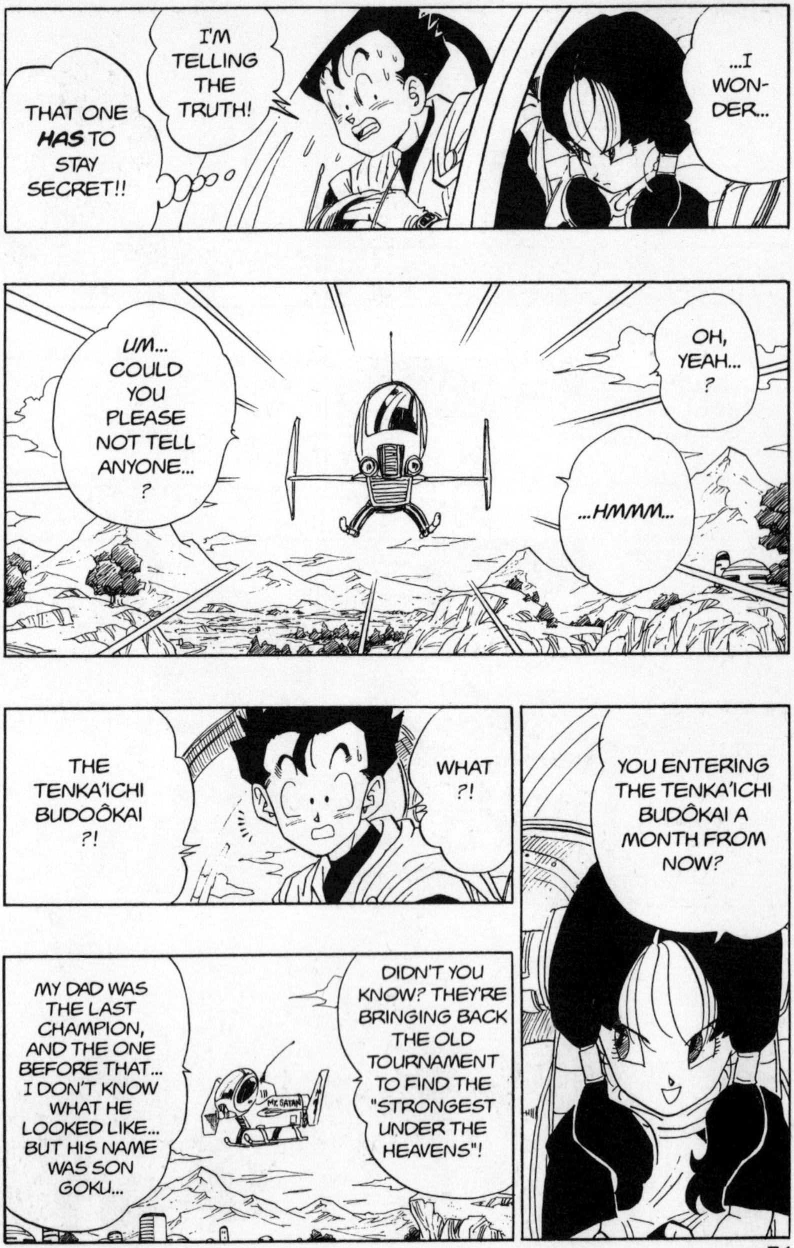
...I WON- DER...
I'M TELLING THE TRUTH!
THAT ONE **HAS** TO STAY SECRET!!
UM... COULD YOU PLEASE NOT TELL ANYONE...?
OH, YEAH...?
...HMMM...
YOU ENTERING THE TENKA'ICHI BUDÔKAI A MONTH FROM NOW?
WHAT ?!
THE TENKA'ICHI BUDOÔKAI ?!
DIDN'T YOU KNOW? THEY'RE BRINGING BACK THE OLD TOURNAMENT TO FIND THE "STRONGEST UNDER THE HEAVENS"!
MR. SATAN
MY DAD WAS THE LAST CHAMPION, AND THE ONE BEFORE THAT... I DON'T KNOW WHAT HE LOOKED LIKE... BUT HIS NAME WAS SON GOKU...

READ THIS WAY

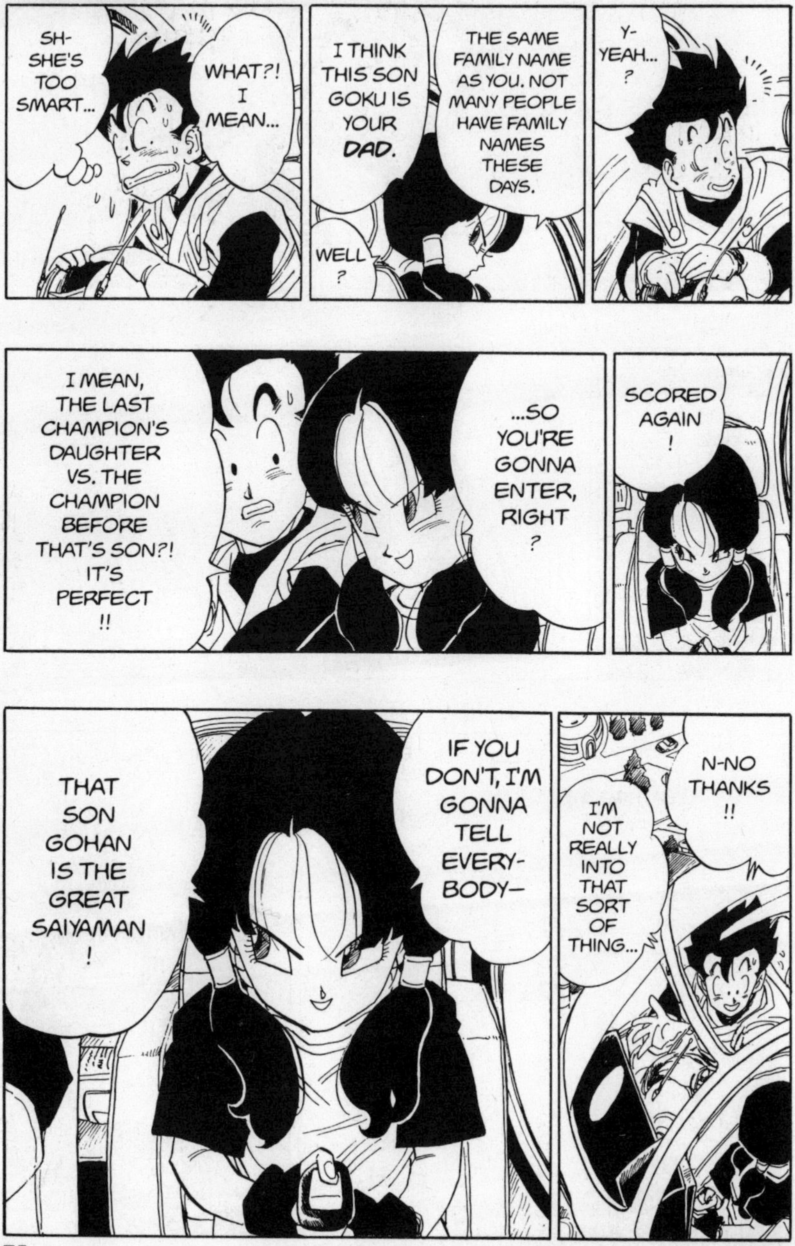
Y- YEAH...?
THE SAME FAMILY NAME AS YOU. NOT MANY PEOPLE HAVE FAMILY NAMES THESE DAYS.
I THINK THIS SON GOKU IS YOUR **DAD**.
WELL?
WHAT?! I MEAN...
SH- SHE'S TOO SMART...
SCORED AGAIN!
...SO YOU'RE GONNA ENTER, RIGHT?
I MEAN, THE LAST CHAMPION'S DAUGHTER VS. THE CHAMPION BEFORE THAT'S SON?! IT'S PERFECT!!
N-NO THANKS!!
I'M NOT REALLY INTO THAT SORT OF THING...
IF YOU DON'T, I'M GONNA TELL EVERYBODY—
THAT SON GOHAN IS THE GREAT SAIYAMAN!

READ THIS WAY

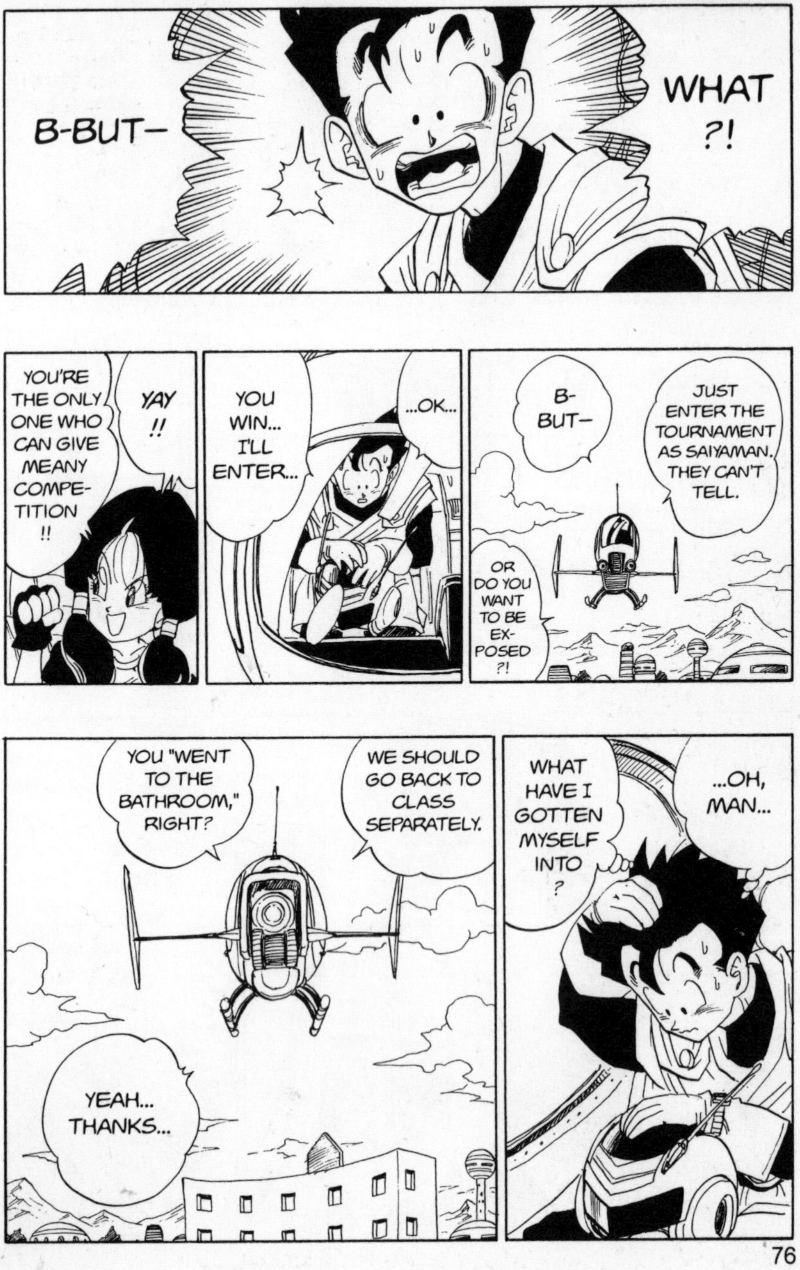
WHAT ?!
B-BUT—
JUST ENTER THE TOURNAMENT AS SAIYAMAN. THEY CAN'T TELL.
B-BUT—
OR DO YOU WANT TO BE EXPOSED ?!
...OK...
YOU WIN... I'LL ENTER...
YAY !!
YOU'RE THE ONLY ONE WHO CAN GIVE ME ANY COMPETITION !!
...OH, MAN...
WHAT HAVE I GOTTEN MYSELF INTO ?
WE SHOULD GO BACK TO CLASS SEPARATELY.
YOU "WENT TO THE BATHROOM," RIGHT?
YEAH... THANKS...

READ THIS WAY

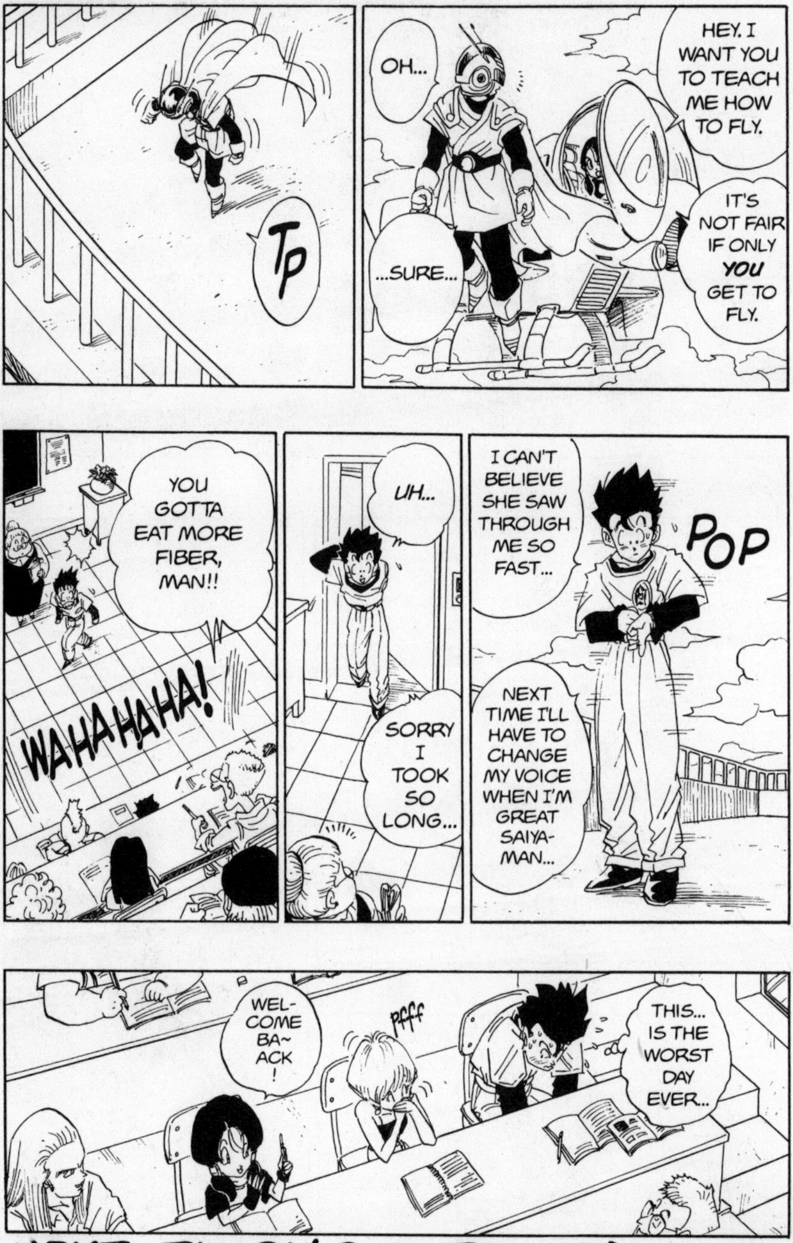
HEY. I WANT YOU TO TEACH ME HOW TO FLY.
OH...
IT'S NOT FAIR IF ONLY YOU GET TO FLY.
...SURE...
TP
I CAN'T BELIEVE SHE SAW THROUGH ME SO FAST...
POP
NEXT TIME I'LL HAVE TO CHANGE MY VOICE WHEN I'M GREAT SAIYA-MAN...
UH...
SORRY I TOOK SO LONG...
YOU GOTTA EAT MORE FIBER, MAN!!
WAHAHAHA!
THIS... IS THE WORST DAY EVER...
pfff
WEL-COME BA~ACK!

NEXT: The Old Gang Returns!

DBZ:232 • Strongest in the Heavens!

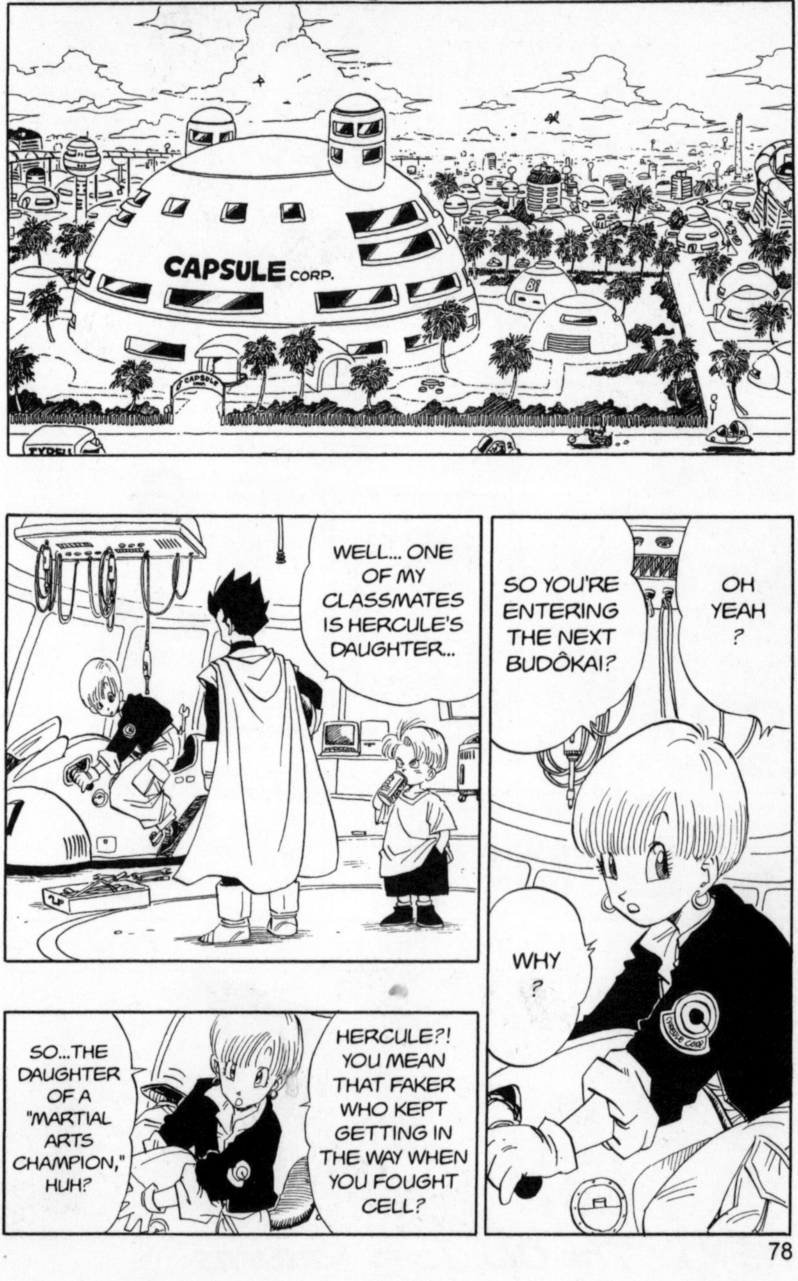
CAPSULE CORP.
OH YEAH ?
SO YOU'RE ENTERING THE NEXT BUDÔKAI?
WHY ?
WELL... ONE OF MY CLASSMATES IS HERCULE'S DAUGHTER...
HERCULE?! YOU MEAN THAT FAKER WHO KEPT GETTING IN THE WAY WHEN YOU FOUGHT CELL?
SO...THE DAUGHTER OF A "MARTIAL ARTS CHAMPION," HUH?

READ THIS WAY

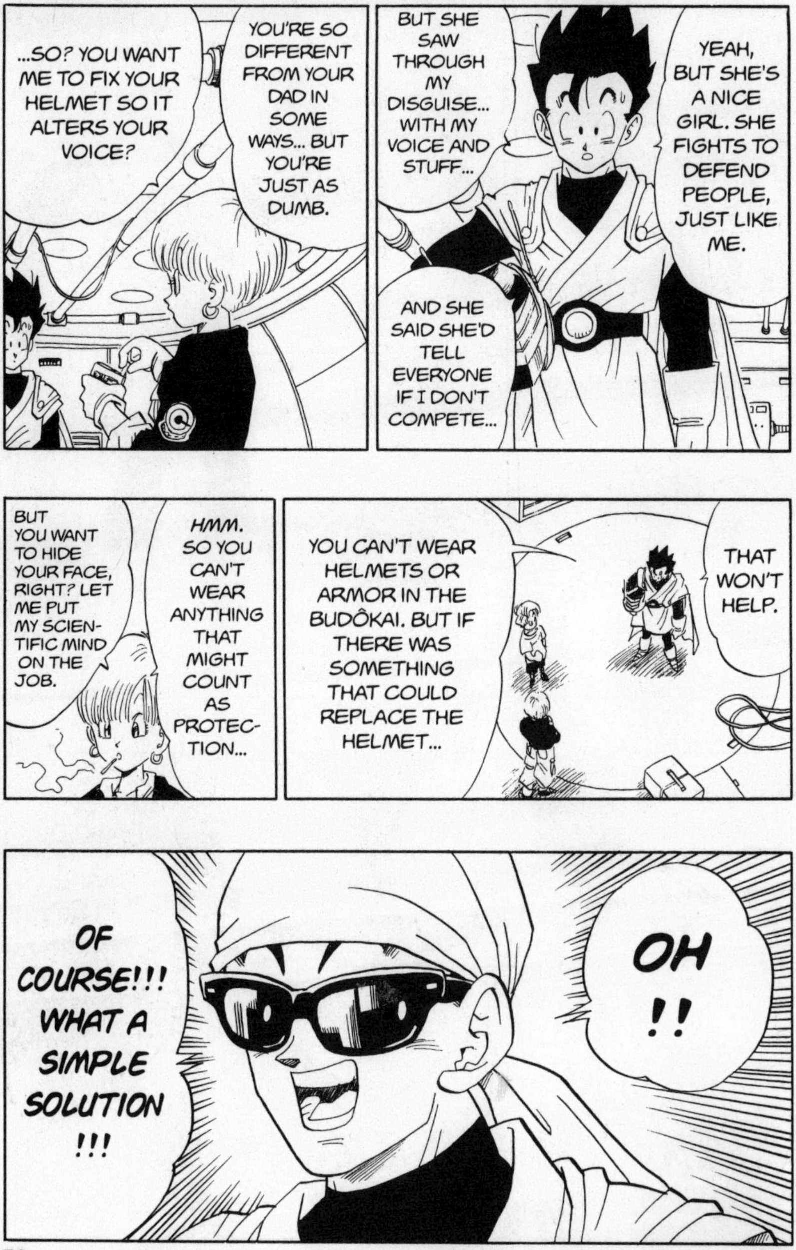
YEAH, BUT SHE'S A NICE GIRL. SHE FIGHTS TO DEFEND PEOPLE, JUST LIKE ME.
BUT SHE SAW THROUGH MY DISGUISE... WITH MY VOICE AND STUFF...
AND SHE SAID SHE'D TELL EVERYONE IF I DON'T COMPETE...
YOU'RE SO DIFFERENT FROM YOUR DAD IN SOME WAYS... BUT YOU'RE JUST AS DUMB.
...SO? YOU WANT ME TO FIX YOUR HELMET SO IT ALTERS YOUR VOICE?
THAT WON'T HELP.
YOU CAN'T WEAR HELMETS OR ARMOR IN THE BUDÔKAI. BUT IF THERE WAS SOMETHING THAT COULD REPLACE THE HELMET...
HMM. SO YOU CAN'T WEAR ANYTHING THAT MIGHT COUNT AS PROTECTION...
BUT YOU WANT TO HIDE YOUR FACE, RIGHT? LET ME PUT MY SCIENTIFIC MIND ON THE JOB.
OH !!
OF COURSE!!! WHAT A SIMPLE SOLUTION !!!

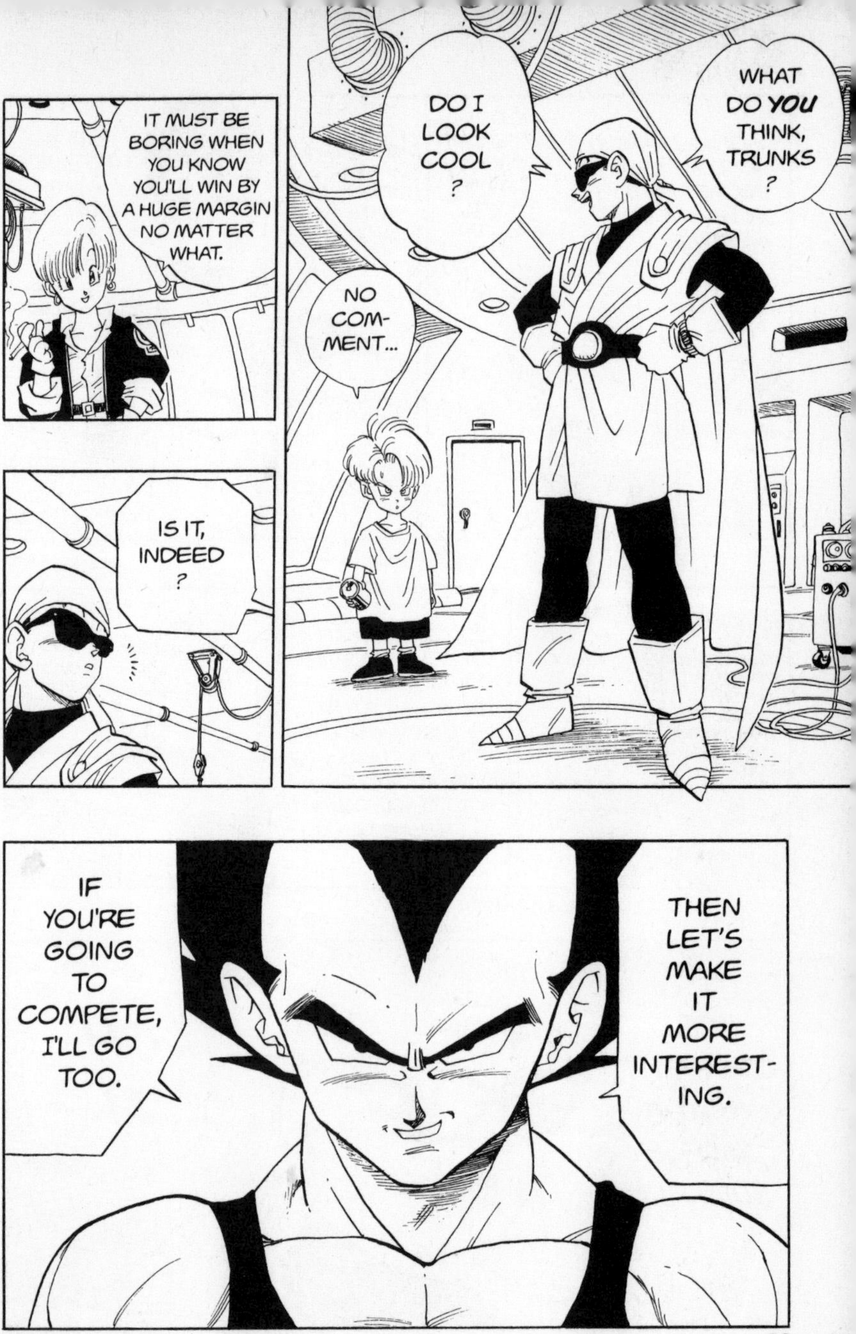
WHAT DO *YOU* THINK, TRUNKS?
DO I LOOK COOL?
NO COM-MENT...
IT MUST BE BORING WHEN YOU KNOW YOU'LL WIN BY A HUGE MARGIN NO MATTER WHAT.
IS IT, INDEED?
THEN LET'S MAKE IT MORE INTEREST-ING.
IF YOU'RE GOING TO COMPETE, I'LL GO TOO.

READ THIS WAY

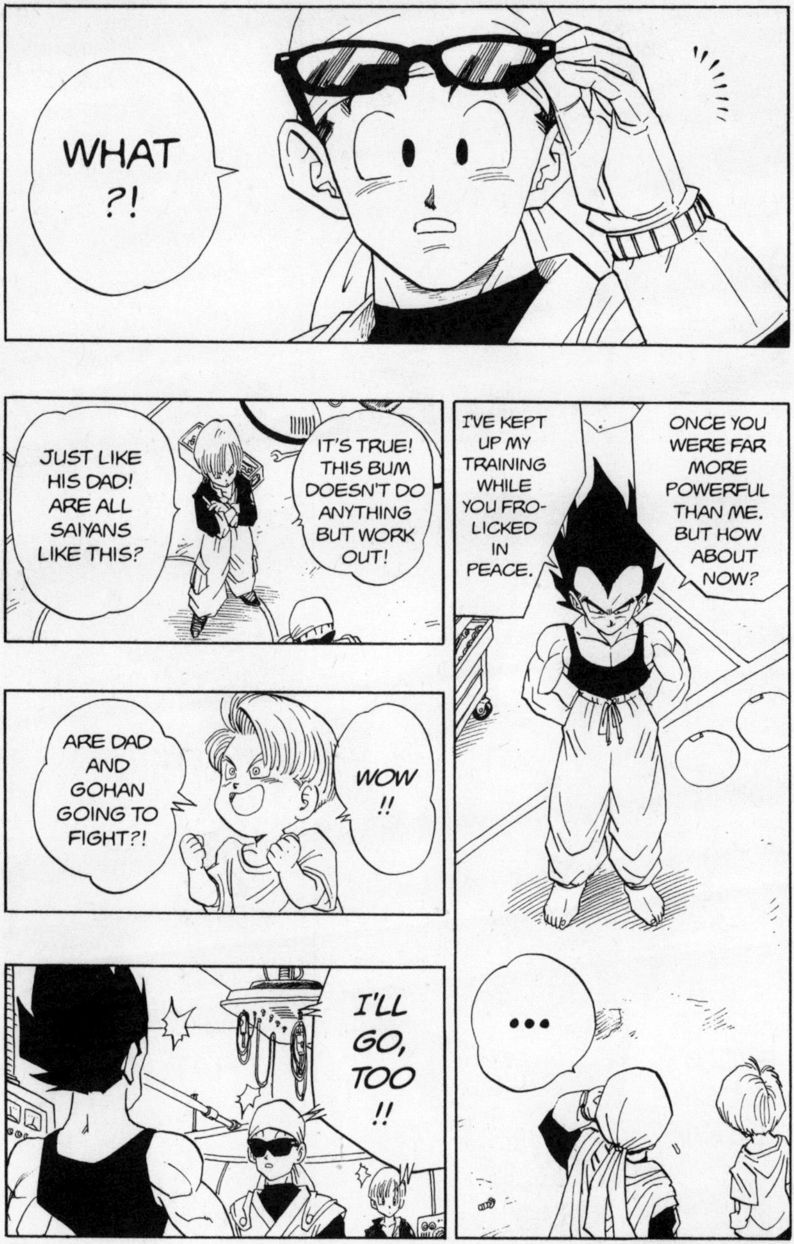

WHAT ?!
ONCE YOU WERE FAR MORE POWERFUL THAN ME. BUT HOW ABOUT NOW?
I'VE KEPT UP MY TRAINING WHILE YOU FRO-LICKED IN PEACE.
IT'S TRUE! THIS BUM DOESN'T DO ANYTHING BUT WORK OUT!
JUST LIKE HIS DAD! ARE ALL SAIYANS LIKE THIS?
WOW !!
ARE DAD AND GOHAN GOING TO FIGHT?!
...
I'LL GO, TOO !!

READ THIS WAY

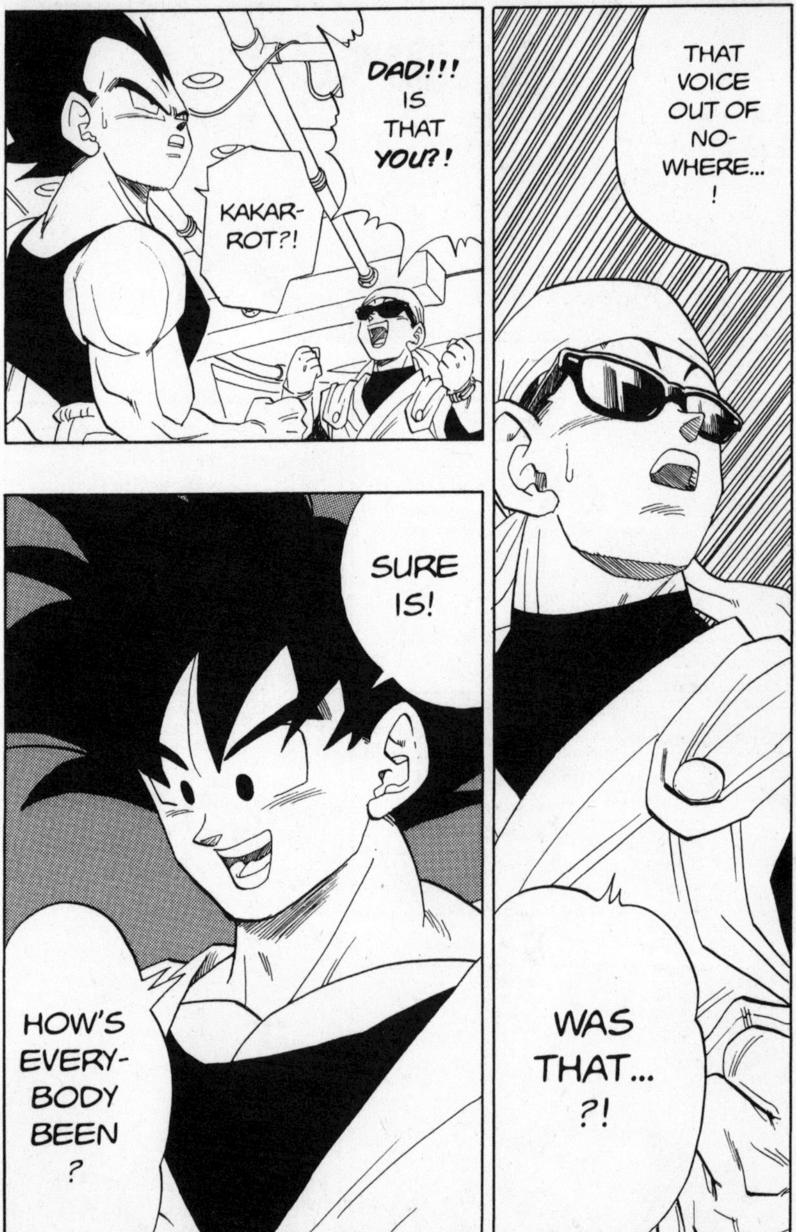
THAT VOICE OUT OF NO-WHERE... !
WAS THAT... ?!
DAD!!! IS THAT YOU?!
KAKAR-ROT?!
SURE IS!
HOW'S EVERY-BODY BEEN ?

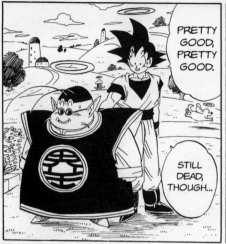

READ THIS WAY

HOW'VE YOU BEEN?!
?
PRETTY GOOD, PRETTY GOOD.
STILL DEAD, THOUGH...
CAN YOU REALLY...
...COME TO THE BUDÔKAI ?!
YEAH! I GET ONE DAY TO VISIT THE LIVING, YOU KNOW, AND I'LL MAKE SURE THAT'S THE DAY I COME BACK! *
IF YOU GUYS ARE BOTH FIGHTING, I WANT TO BE IN ON IT TOO!

* SEE DRAGON BALL VOL. 9 FOR DETAILS!

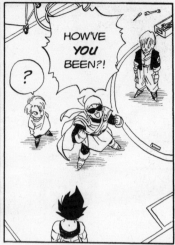

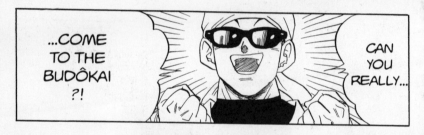

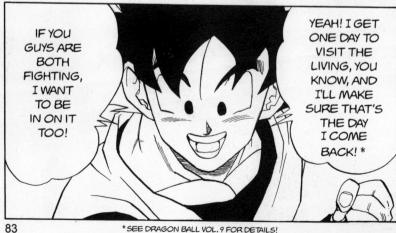

READ THIS WAY

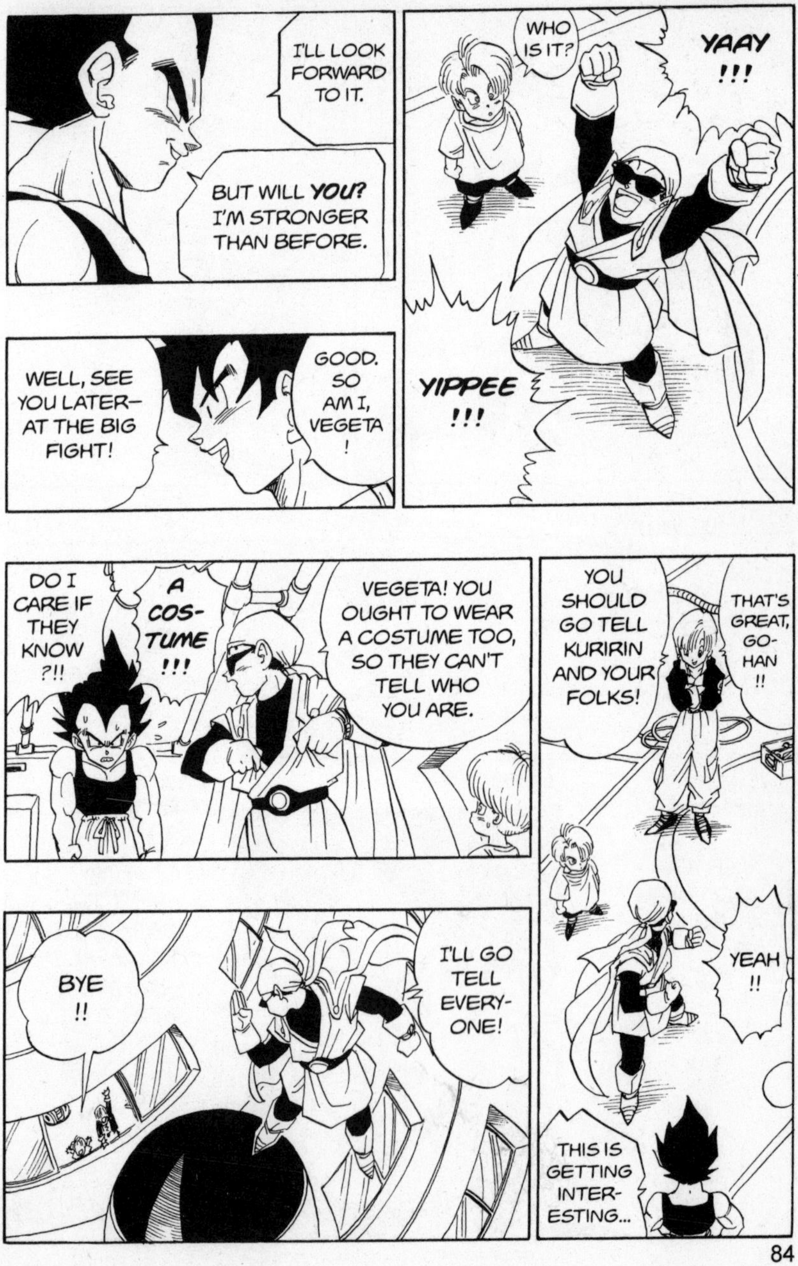
WHO IS IT?
YAAY !!!
YIPPEE !!!
I'LL LOOK FORWARD TO IT.
BUT WILL YOU? I'M STRONGER THAN BEFORE.
GOOD. SO AM I, VEGETA !
WELL, SEE YOU LATER— AT THE BIG FIGHT!
THAT'S GREAT, GO-HAN !!
YOU SHOULD GO TELL KURIRIN AND YOUR FOLKS!
YEAH !!
THIS IS GETTING INTER-ESTING...
VEGETA! YOU OUGHT TO WEAR A COSTUME TOO, SO THEY CAN'T TELL WHO YOU ARE.
A COS-TUME !!!
DO I CARE IF THEY KNOW ?!!
I'LL GO TELL EVERY-ONE!
BYE !!

READ THIS WAY

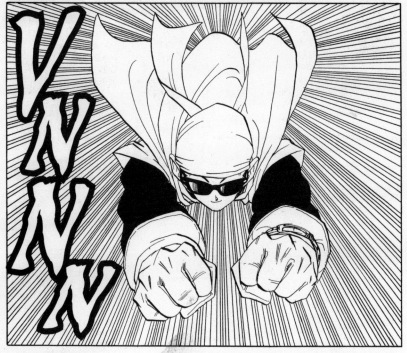

GOKU?! REALLY?!

KURIRIN QUIT SHAVING HIS HEAD WHEN THE FIGHTING STOPPED.

85

READ THIS WAY

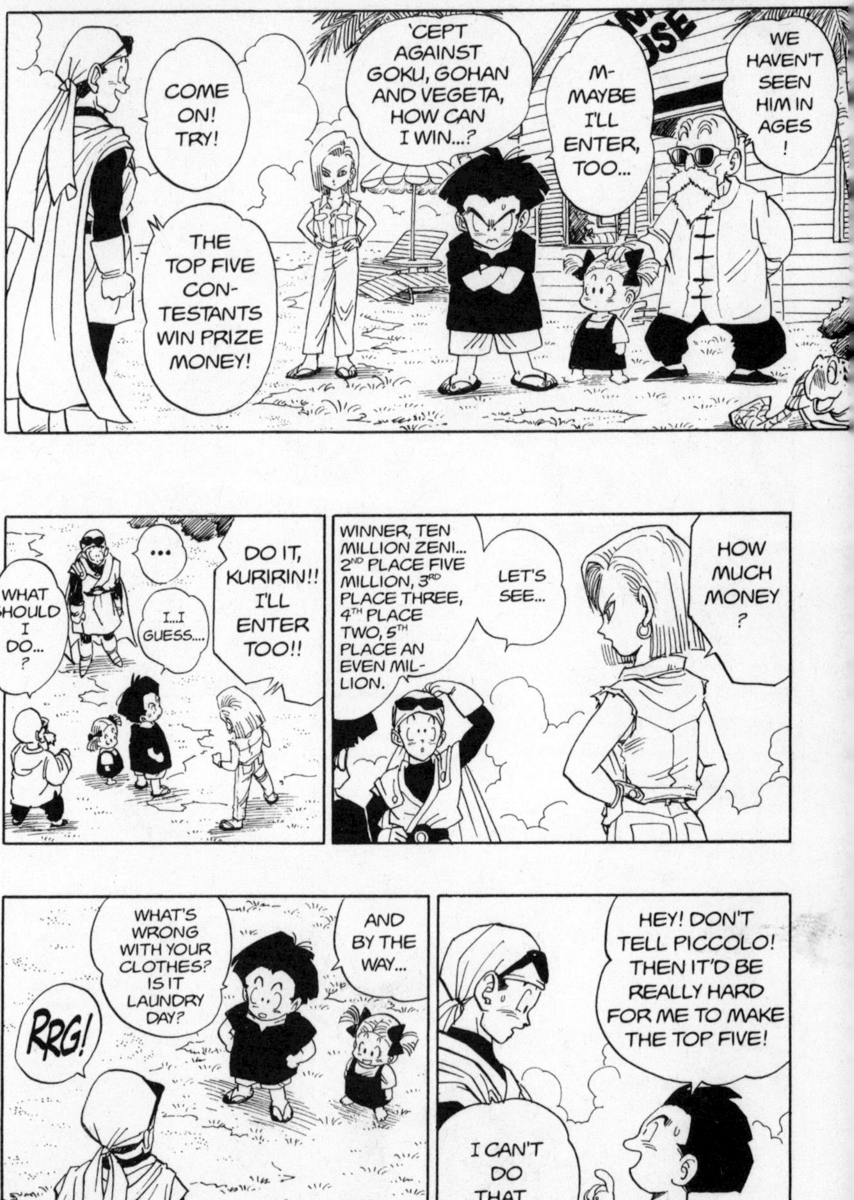
WE HAVEN'T SEEN HIM IN AGES!
M-MAYBE I'LL ENTER, TOO...
'CEPT AGAINST GOKU, GOHAN AND VEGETA, HOW CAN I WIN...?
COME ON! TRY!
THE TOP FIVE CON-TESTANTS WIN PRIZE MONEY!
HOW MUCH MONEY?
LET'S SEE...
WINNER, TEN MILLION ZENI... 2ND PLACE FIVE MILLION, 3RD PLACE THREE, 4TH PLACE TWO, 5TH PLACE AN EVEN MIL-LION.
DO IT, KURIRIN!! I'LL ENTER TOO!!
...
I...I GUESS....
WHAT SHOULD I DO...?
HEY! DON'T TELL PICCOLO! THEN IT'D BE REALLY HARD FOR ME TO MAKE THE TOP FIVE!
I CAN'T DO THAT...
AND BY THE WAY...
WHAT'S WRONG WITH YOUR CLOTHES? IS IT LAUNDRY DAY?
RRG!

READ THIS WAY

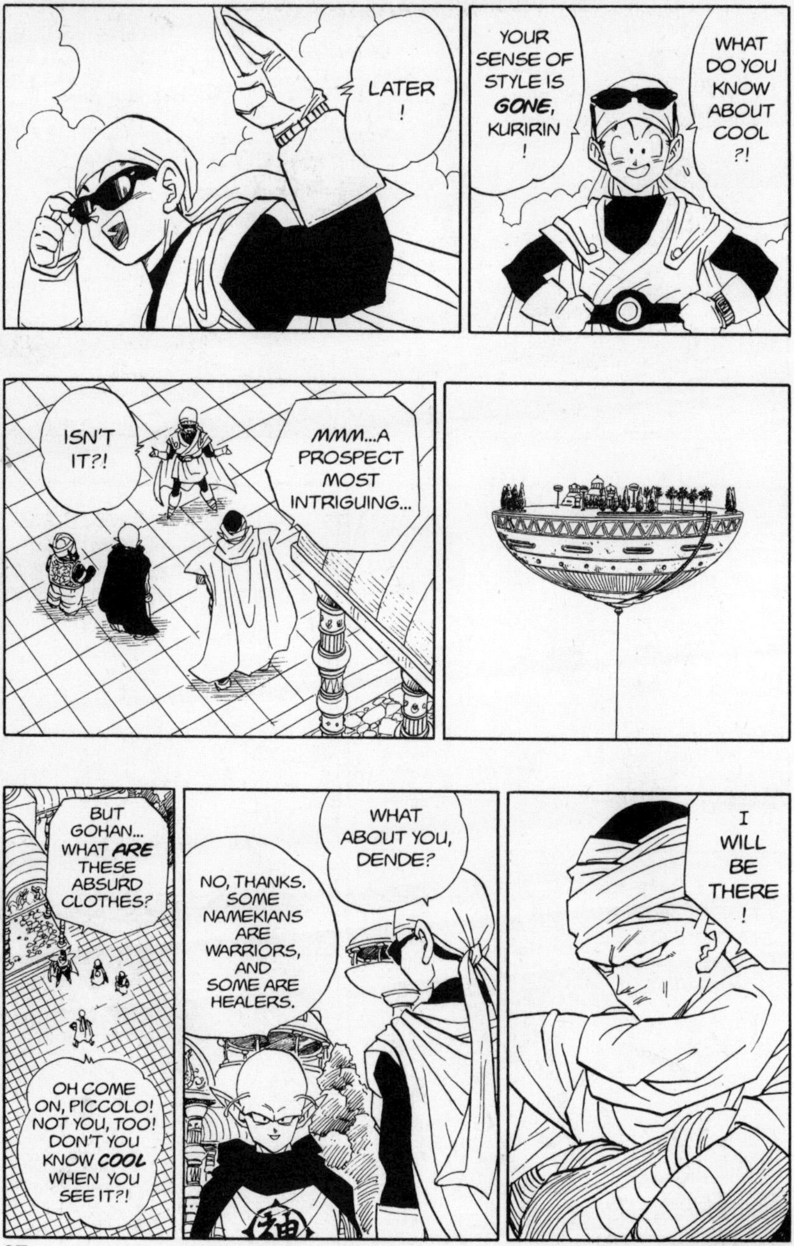

WHAT DO YOU KNOW ABOUT COOL?!
YOUR SENSE OF STYLE IS GONE, KURIRIN!
LATER!
MMM...A PROSPECT MOST INTRIGUING...
ISN'T IT?!
I WILL BE THERE!
WHAT ABOUT YOU, DENDE?
NO, THANKS. SOME NAMEKIANS ARE WARRIORS, AND SOME ARE HEALERS.
BUT GOHAN... WHAT ARE THESE ABSURD CLOTHES?
OH COME ON, PICCOLO! NOT YOU, TOO! DON'T YOU KNOW COOL WHEN YOU SEE IT?!

READ THIS WAY

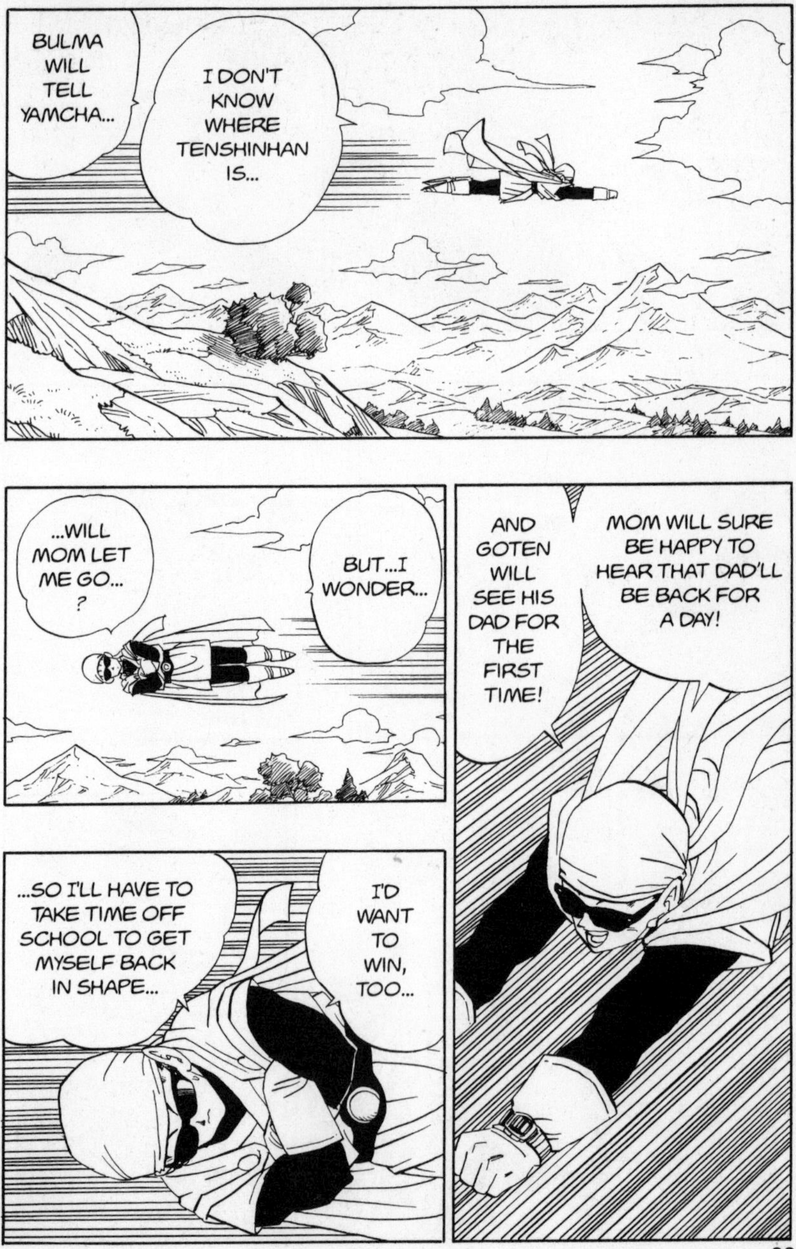
I DON'T KNOW WHERE TENSHINHAN IS...
BULMA WILL TELL YAMCHA...
MOM WILL SURE BE HAPPY TO HEAR THAT DAD'LL BE BACK FOR A DAY!
AND GOTEN WILL SEE HIS DAD FOR THE FIRST TIME!
BUT...I WONDER...
...WILL MOM LET ME GO... ?
I'D WANT TO WIN, TOO...
...SO I'LL HAVE TO TAKE TIME OFF SCHOOL TO GET MYSELF BACK IN SHAPE...

READ THIS WAY

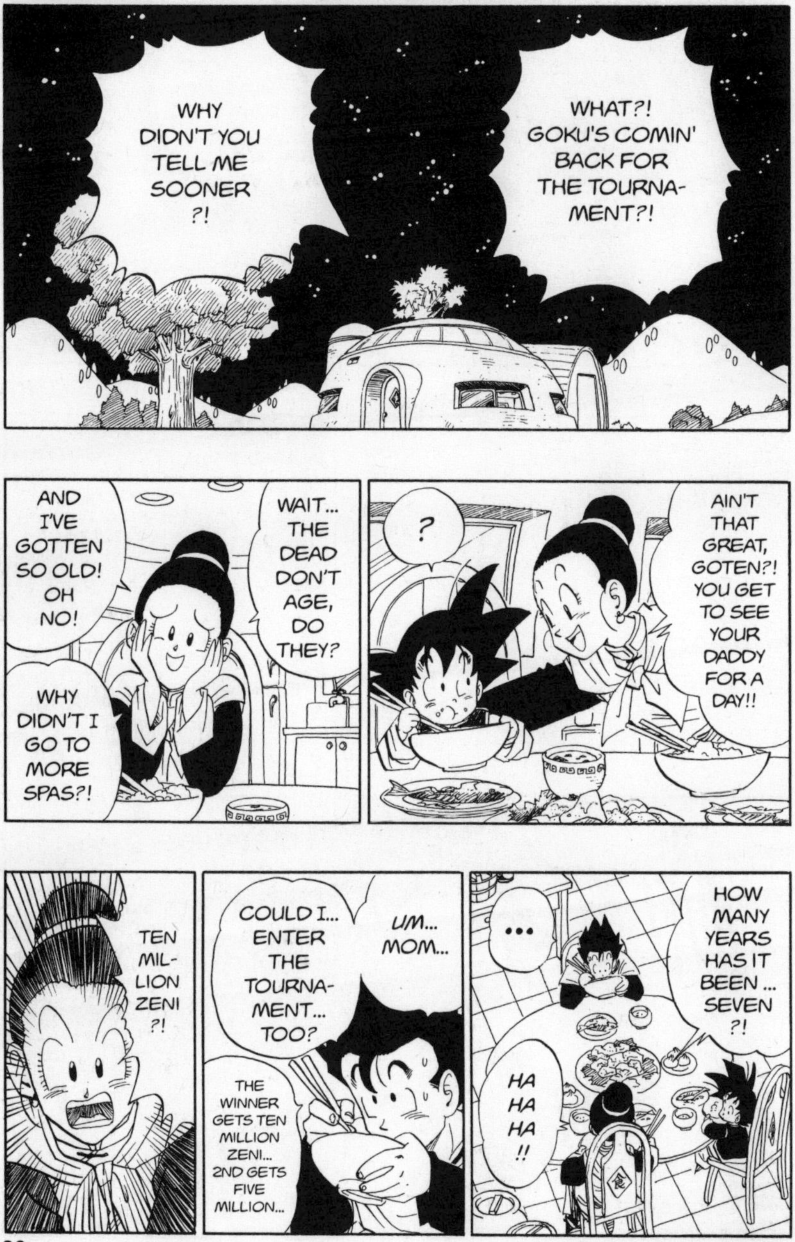

WHAT?! GOKU'S COMIN' BACK FOR THE TOURNAMENT?!
WHY DIDN'T YOU TELL ME SOONER?!
AIN'T THAT GREAT, GOTEN?! YOU GET TO SEE YOUR DADDY FOR A DAY!!
?
WAIT... THE DEAD DON'T AGE, DO THEY?
AND I'VE GOTTEN SO OLD! OH NO!
WHY DIDN'T I GO TO MORE SPAS?!
HOW MANY YEARS HAS IT BEEN... SEVEN?!
...
HA HA HA!!
UM... MOM...
COULD I... ENTER THE TOURNAMENT... TOO?
THE WINNER GETS TEN MILLION ZENI... 2ND GETS FIVE MILLION...
TEN MILLION ZENI?!

READ THIS WAY

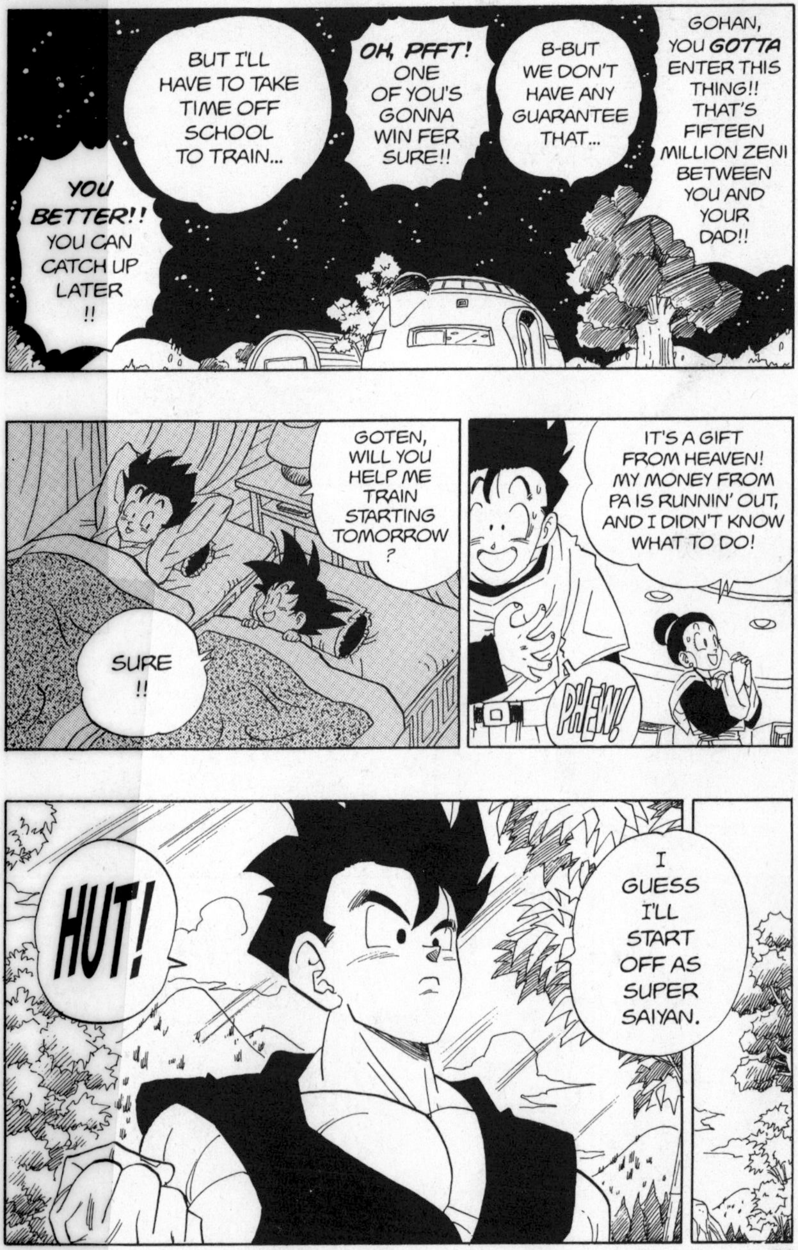

GOHAN, YOU GOTTA ENTER THIS THING!! THAT'S FIFTEEN MILLION ZENI BETWEEN YOU AND YOUR DAD!!
B-BUT WE DON'T HAVE ANY GUARANTEE THAT...
OH, PFFT! ONE OF YOU'S GONNA WIN FER SURE!!
BUT I'LL HAVE TO TAKE TIME OFF SCHOOL TO TRAIN...
YOU BETTER!! YOU CAN CATCH UP LATER !!
IT'S A GIFT FROM HEAVEN! MY MONEY FROM PA IS RUNNIN' OUT, AND I DIDN'T KNOW WHAT TO DO!
PHEW!
GOTEN, WILL YOU HELP ME TRAIN STARTING TOMORROW ?
SURE !!
I GUESS I'LL START OFF AS SUPER SAIYAN.
HUT!

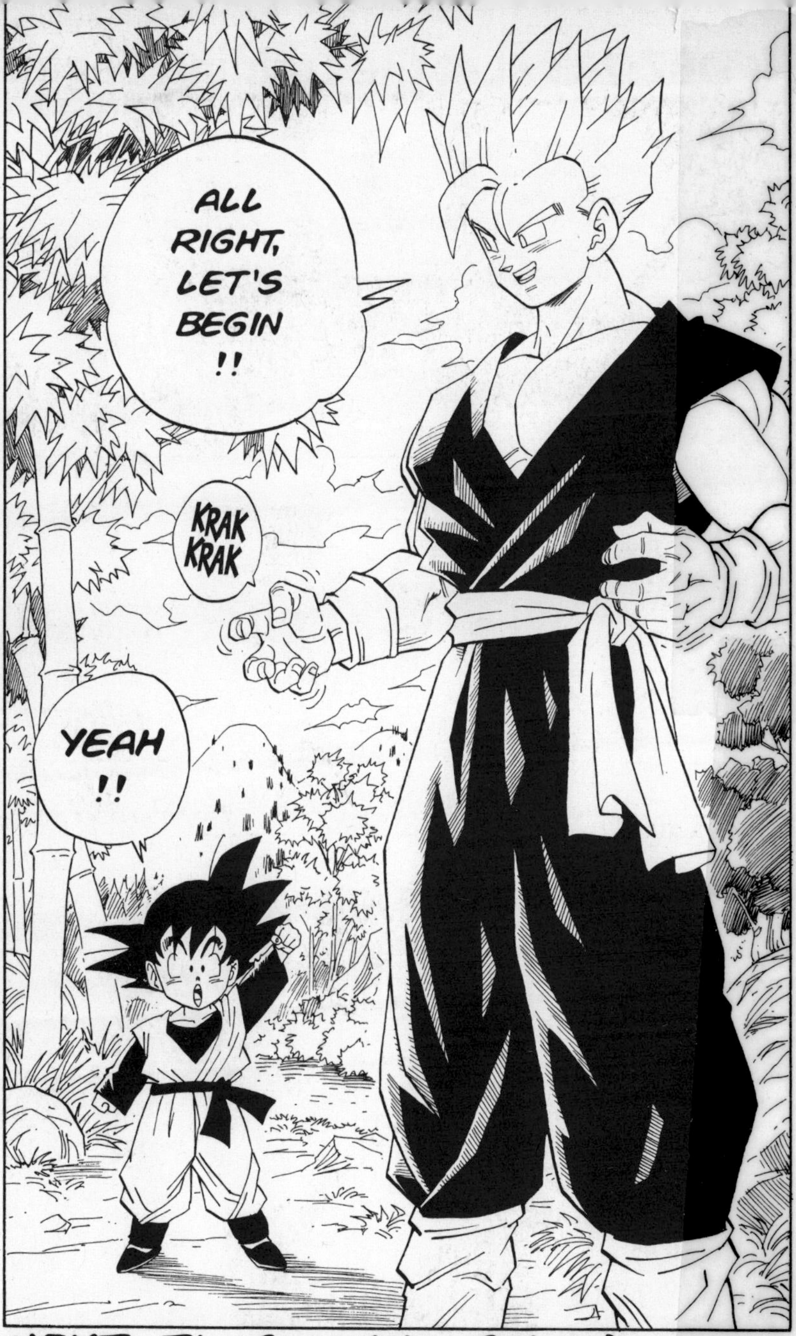
ALL RIGHT, LET'S BEGIN !!
KRAK KRAK
YEAH !!

NEXT: The Surprising Saiyan!

DBZ:233 • Let the Training Begin!

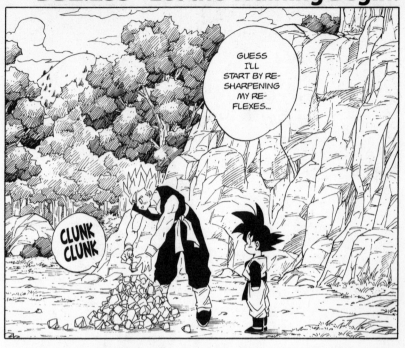

GUESS I'LL START BY RE-SHARPENING MY RE-FLEXES...
CLUNK CLUNK
GOTEN, THROW ROCKS AT ME FROM BEHIND THIS LINE.
ZSH
'KAY...
I'M READY!
HUH?! FROM *THIS* CLOSE?!

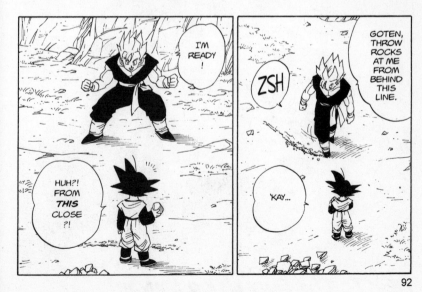

READ THIS WAY

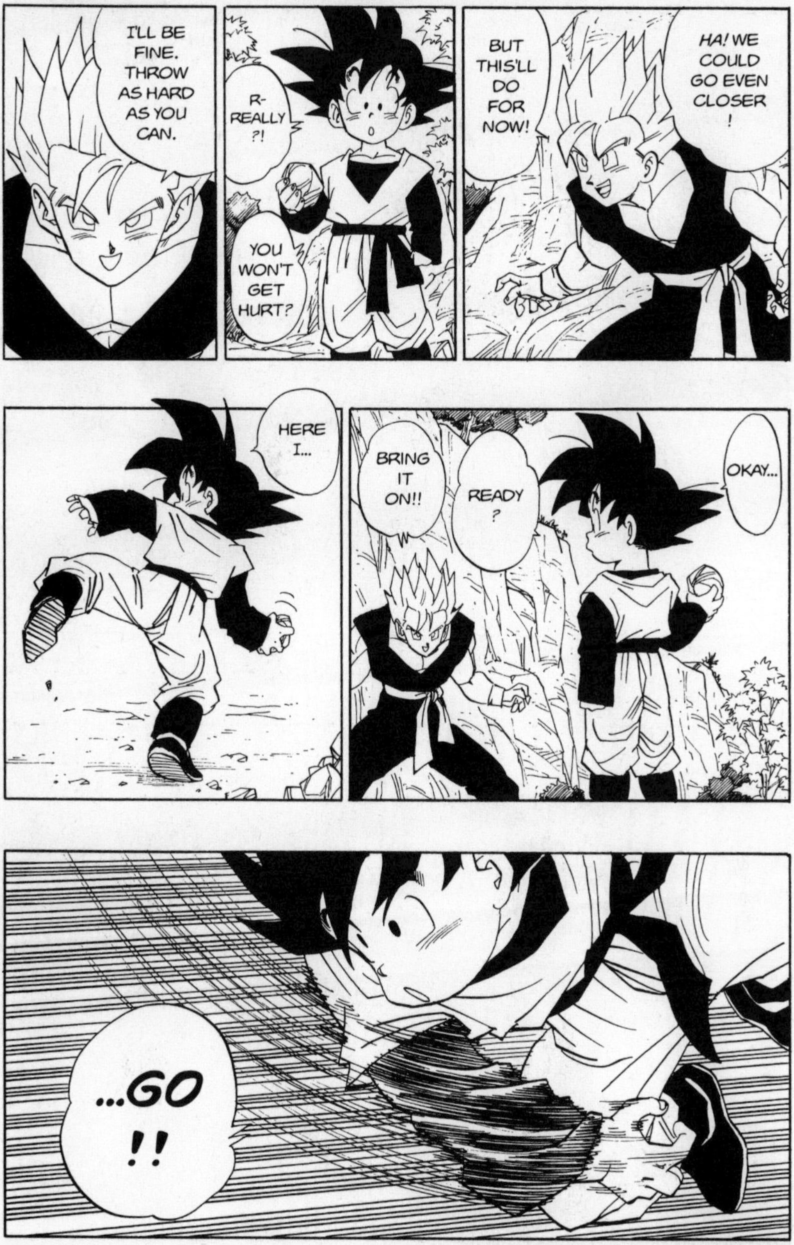
HA! WE COULD GO EVEN CLOSER!
BUT THIS'LL DO FOR NOW!
R-REALLY?!
YOU WON'T GET HURT?
I'LL BE FINE. THROW AS HARD AS YOU CAN.
OKAY...
READY?
BRING IT ON!!
HERE I...
...GO!!

READ THIS WAY

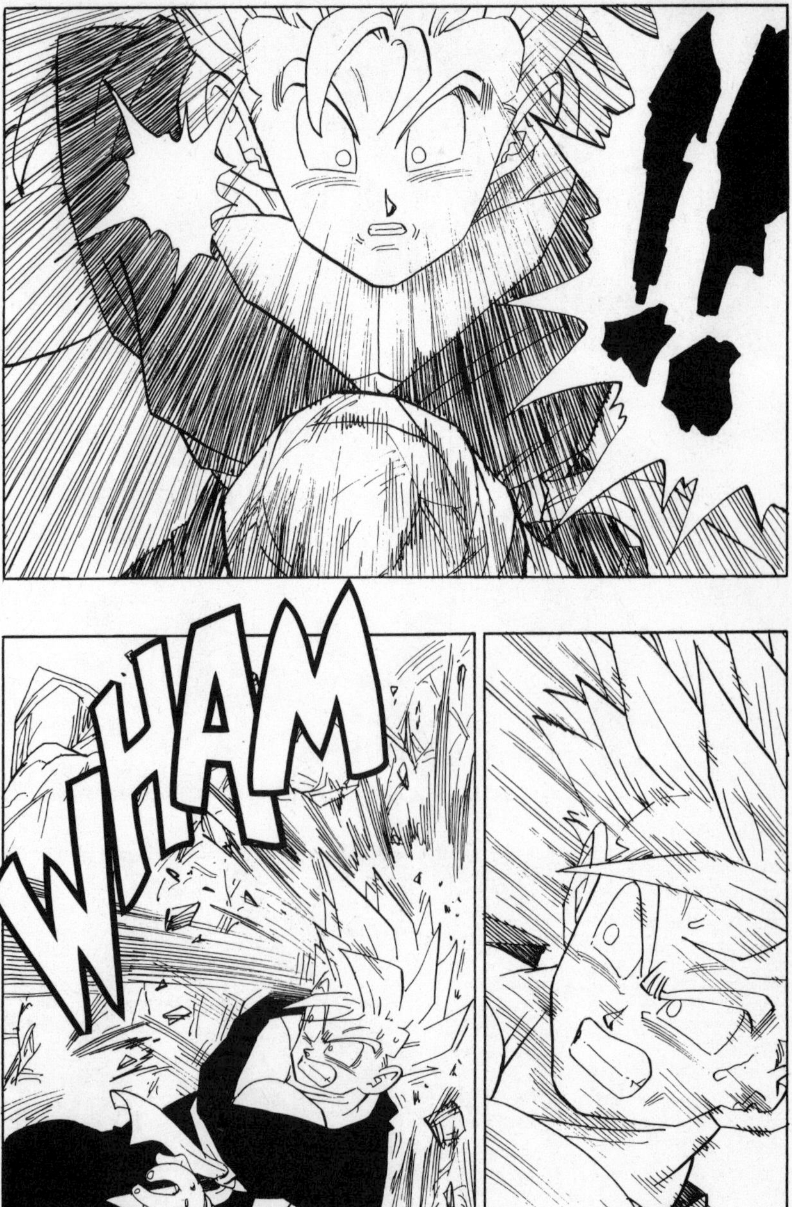
!!
WHAM

READ THIS WAY

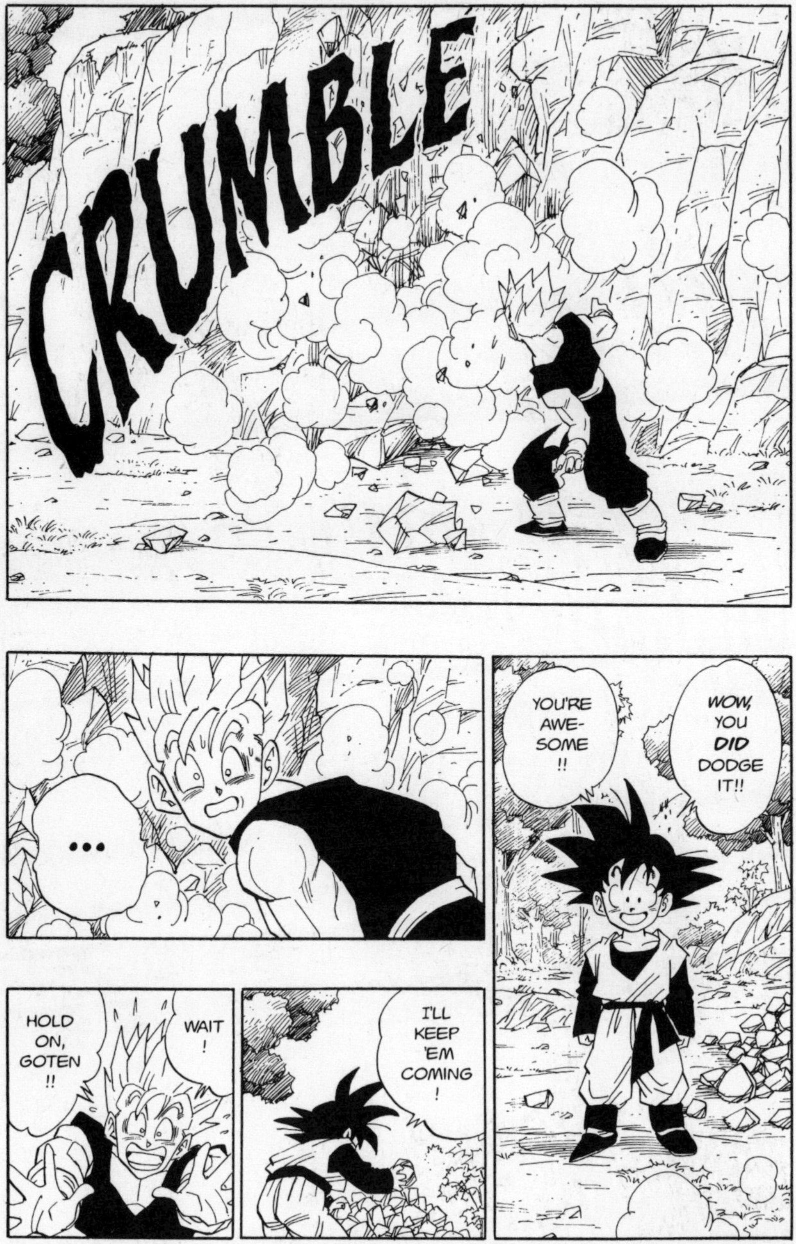
CRUMBLE
WOW, YOU DID DODGE IT!!
YOU'RE AWE-SOME!!
...
I'LL KEEP 'EM COMING!
WAIT!
HOLD ON, GOTEN!!

READ THIS WAY

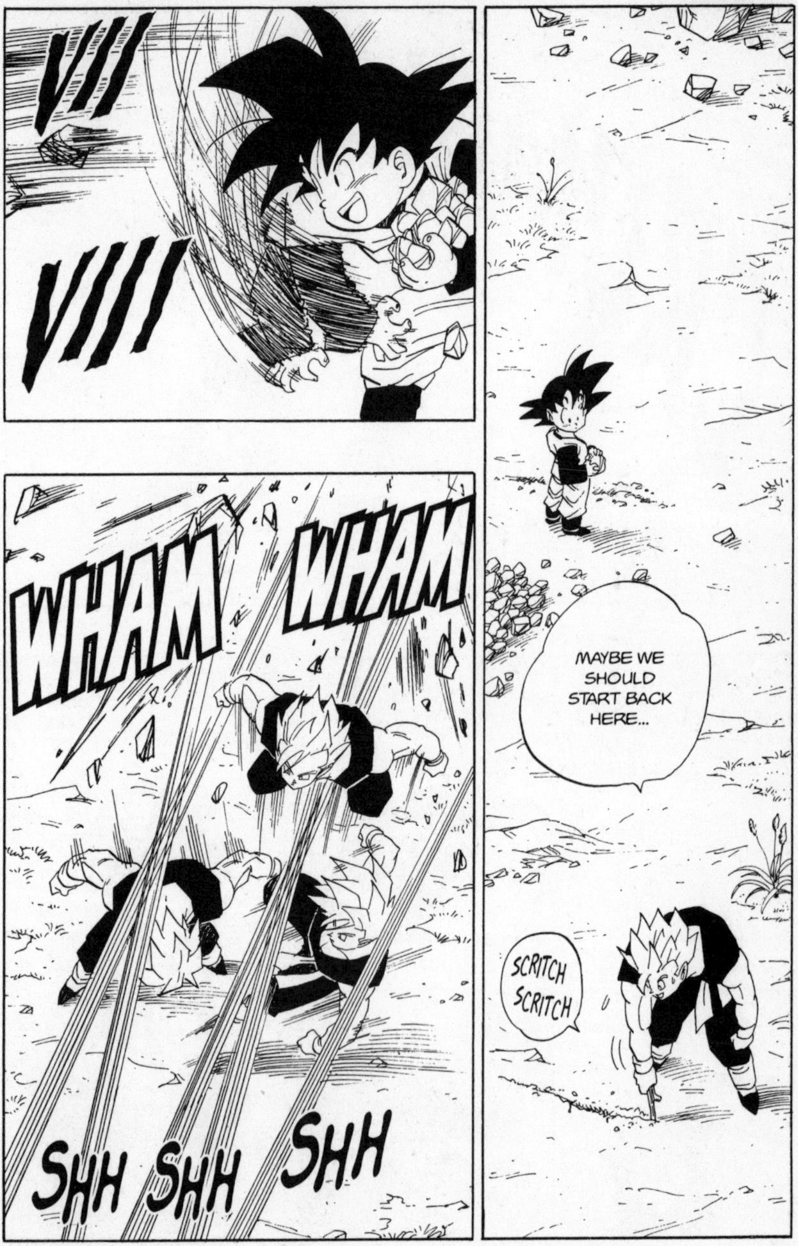
MAYBE WE SHOULD START BACK HERE...
SCRITCH SCRITCH
VII
VIII
WHAM
WHAM
SHH SHH SHH

READ THIS WAY

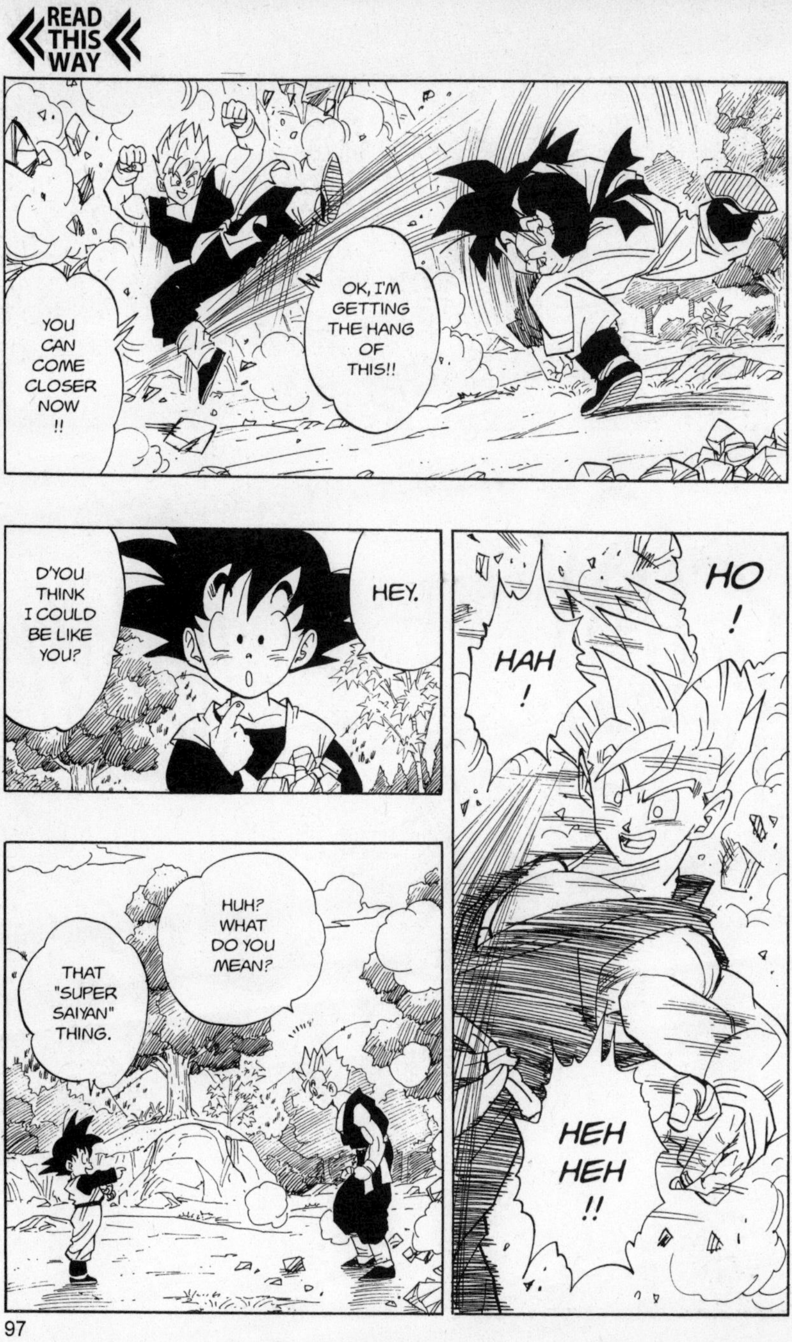
OK, I'M GETTING THE HANG OF THIS!!
YOU CAN COME CLOSER NOW !!
HO !
HAH !
HEH HEH !!
HEY.
D'YOU THINK I COULD BE LIKE YOU?
HUH? WHAT DO YOU MEAN?
THAT "SUPER SAIYAN" THING.

READ THIS WAY

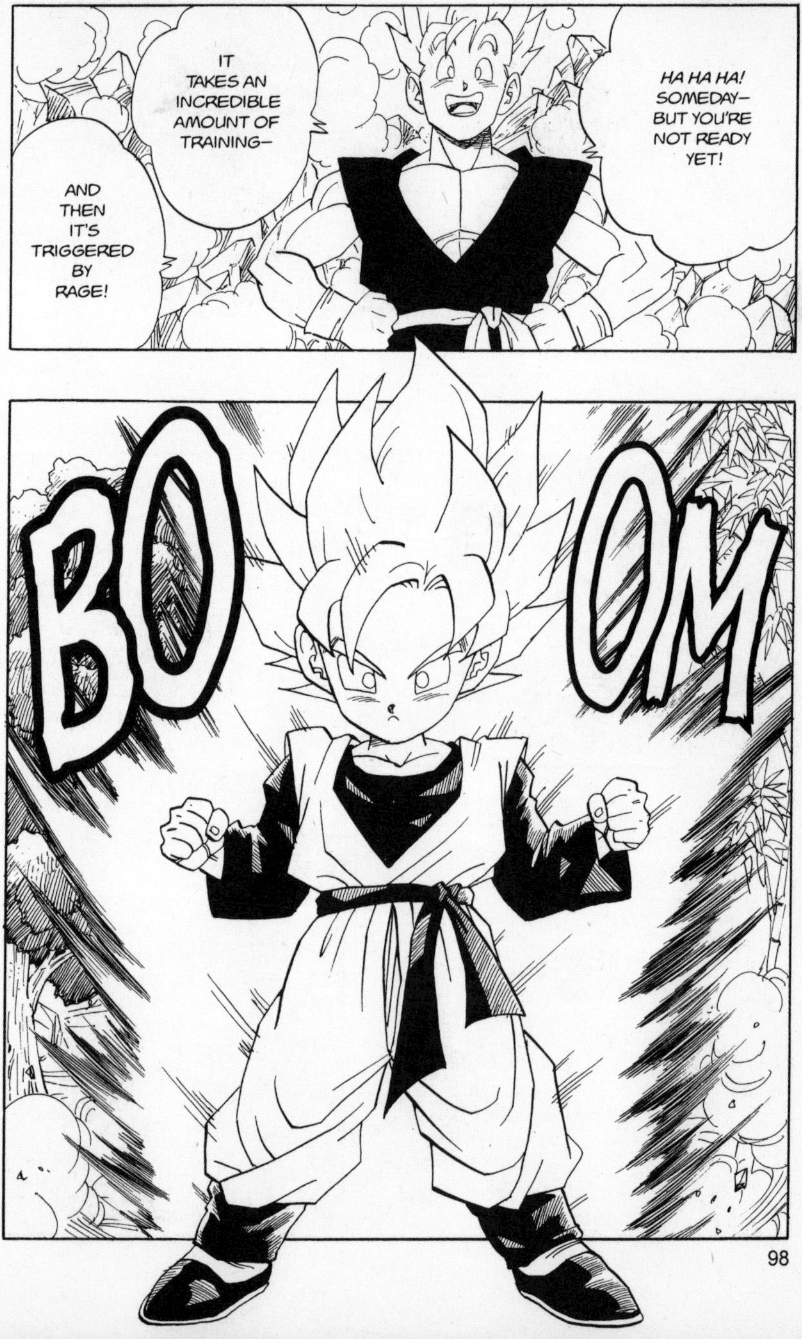

HA HA HA! SOMEDAY— BUT YOU'RE NOT READY YET!
IT TAKES AN INCREDIBLE AMOUNT OF TRAINING—
AND THEN IT'S TRIGGERED BY RAGE!
BOOM

READ THIS WAY

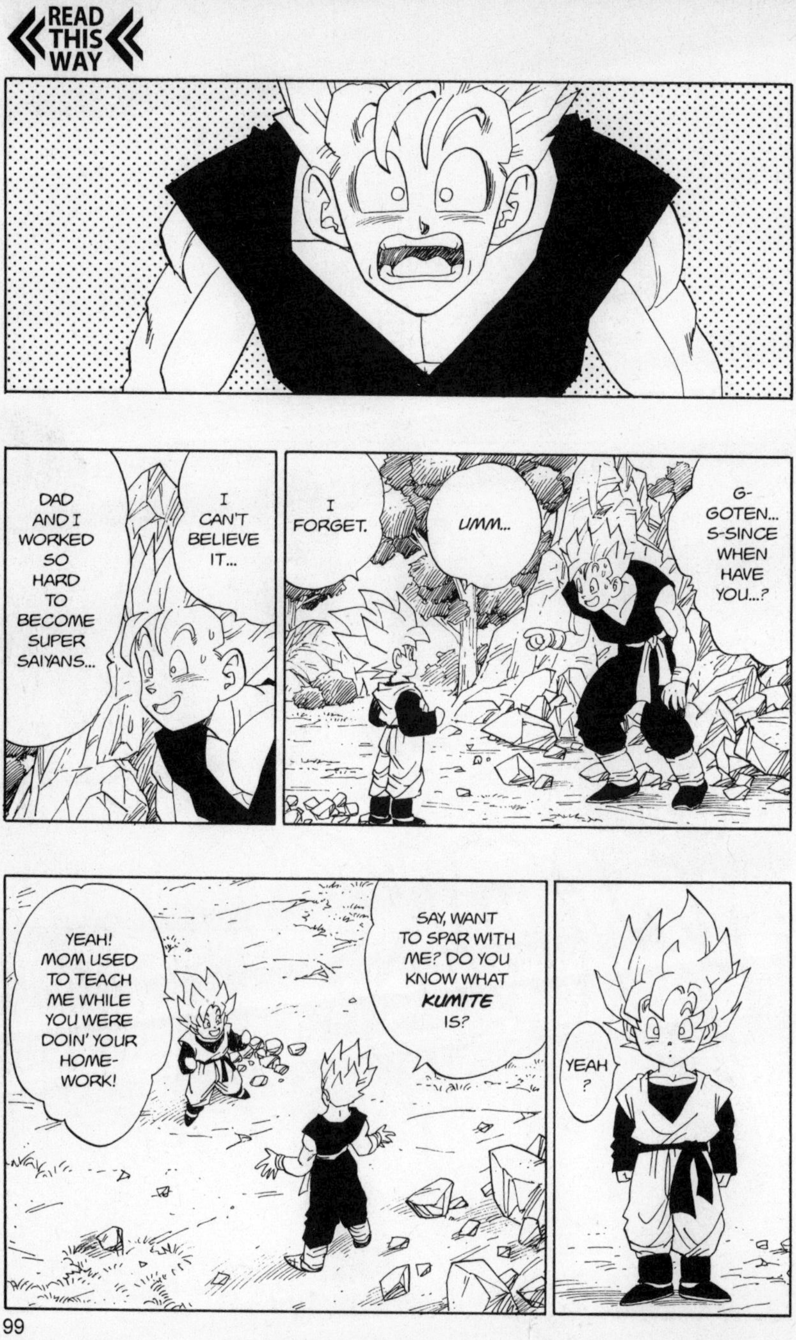
G- GOTEN... S-SINCE WHEN HAVE YOU...?
UMM...
I FORGET.
I CAN'T BELIEVE IT...
DAD AND I WORKED SO HARD TO BECOME SUPER SAIYANS...
YEAH?
SAY, WANT TO SPAR WITH ME? DO YOU KNOW WHAT **KUMITE** IS?
YEAH! MOM USED TO TEACH ME WHILE YOU WERE DOIN' YOUR HOME-WORK!

READ THIS WAY

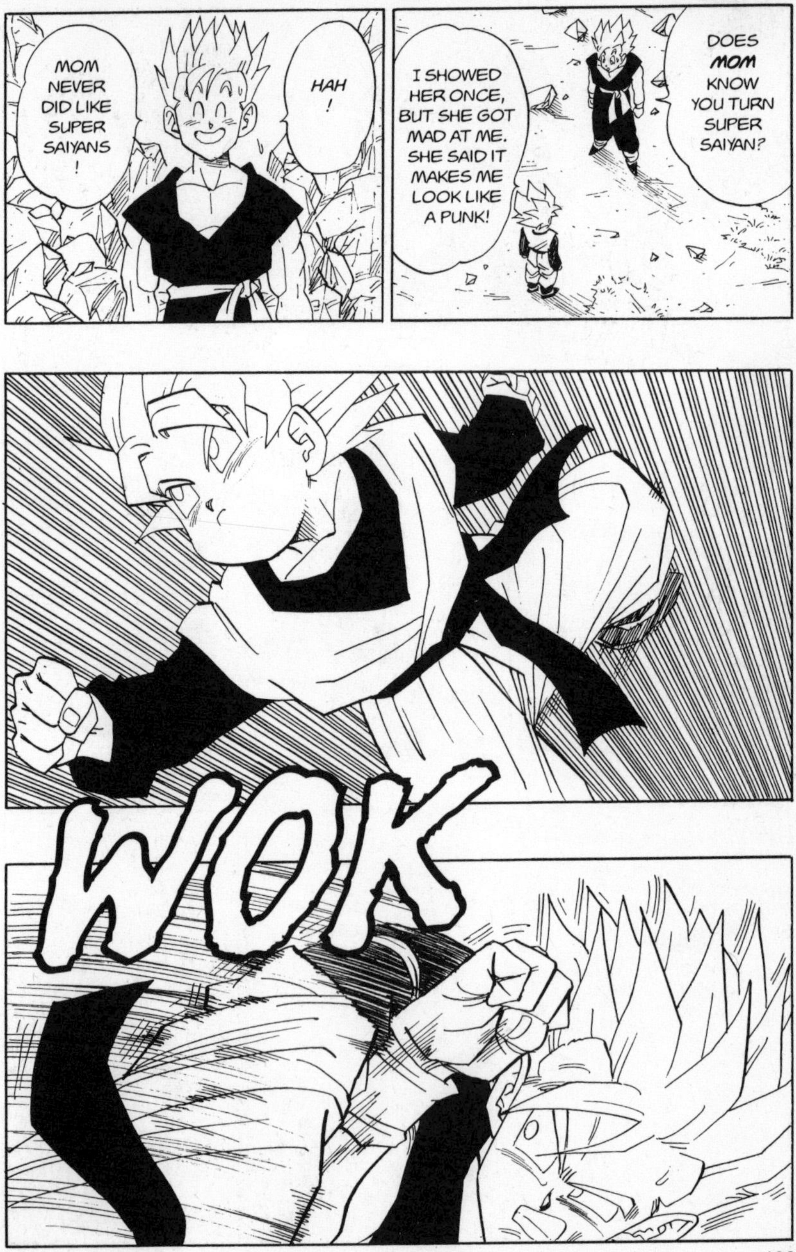
DOES MOM KNOW YOU TURN SUPER SAIYAN?
I SHOWED HER ONCE, BUT SHE GOT MAD AT ME. SHE SAID IT MAKES ME LOOK LIKE A PUNK!
HAH!
MOM NEVER DID LIKE SUPER SAIYANS!
WOK

READ THIS WAY

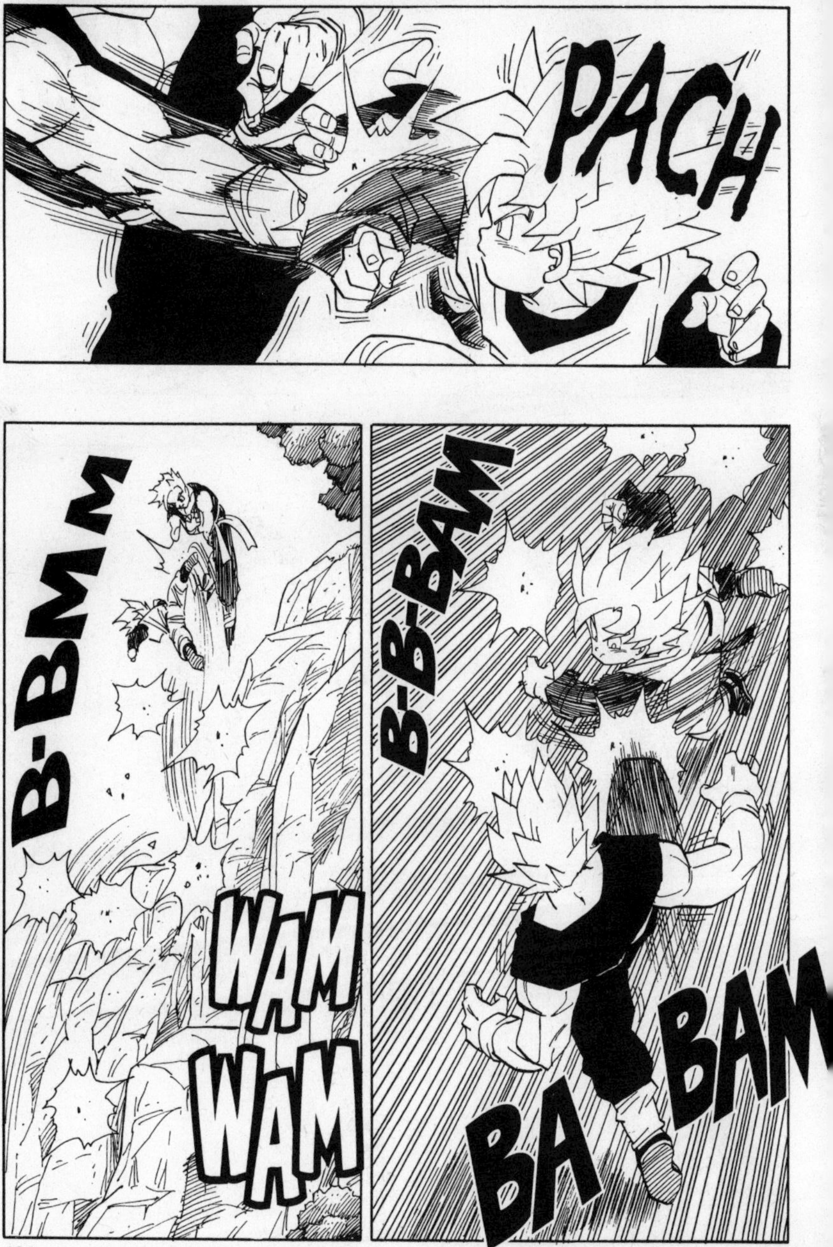
PACH
B-B-BAM
BA BAM
B-BMM
WAM WAM

READ THIS WAY

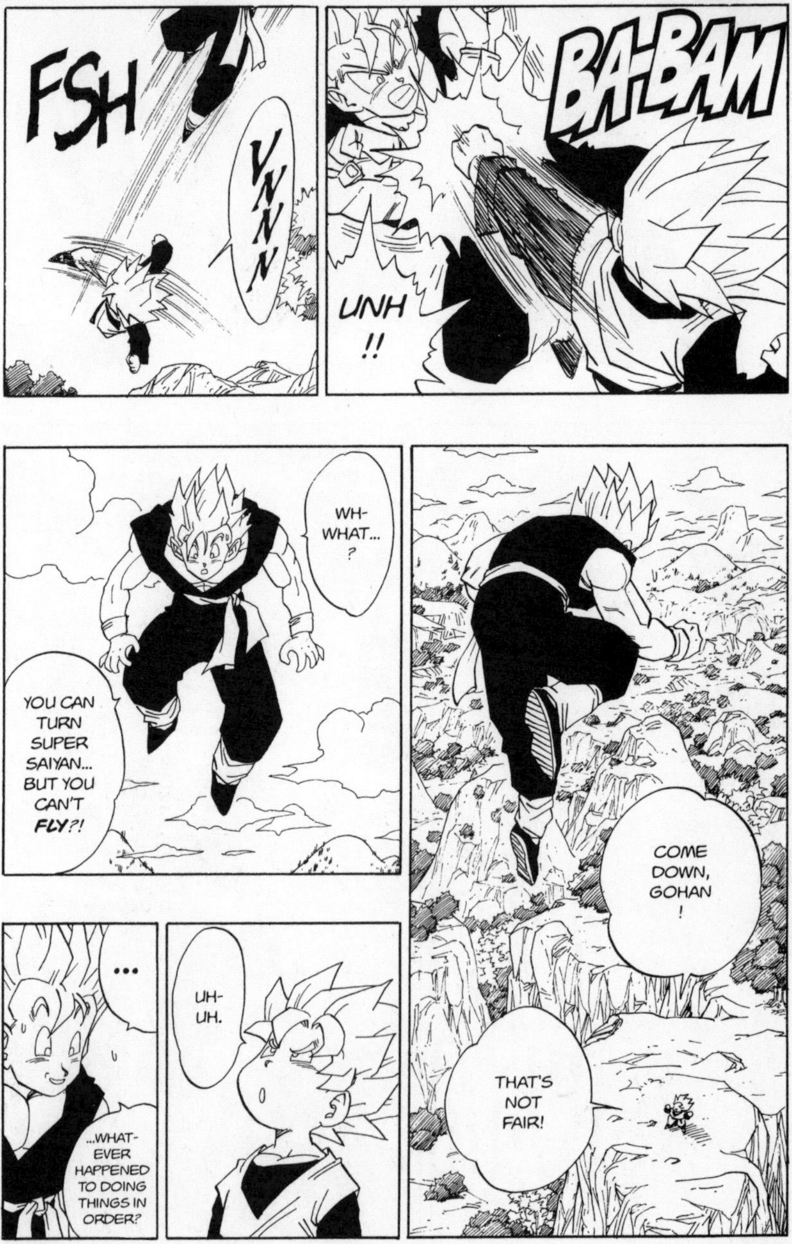
BA-BAM
UNH !!
VNNN
FSH
COME DOWN, GOHAN !
THAT'S NOT FAIR!
WH- WHAT... ?
YOU CAN TURN SUPER SAIYAN... BUT YOU CAN'T *FLY*?!
UH- UH.
...
...WHAT- EVER HAPPENED TO DOING THINGS IN ORDER?

READ THIS WAY

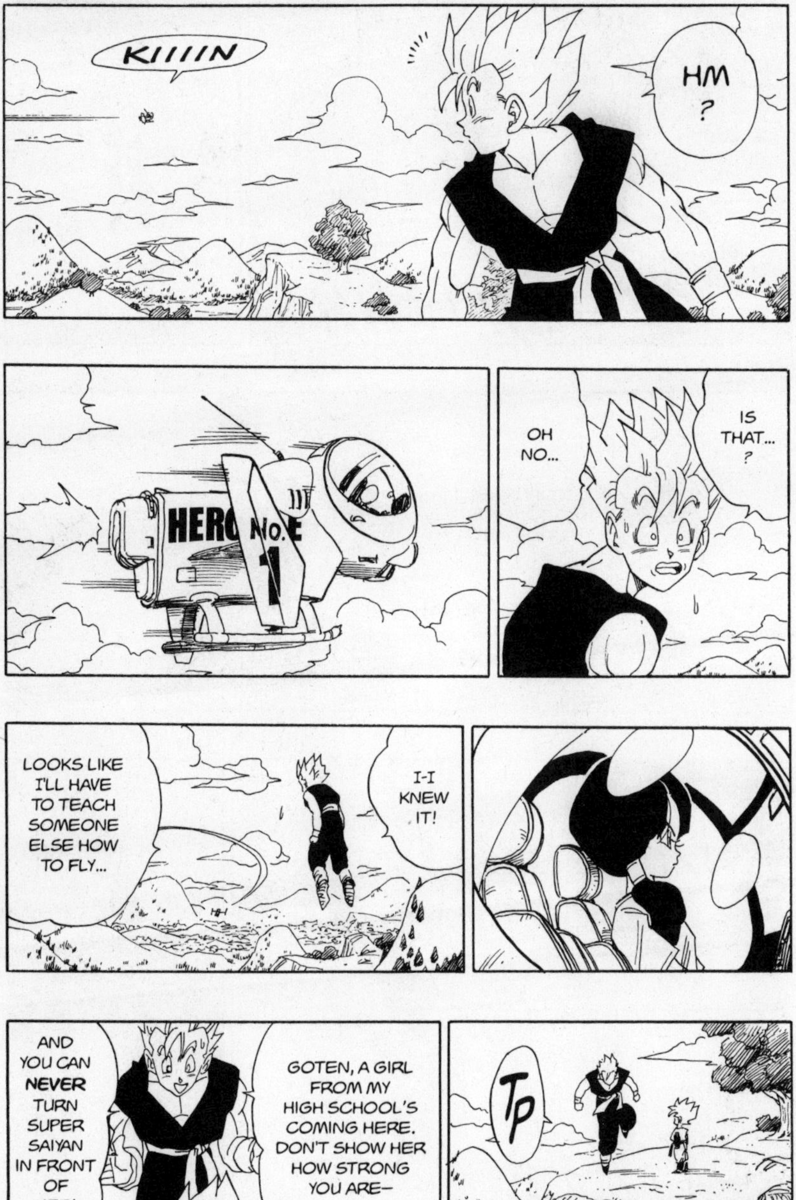
HM ?
KIIIIN
IS THAT... ?
OH NO...
I-I KNEW IT!
LOOKS LIKE I'LL HAVE TO TEACH SOMEONE ELSE HOW TO FLY...
TP
GOTEN, A GIRL FROM MY HIGH SCHOOL'S COMING HERE. DON'T SHOW HER HOW STRONG YOU ARE—
AND YOU CAN **NEVER** TURN SUPER SAIYAN IN FRONT OF HER!

READ THIS WAY

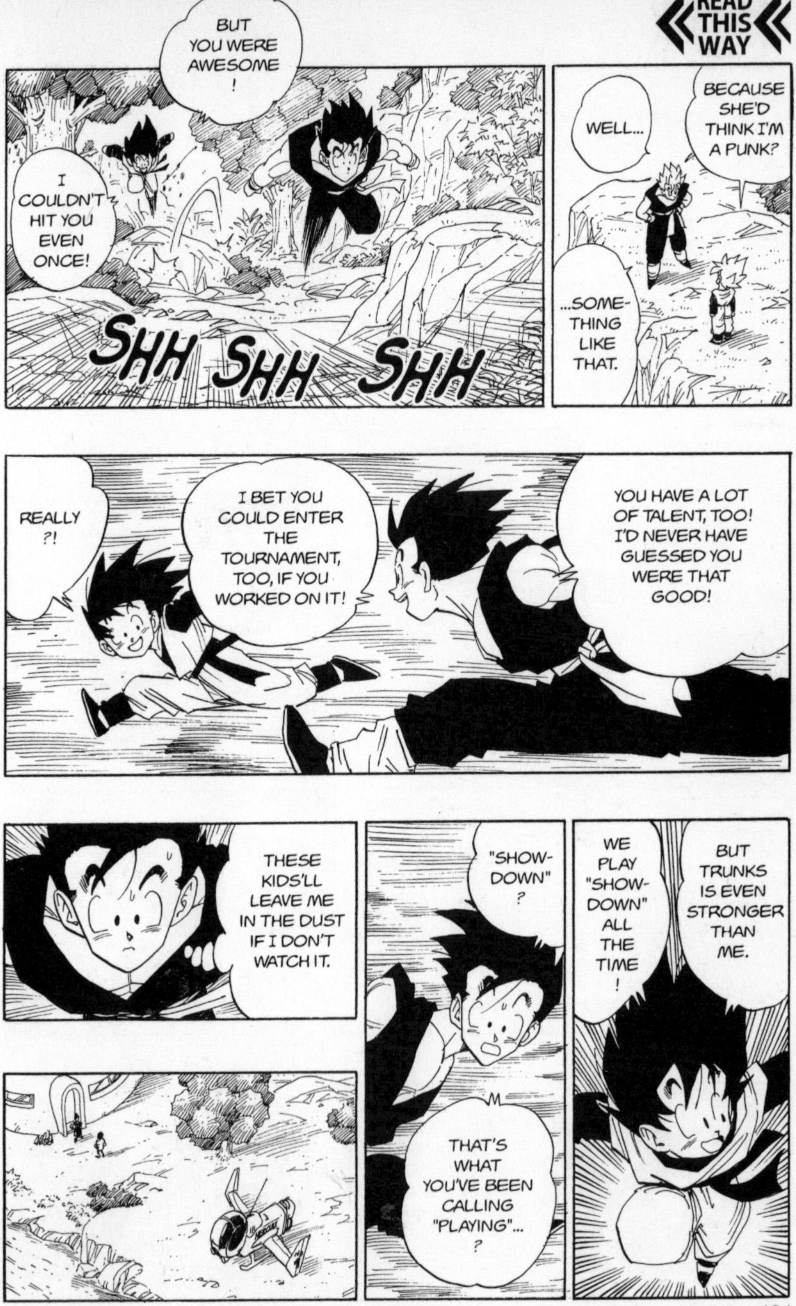
BECAUSE SHE'D THINK I'M A PUNK?
WELL...
...SOME-THING LIKE THAT.
BUT YOU WERE AWESOME!
I COULDN'T HIT YOU EVEN ONCE!
SHH SHH SHH
YOU HAVE A LOT OF TALENT, TOO! I'D NEVER HAVE GUESSED YOU WERE THAT GOOD!
I BET YOU COULD ENTER THE TOURNAMENT, TOO, IF YOU WORKED ON IT!
REALLY?!
BUT TRUNKS IS EVEN STRONGER THAN ME.
WE PLAY "SHOW-DOWN" ALL THE TIME!
"SHOW-DOWN"?
THAT'S WHAT YOU'VE BEEN CALLING "PLAYING"...?
THESE KIDS'LL LEAVE ME IN THE DUST IF I DON'T WATCH IT.

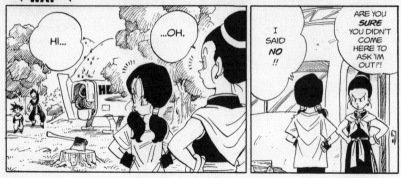

READ THIS WAY

ARE YOU SURE YOU DIDN'T COME HERE TO ASK 'IM OUT?!
I SAID NO !!
...OH.
HI...
UM... HOW'D YOU FIND MY HOUSE ?
I LOOKED ON THE STUDENT ROSTER. DUH.
SO WHAT'S THE IDEA OF CUTTING OUT LIKE THAT ?
YOU SAID YOU'D TEACH ME TO FLY!
R-RIGHT... I WAS STILL PLANNING TO...
GOHAN, IS SHE REALLY GONNA BE IN THIS TOURNAMENT?!
YEAH, SHE IS, MOM.
SHE WAS THE ONE WHO TOLD ME ABOUT THE TOURNAMENT TO BEGIN WITH. I PROMISED TO TEACH HER HOW TO FLY.
HMPH.
WELL, ALL RIGHT THEN.
BUT YOU'D BETTER NOT BE THINKIN' YOU'RE GONNA USE THIS TO SNAG 'IM!
OH, I'M SURE !!
PBB TTHH !!!
...
...HEH HEH...
I JUST WANT TO TRAIN QUIETLY...

NEXT: As Above, So Below

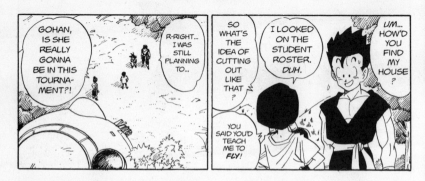

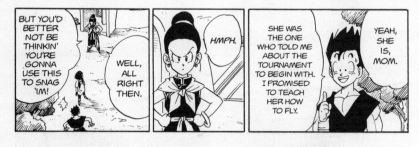

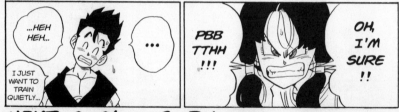

DBZ:234 • Videl Learns to Fly

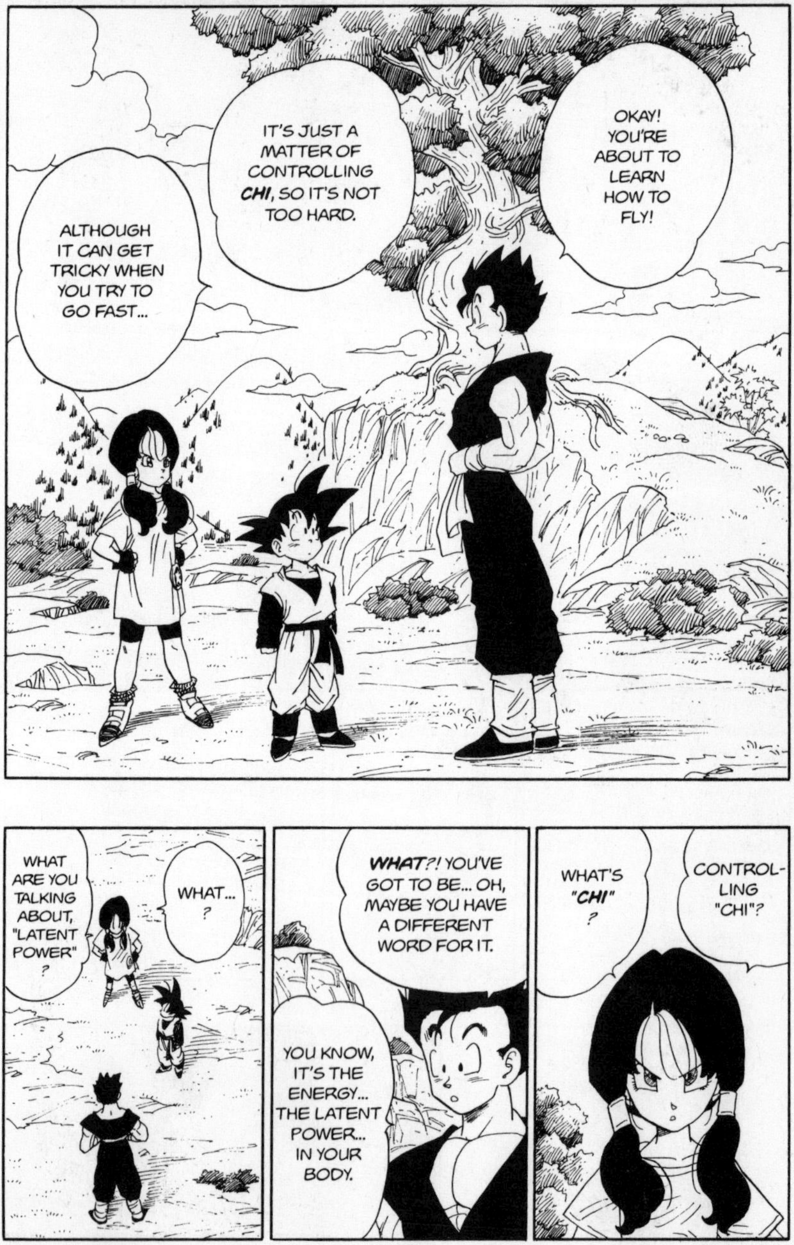
OKAY! YOU'RE ABOUT TO LEARN HOW TO FLY!
IT'S JUST A MATTER OF CONTROLLING **CHI**, SO IT'S NOT TOO HARD.
ALTHOUGH IT CAN GET TRICKY WHEN YOU TRY TO GO FAST...
CONTROL-LING "CHI"?
WHAT'S "**CHI**" ?
WHAT?! YOU'VE GOT TO BE... OH, MAYBE YOU HAVE A DIFFERENT WORD FOR IT.
YOU KNOW, IT'S THE ENERGY... THE LATENT POWER... IN YOUR BODY.
WHAT... ?
WHAT ARE YOU TALKING ABOUT, "LATENT POWER" ?

READ THIS WAY

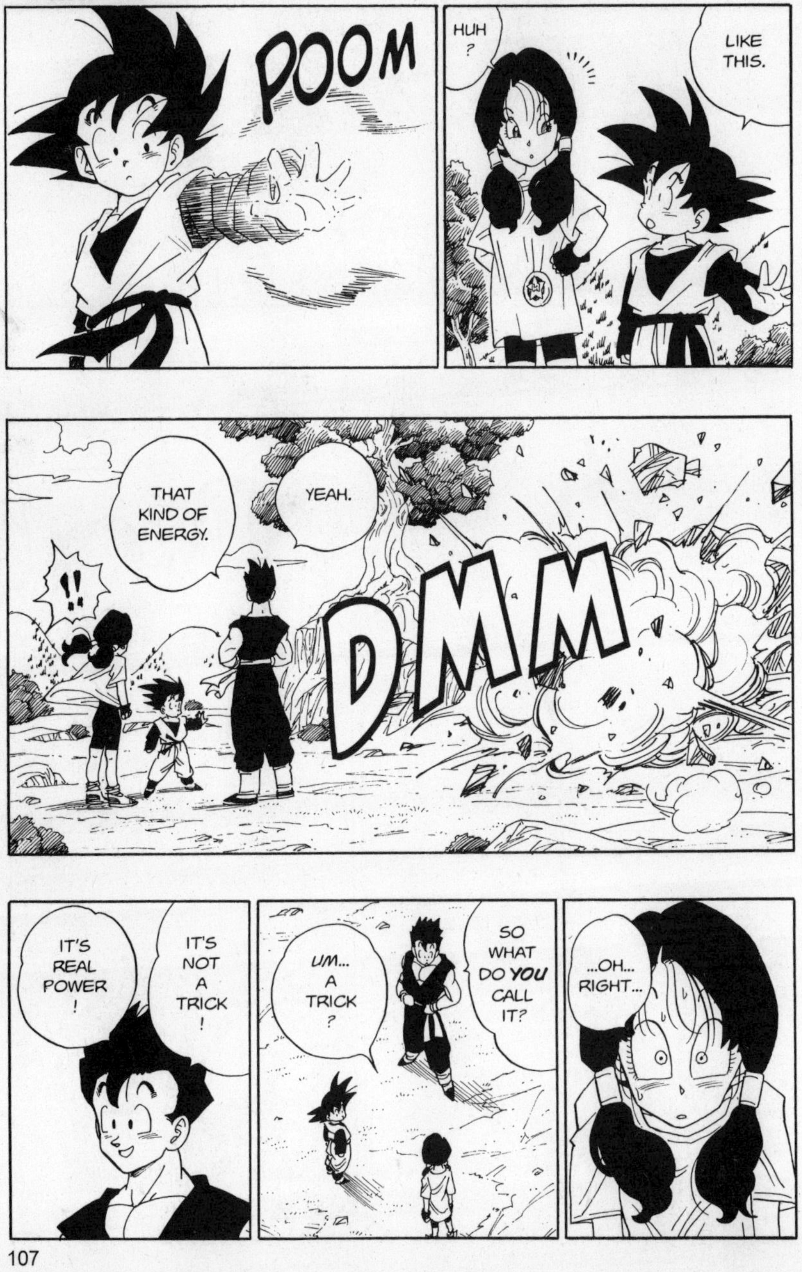
LIKE THIS.
HUH ?
POOM
YEAH.
THAT KIND OF ENERGY.
DMM
!!
...OH... RIGHT...
SO WHAT DO *YOU* CALL IT?
UM... A TRICK ?
IT'S NOT A TRICK !
IT'S REAL POWER !

READ THIS WAY

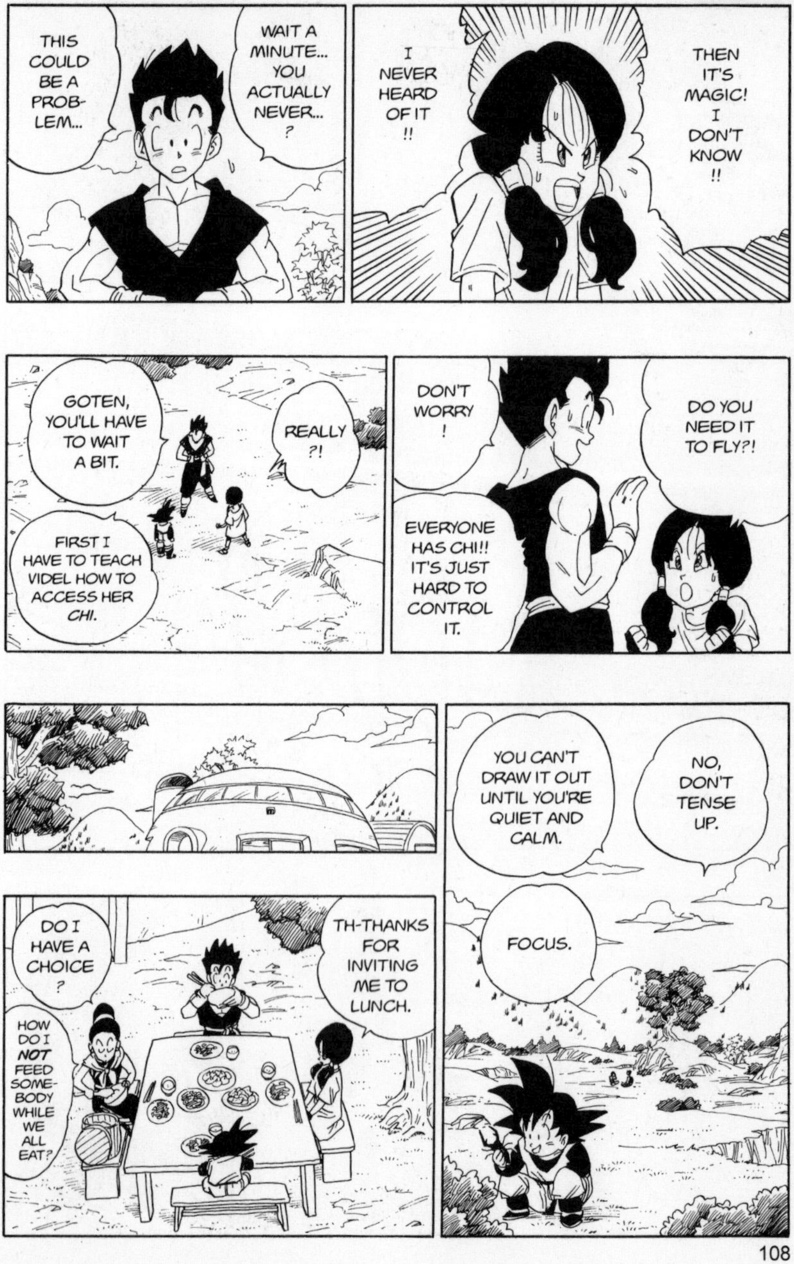
THEN IT'S MAGIC! I DON'T KNOW !!
I NEVER HEARD OF IT !!
WAIT A MINUTE... YOU ACTUALLY NEVER... ?
THIS COULD BE A PROB-LEM...
DO YOU NEED IT TO FLY?!
DON'T WORRY !
EVERYONE HAS CHI!! IT'S JUST HARD TO CONTROL IT.
REALLY ?!
GOTEN, YOU'LL HAVE TO WAIT A BIT.
FIRST I HAVE TO TEACH VIDEL HOW TO ACCESS HER *CHI*.
NO, DON'T TENSE UP.
YOU CAN'T DRAW IT OUT UNTIL YOU'RE QUIET AND CALM.
FOCUS.
TH-THANKS FOR INVITING ME TO LUNCH.
DO I HAVE A CHOICE ?
HOW DO I **NOT** FEED SOME-BODY WHILE WE ALL EAT?

READ THIS WAY

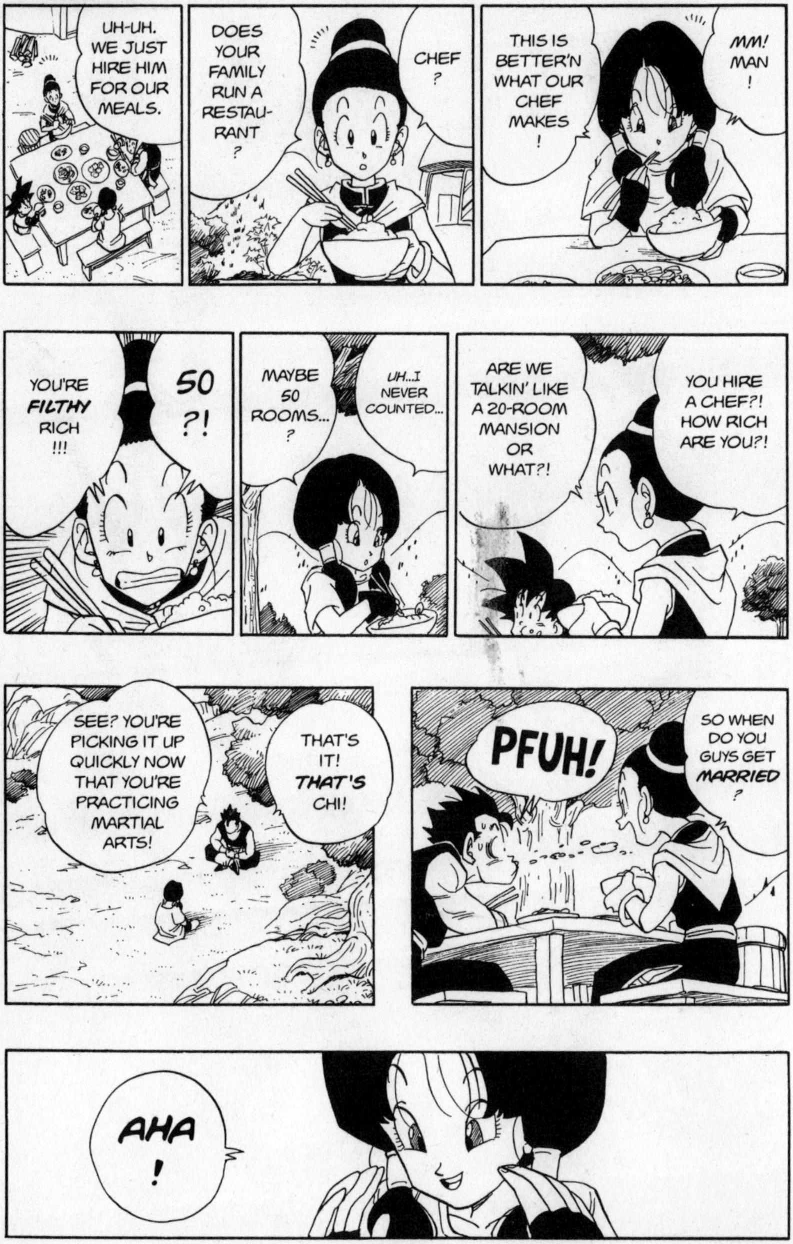
MM! MAN!
THIS IS BETTER'N WHAT OUR CHEF MAKES!
CHEF?
DOES YOUR FAMILY RUN A RESTAURANT?
UH-UH. WE JUST HIRE HIM FOR OUR MEALS.
YOU HIRE A CHEF?! HOW RICH ARE YOU?!
ARE WE TALKIN' LIKE A 20-ROOM MANSION OR WHAT?!
UH...I NEVER COUNTED...
MAYBE 50 ROOMS...?
50?!
YOU'RE FILTHY RICH!!!
SO WHEN DO YOU GUYS GET MARRIED?
PFUH!
THAT'S IT! THAT'S CHI!
SEE? YOU'RE PICKING IT UP QUICKLY NOW THAT YOU'RE PRACTICING MARTIAL ARTS!
AHA!

READ THIS WAY

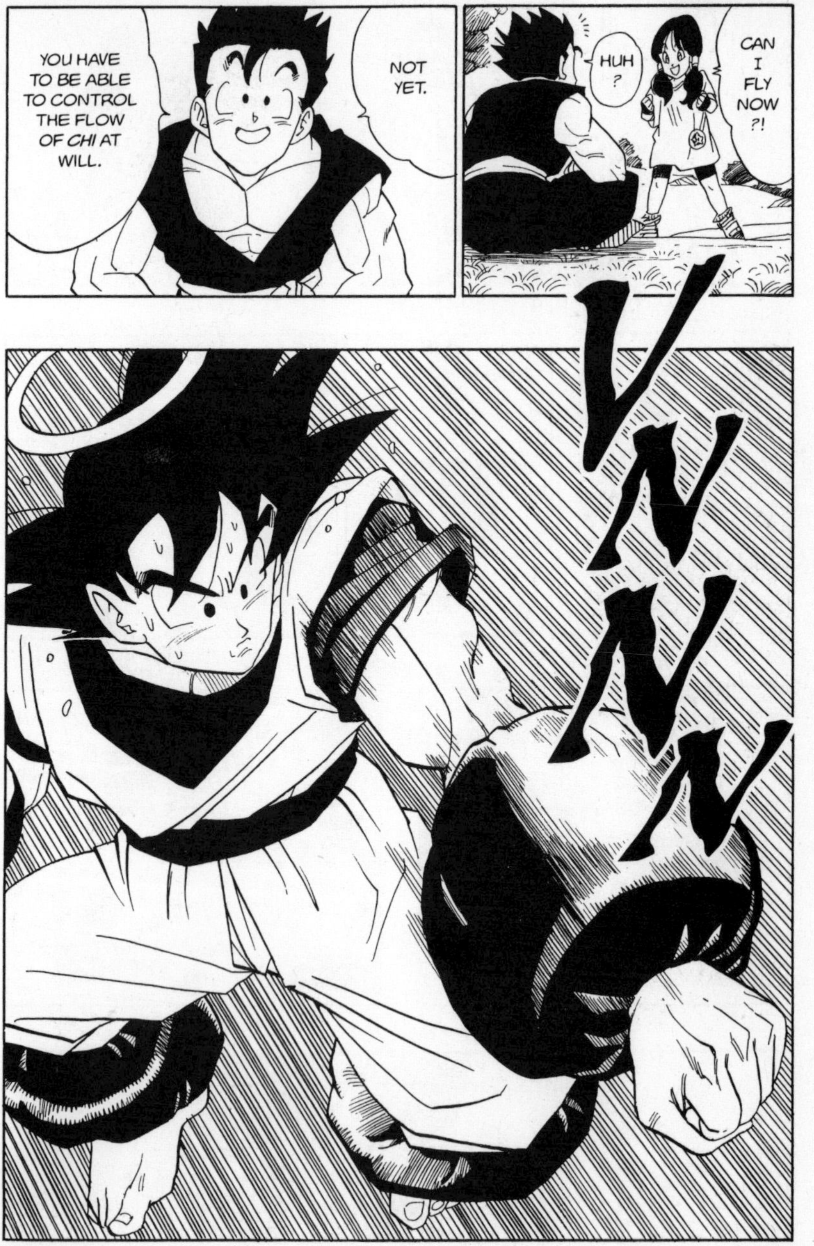
CAN I FLY NOW ?!
HUH ?
NOT YET.
YOU HAVE TO BE ABLE TO CONTROL THE FLOW OF *CHI* AT WILL.
VNNN

READ THIS WAY

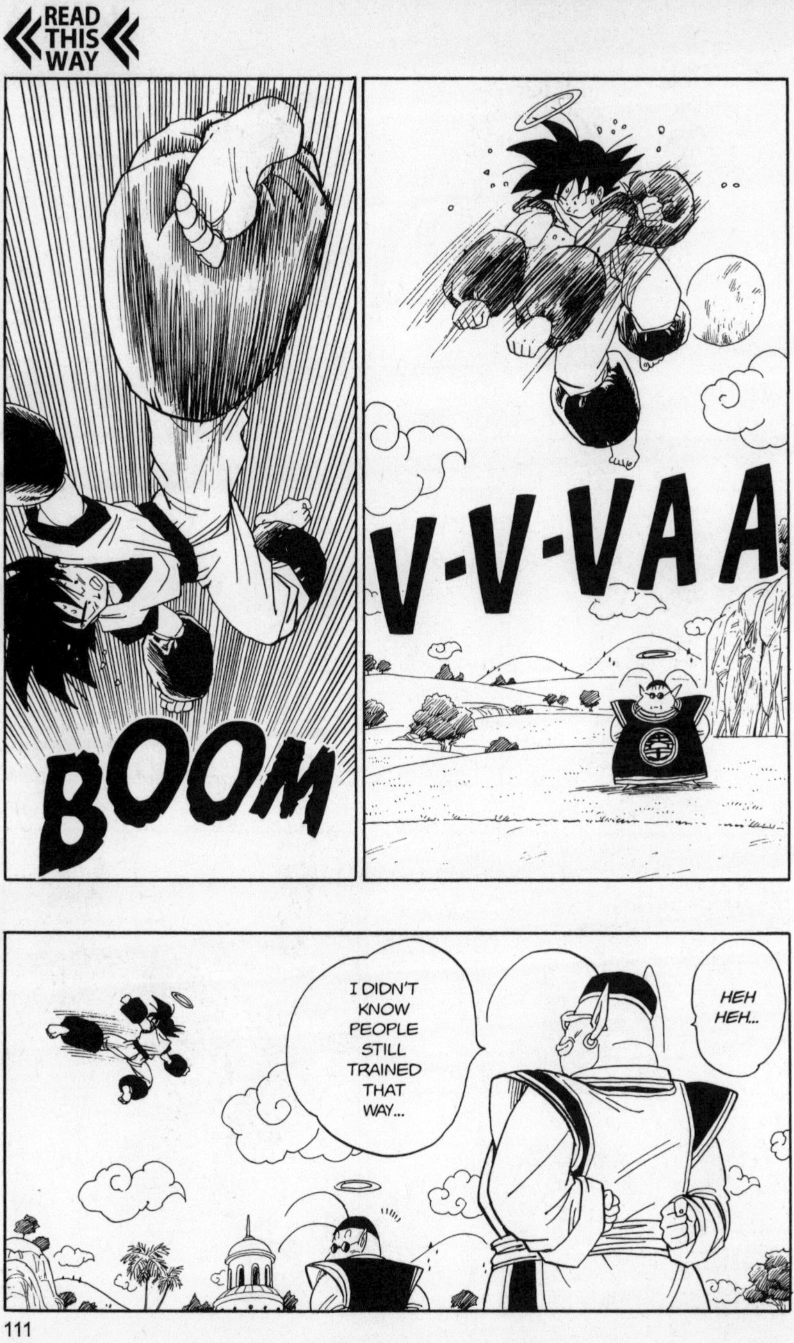
V-V-VAA
BOOM
HEH HEH...
I DIDN'T KNOW PEOPLE STILL TRAINED THAT WAY...

READ THIS WAY

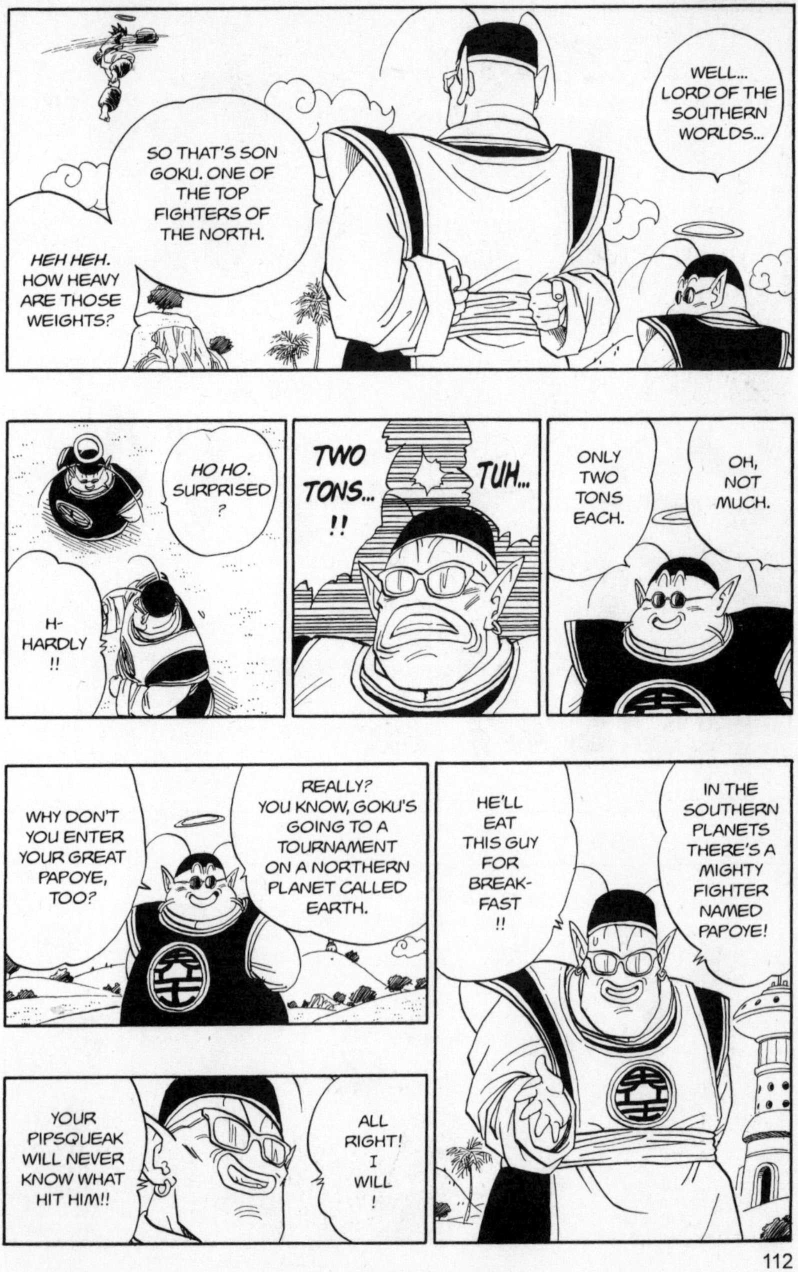
WELL... LORD OF THE SOUTHERN WORLDS...
SO THAT'S SON GOKU. ONE OF THE TOP FIGHTERS OF THE NORTH.
HEH HEH. HOW HEAVY ARE THOSE WEIGHTS?
OH, NOT MUCH.
ONLY TWO TONS EACH.
TUH...
TWO TONS... !!
HO HO. SURPRISED?
H-HARDLY!!
IN THE SOUTHERN PLANETS THERE'S A MIGHTY FIGHTER NAMED PAPOYE!
HE'LL EAT THIS GUY FOR BREAKFAST!!
REALLY? YOU KNOW, GOKU'S GOING TO A TOURNAMENT ON A NORTHERN PLANET CALLED EARTH.
WHY DON'T YOU ENTER YOUR GREAT PAPOYE, TOO?
ALL RIGHT! I WILL!
YOUR PIPSQUEAK WILL NEVER KNOW WHAT HIT HIM!!

READ THIS WAY

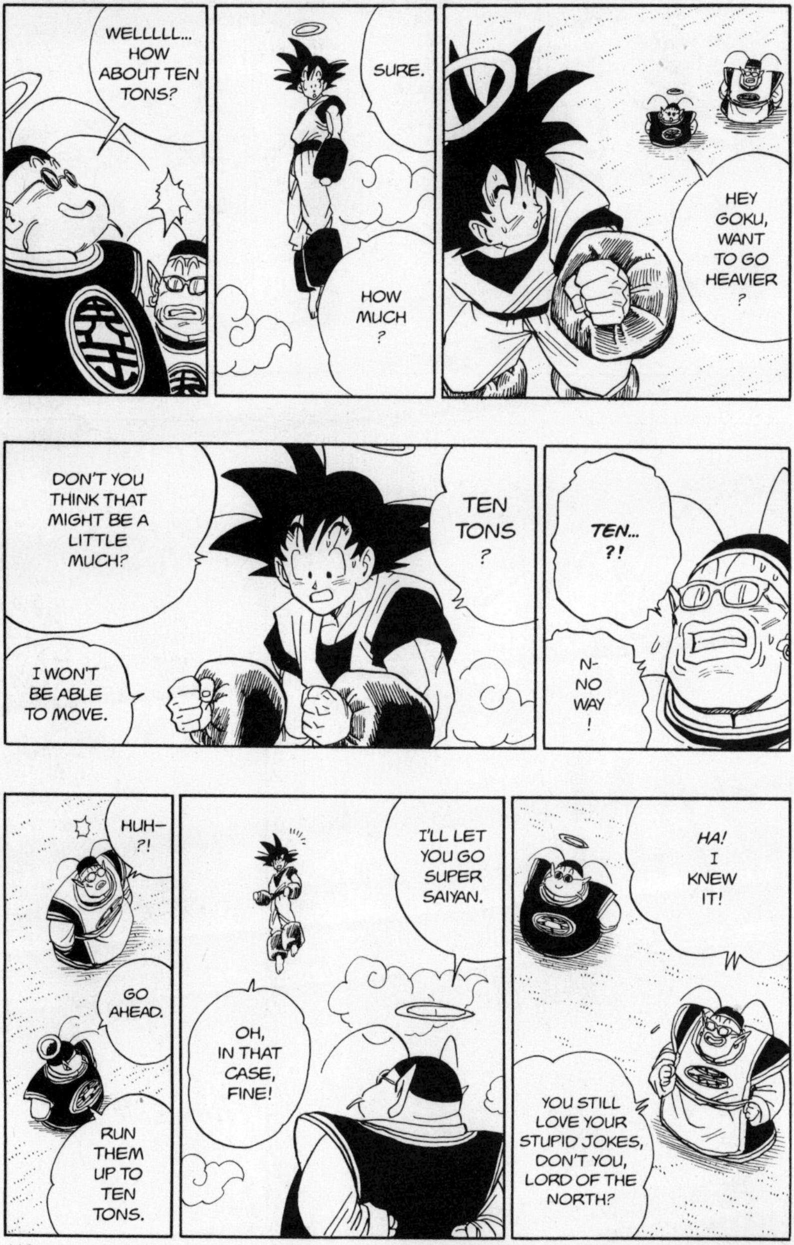

HEY GOKU, WANT TO GO HEAVIER?
SURE.
HOW MUCH?
WELLLLL... HOW ABOUT TEN TONS?
TEN...?!
N-NO WAY!
TEN TONS?
DON'T YOU THINK THAT MIGHT BE A LITTLE MUCH?
I WON'T BE ABLE TO MOVE.
HA! I KNEW IT!
YOU STILL LOVE YOUR STUPID JOKES, DON'T YOU, LORD OF THE NORTH?
I'LL LET YOU GO SUPER SAIYAN.
OH, IN THAT CASE, FINE!
HUH-?!
GO AHEAD.
RUN THEM UP TO TEN TONS.

READ THIS WAY

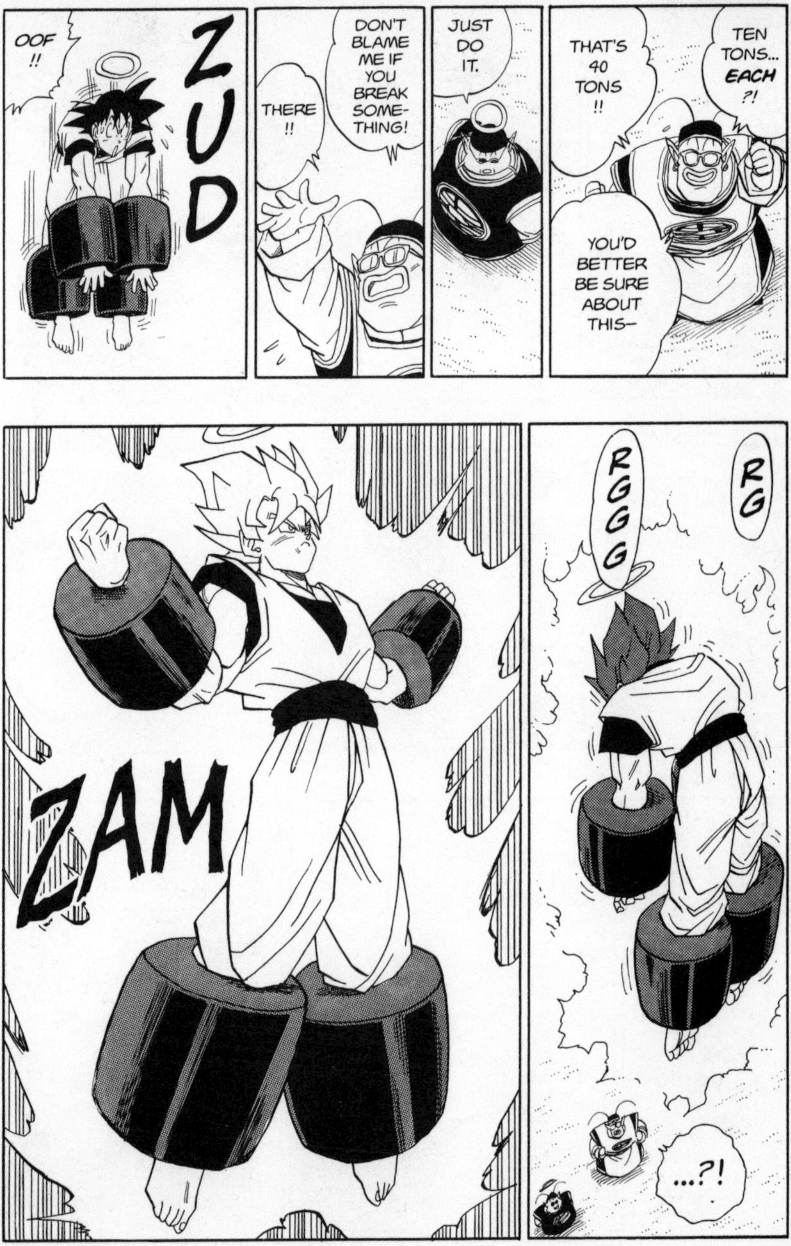

TEN TONS... EACH ?!
THAT'S 40 TONS !!
YOU'D BETTER BE SURE ABOUT THIS—
JUST DO IT.
DON'T BLAME ME IF YOU BREAK SOME-THING!
THERE !!
ZUD
OOF !!
RG
RGGG
...?!
ZAM

READ THIS WAY

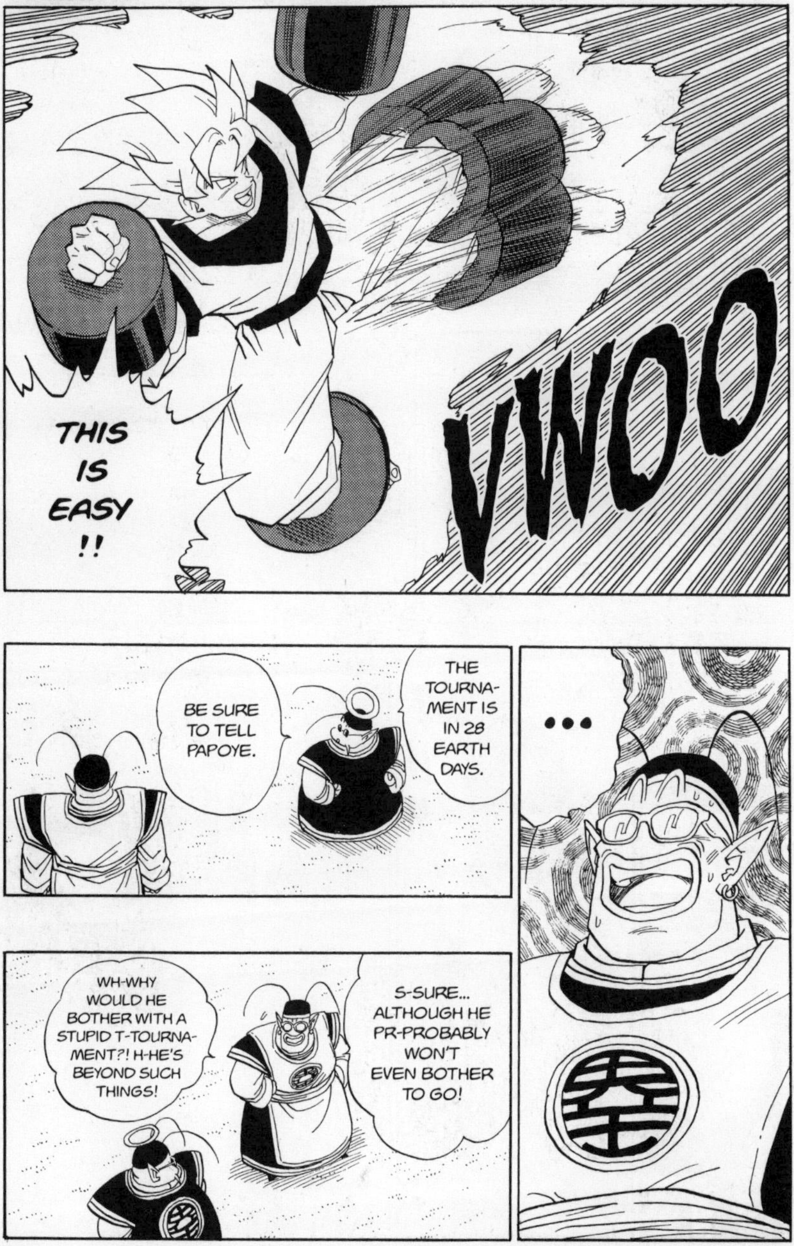
VWOO
THIS IS EASY!!
...
THE TOURNAMENT IS IN 28 EARTH DAYS.
BE SURE TO TELL PAPOYE.
S-SURE... ALTHOUGH HE PR-PROBABLY WON'T EVEN BOTHER TO GO!
WH-WHY WOULD HE BOTHER WITH A STUPID T-TOURNAMENT?! H-HE'S BEYOND SUCH THINGS!

READ THIS WAY

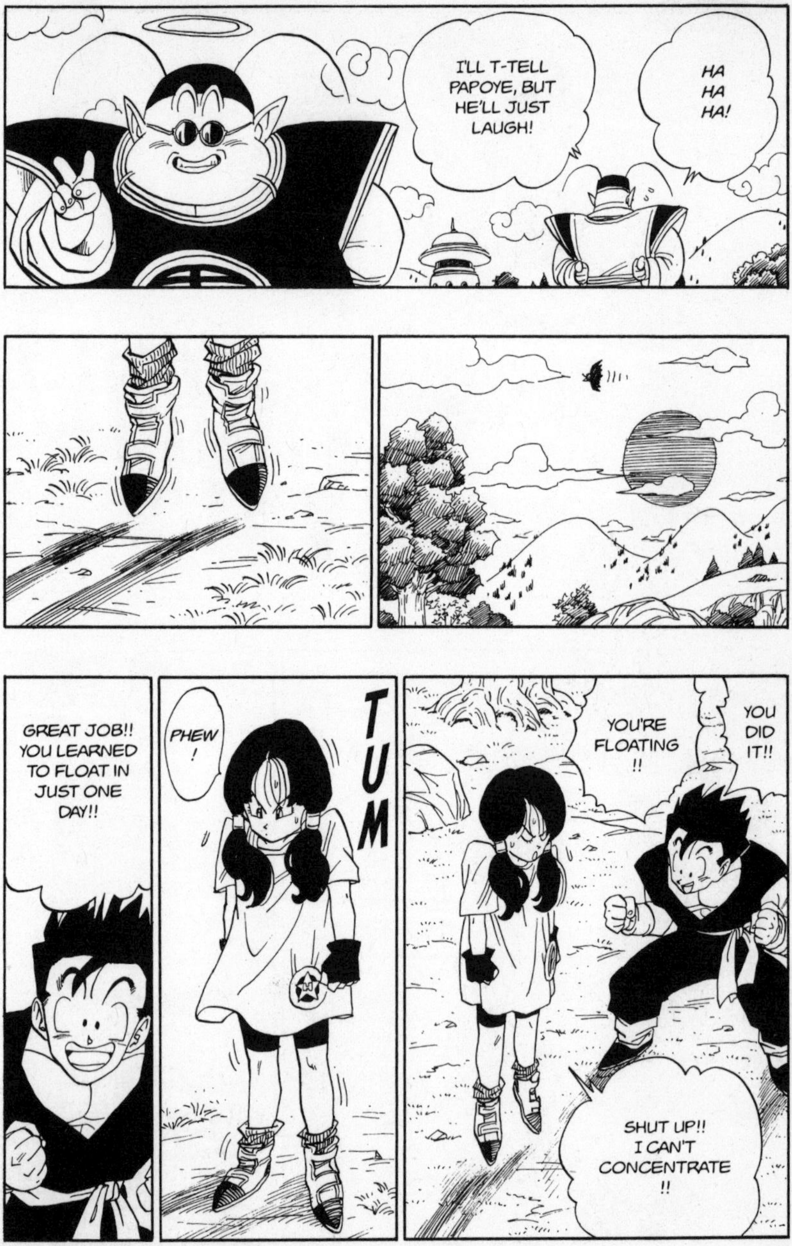

HA HA HA!
I'LL T-TELL PAPOYE, BUT HE'LL JUST LAUGH!
YOU DID IT!!
YOU'RE FLOATING !!
SHUT UP!! I CAN'T CONCENTRATE !!
TUM
PHEW !
GREAT JOB!! YOU LEARNED TO FLOAT IN JUST ONE DAY!!

READ THIS WAY

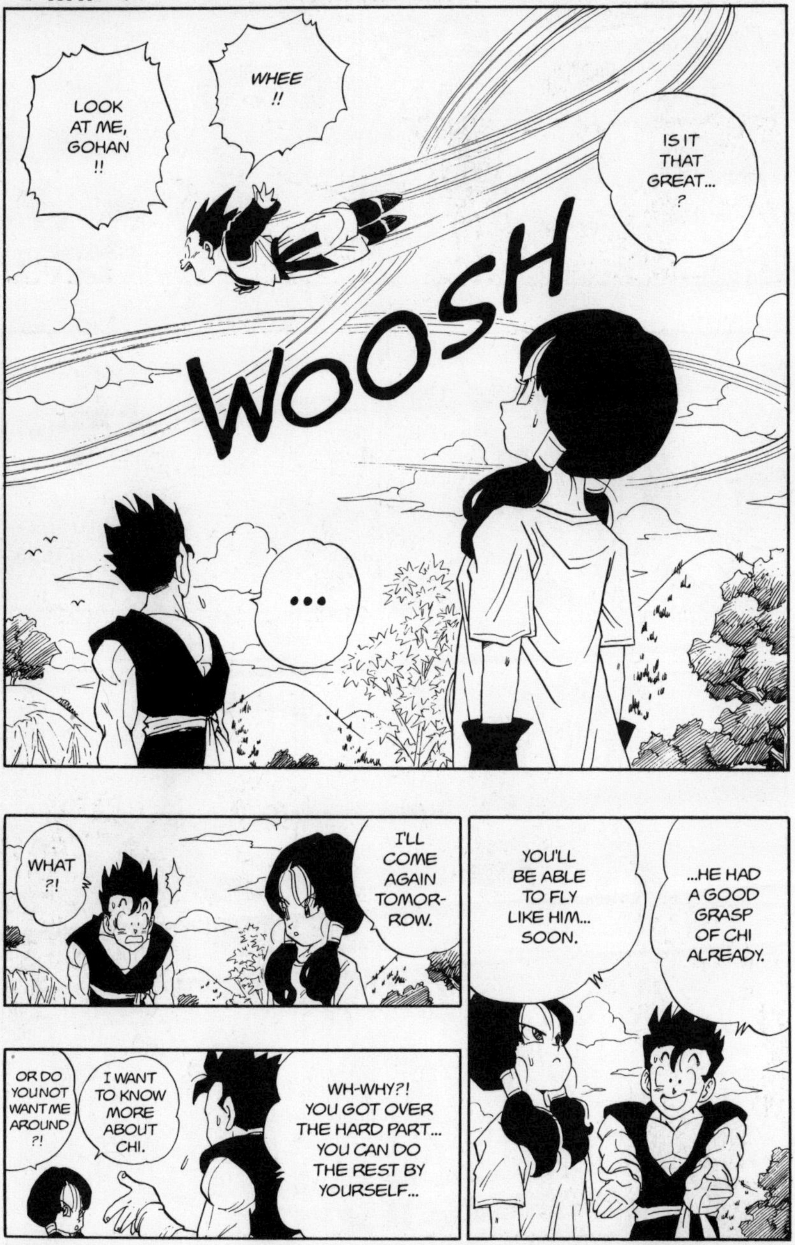
IS IT THAT GREAT...?
WHEE!!
LOOK AT ME, GOHAN!!
WOOSH
...
...HE HAD A GOOD GRASP OF CHI ALREADY.
YOU'LL BE ABLE TO FLY LIKE HIM... SOON.
I'LL COME AGAIN TOMORROW.
WHAT?!
WH-WHY?! YOU GOT OVER THE HARD PART... YOU CAN DO THE REST BY YOURSELF...
I WANT TO KNOW MORE ABOUT CHI.
OR DO YOU NOT WANT ME AROUND?!

READ THIS WAY

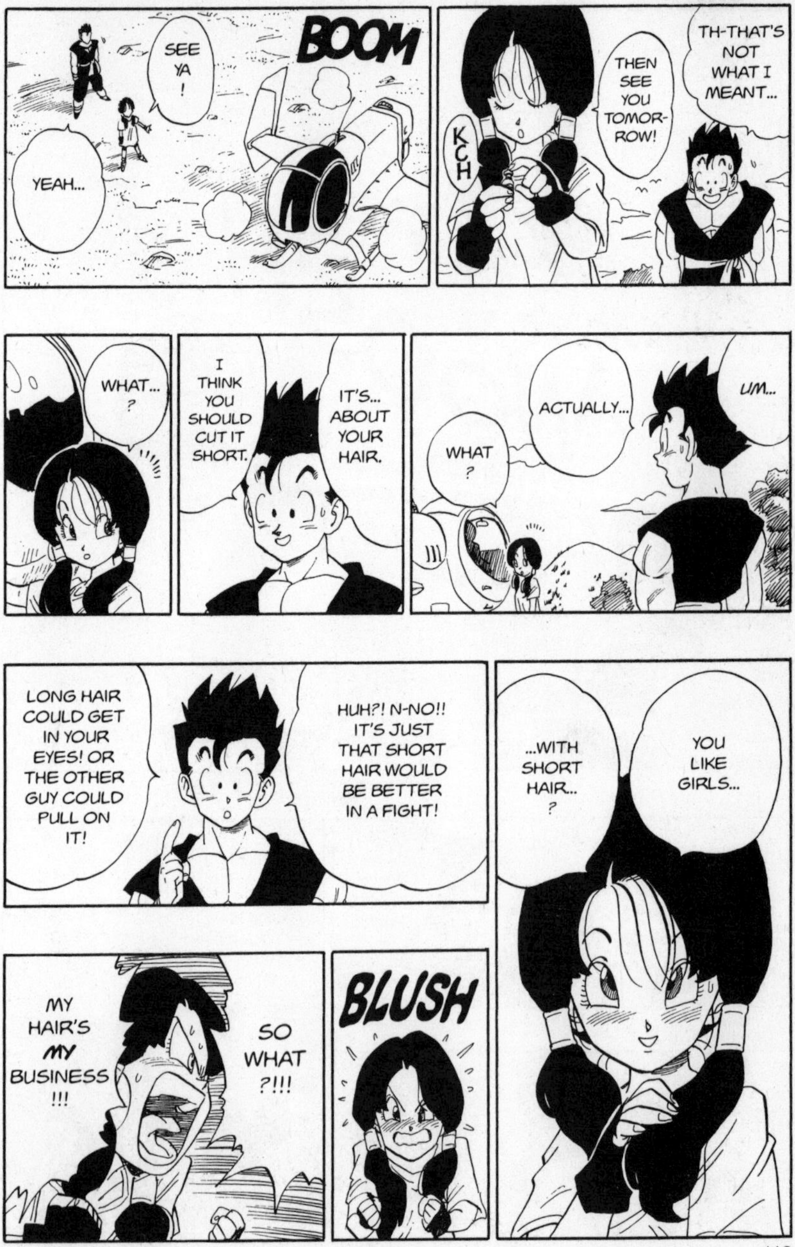
TH-THAT'S NOT WHAT I MEANT...
THEN SEE YOU TOMORROW!
KCH
BOOM
SEE YA!
YEAH...
UM...
ACTUALLY...
WHAT?
IT'S... ABOUT YOUR HAIR.
I THINK YOU SHOULD CUT IT SHORT.
WHAT...?
YOU LIKE GIRLS...
...WITH SHORT HAIR...?
HUH?! N-NO!! IT'S JUST THAT SHORT HAIR WOULD BE BETTER IN A FIGHT!
LONG HAIR COULD GET IN YOUR EYES! OR THE OTHER GUY COULD PULL ON IT!
BLUSH
SO WHAT?!!!
MY HAIR'S MY BUSINESS!!!

READ THIS WAY

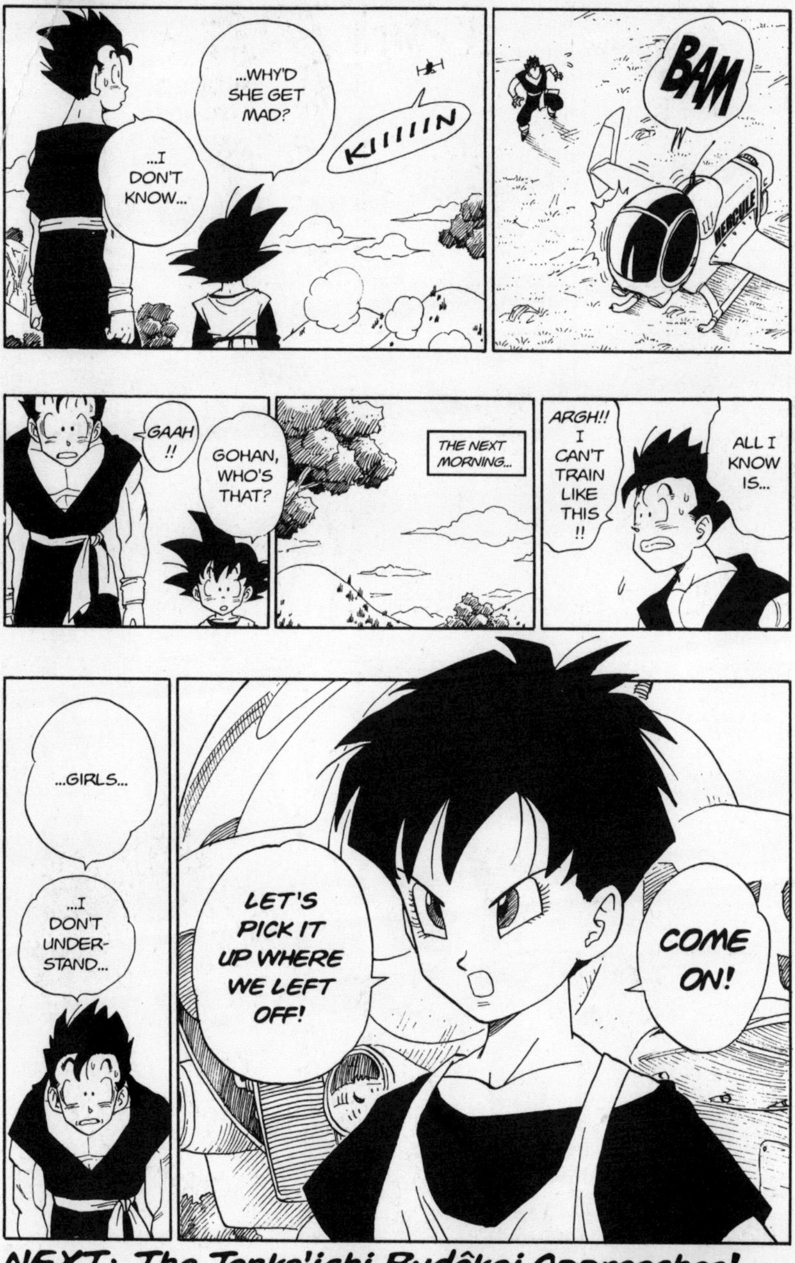
BAM
...WHY'D SHE GET MAD?
KIIIIIN
...I DON'T KNOW...
ARGH!! I CAN'T TRAIN LIKE THIS!!
ALL I KNOW IS...
THE NEXT MORNING...
GOHAN, WHO'S THAT?
GAAH!!
COME ON!
LET'S PICK IT UP WHERE WE LEFT OFF!
...GIRLS...
...I DON'T UNDERSTAND...

NEXT: The Tenka'ichi Budôkai Approaches!

DBZ:235 • Fathers

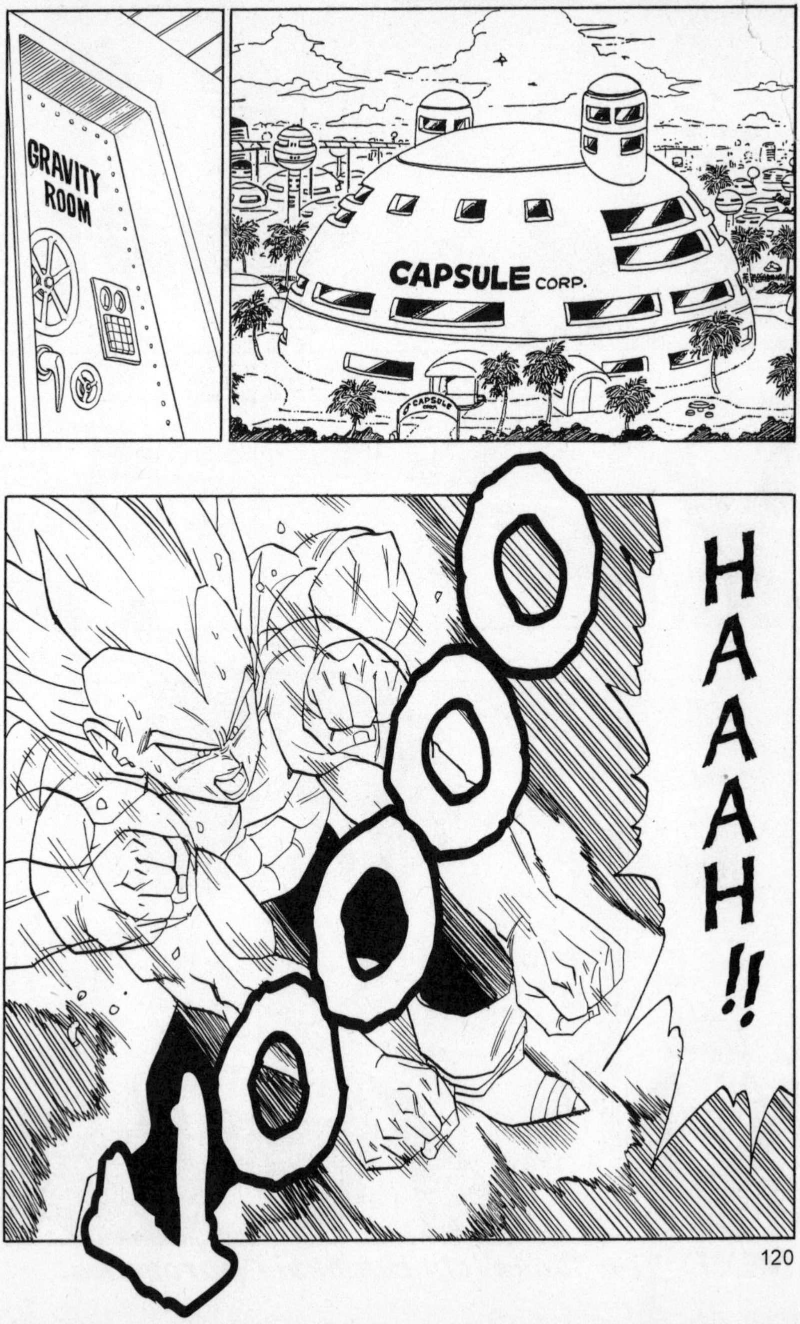
CAPSULE CORP.
CAPSULE CORP.
GRAVITY ROOM
HAAAH!!

READ THIS WAY

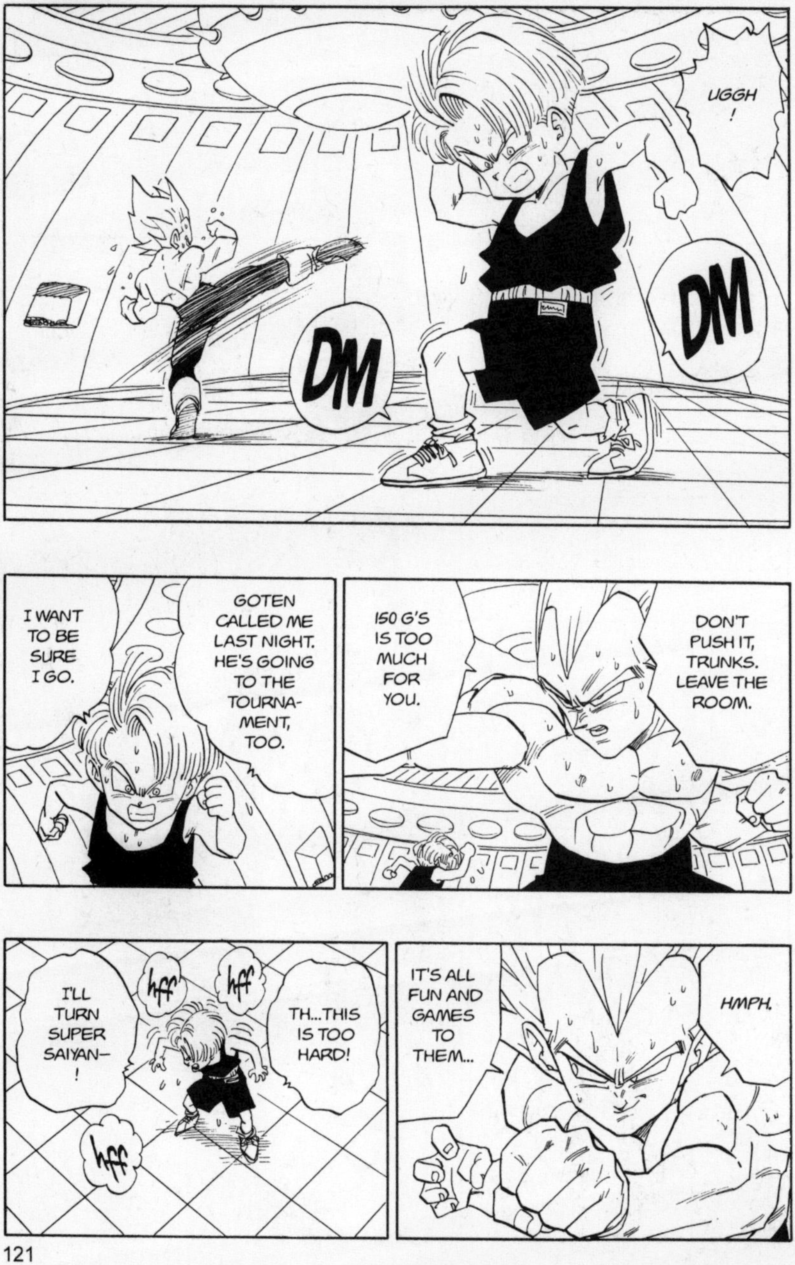
UGGH!
DM
DM
DON'T PUSH IT, TRUNKS. LEAVE THE ROOM.
150 G'S IS TOO MUCH FOR YOU.
GOTEN CALLED ME LAST NIGHT. HE'S GOING TO THE TOURNAMENT, TOO.
I WANT TO BE SURE I GO.
HMPH.
IT'S ALL FUN AND GAMES TO THEM...
TH...THIS IS TOO HARD!
hff
hff
I'LL TURN SUPER SAIYAN-!
hff

READ THIS WAY

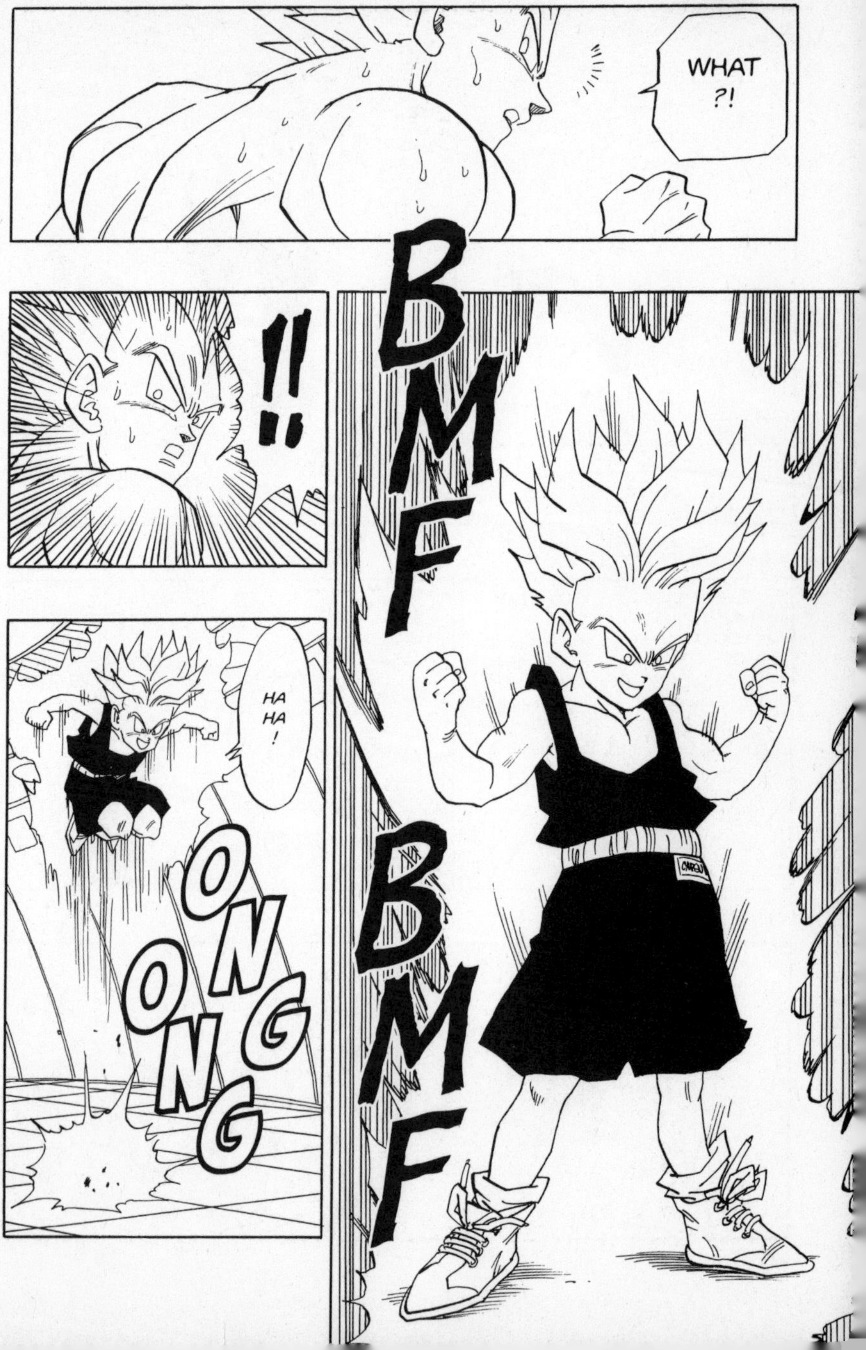
WHAT ?!
BMF
BMF
!!
HA HA!
ONG
ONG

READ THIS WAY

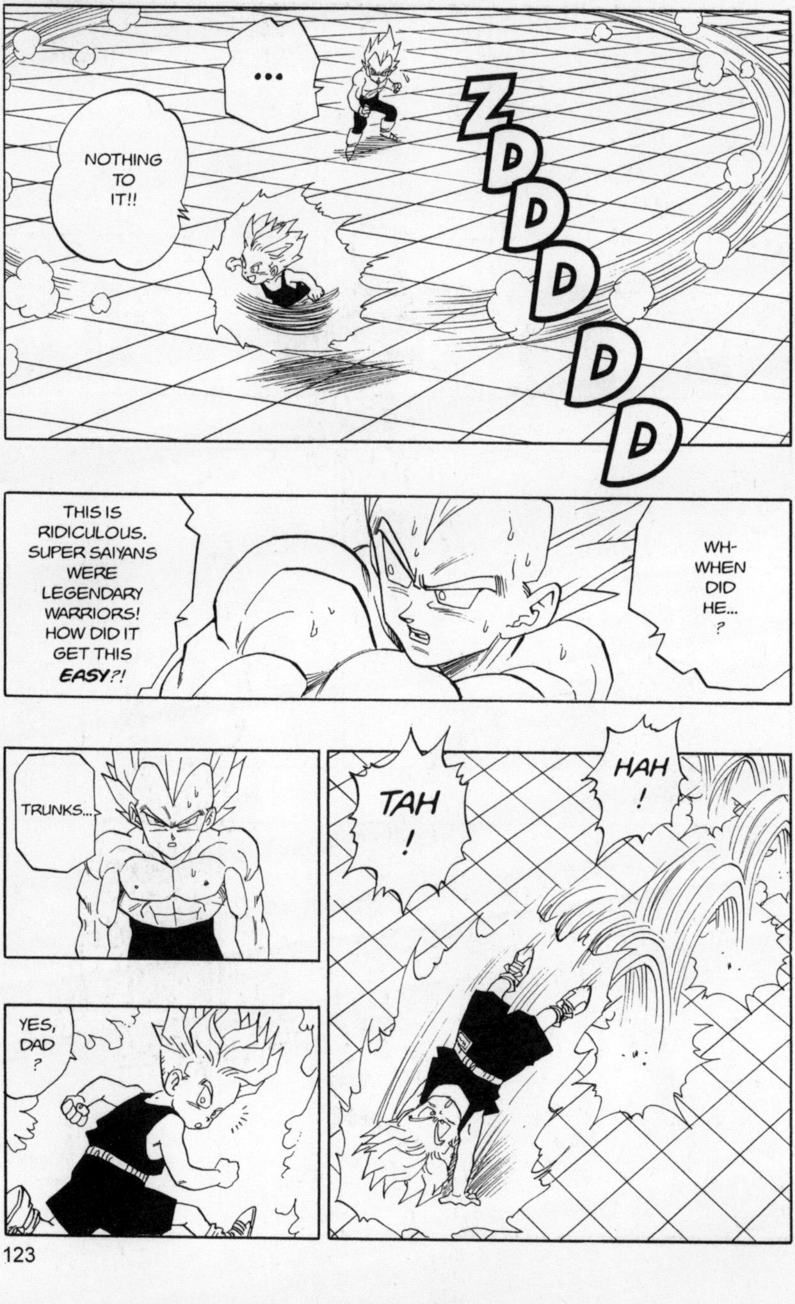

...
ZDDDDD
NOTHING TO IT!!
WH- WHEN DID HE...?
THIS IS RIDICULOUS. SUPER SAIYANS WERE LEGENDARY WARRIORS! HOW DID IT GET THIS *EASY*?!
HAH!
TAH!
TRUNKS...
YES, DAD?

READ THIS WAY

CAN SON GOHAN'S BROTHER TURN SUPER SAIYAN, TOO?
YES.
...
...IT'S A BARGAIN SALE ON SUPER SAIYANS...
TRY TO HIT ME.
HUH ?!
TH- THAT'S IMPOS- SIBLE, DAD !
YOU'RE TOO STRONG !
JUST DO IT.
IF YOU LAND ONE BLOW ON MY FACE, I'LL TAKE YOU TO THE AMUSEMENT PARK.
REALLY ?!
YOU ?!
O- KAY !
BRING EVERY- THING YOU'VE GOT!

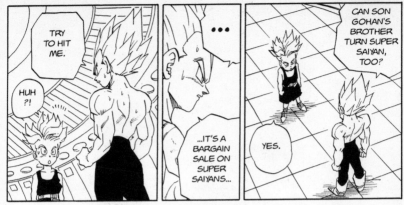

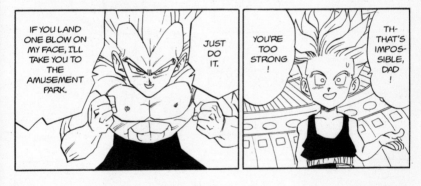

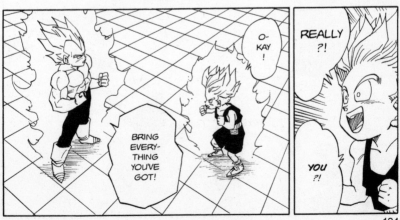

READ THIS WAY

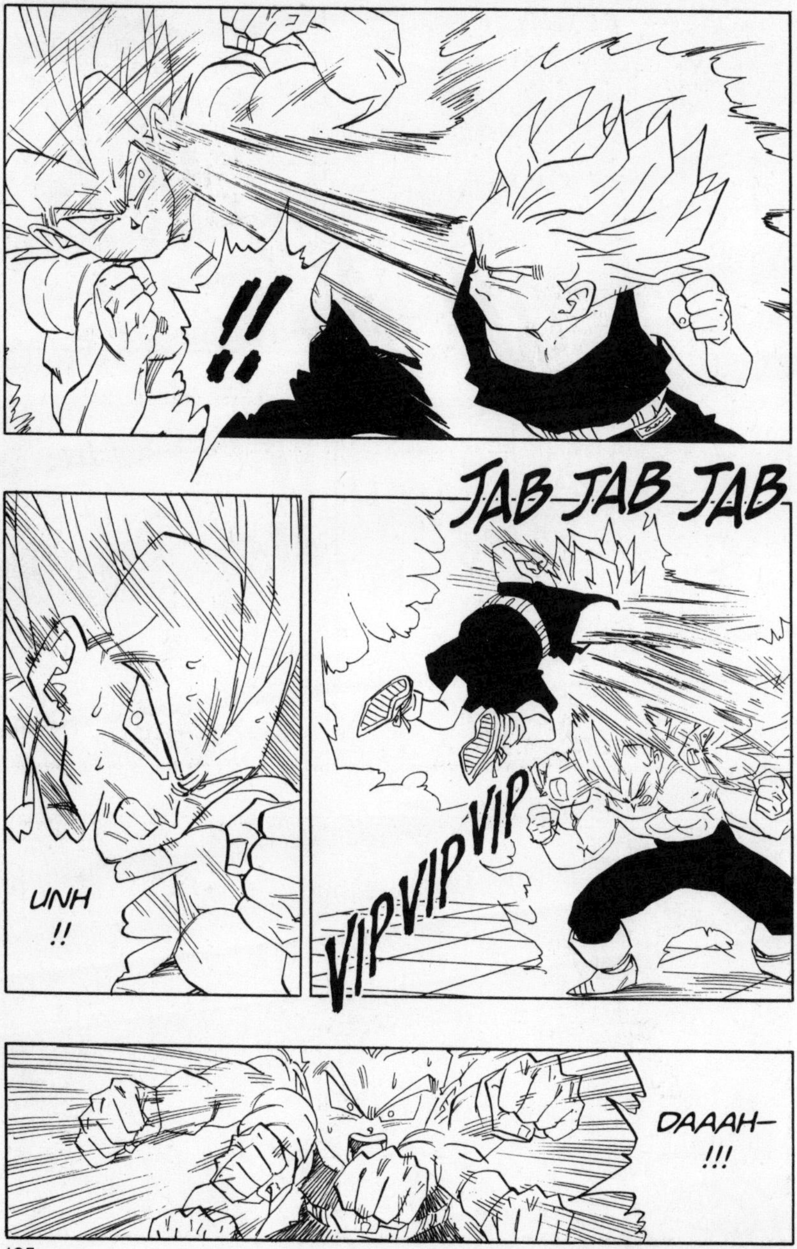
!!
JAB JAB JAB
VIP VIP VIP
UNH !!
DAAAH— !!!

READ THIS WAY

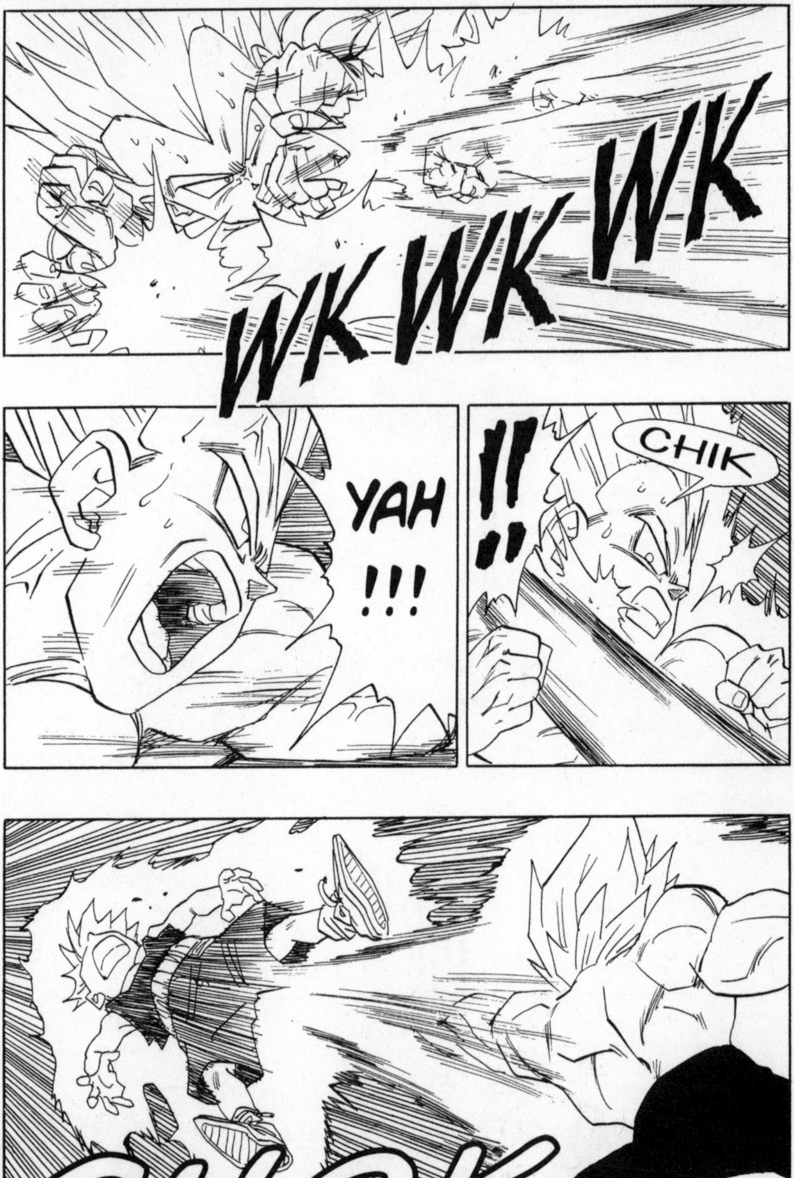
WK WK WK
!!
CHIK
YAH !!!
CHOK

READ THIS WAY

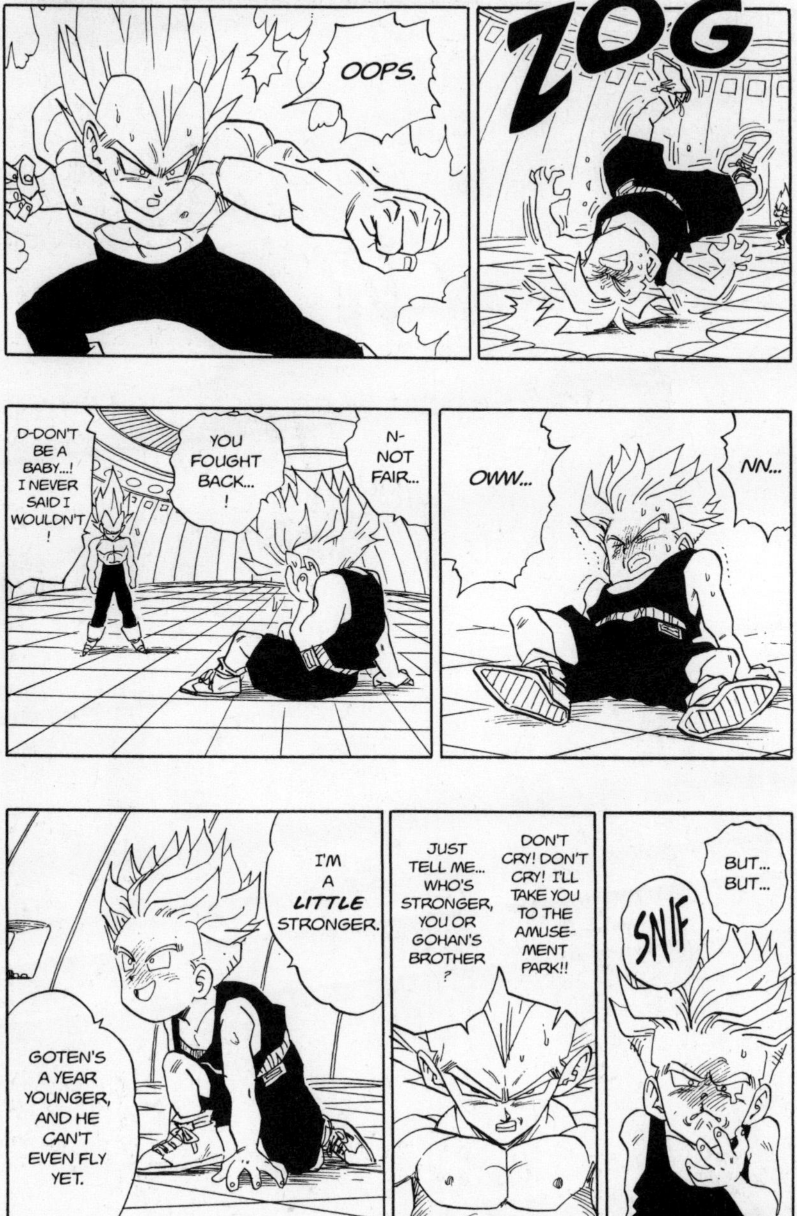
ZOG
OOPS.
NN...
OWW...
N- NOT FAIR...
YOU FOUGHT BACK...!
D-DON'T BE A BABY...! I NEVER SAID I WOULDN'T!
BUT... BUT...
SNIF
DON'T CRY! DON'T CRY! I'LL TAKE YOU TO THE AMUSEMENT PARK!!
JUST TELL ME... WHO'S STRONGER, YOU OR GOHAN'S BROTHER?
I'M A LITTLE STRONGER.
GOTEN'S A YEAR YOUNGER, AND HE CAN'T EVEN FLY YET.

READ THIS WAY

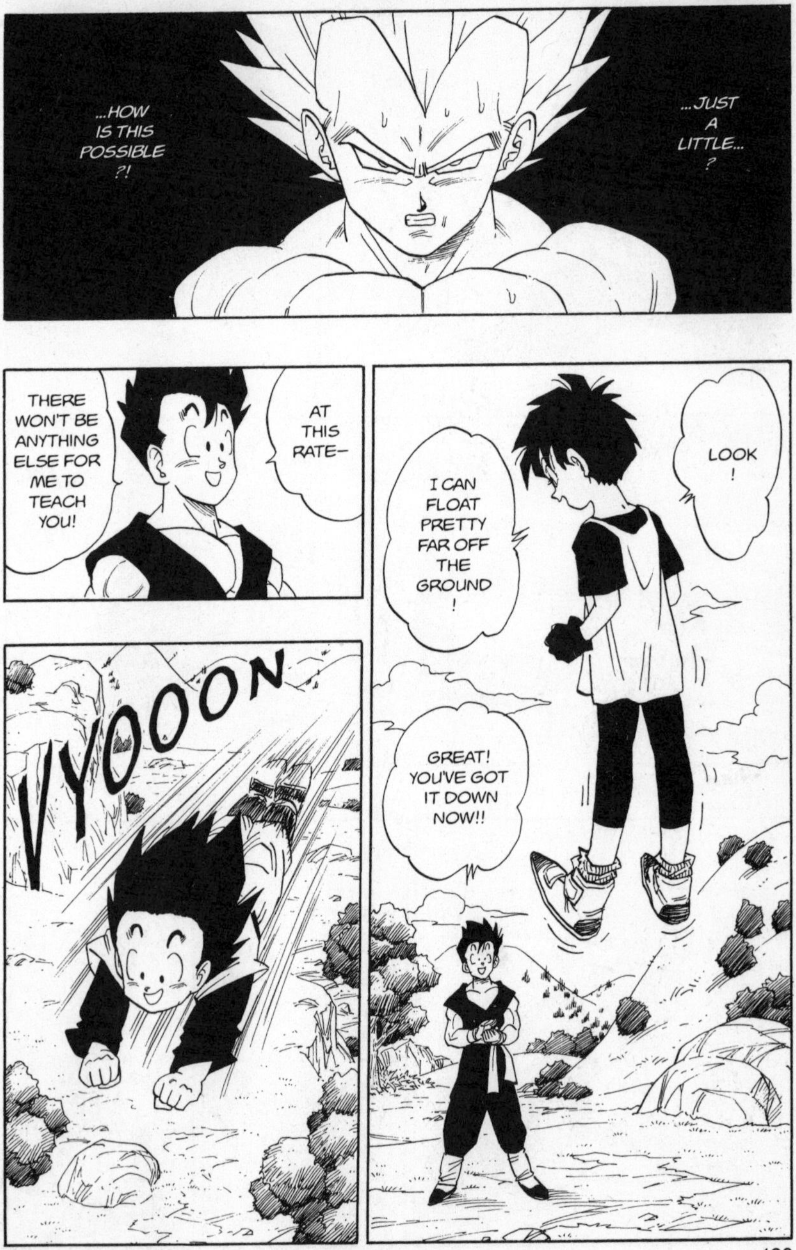
...JUST A LITTLE...?
...HOW IS THIS POSSIBLE?!
LOOK!
I CAN FLOAT PRETTY FAR OFF THE GROUND!
GREAT! YOU'VE GOT IT DOWN NOW!!
AT THIS RATE—
THERE WON'T BE ANYTHING ELSE FOR ME TO TEACH YOU!
VYOOON

READ THIS WAY

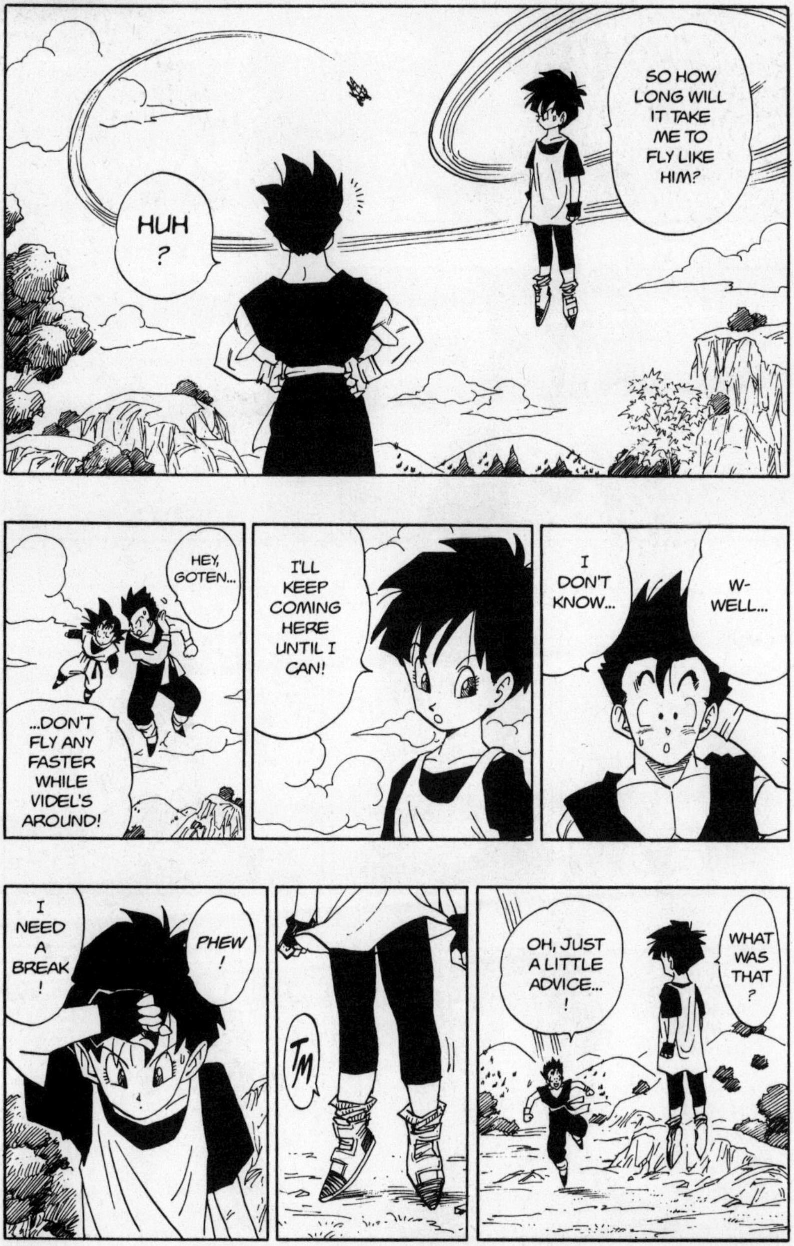
SO HOW LONG WILL IT TAKE ME TO FLY LIKE HIM?
HUH ?
W- WELL...
I DON'T KNOW...
I'LL KEEP COMING HERE UNTIL I CAN!
HEY, GOTEN...
...DON'T FLY ANY FASTER WHILE VIDEL'S AROUND!
WHAT WAS THAT ?
OH, JUST A LITTLE ADVICE... !
TM
PHEW !
I NEED A BREAK !

READ THIS WAY

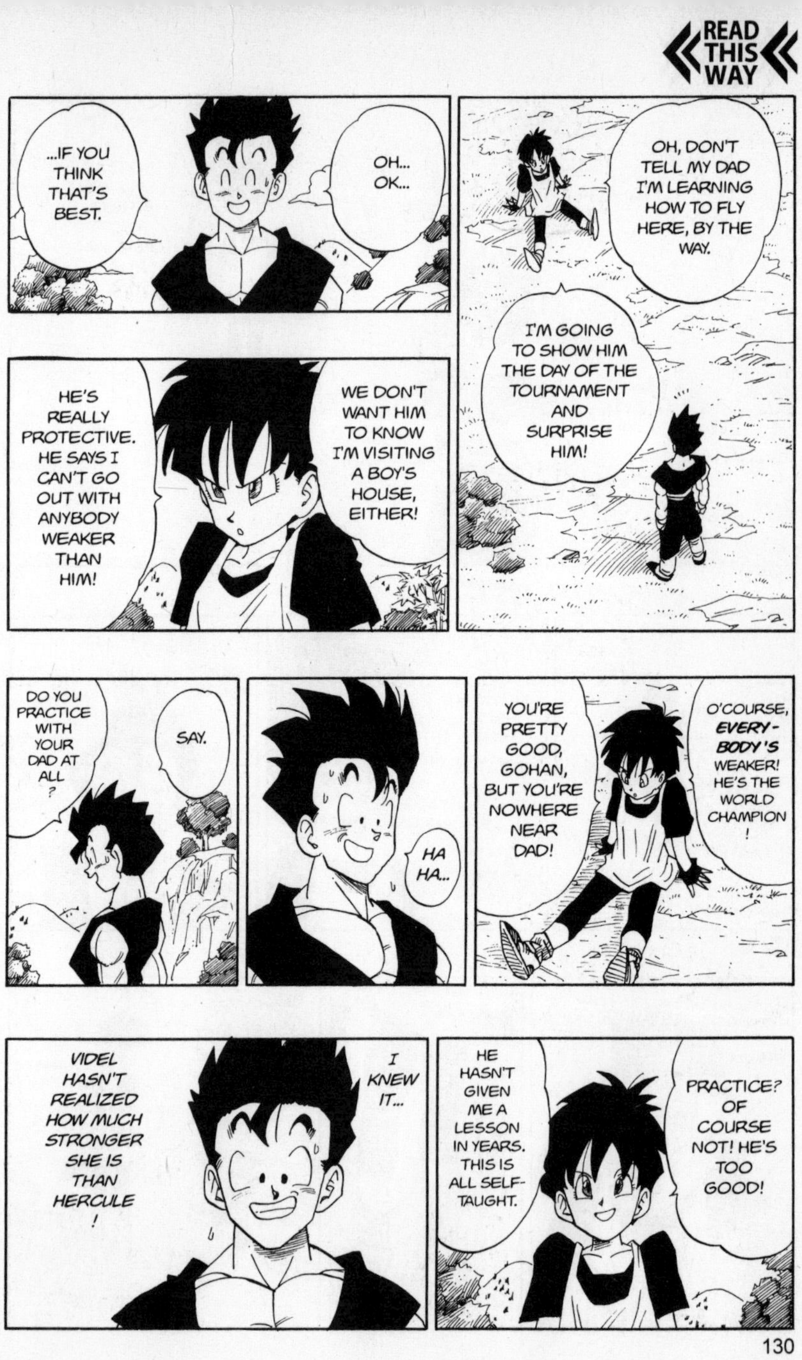

OH, DON'T TELL MY DAD I'M LEARNING HOW TO FLY HERE, BY THE WAY.
I'M GOING TO SHOW HIM THE DAY OF THE TOURNAMENT AND SURPRISE HIM!
OH... OK...
...IF YOU THINK THAT'S BEST.
WE DON'T WANT HIM TO KNOW I'M VISITING A BOY'S HOUSE, EITHER!
HE'S REALLY PROTECTIVE. HE SAYS I CAN'T GO OUT WITH ANYBODY WEAKER THAN HIM!
O'COURSE, ***EVERY-BODY'S*** WEAKER! HE'S THE WORLD CHAMPION!
YOU'RE PRETTY GOOD, GOHAN, BUT YOU'RE NOWHERE NEAR DAD!
HA HA...
SAY.
DO YOU PRACTICE WITH YOUR DAD AT ALL?
PRACTICE? OF COURSE NOT! HE'S TOO GOOD!
HE HASN'T GIVEN ME A LESSON IN YEARS. THIS IS ALL SELF-TAUGHT.
I KNEW IT...
VIDEL HASN'T REALIZED HOW MUCH STRONGER SHE IS THAN HERCULE!

READ THIS WAY

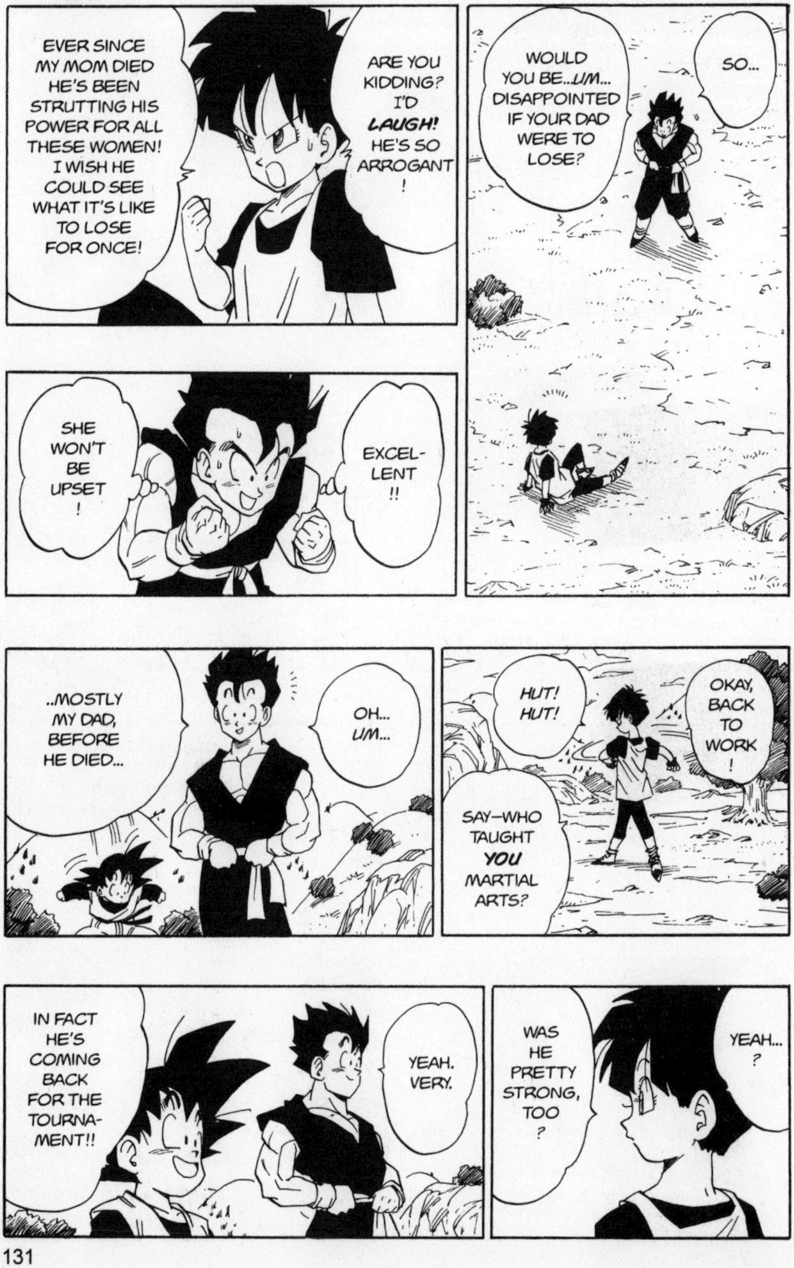
SO...
WOULD YOU BE...UM... DISAPPOINTED IF YOUR DAD WERE TO LOSE?
ARE YOU KIDDING? I'D LAUGH! HE'S SO ARROGANT!
EVER SINCE MY MOM DIED HE'S BEEN STRUTTING HIS POWER FOR ALL THESE WOMEN! I WISH HE COULD SEE WHAT IT'S LIKE TO LOSE FOR ONCE!
EXCEL-LENT!!
SHE WON'T BE UPSET!
OKAY, BACK TO WORK!
HUT! HUT!
SAY—WHO TAUGHT YOU MARTIAL ARTS?
OH... UM...
..MOSTLY MY DAD, BEFORE HE DIED...
YEAH...?
WAS HE PRETTY STRONG, TOO?
YEAH. VERY.
IN FACT HE'S COMING BACK FOR THE TOURNA-MENT!!

READ THIS WAY

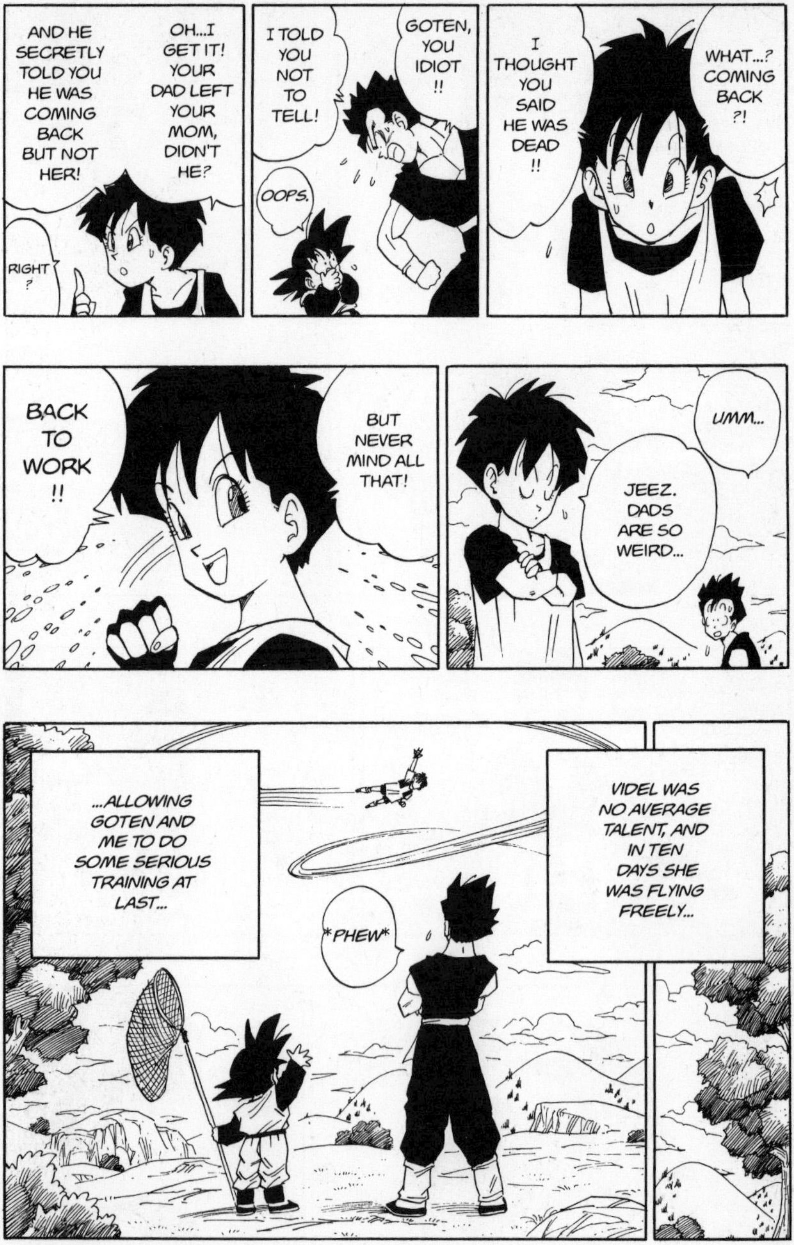
WHAT...? COMING BACK ?!
I THOUGHT YOU SAID HE WAS DEAD !!
GOTEN, YOU IDIOT !!
I TOLD YOU NOT TO TELL!
OOPS.
OH...I GET IT! YOUR DAD LEFT YOUR MOM, DIDN'T HE?
AND HE SECRETLY TOLD YOU HE WAS COMING BACK BUT NOT HER!
RIGHT ?
UMM...
JEEZ. DADS ARE SO WEIRD...
BUT NEVER MIND ALL THAT!
BACK TO WORK !!
VIDEL WAS NO AVERAGE TALENT, AND IN TEN DAYS SHE WAS FLYING FREELY...
PHEW
...ALLOWING GOTEN AND ME TO DO SOME SERIOUS TRAINING AT LAST...

READ THIS WAY

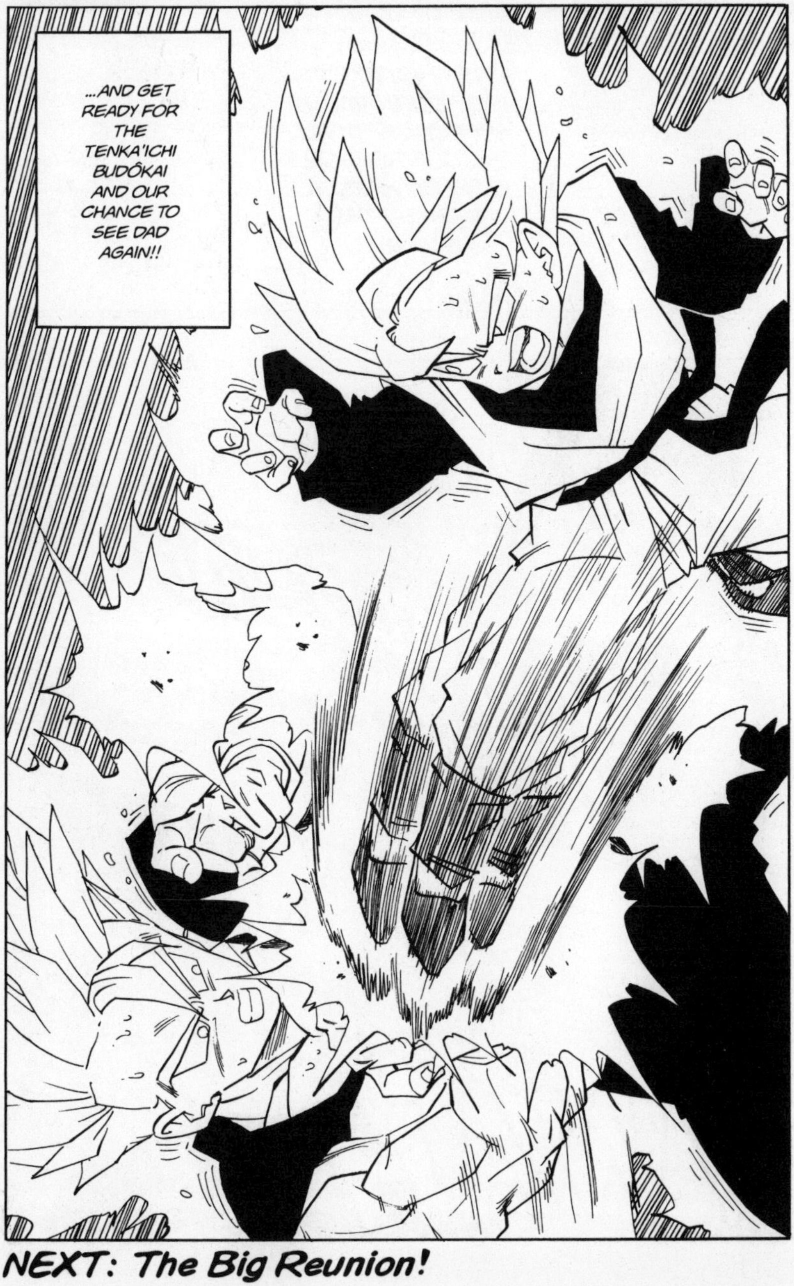
...AND GET READY FOR THE TENKA'ICHI BUDÔKAI AND OUR CHANCE TO SEE DAD AGAIN!!

NEXT: The Big Reunion!

DBZ:236 • The Dragon Team Returns!

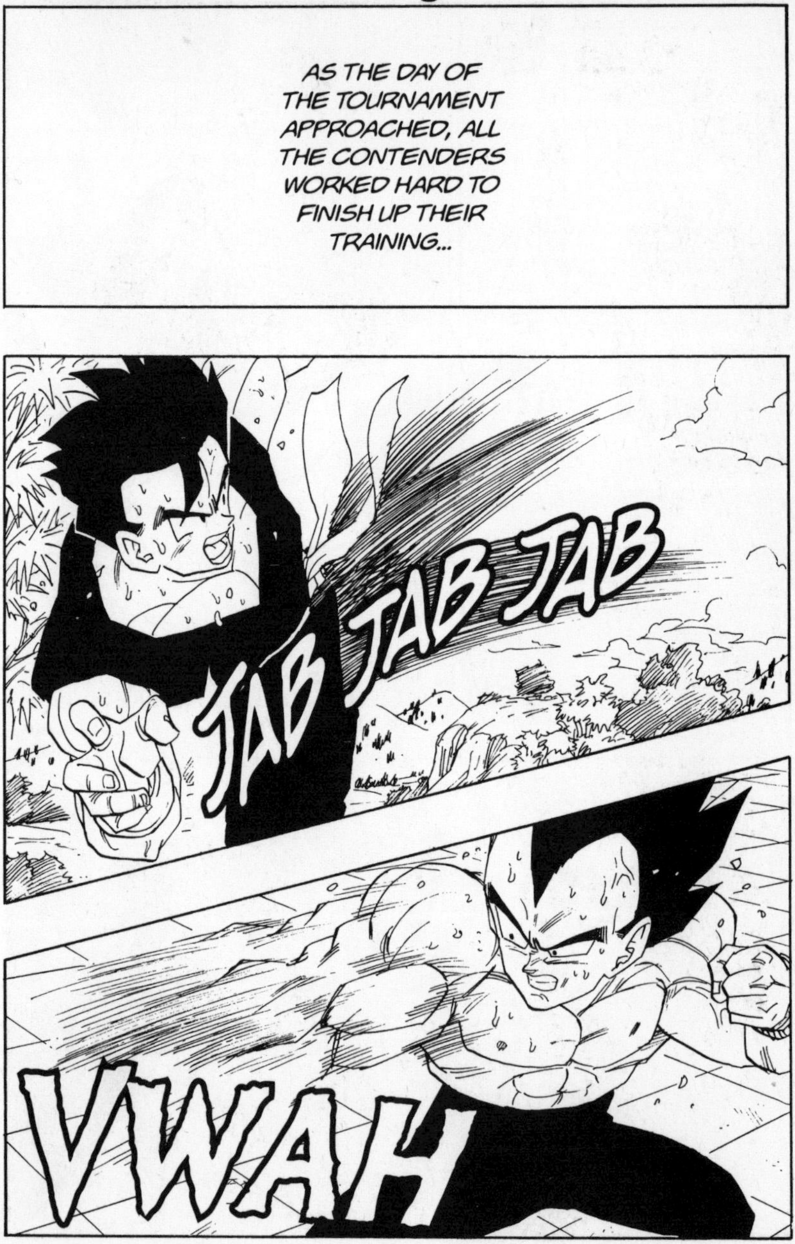
AS THE DAY OF THE TOURNAMENT APPROACHED, ALL THE CONTENDERS WORKED HARD TO FINISH UP THEIR TRAINING...
JAB JAB JAB
VWAH

READ THIS WAY

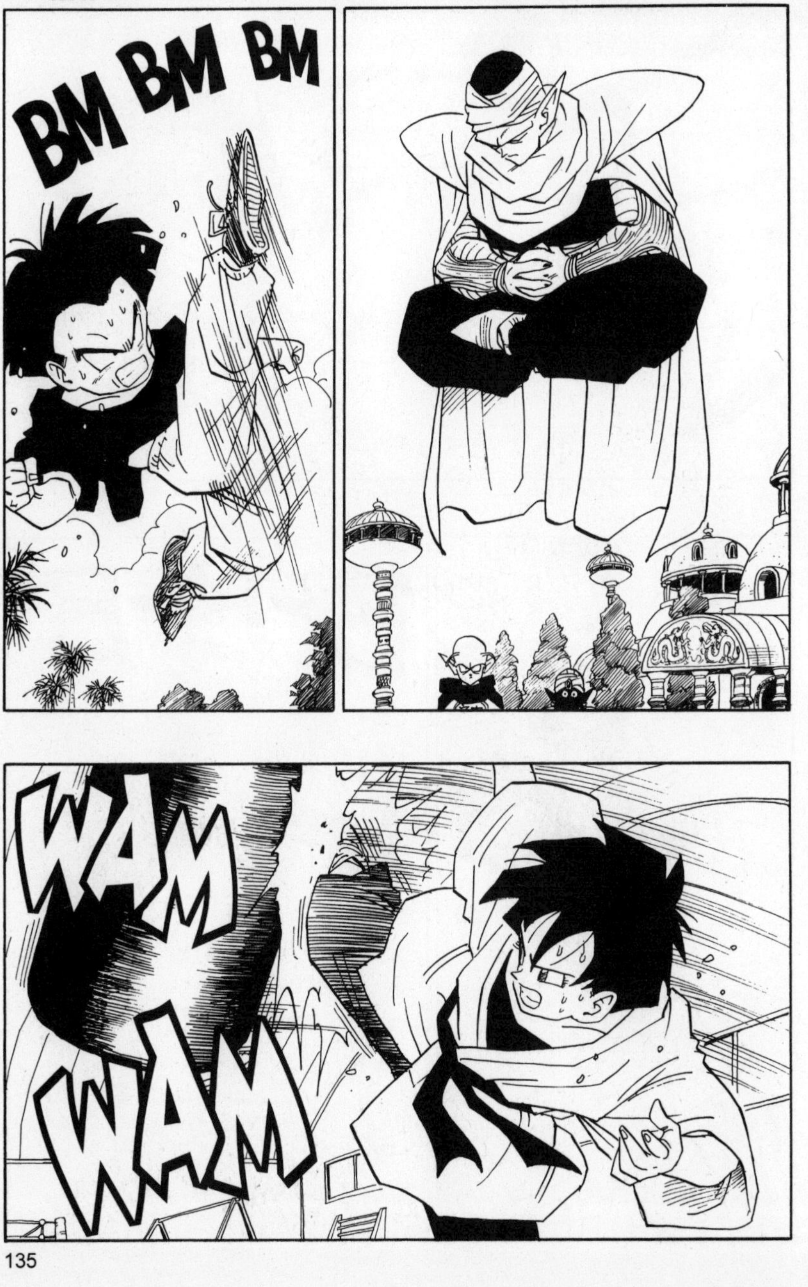
BM BM BM
WAM
WAM

READ THIS WAY

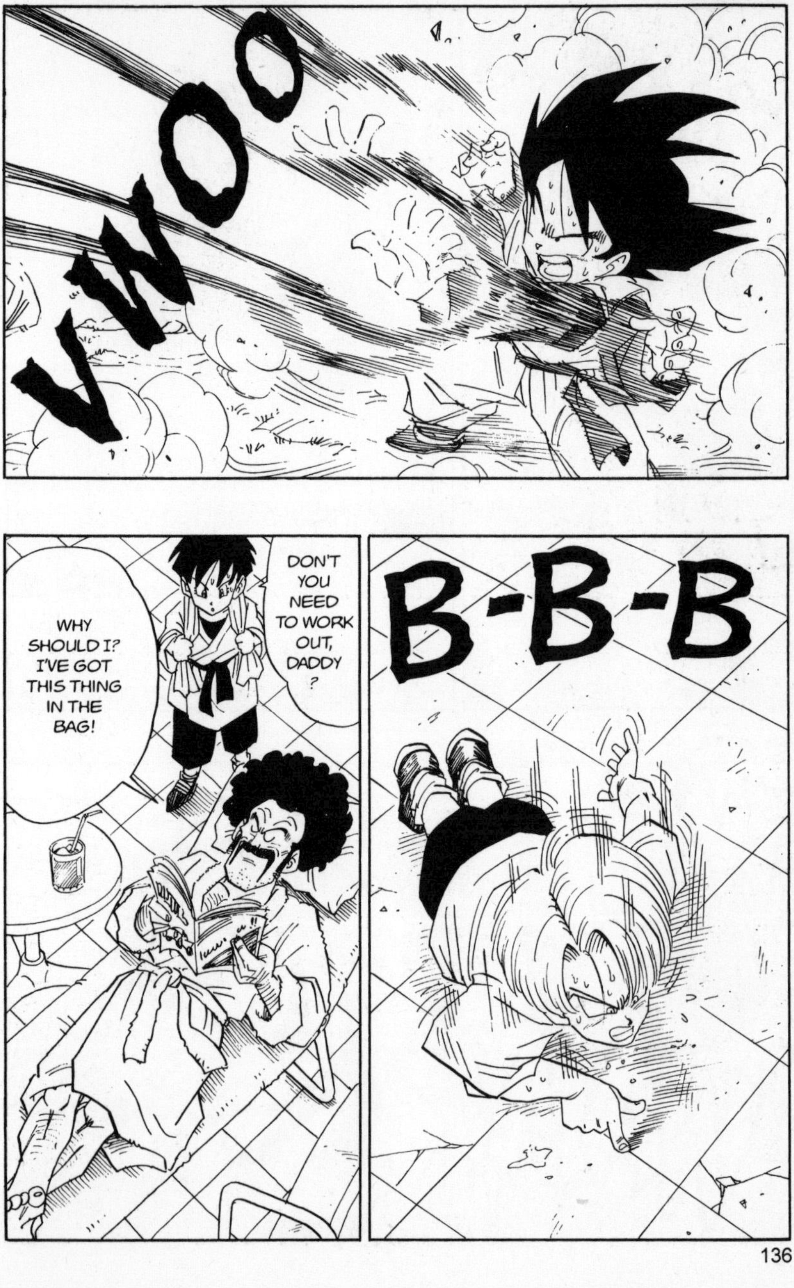
VWOOO
B-B-B
DON'T YOU NEED TO WORK OUT, DADDY?
WHY SHOULD I? I'VE GOT THIS THING IN THE BAG!

READ THIS WAY

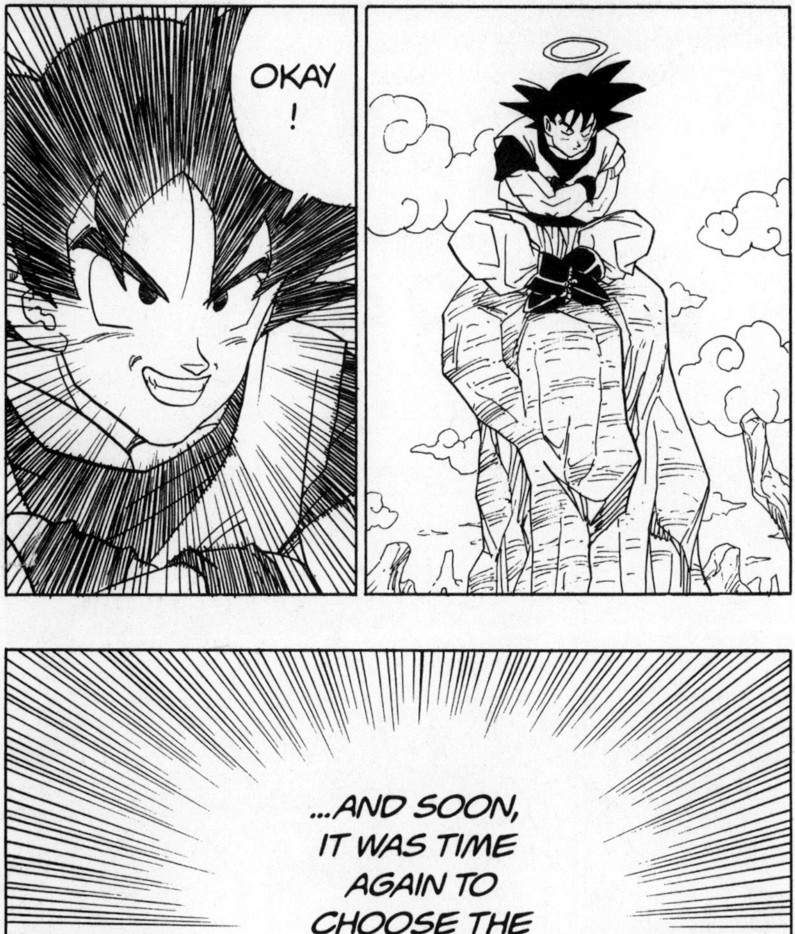
OKAY !
...AND SOON, IT WAS TIME AGAIN TO CHOOSE THE "STRONGEST UNDER THE HEAVENS"!!!

READ THIS WAY

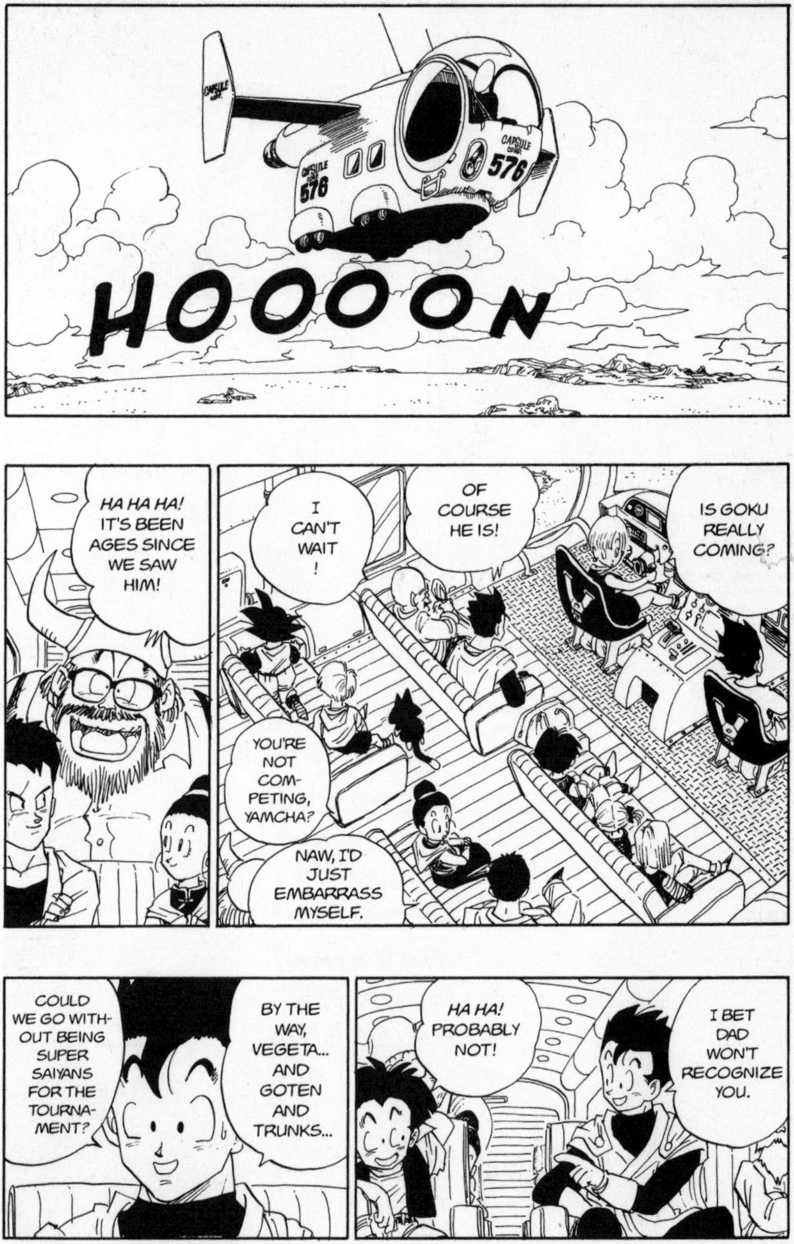
HOOOON
IS GOKU REALLY COMING?
OF COURSE HE IS!
I CAN'T WAIT!
YOU'RE NOT COM-PETING, YAMCHA?
NAW, I'D JUST EMBARRASS MYSELF.
HA HA HA! IT'S BEEN AGES SINCE WE SAW HIM!
I BET DAD WON'T RECOGNIZE YOU.
HA HA! PROBABLY NOT!
BY THE WAY, VEGETA... AND GOTEN AND TRUNKS...
COULD WE GO WITH-OUT BEING SUPER SAIYANS FOR THE TOURNA-MENT?

READ THIS WAY

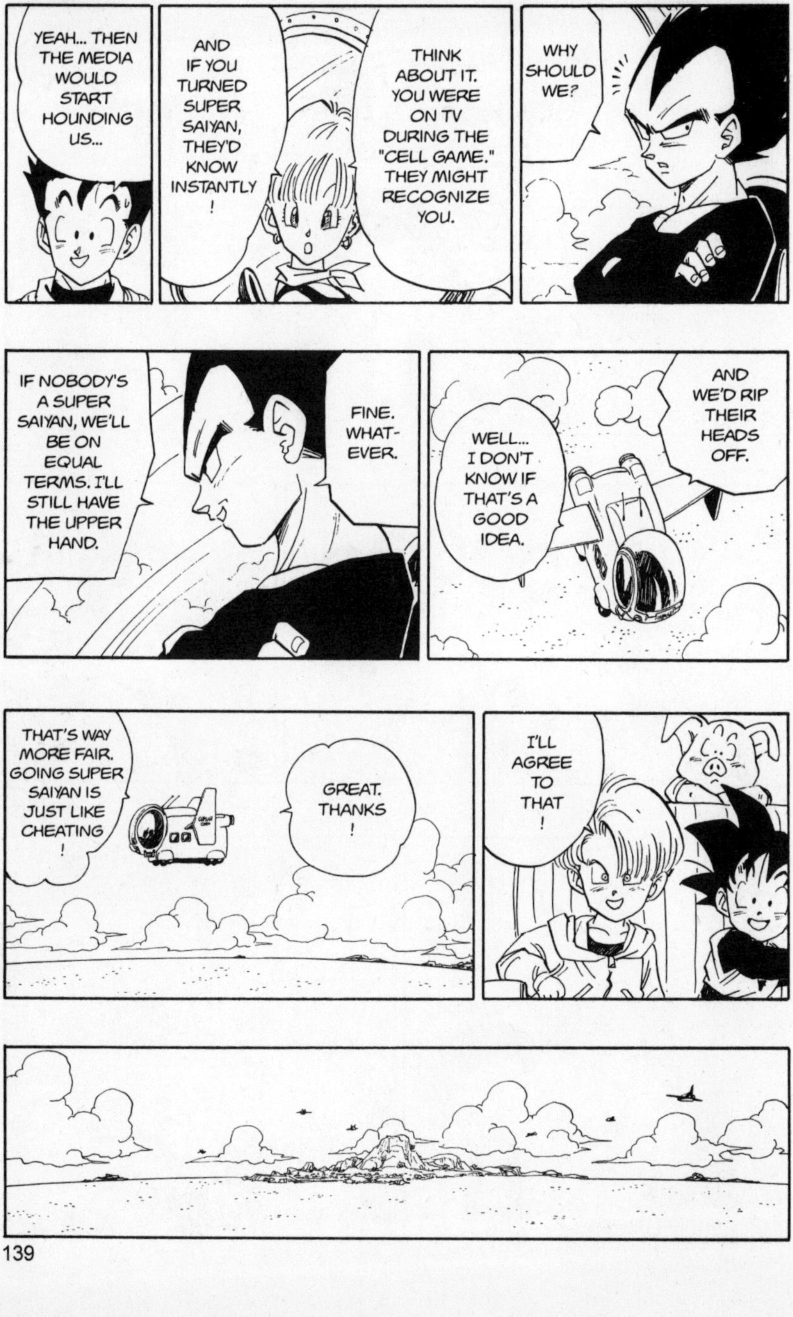
WHY SHOULD WE?
THINK ABOUT IT. YOU WERE ON TV DURING THE "CELL GAME." THEY MIGHT RECOGNIZE YOU.
AND IF YOU TURNED SUPER SAIYAN, THEY'D KNOW INSTANTLY!
YEAH... THEN THE MEDIA WOULD START HOUNDING US...
AND WE'D RIP THEIR HEADS OFF.
WELL... I DON'T KNOW IF THAT'S A GOOD IDEA.
FINE. WHAT-EVER.
IF NOBODY'S A SUPER SAIYAN, WE'LL BE ON EQUAL TERMS. I'LL STILL HAVE THE UPPER HAND.
I'LL AGREE TO THAT!
GREAT. THANKS!
THAT'S WAY MORE FAIR. GOING SUPER SAIYAN IS JUST LIKE CHEATING!

READ THIS WAY

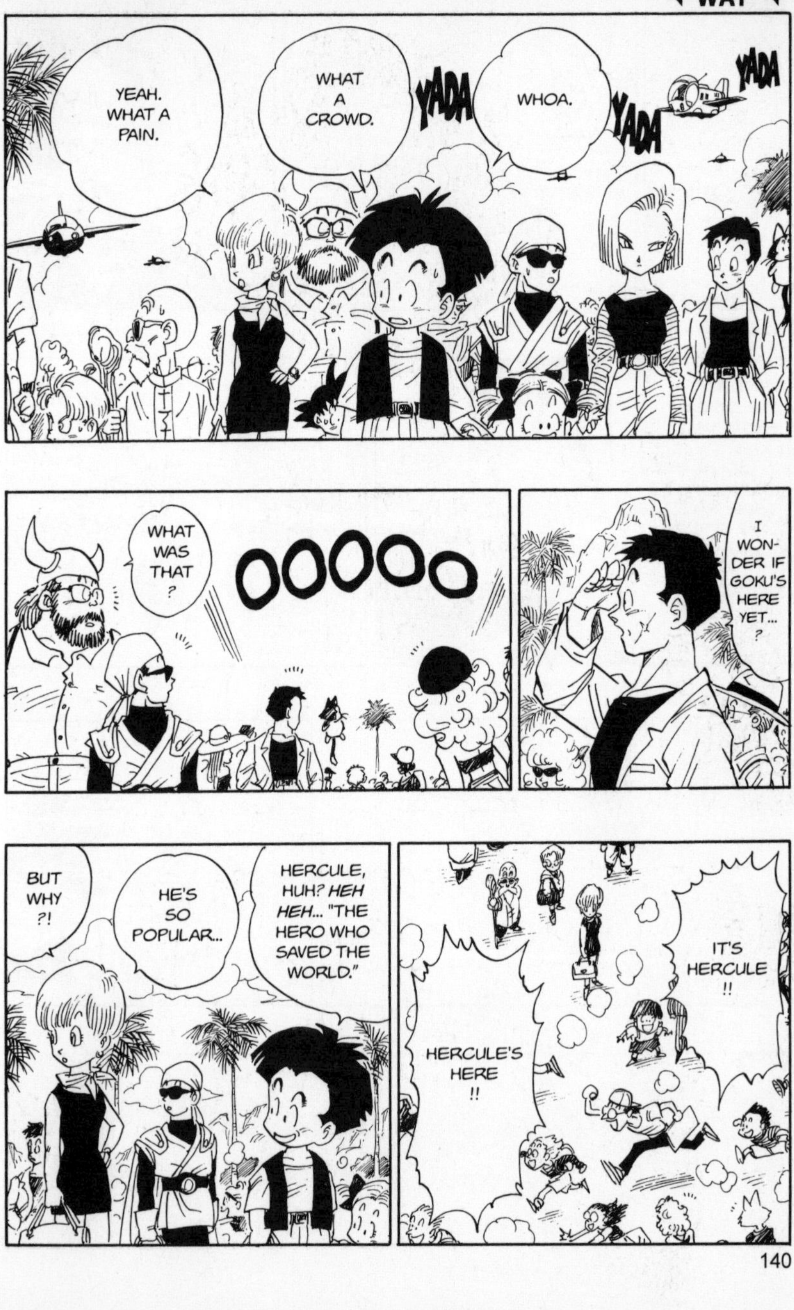
YADA
YADA
WHOA.
YADA
WHAT A CROWD.
YEAH. WHAT A PAIN.
I WONDER IF GOKU'S HERE YET...?
OOOOO
WHAT WAS THAT?
IT'S HERCULE!!
HERCULE'S HERE!!
HERCULE, HUH? *HEH HEH*... "THE HERO WHO SAVED THE WORLD."
HE'S SO POPULAR...
BUT WHY?!

READ THIS WAY

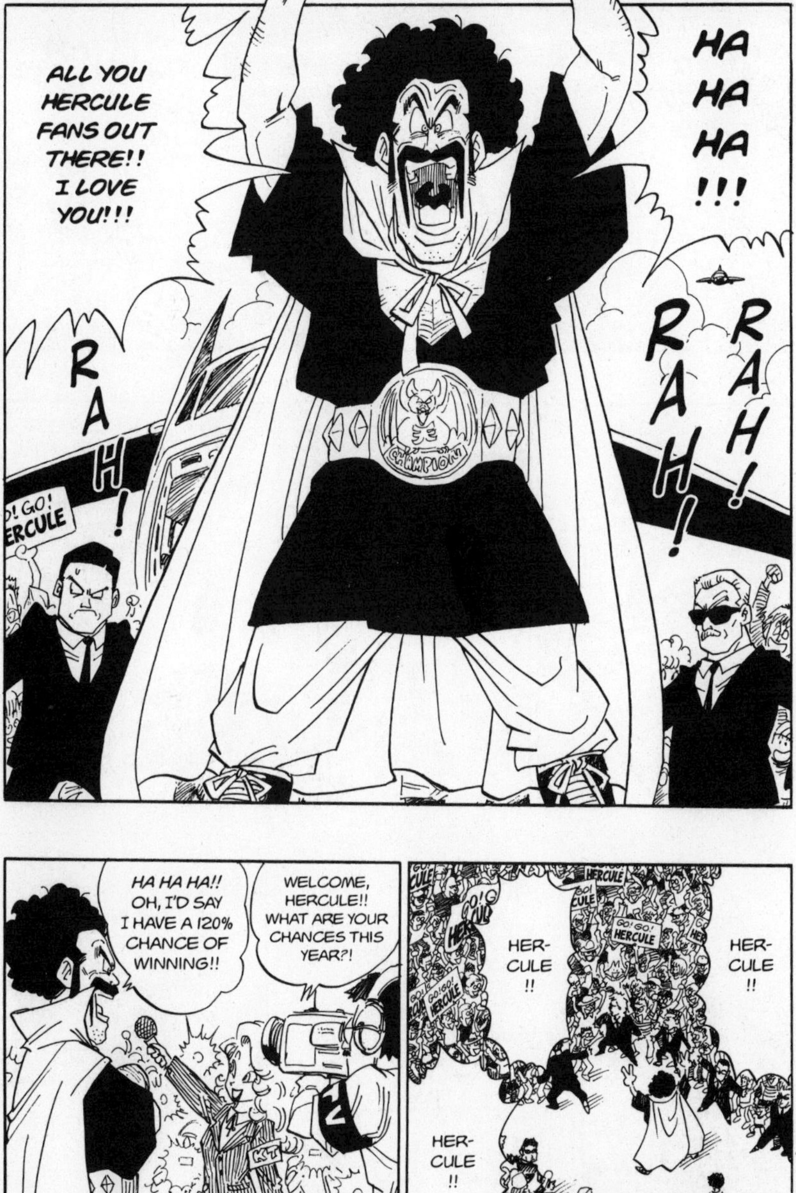
HA HA HA!!!
ALL YOU HERCULE FANS OUT THERE!! I LOVE YOU!!!
RAH RAH!
RAH!
RAH!
HER-CULE!!
HER-CULE!!
GO! GO! HERCULE
HER-CULE!!
WELCOME, HERCULE!! WHAT ARE YOUR CHANCES THIS YEAR?!
HA HA HA!! OH, I'D SAY I HAVE A 120% CHANCE OF WINNING!!

READ THIS WAY

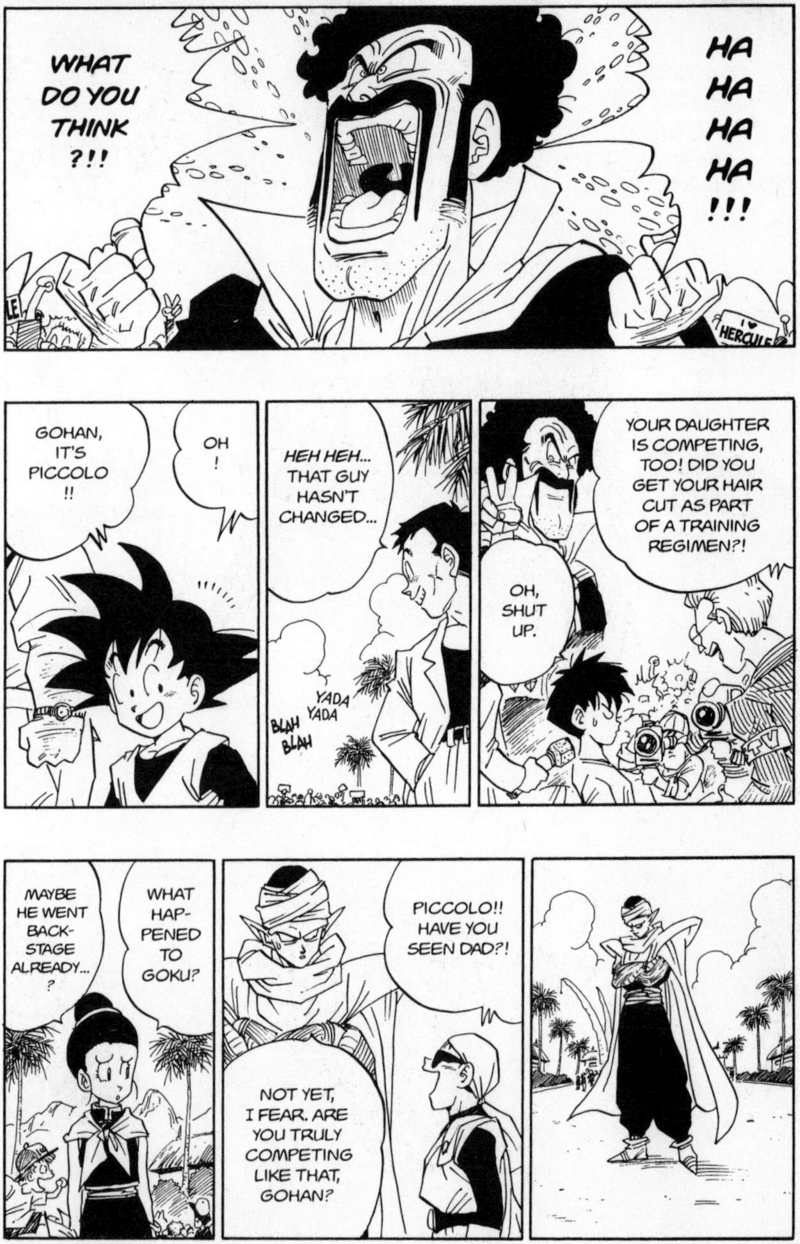
HA HA HA HA!!!
WHAT DO YOU THINK?!!
I ♥ HERCULE
YOUR DAUGHTER IS COMPETING, TOO! DID YOU GET YOUR HAIR CUT AS PART OF A TRAINING REGIMEN?!
OH, SHUT UP.
TV
HEH HEH... THAT GUY HASN'T CHANGED...
YADA YADA
BLAH BLAH
OH!
GOHAN, IT'S PICCOLO!!
PICCOLO!! HAVE YOU SEEN DAD?!
NOT YET, I FEAR. ARE YOU TRULY COMPETING LIKE THAT, GOHAN?
WHAT HAP-PENED TO GOKU?
MAYBE HE WENT BACK-STAGE ALREADY...?

READ THIS WAY

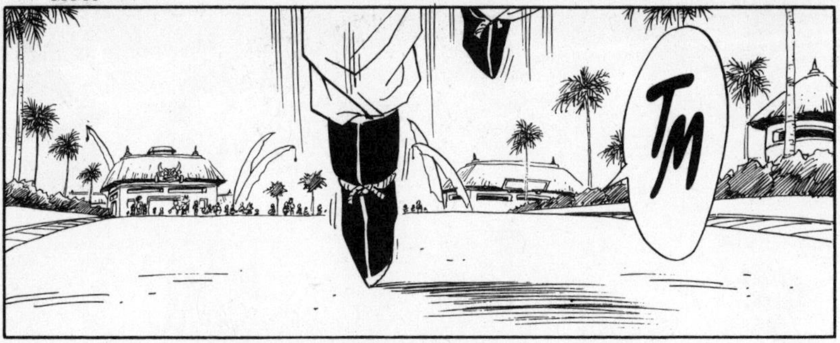
TM

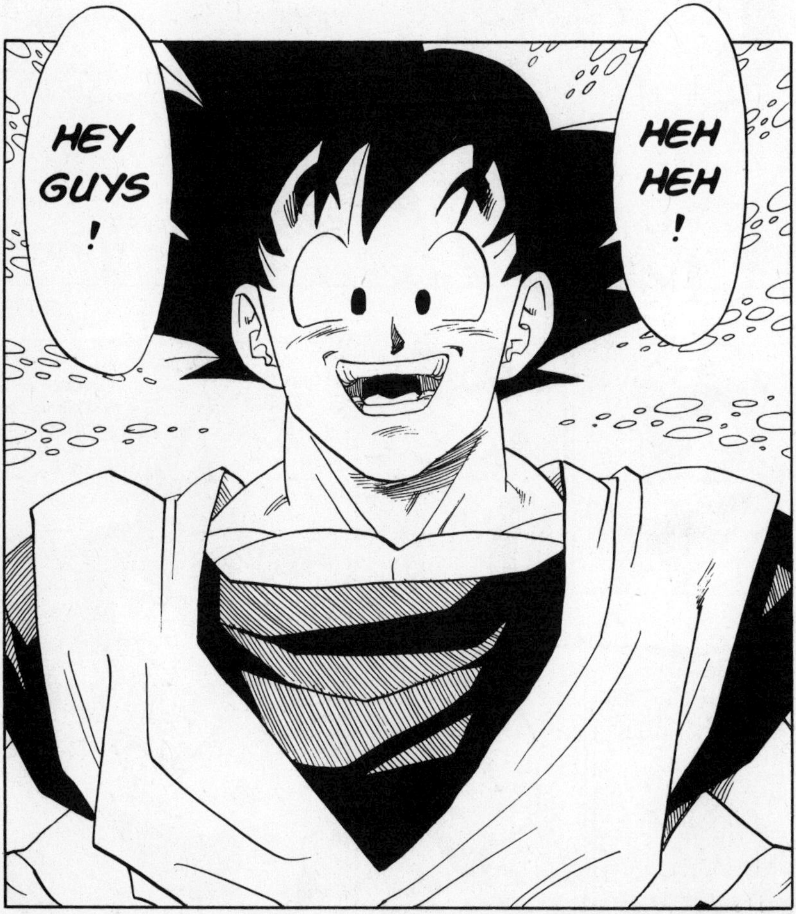
HEH HEH !
HEY GUYS !

READ THIS WAY

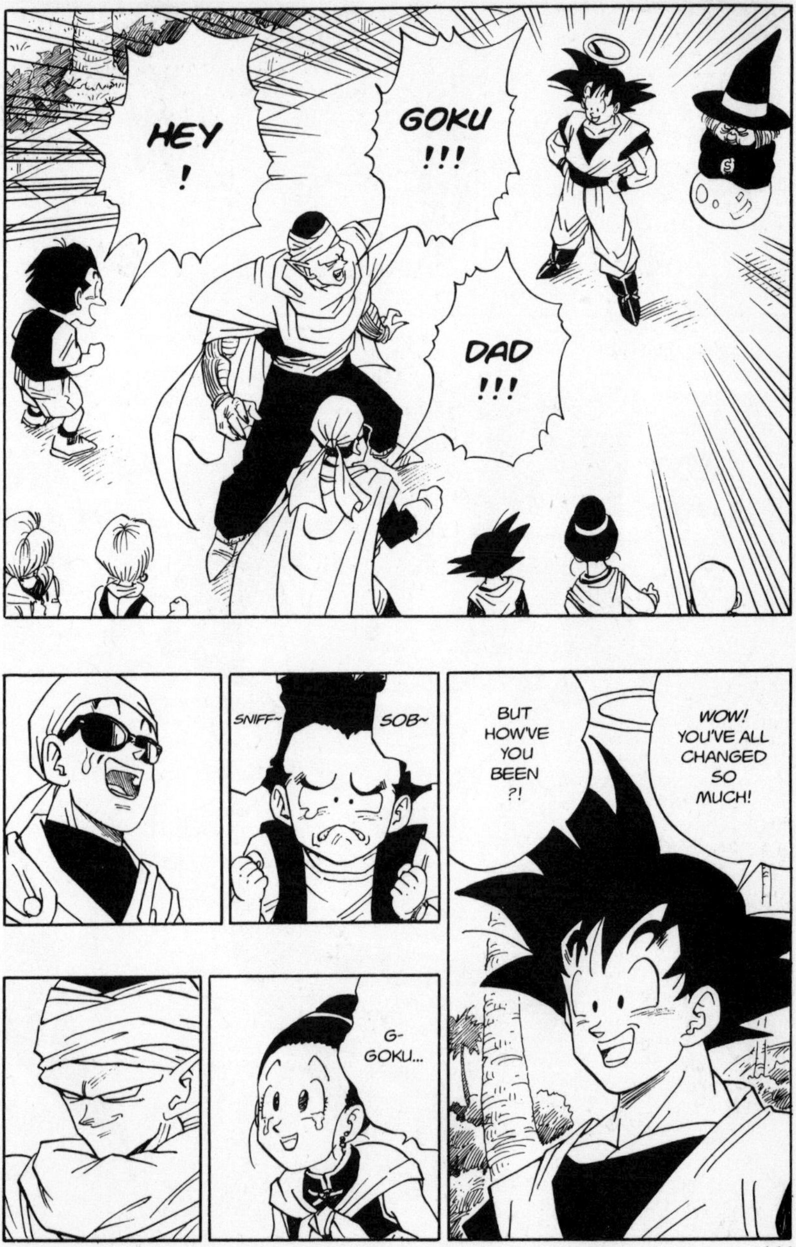

GOKU !!!
DAD !!!
HEY !
WOW! YOU'VE ALL CHANGED SO MUCH!
BUT HOW'VE YOU BEEN ?!
SNIFF~
SOB~
G-GOKU...

READ THIS WAY

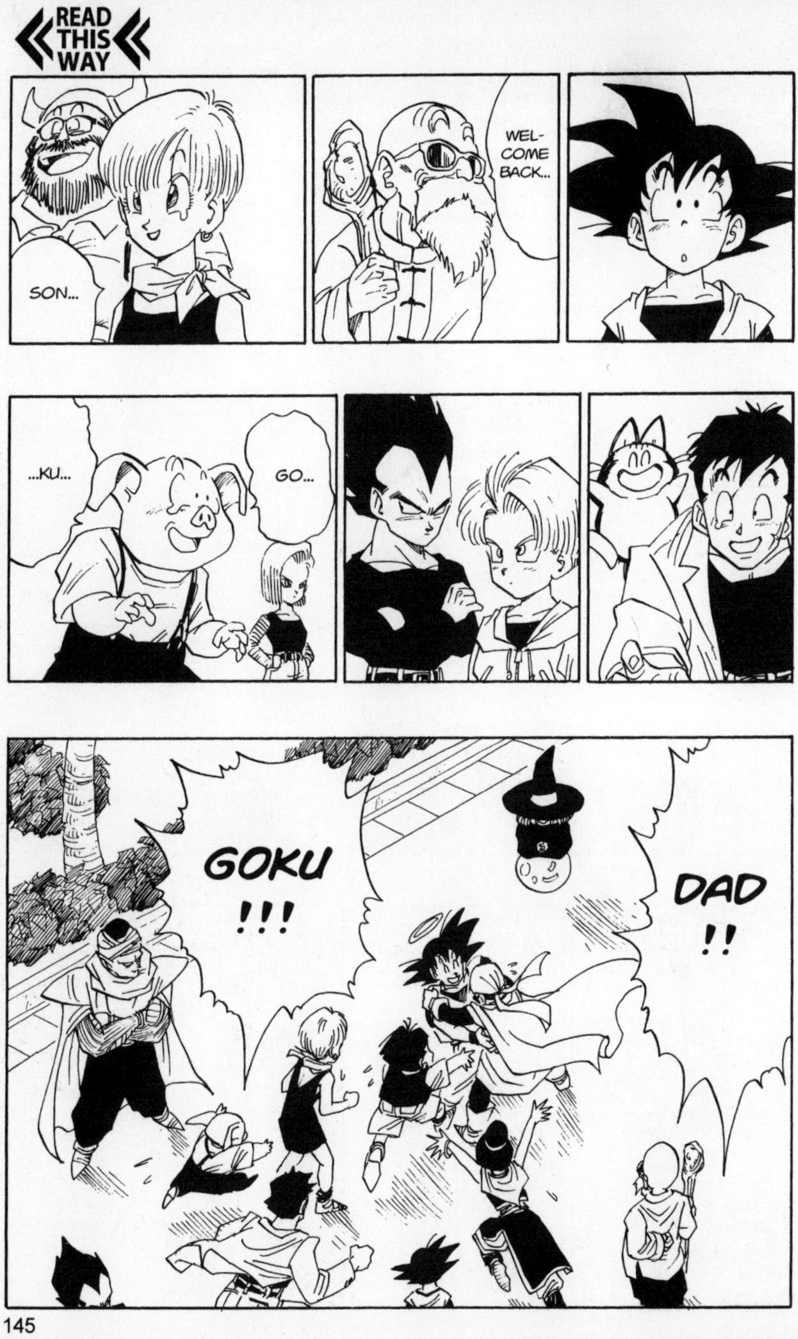
WEL-COME BACK...
SON...
GO...
...KU...
DAD!!
GOKU!!!

READ THIS WAY

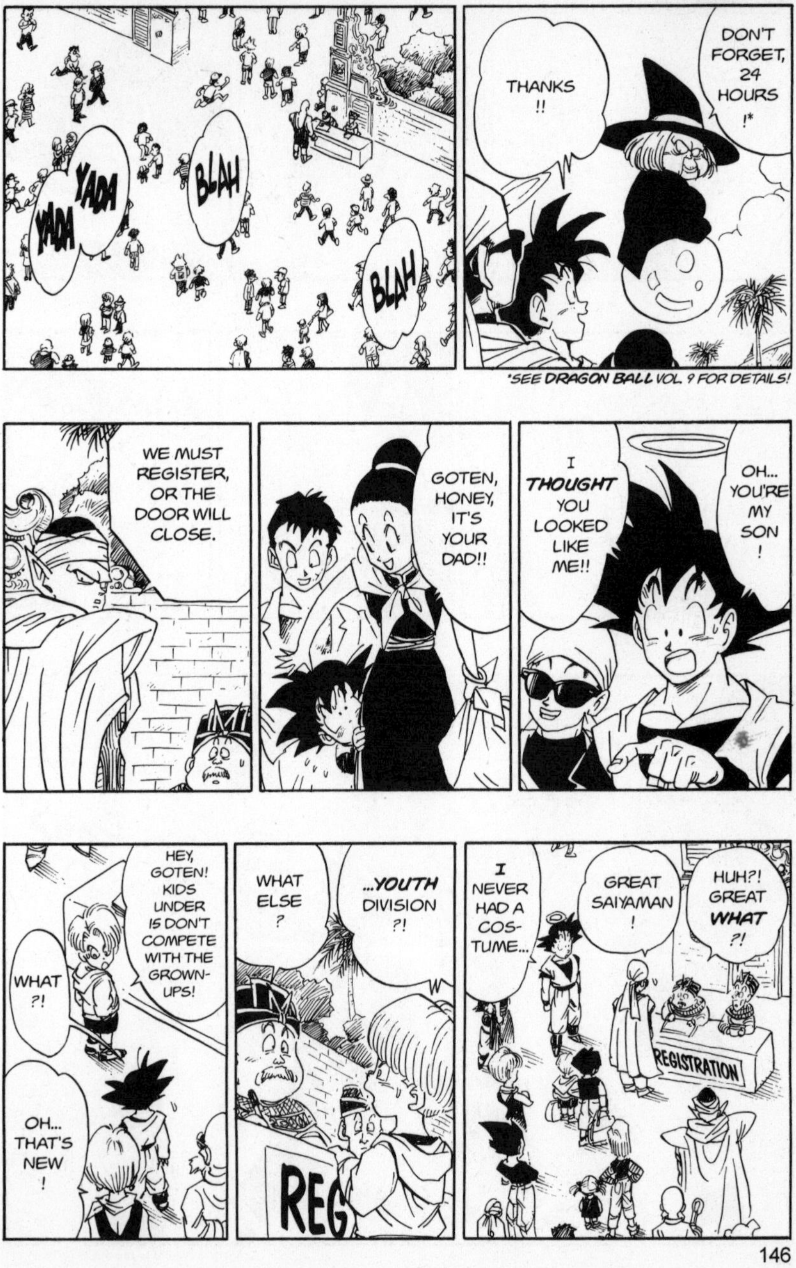
DON'T FORGET, 24 HOURS !*
THANKS !!
*SEE DRAGON BALL VOL. 9 FOR DETAILS!
BLAH
BLAH
YADA
YADA
OH... YOU'RE MY SON !
I THOUGHT YOU LOOKED LIKE ME!!
GOTEN, HONEY, IT'S YOUR DAD!!
WE MUST REGISTER, OR THE DOOR WILL CLOSE.
HUH?! GREAT WHAT ?!
GREAT SAIYAMAN !
I NEVER HAD A COS-TUME...
REGISTRATION
...YOUTH DIVISION ?!
WHAT ELSE ?
REG
HEY, GOTEN! KIDS UNDER 15 DON'T COMPETE WITH THE GROWN-UPS!
WHAT ?!
OH... THAT'S NEW !

READ THIS WAY

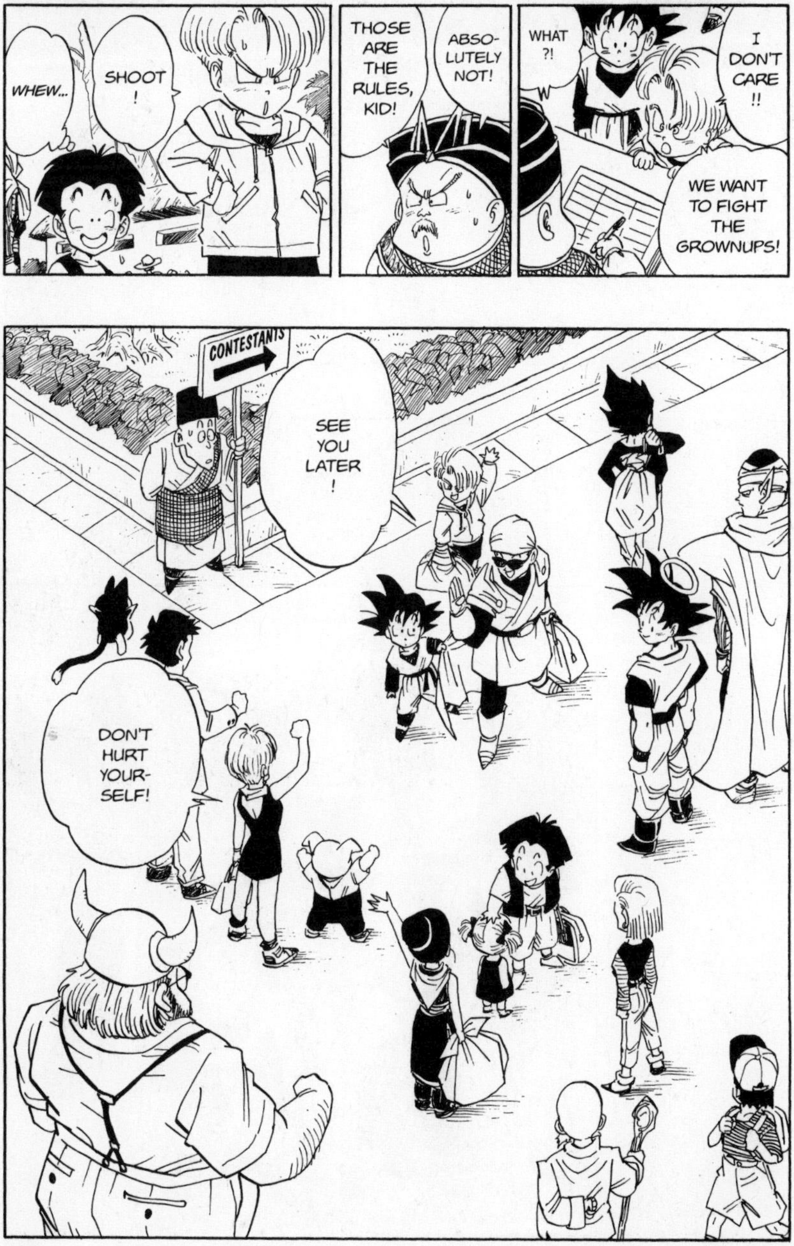
WHAT ?!
I DON'T CARE !!
WE WANT TO FIGHT THE GROWNUPS!
ABSO-LUTELY NOT!
THOSE ARE THE RULES, KID!
SHOOT !
WHEW...
CONTESTANTS
SEE YOU LATER !
DON'T HURT YOUR-SELF!

DBZ:237
The Preliminaries Begin

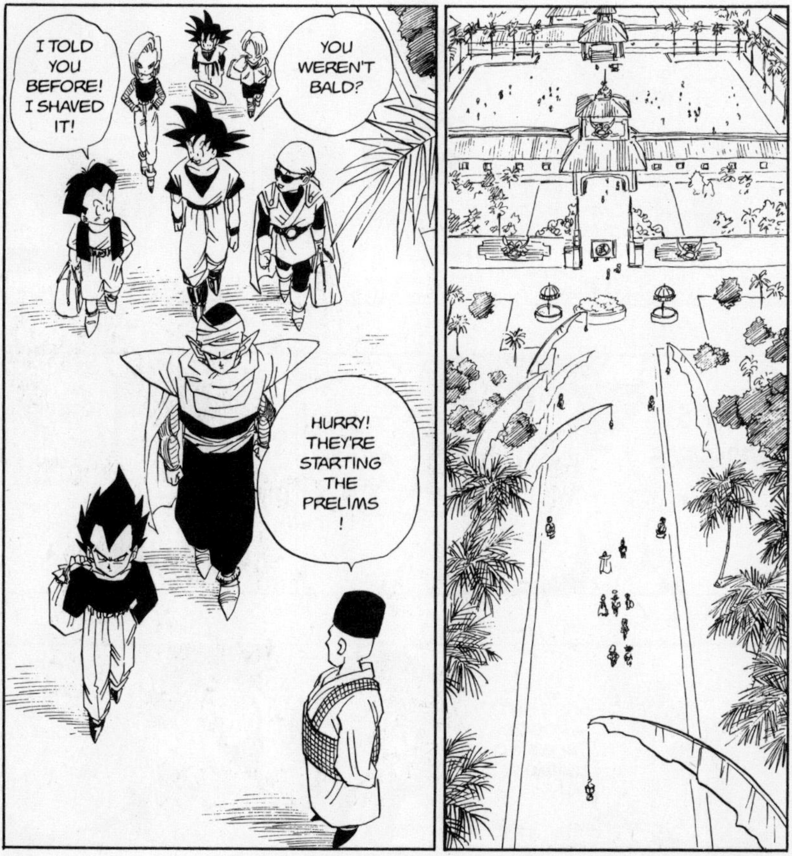
YOU WEREN'T BALD?
I TOLD YOU BEFORE! I SHAVED IT!
HURRY! THEY'RE STARTING THE PRELIMS!

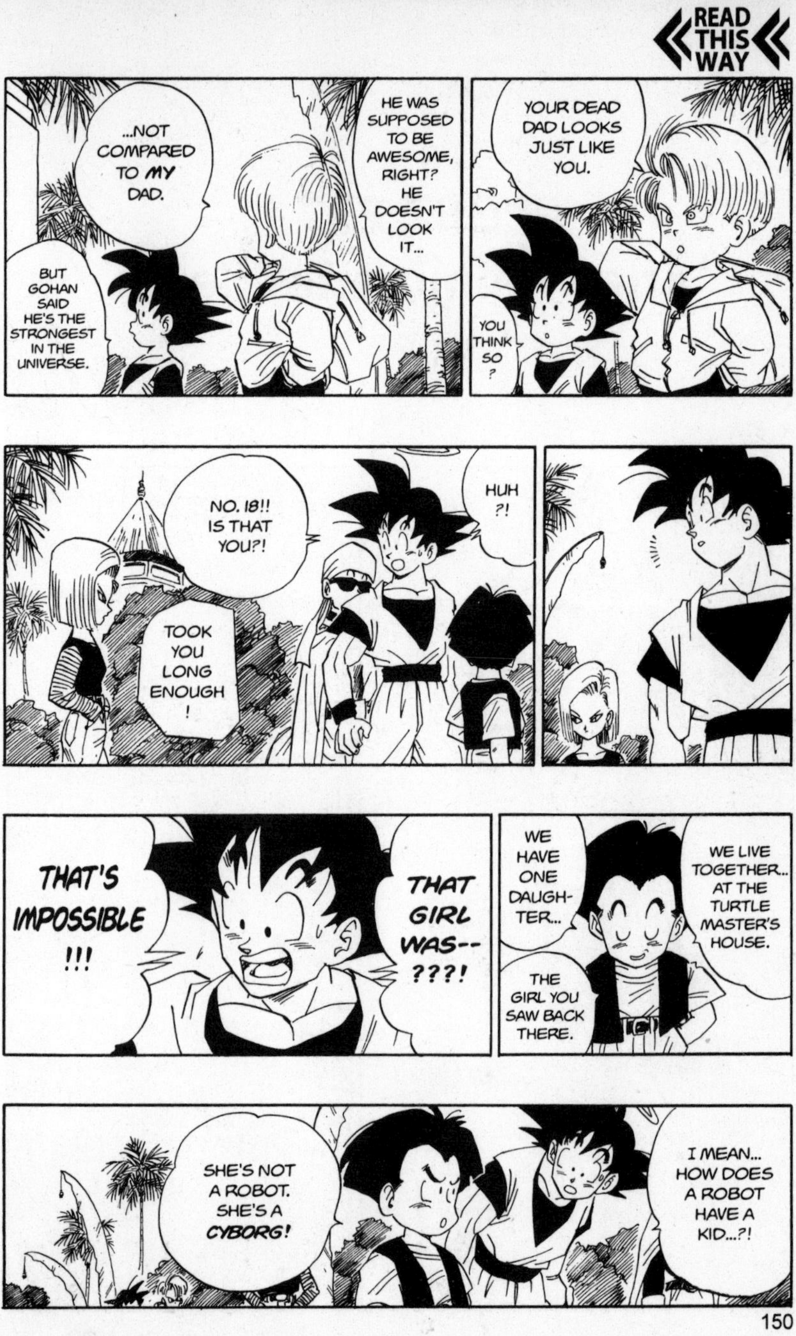
YOUR DEAD DAD LOOKS JUST LIKE YOU.
YOU THINK SO?
HE WAS SUPPOSED TO BE AWESOME, RIGHT? HE DOESN'T LOOK IT...
...NOT COMPARED TO MY DAD.
BUT GOHAN SAID HE'S THE STRONGEST IN THE UNIVERSE.
HUH?!
NO. 18!! IS THAT YOU?!
TOOK YOU LONG ENOUGH!
WE LIVE TOGETHER... AT THE TURTLE MASTER'S HOUSE.
WE HAVE ONE DAUGHTER...
THE GIRL YOU SAW BACK THERE.
THAT GIRL WAS--???!
THAT'S IMPOSSIBLE!!!
I MEAN... HOW DOES A ROBOT HAVE A KID...?!
SHE'S NOT A ROBOT. SHE'S A CYBORG!

READ THIS WAY

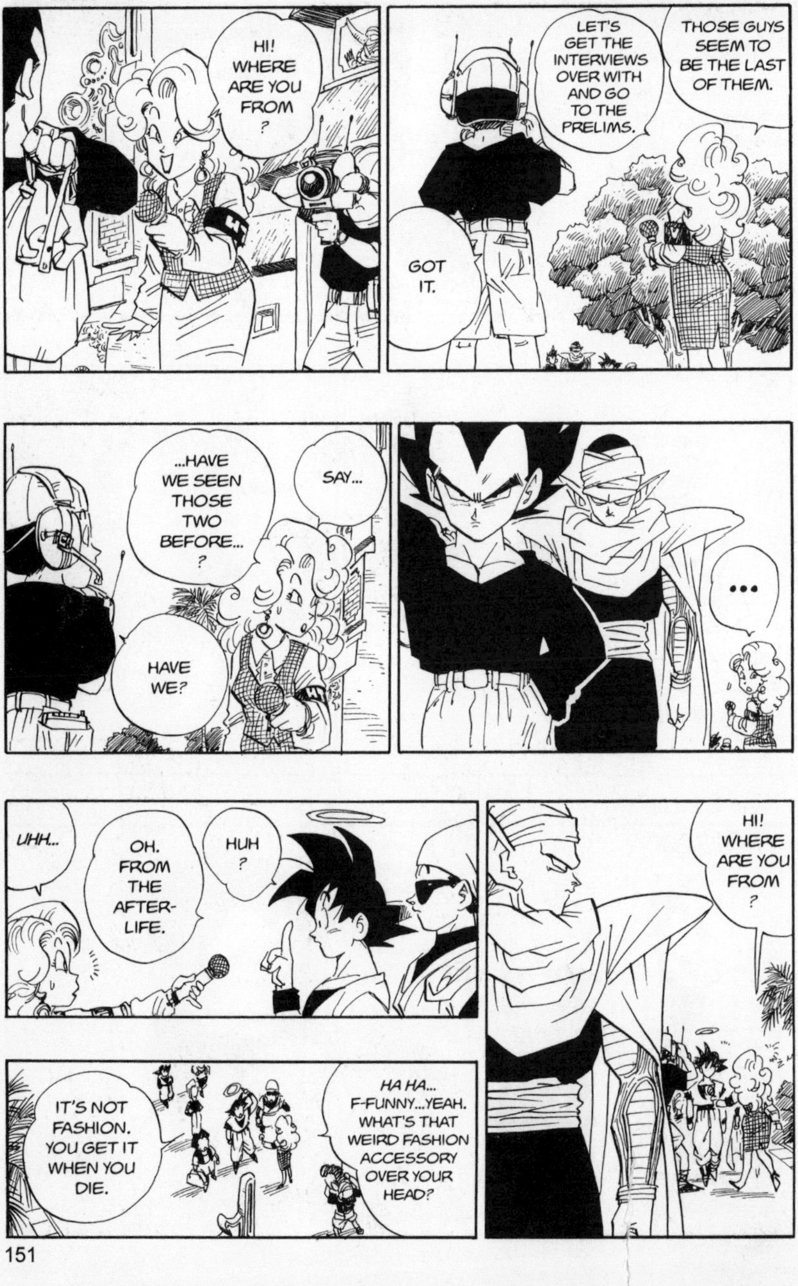
THOSE GUYS SEEM TO BE THE LAST OF THEM.
LET'S GET THE INTERVIEWS OVER WITH AND GO TO THE PRELIMS.
GOT IT.
HI! WHERE ARE YOU FROM ?
...
SAY...
...HAVE WE SEEN THOSE TWO BEFORE... ?
HAVE WE?
HI! WHERE ARE YOU FROM ?
HUH ?
OH. FROM THE AFTER-LIFE.
UHH...
HA HA... F-FUNNY...YEAH. WHAT'S THAT WEIRD FASHION ACCESSORY OVER YOUR HEAD?
IT'S NOT FASHION. YOU GET IT WHEN YOU DIE.

READ THIS WAY

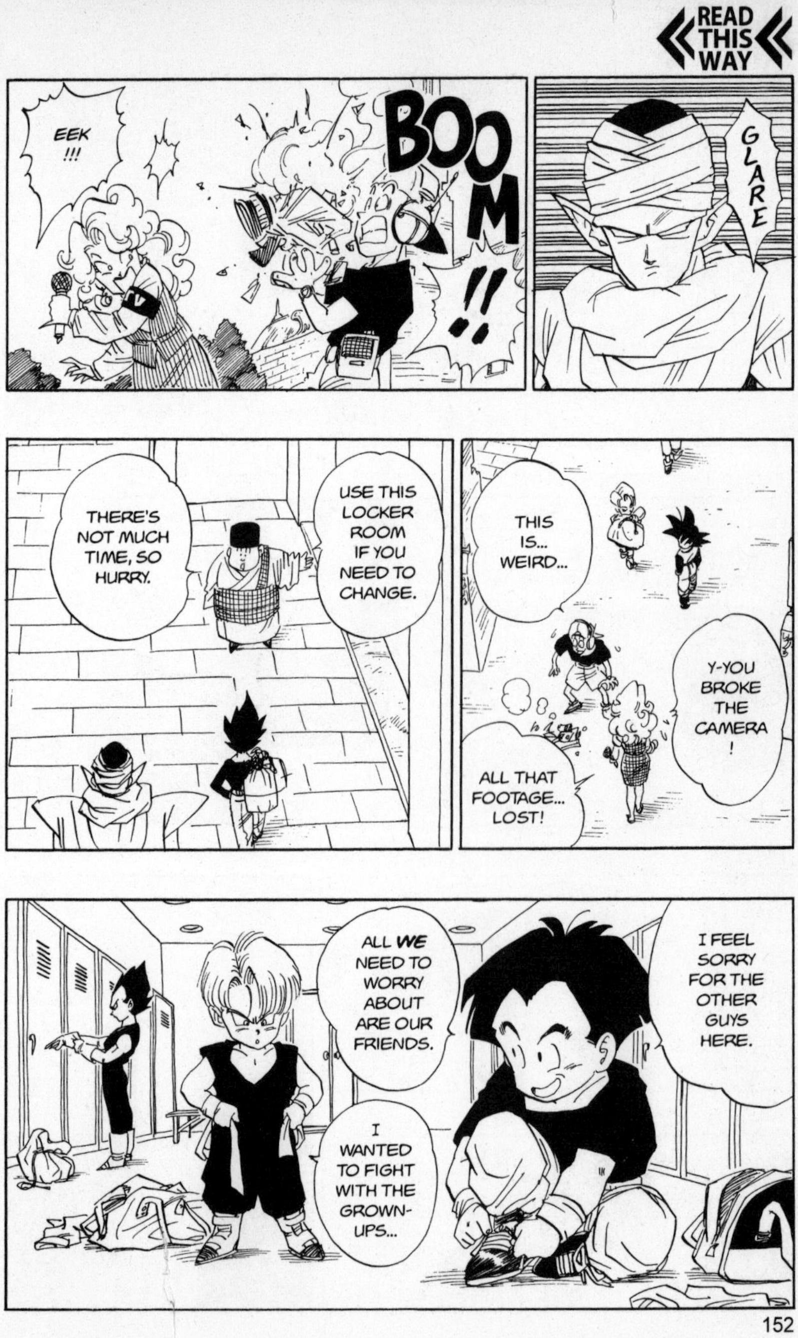
GLARE
BOOM!!
EEK!!!
THIS IS... WEIRD...
Y-YOU BROKE THE CAMERA!
ALL THAT FOOTAGE... LOST!
USE THIS LOCKER ROOM IF YOU NEED TO CHANGE.
THERE'S NOT MUCH TIME, SO HURRY.
I FEEL SORRY FOR THE OTHER GUYS HERE.
ALL *WE* NEED TO WORRY ABOUT ARE OUR FRIENDS.
I WANTED TO FIGHT WITH THE GROWN-UPS...

READ THIS WAY

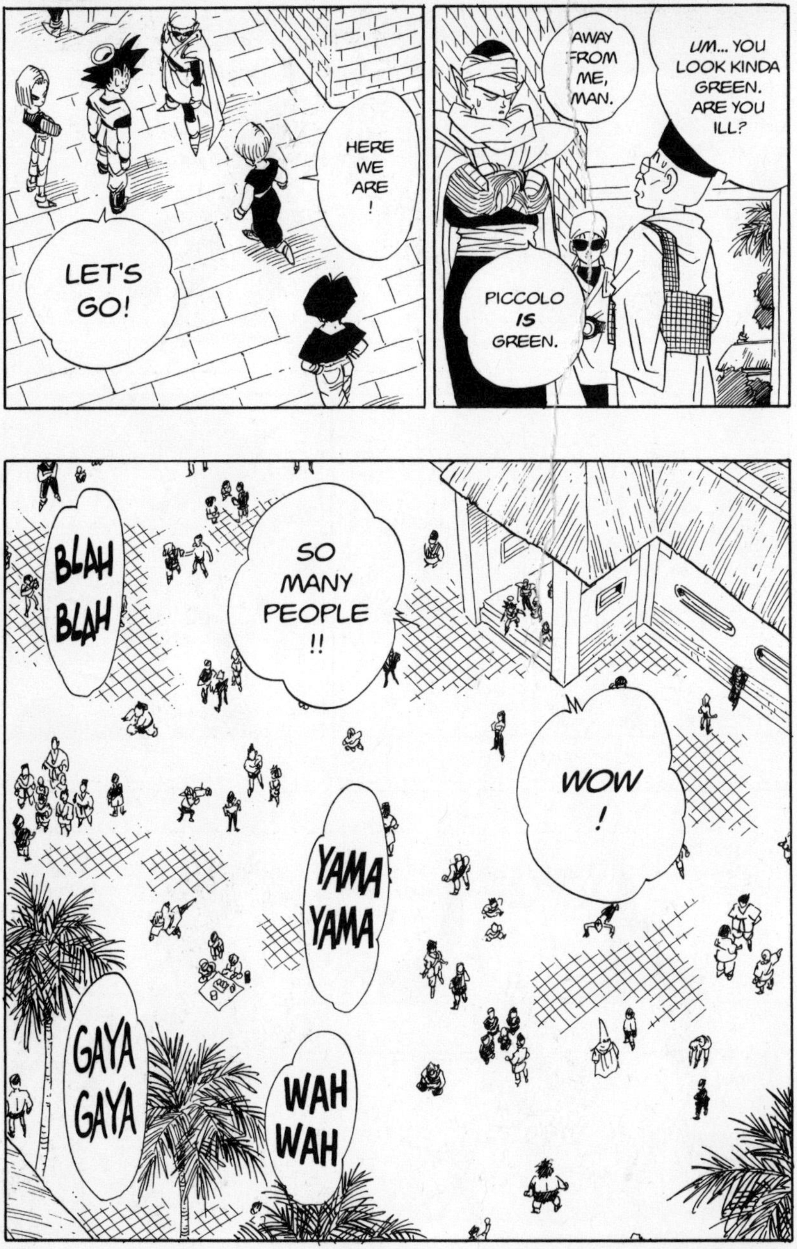

UM... YOU LOOK KINDA GREEN. ARE YOU ILL?
AWAY FROM ME, MAN.
PICCOLO IS GREEN.
HERE WE ARE!
LET'S GO!
WOW!
SO MANY PEOPLE!!
BLAH BLAH
YAMA YAMA
WAH WAH
GAYA GAYA

READ THIS WAY

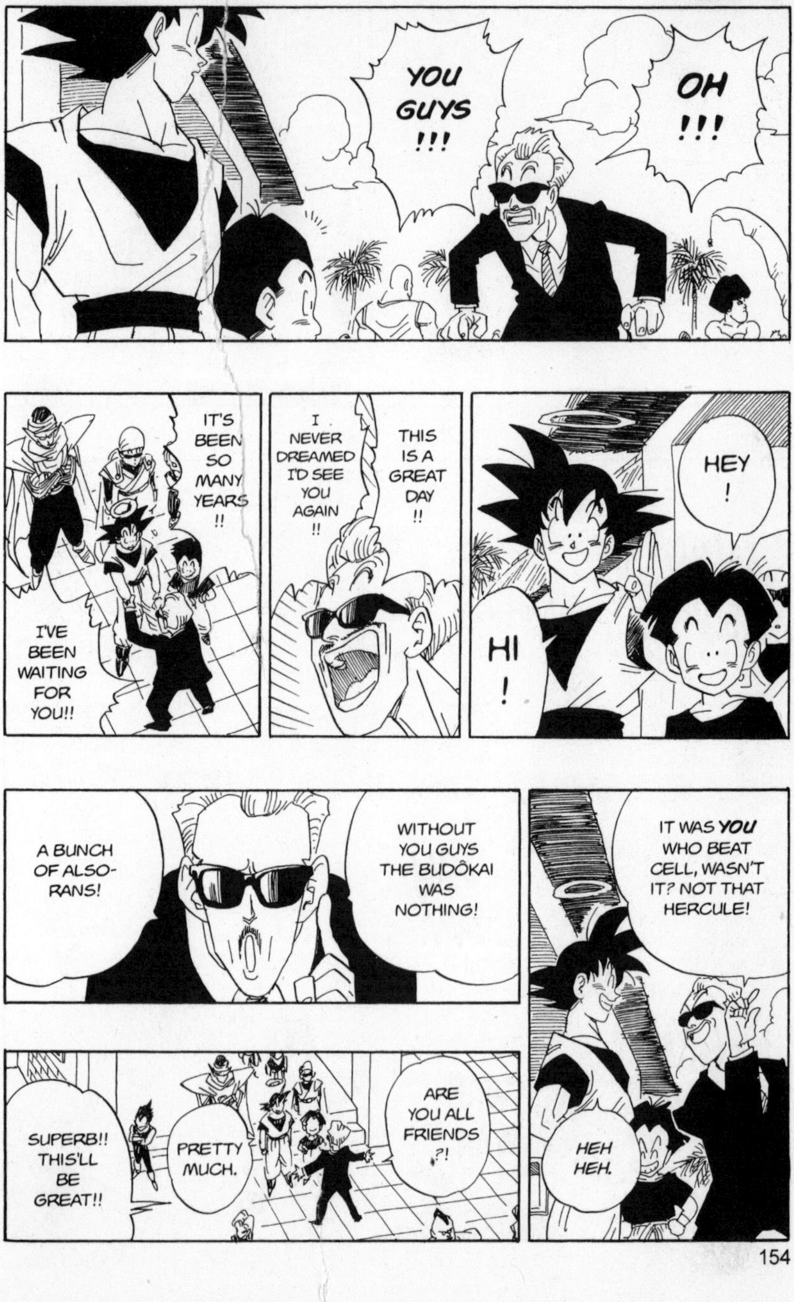
OH !!!
YOU GUYS !!!
HEY !
HI !
THIS IS A GREAT DAY !!
I NEVER DREAMED I'D SEE YOU AGAIN !!
IT'S BEEN SO MANY YEARS !!
I'VE BEEN WAITING FOR YOU!!
IT WAS ***YOU*** WHO BEAT CELL, WASN'T IT? NOT THAT HERCULE!
HEH HEH.
WITHOUT YOU GUYS THE BUDÔKAI WAS NOTHING!
A BUNCH OF ALSO-RANS!
ARE YOU ALL FRIENDS ?!
PRETTY MUCH.
SUPERB!! THIS'LL BE GREAT!!

READ THIS WAY

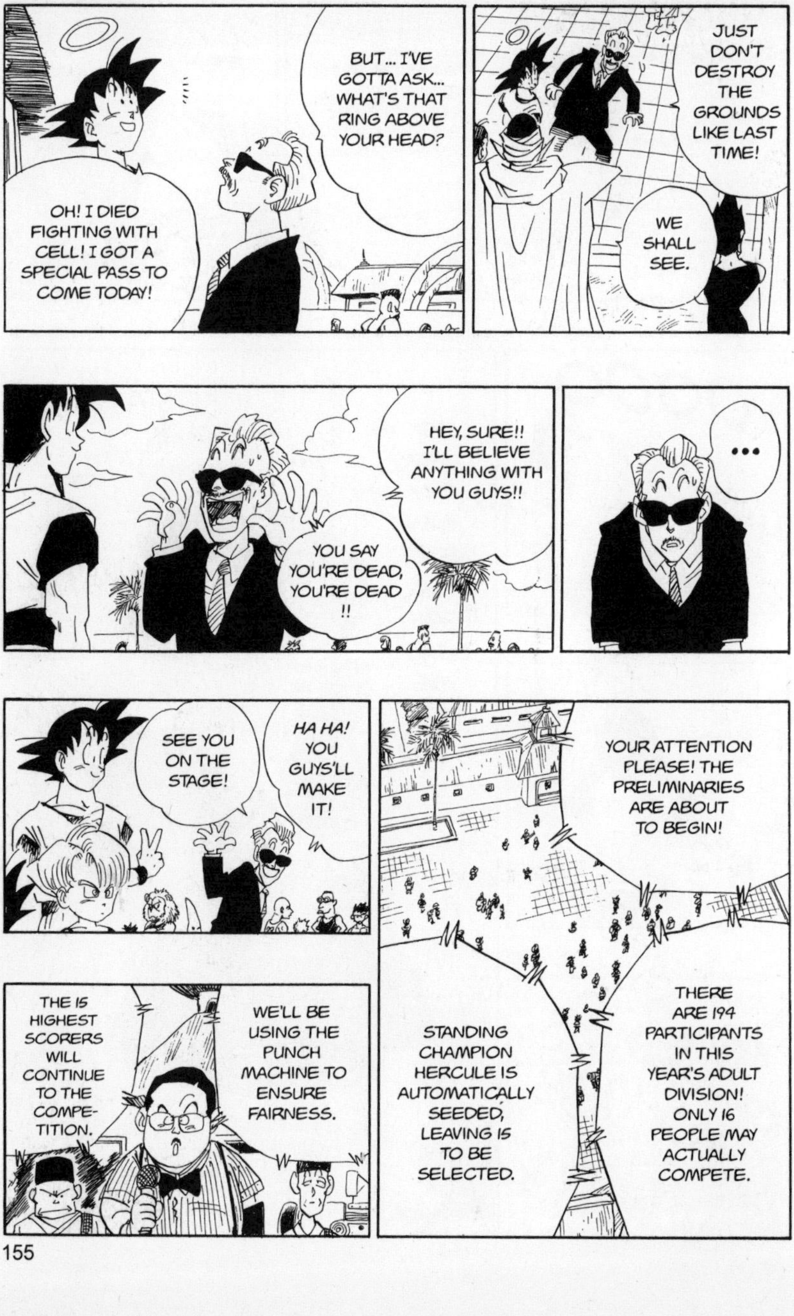
JUST DON'T DESTROY THE GROUNDS LIKE LAST TIME!
WE SHALL SEE.
BUT... I'VE GOTTA ASK... WHAT'S THAT RING ABOVE YOUR HEAD?
OH! I DIED FIGHTING WITH CELL! I GOT A SPECIAL PASS TO COME TODAY!
...
HEY, SURE!! I'LL BELIEVE ANYTHING WITH YOU GUYS!!
YOU SAY YOU'RE DEAD, YOU'RE DEAD !!
YOUR ATTENTION PLEASE! THE PRELIMINARIES ARE ABOUT TO BEGIN!
THERE ARE 194 PARTICIPANTS IN THIS YEAR'S ADULT DIVISION! ONLY 16 PEOPLE MAY ACTUALLY COMPETE.
STANDING CHAMPION HERCULE IS AUTOMATICALLY SEEDED, LEAVING 15 TO BE SELECTED.
HA HA! YOU GUYS'LL MAKE IT!
SEE YOU ON THE STAGE!
WE'LL BE USING THE PUNCH MACHINE TO ENSURE FAIRNESS.
THE 15 HIGHEST SCORERS WILL CONTINUE TO THE COMPETITION.

READ THIS WAY

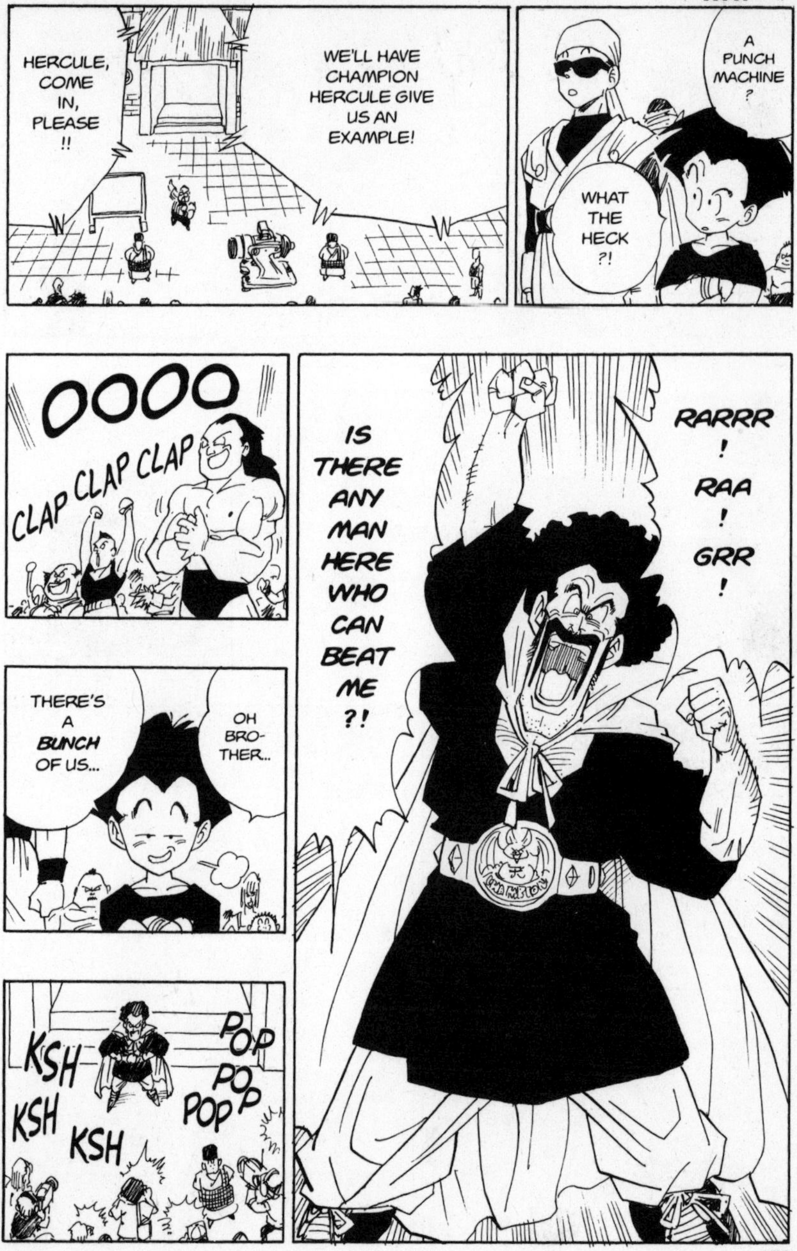

A PUNCH MACHINE?
WHAT THE HECK?!
WE'LL HAVE CHAMPION HERCULE GIVE US AN EXAMPLE!
HERCULE, COME IN, PLEASE!!
RARRR! RAA! GRR!
IS THERE ANY MAN HERE WHO CAN BEAT ME?!
OOOO
CLAP CLAP CLAP
OH BROTHER...
THERE'S A *BUNCH* OF US...
POP POP POP
KSH KSH KSH

READ THIS WAY

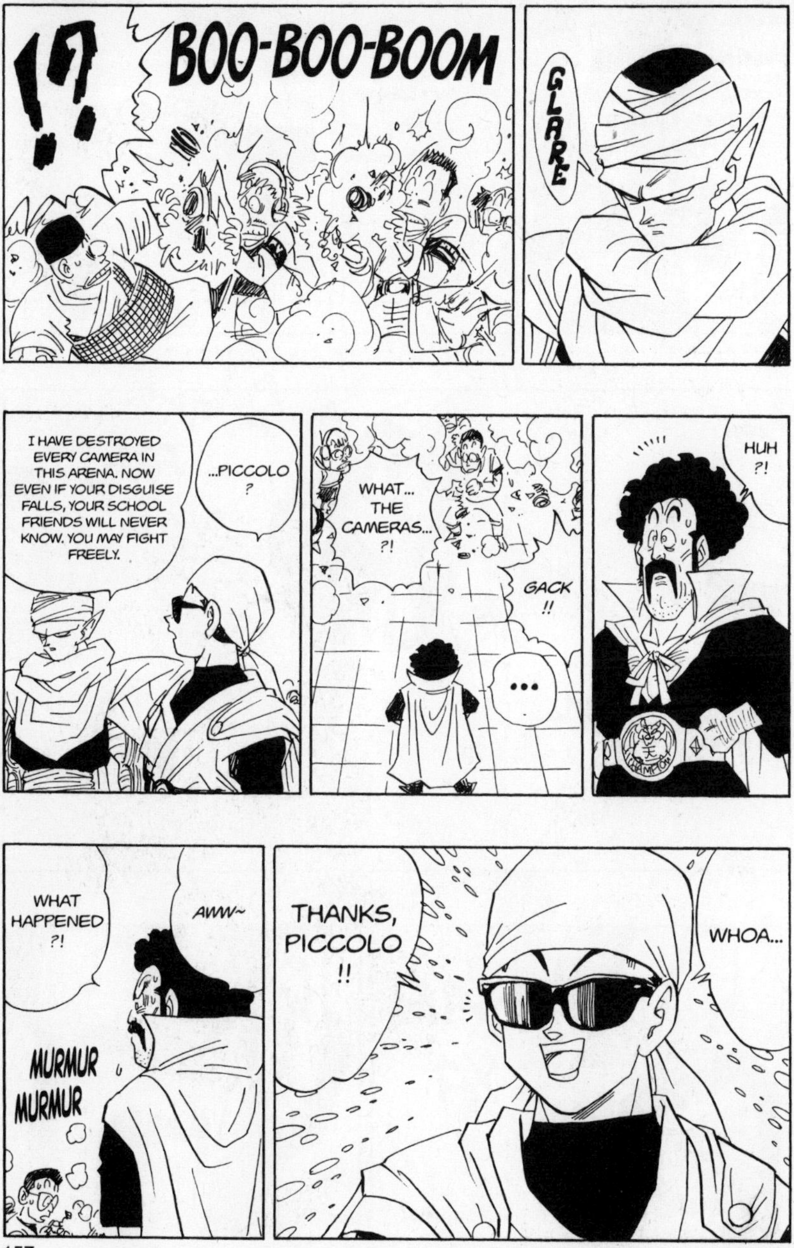
GLARE
BOO-BOO-BOOM
!?
HUH ?!
WHAT... THE CAMERAS... ?!
GACK !!
...
...PICCOLO ?
I HAVE DESTROYED EVERY CAMERA IN THIS ARENA. NOW EVEN IF YOUR DISGUISE FALLS, YOUR SCHOOL FRIENDS WILL NEVER KNOW. YOU MAY FIGHT FREELY.
WHOA...
THANKS, PICCOLO !!
AWW~
WHAT HAPPENED ?!
MURMUR MURMUR

READ THIS WAY

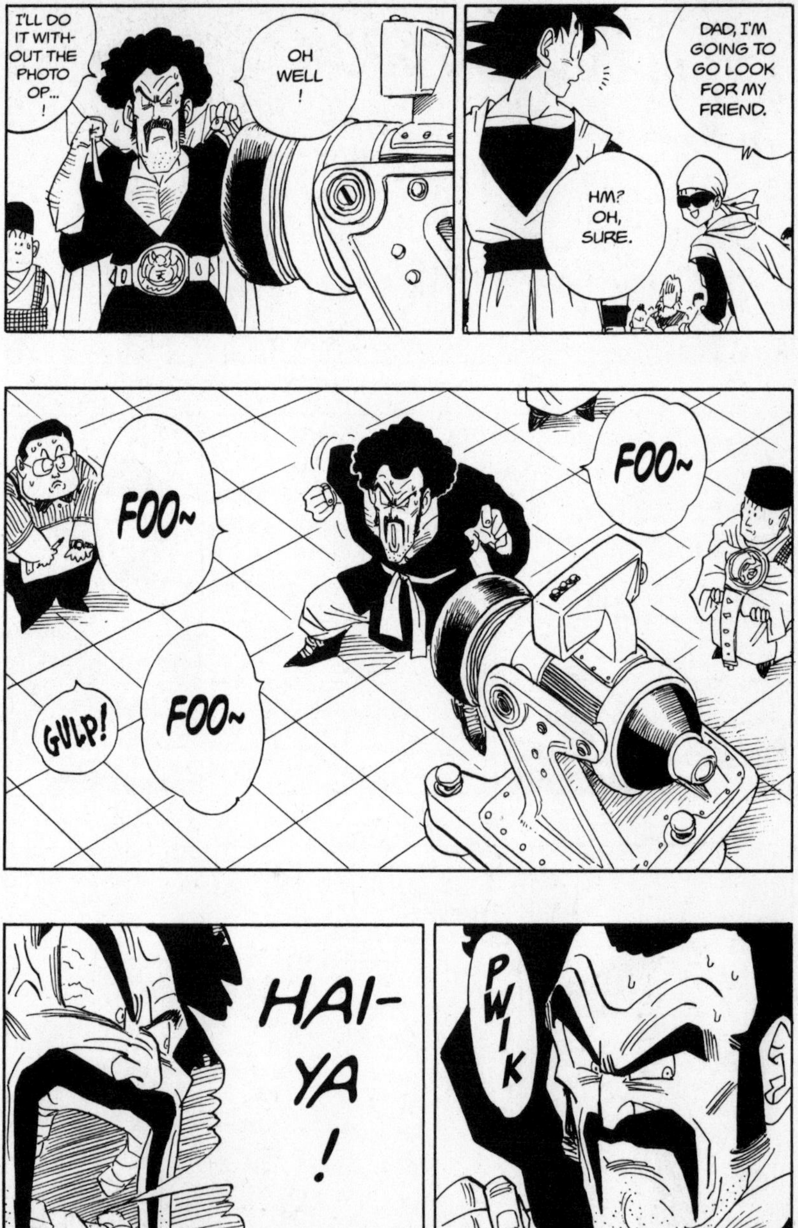
DAD, I'M GOING TO GO LOOK FOR MY FRIEND.
HM? OH, SURE.
OH WELL!
I'LL DO IT WITH-OUT THE PHOTO OP...!
FOO~
FOO~
FOO~
GULP!
PWIK
HAI-YA!

READ THIS WAY

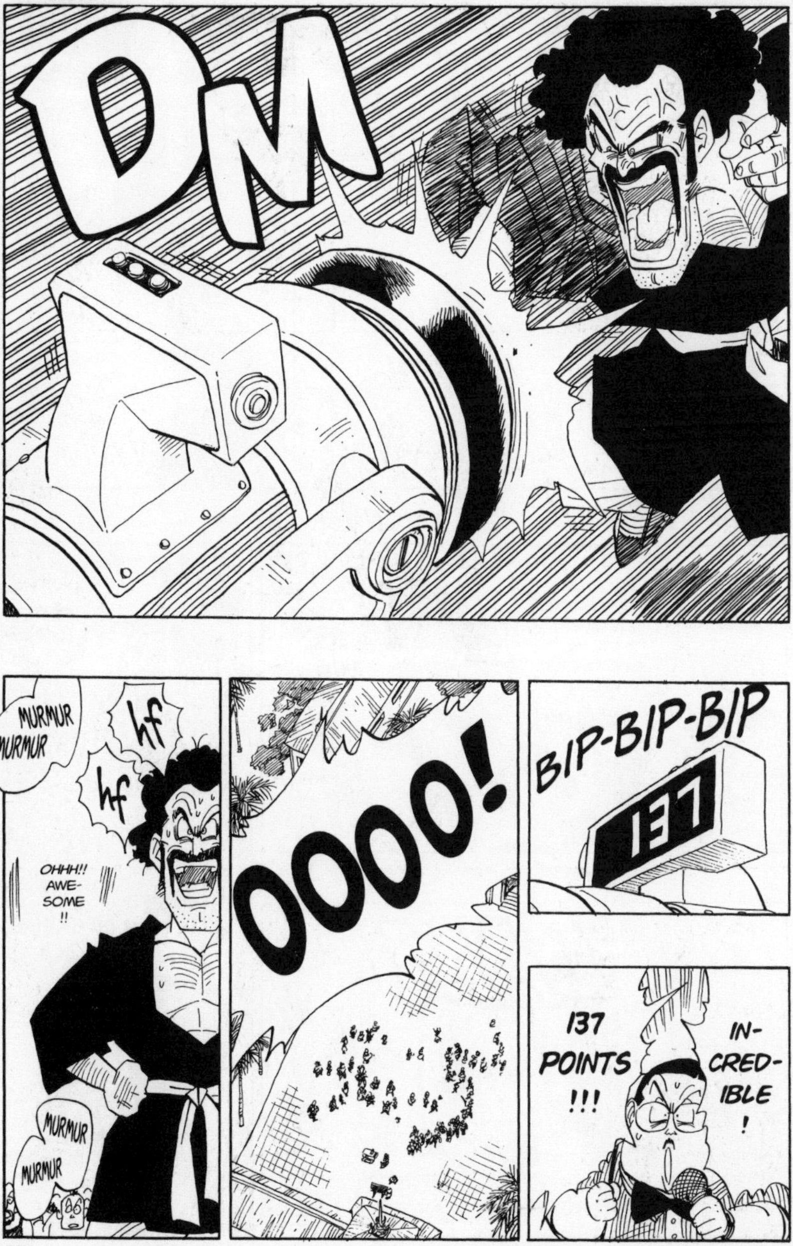
DM
BIP-BIP-BIP
IN-CRED-IBLE!
137 POINTS!!!
OOOO!
hf
hf
MURMUR MURMUR
OHHH!! AWE-SOME!!
MURMUR
MURMUR

READ THIS WAY

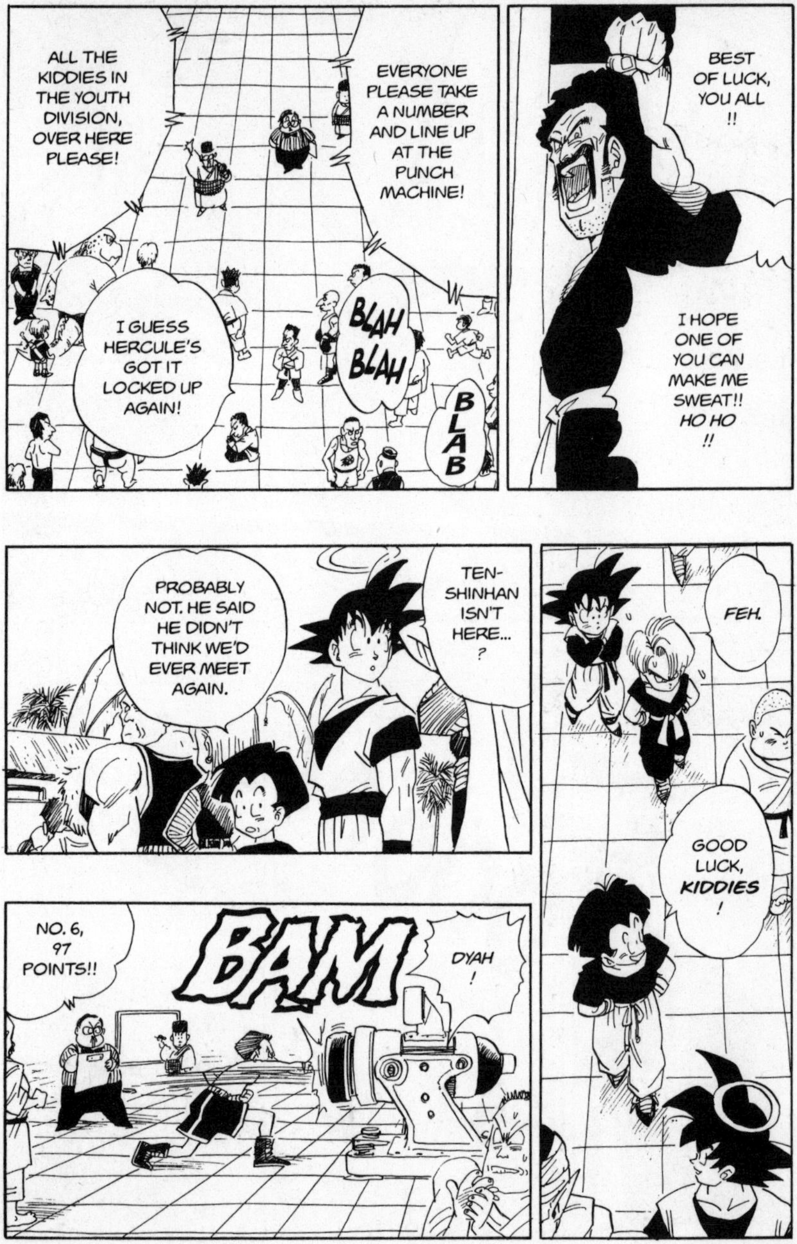

BEST OF LUCK, YOU ALL !!
I HOPE ONE OF YOU CAN MAKE ME SWEAT!! HO HO !!
EVERYONE PLEASE TAKE A NUMBER AND LINE UP AT THE PUNCH MACHINE!
ALL THE KIDDIES IN THE YOUTH DIVISION, OVER HERE PLEASE!
BLAB
BLAH BLAH
I GUESS HERCULE'S GOT IT LOCKED UP AGAIN!
FEH.
GOOD LUCK, KIDDIES !
TEN-SHINHAN ISN'T HERE...?
PROBABLY NOT. HE SAID HE DIDN'T THINK WE'D EVER MEET AGAIN.
DYAH !
BAM
NO. 6, 97 POINTS!!

READ THIS WAY

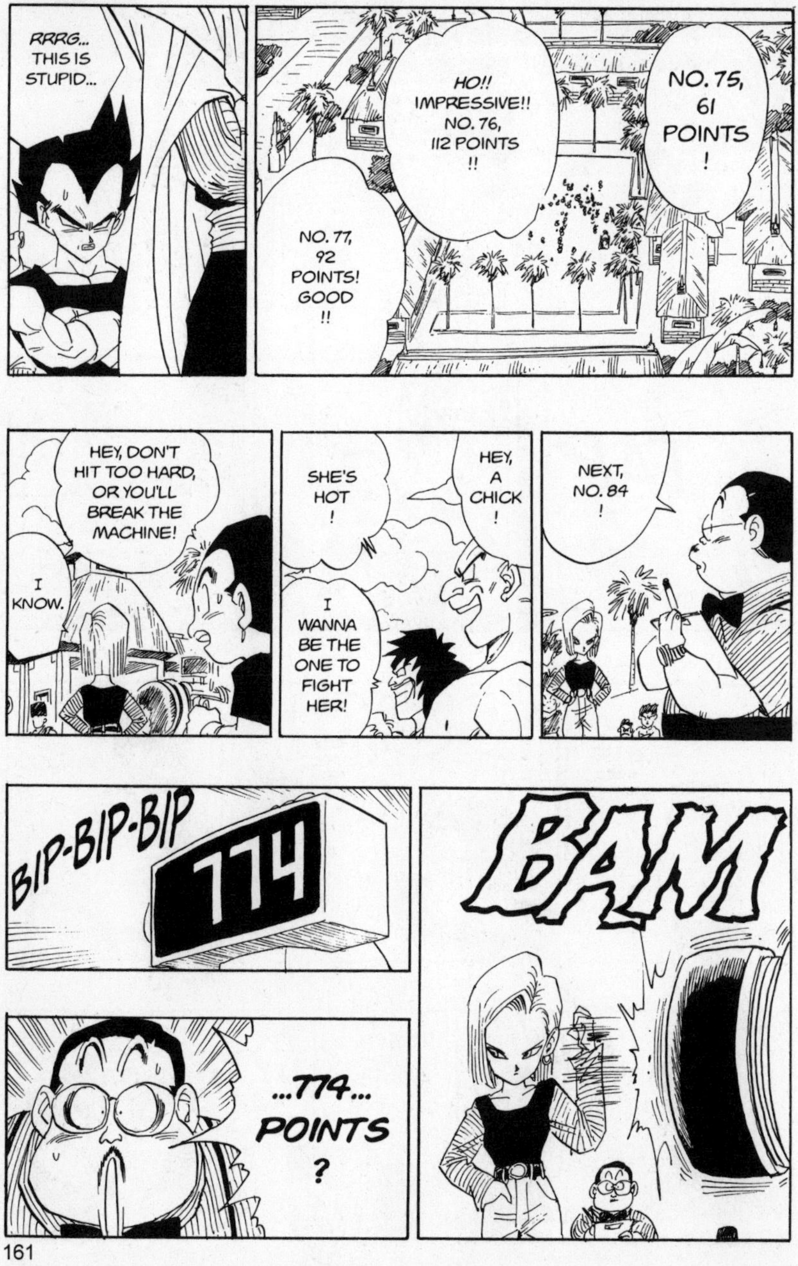

NO. 75, 61 POINTS !
HO!! IMPRESSIVE!! NO. 76, 112 POINTS !!
NO. 77, 92 POINTS! GOOD !!
RRRG... THIS IS STUPID...
NEXT, NO. 84 !
HEY, A CHICK !
SHE'S HOT !
I WANNA BE THE ONE TO FIGHT HER!
HEY, DON'T HIT TOO HARD, OR YOU'LL BREAK THE MACHINE!
I KNOW.
BAM
BIP-BIP-BIP
774
...774... POINTS ?

READ THIS WAY

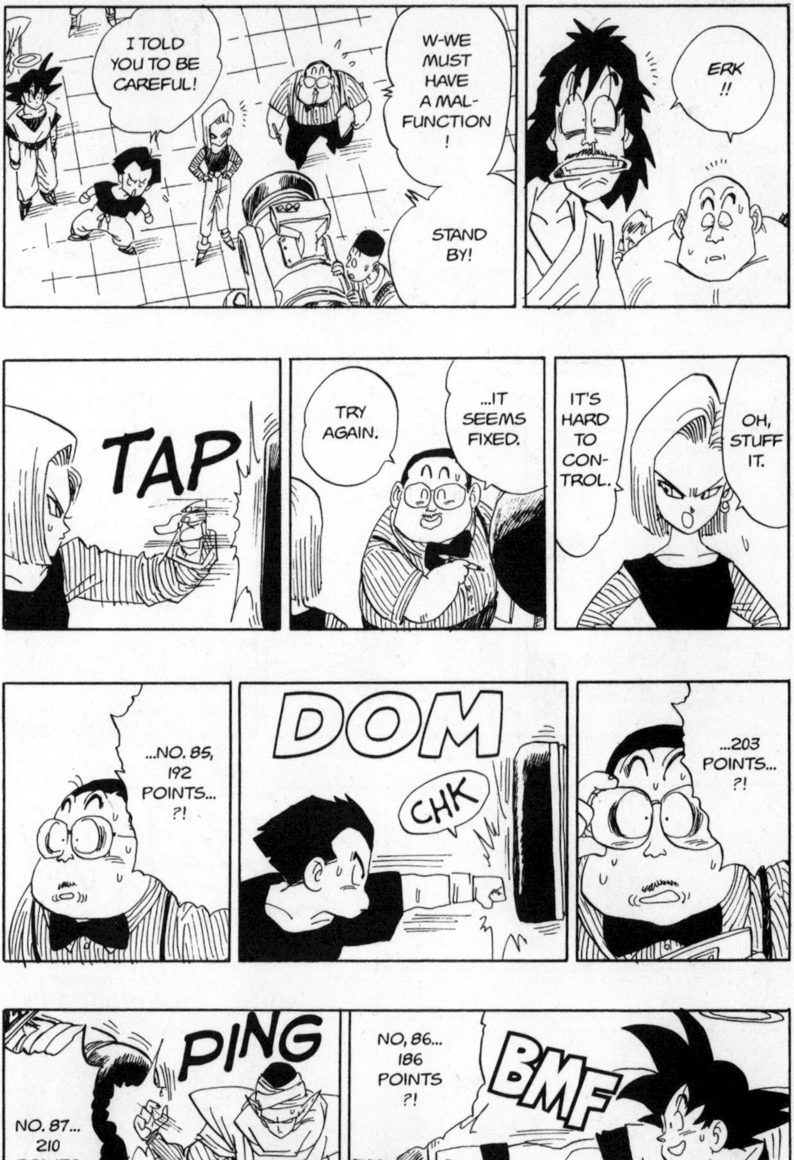
ERK !!
W-WE MUST HAVE A MAL-FUNCTION !
STAND BY!
I TOLD YOU TO BE CAREFUL!
OH, STUFF IT.
IT'S HARD TO CON-TROL.
...IT SEEMS FIXED.
TRY AGAIN.
TAP
...203 POINTS... ?!
DOM
CHK
...NO. 85, 192 POINTS... ?!
BMF
NO, 86... 186 POINTS ?!
PING
NO. 87... 210 POINTS ?!

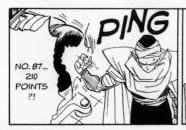

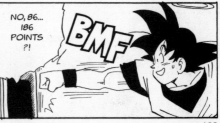

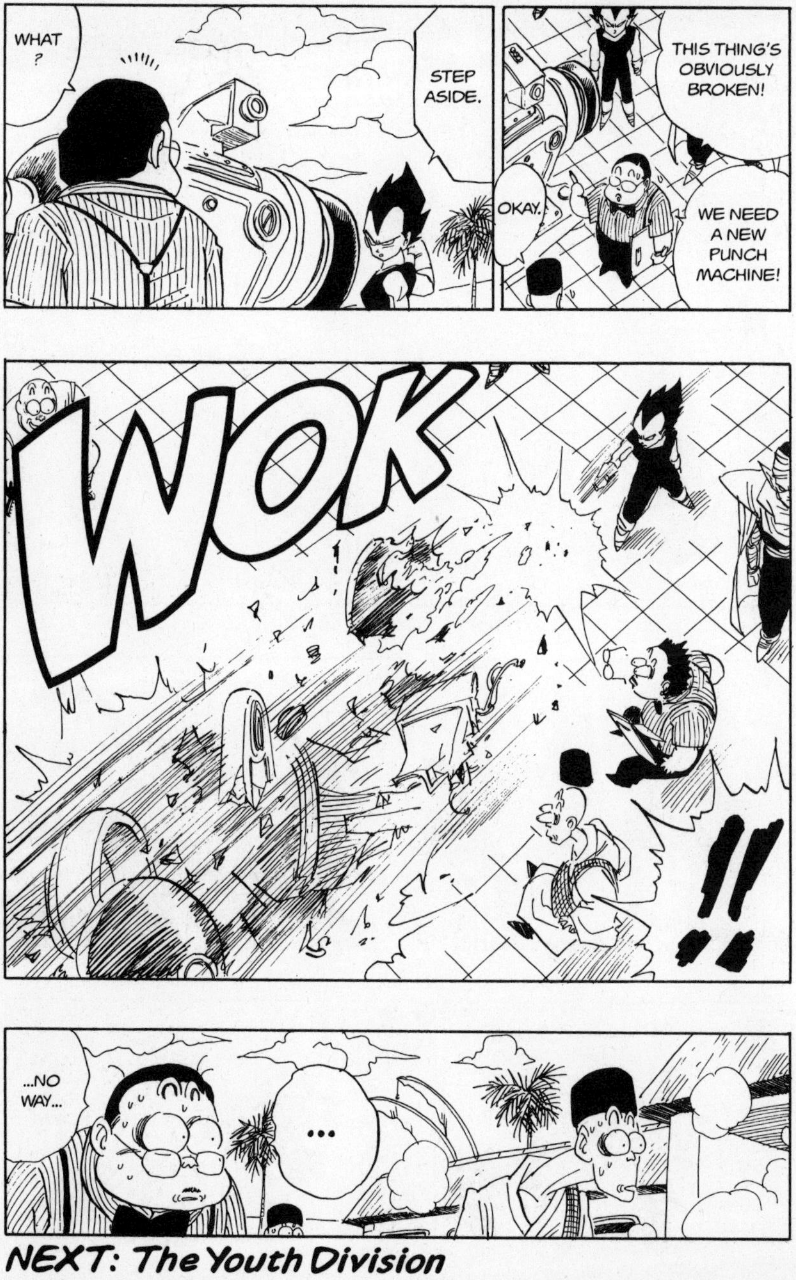
THIS THING'S OBVIOUSLY BROKEN!
WE NEED A NEW PUNCH MACHINE!
OKAY.
STEP ASIDE.
WHAT?
WOK
!!
...
...NO WAY...

NEXT: The Youth Division

DBZ:238 • The Two Little Warriors

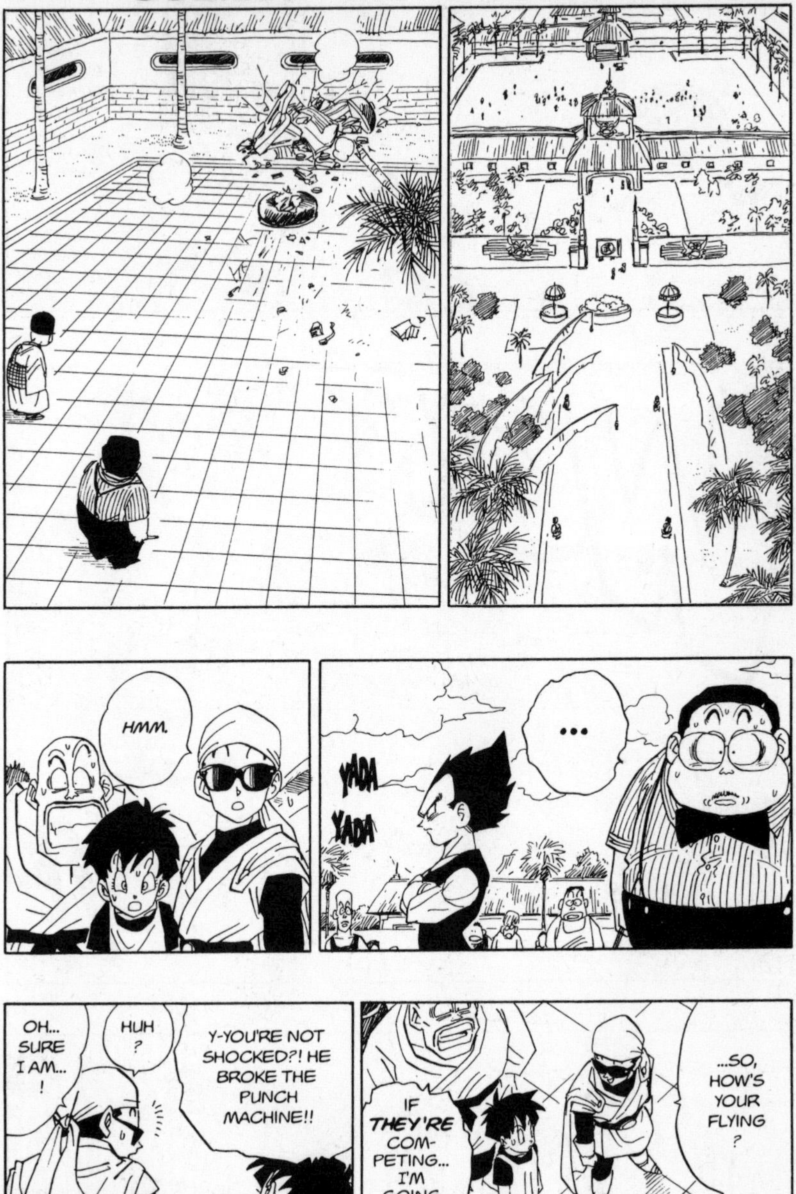
...
YADA YADA
HMM.
...SO, HOW'S YOUR FLYING?
IF THEY'RE COMPETING... I'M GOING HOME.
Y-YOU'RE NOT SHOCKED?! HE BROKE THE PUNCH MACHINE!!
HUH?
OH... SURE I AM...!

READ THIS WAY

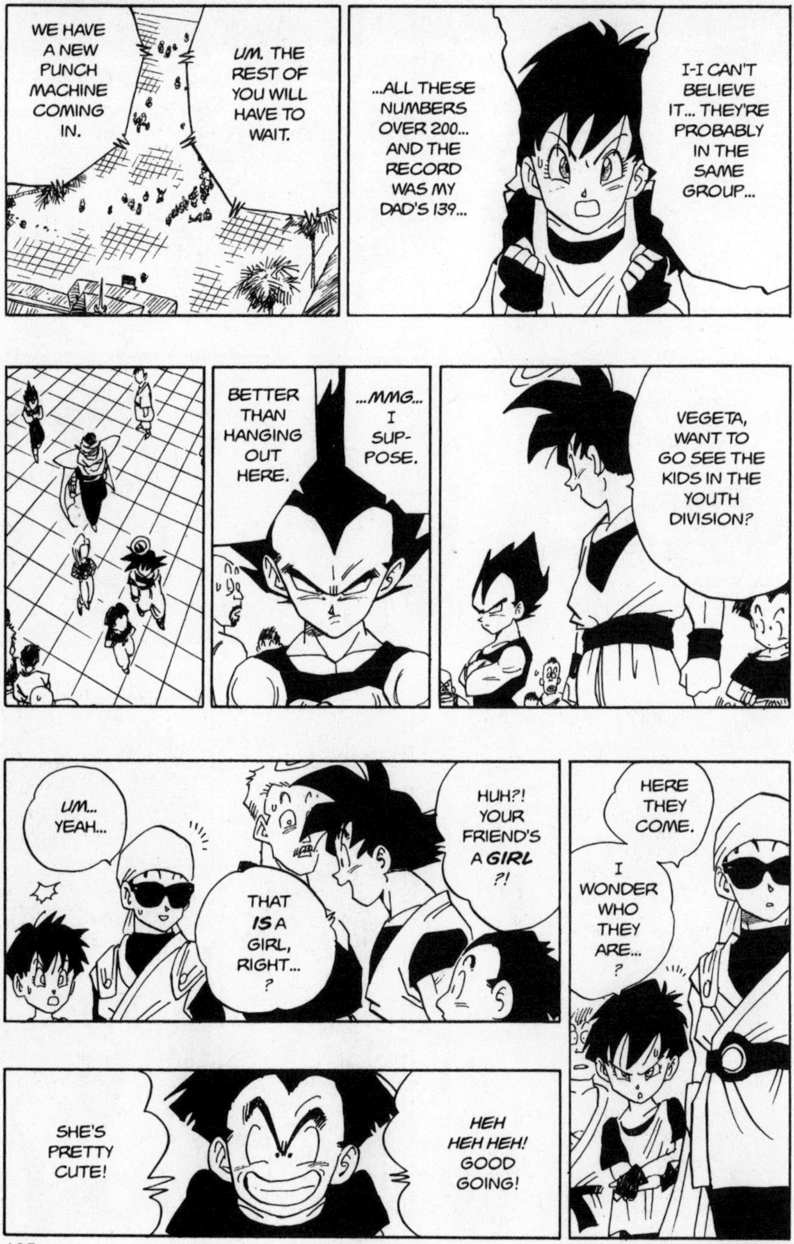
I-I CAN'T BELIEVE IT... THEY'RE PROBABLY IN THE SAME GROUP...
...ALL THESE NUMBERS OVER 200... AND THE RECORD WAS MY DAD'S 139...
UM. THE REST OF YOU WILL HAVE TO WAIT.
WE HAVE A NEW PUNCH MACHINE COMING IN.
VEGETA, WANT TO GO SEE THE KIDS IN THE YOUTH DIVISION?
...MMG... I SUPPOSE.
BETTER THAN HANGING OUT HERE.
HERE THEY COME.
I WONDER WHO THEY ARE... ?
HUH?! YOUR FRIEND'S A GIRL ?!
THAT IS A GIRL, RIGHT... ?
UM... YEAH...
HEH HEH HEH! GOOD GOING!
SHE'S PRETTY CUTE!

READ THIS WAY

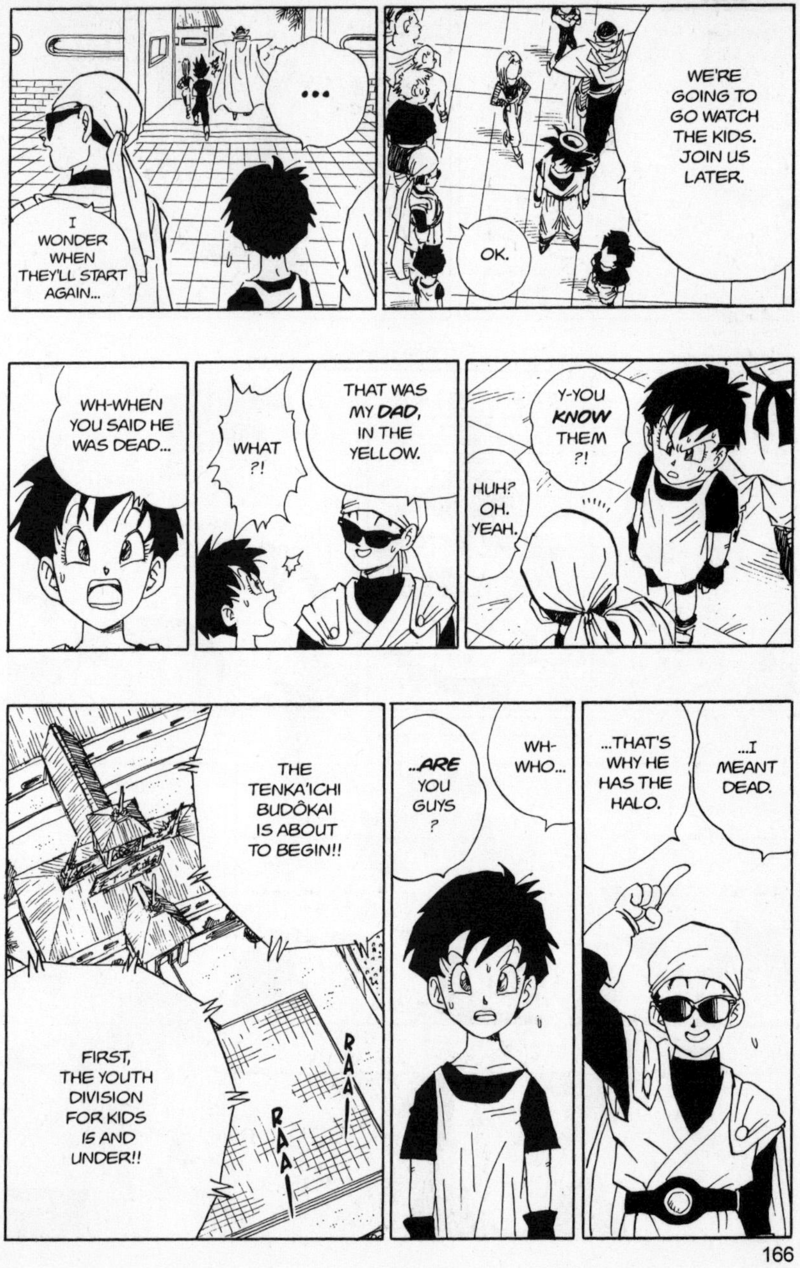
WE'RE GOING TO GO WATCH THE KIDS. JOIN US LATER.
OK.
...
I WONDER WHEN THEY'LL START AGAIN...
Y-YOU **KNOW** THEM ?!
HUH? OH. YEAH.
THAT WAS MY **DAD**, IN THE YELLOW.
WHAT ?!
WH-WHEN YOU SAID HE WAS DEAD...
...I MEANT DEAD.
...THAT'S WHY HE HAS THE HALO.
WH-WHO...
...**ARE** YOU GUYS ?
THE TENKA'ICHI BUDÔKAI IS ABOUT TO BEGIN!!
RAA!
RAA!
FIRST, THE YOUTH DIVISION FOR KIDS 15 AND UNDER!!

READ THIS WAY

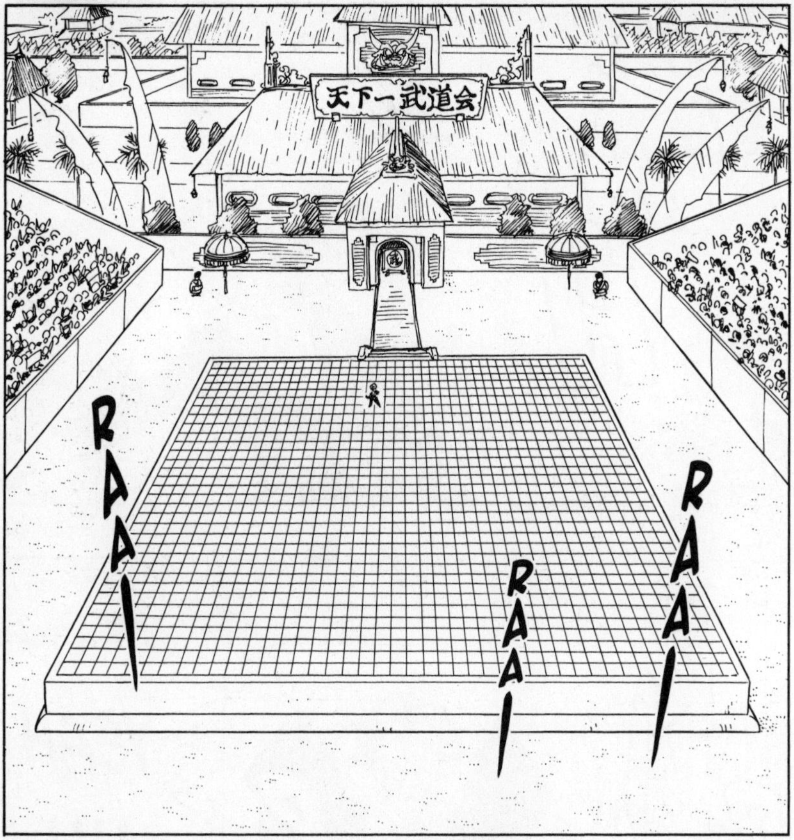
天下一武道会
RAA!
RAA!
RAA!

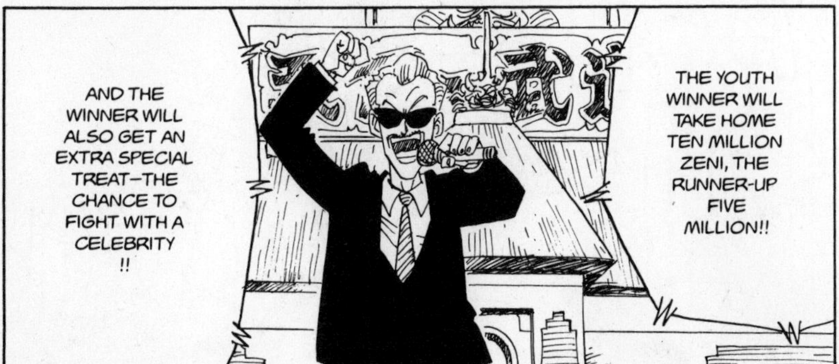
THE YOUTH WINNER WILL TAKE HOME TEN MILLION ZENI, THE RUNNER-UP FIVE MILLION!!
AND THE WINNER WILL ALSO GET AN EXTRA SPECIAL TREAT—THE CHANCE TO FIGHT WITH A CELEBRITY!!

READ THIS WAY

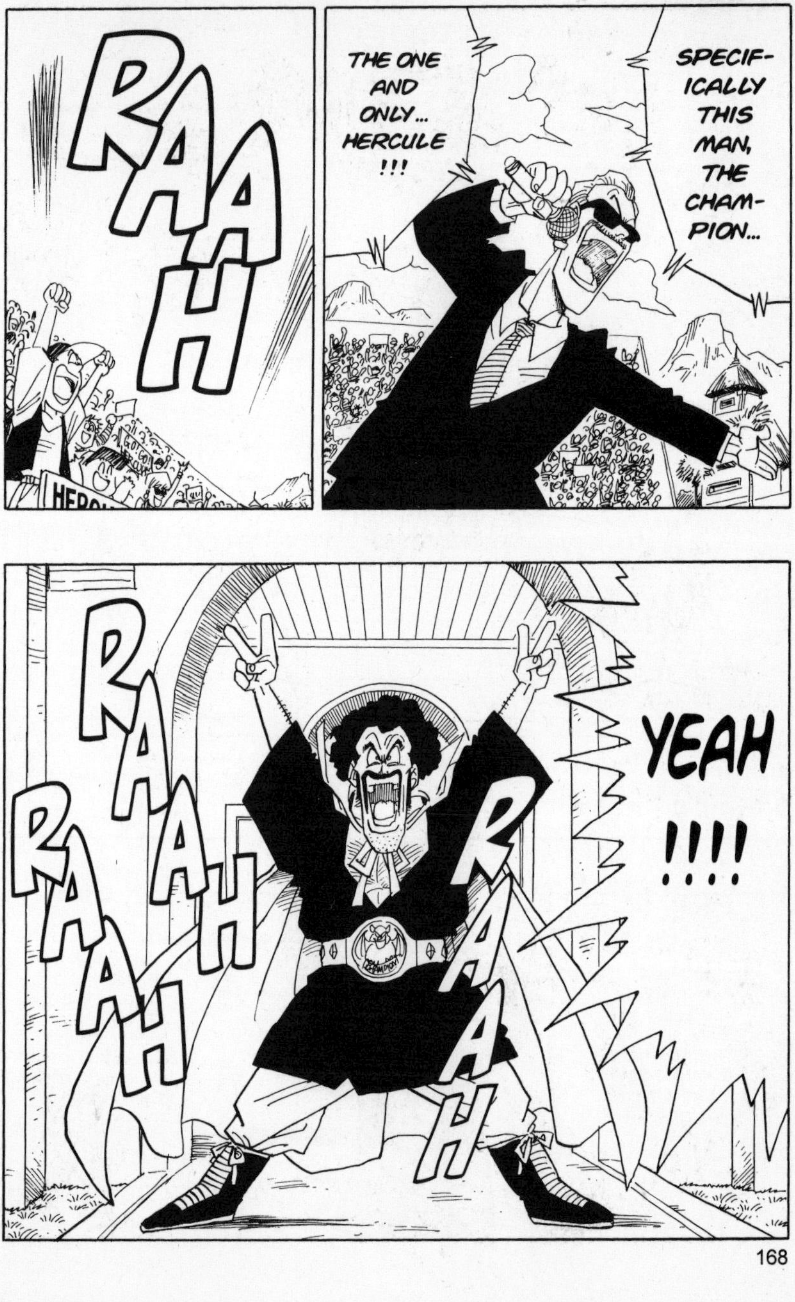

SPECIFICALLY THIS MAN, THE CHAMPION...
THE ONE AND ONLY... HERCULE !!!
RAAH
YEAH !!!!
RAAH
RAAH
RAAH

READ THIS WAY

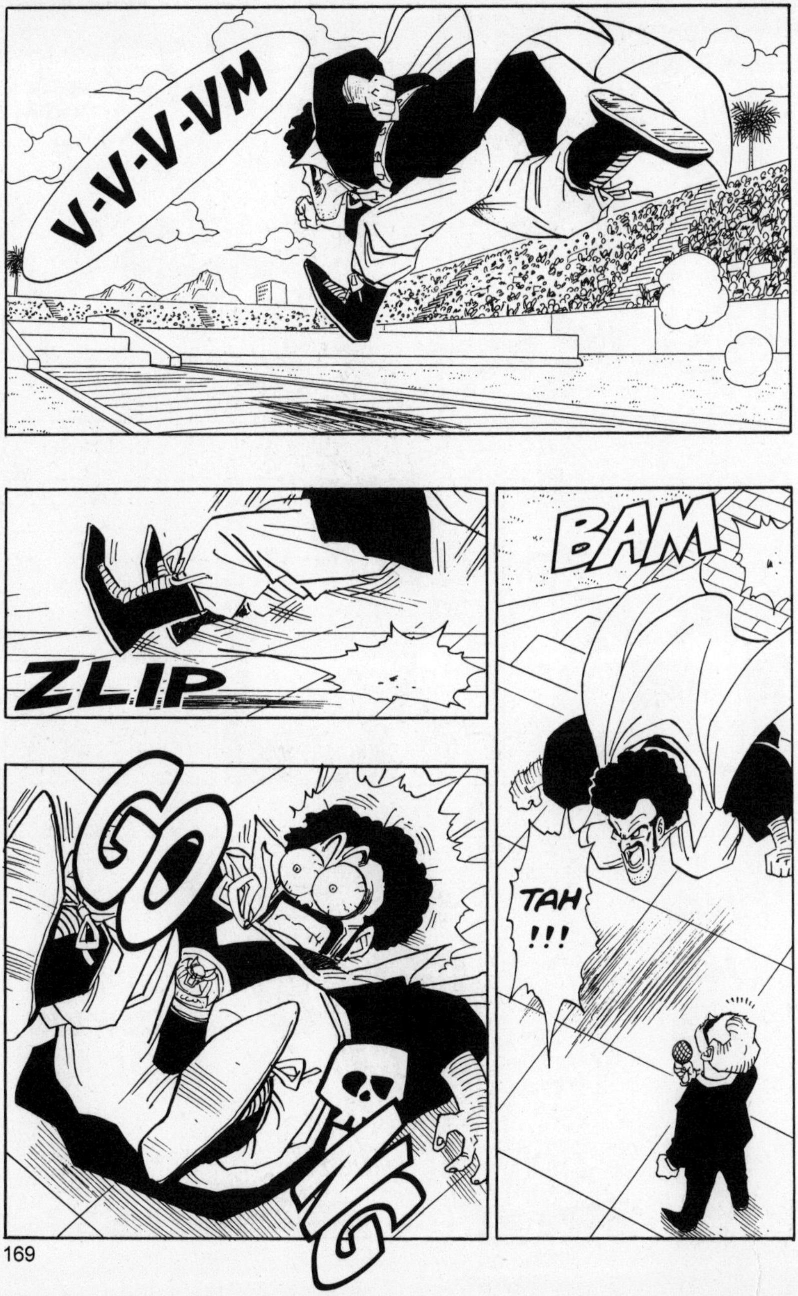
V-V-V-VM
BAM
TAH !!!
ZLIP
GONG

READ THIS WAY

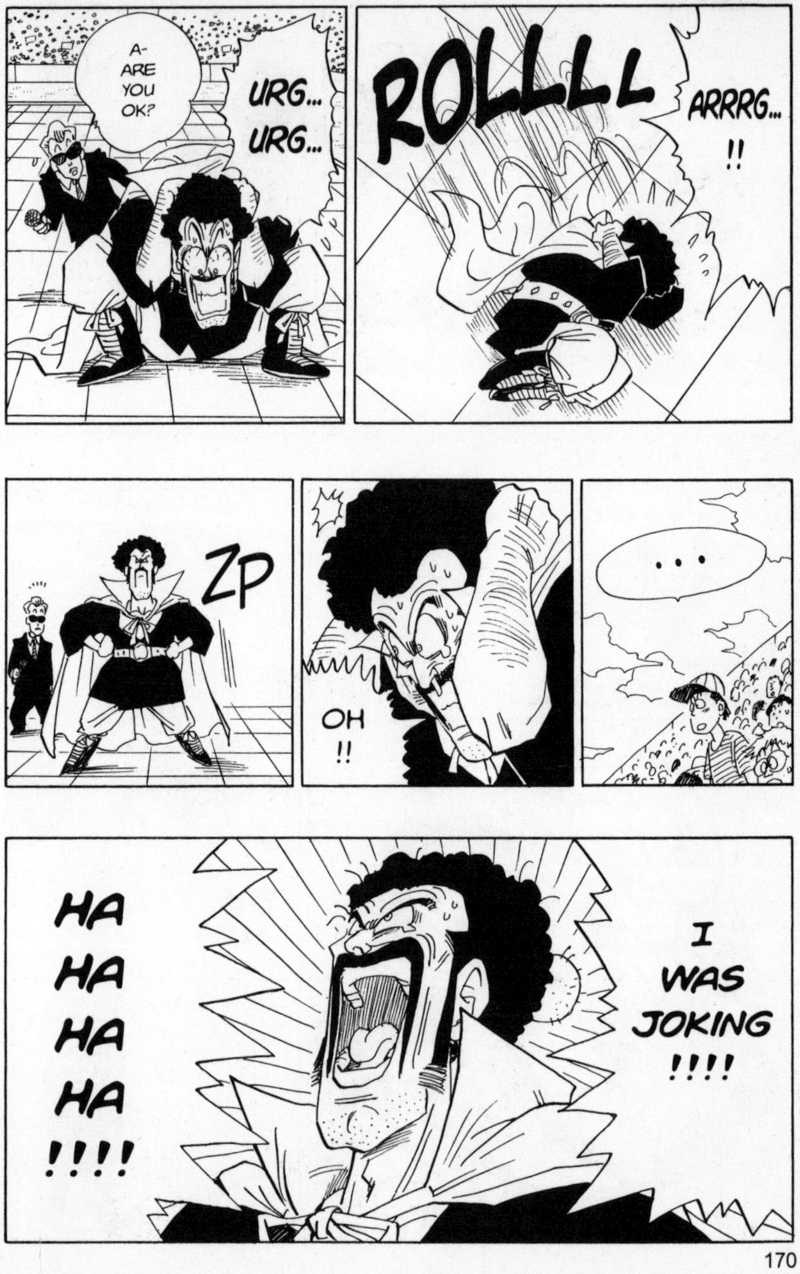
ROLLLL
ARRRG... !!
URG... URG...
A- ARE YOU OK?
...
OH !!
ZP
I WAS JOKING !!!!
HA HA HA HA !!!!

READ THIS WAY

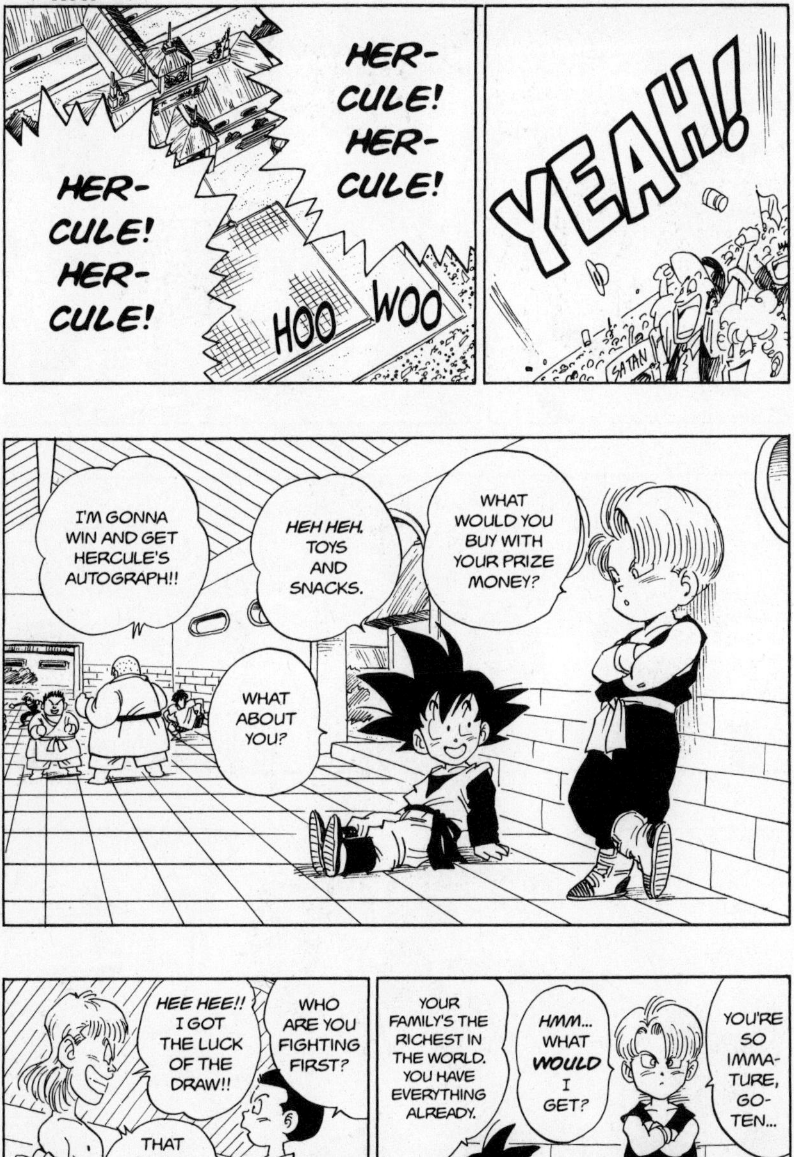
YEAH!
SATAN
HER-CULE! HER-CULE!
WOO
HOO
HER-CULE! HER-CULE!
WHAT WOULD YOU BUY WITH YOUR PRIZE MONEY?
HEH HEH. TOYS AND SNACKS.
WHAT ABOUT YOU?
I'M GONNA WIN AND GET HERCULE'S AUTOGRAPH!!
YOU'RE SO IMMA-TURE, GO-TEN...
HMM... WHAT WOULD I GET?
YOUR FAMILY'S THE RICHEST IN THE WORLD. YOU HAVE EVERYTHING ALREADY.
WHO ARE YOU FIGHTING FIRST?
HEE HEE!! I GOT THE LUCK OF THE DRAW!!
THAT SHRIMP OVER THERE!!

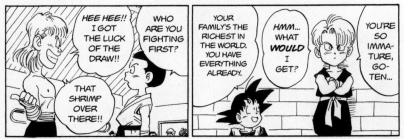

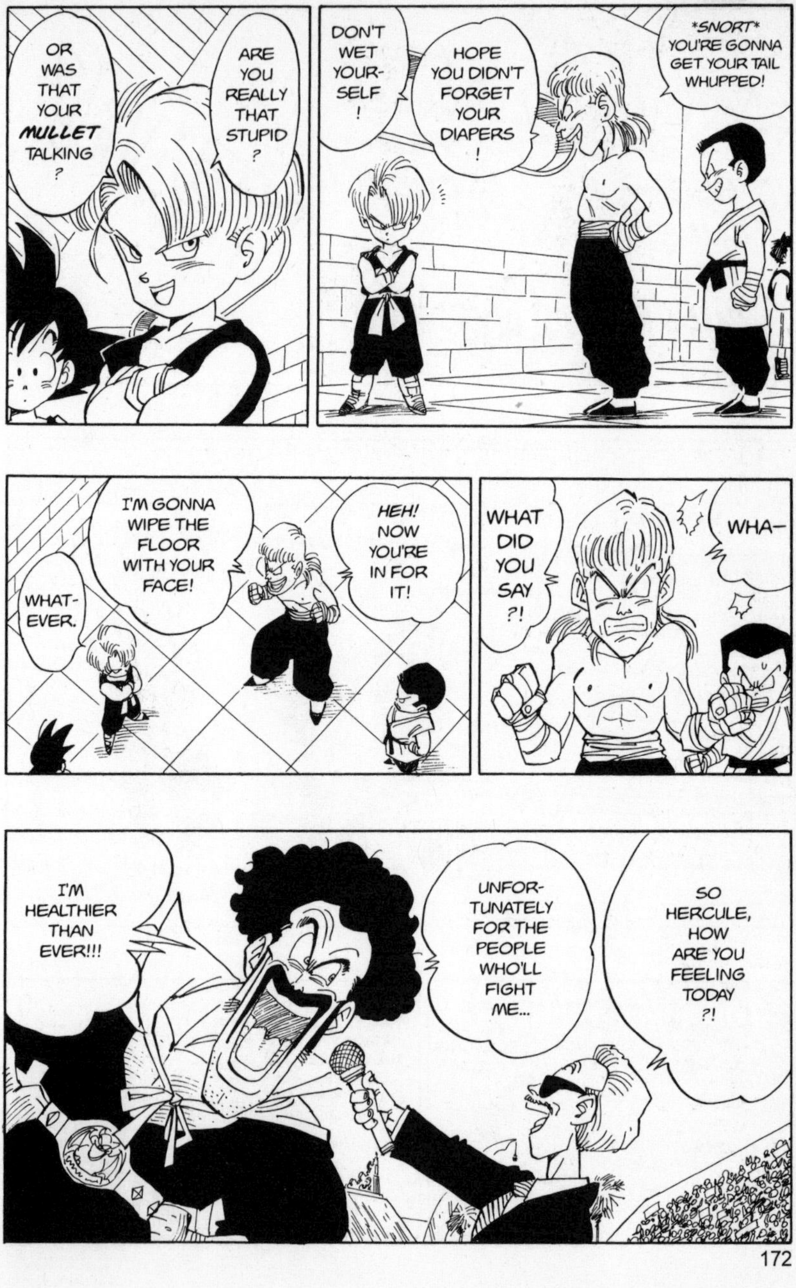
SNORT YOU'RE GONNA GET YOUR TAIL WHUPPED!
HOPE YOU DIDN'T FORGET YOUR DIAPERS!
DON'T WET YOURSELF!
ARE YOU REALLY THAT STUPID?
OR WAS THAT YOUR MULLET TALKING?
WHA-
WHAT DID YOU SAY?!
HEH! NOW YOU'RE IN FOR IT!
I'M GONNA WIPE THE FLOOR WITH YOUR FACE!
WHAT-EVER.
SO HERCULE, HOW ARE YOU FEELING TODAY?!
UNFOR-TUNATELY FOR THE PEOPLE WHO'LL FIGHT ME...
I'M HEALTHIER THAN EVER!!!

READ THIS WAY

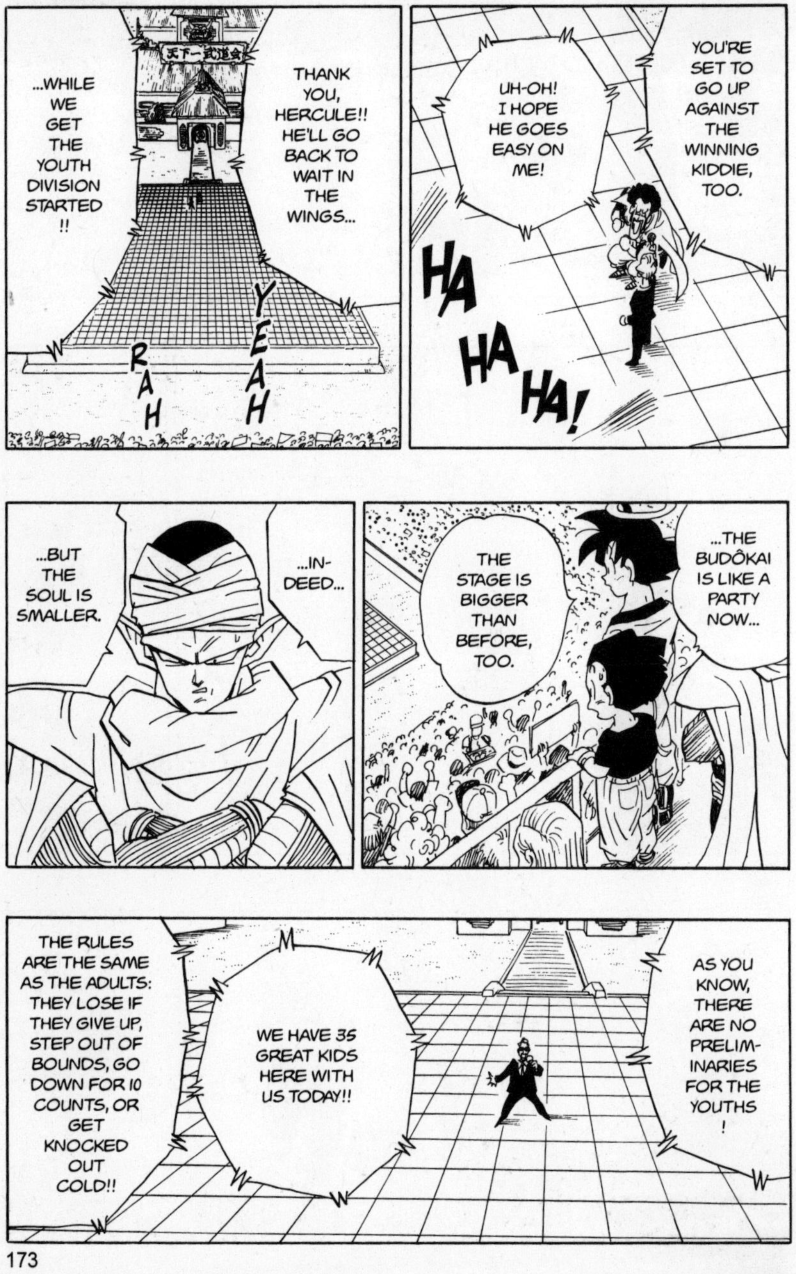

YOU'RE SET TO GO UP AGAINST THE WINNING KIDDIE, TOO.
UH-OH! I HOPE HE GOES EASY ON ME!
HA HA HA!
天下一武道会
THANK YOU, HERCULE!! HE'LL GO BACK TO WAIT IN THE WINGS...
...WHILE WE GET THE YOUTH DIVISION STARTED!!
YEAH
RAH
...THE BUDÔKAI IS LIKE A PARTY NOW...
THE STAGE IS BIGGER THAN BEFORE, TOO.
...IN-DEED...
...BUT THE SOUL IS SMALLER.
AS YOU KNOW, THERE ARE NO PRELIM-INARIES FOR THE YOUTHS!
WE HAVE 35 GREAT KIDS HERE WITH US TODAY!!
THE RULES ARE THE SAME AS THE ADULTS: THEY LOSE IF THEY GIVE UP, STEP OUT OF BOUNDS, GO DOWN FOR 10 COUNTS, OR GET KNOCKED OUT COLD!!

READ THIS WAY

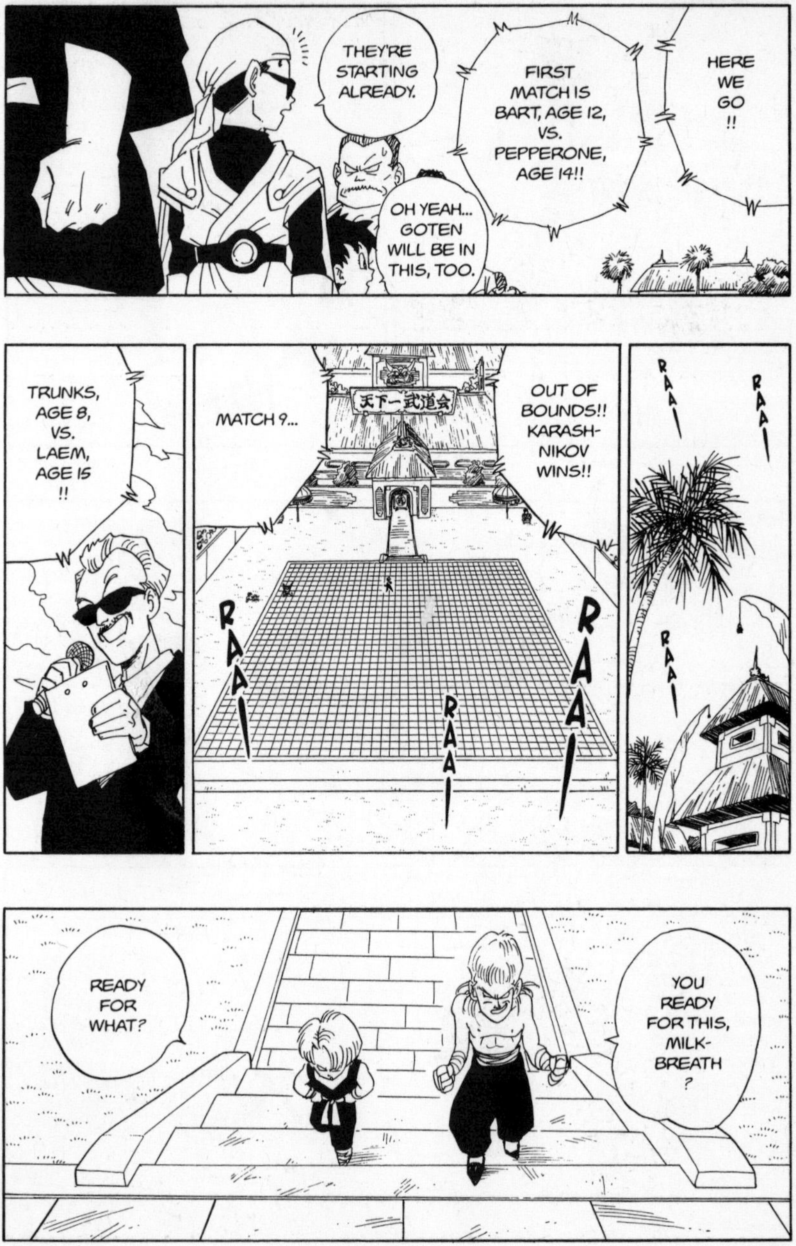
HERE WE GO!!
FIRST MATCH IS BART, AGE 12, VS. PEPPERONE, AGE 14!!
THEY'RE STARTING ALREADY.
OH YEAH... GOTEN WILL BE IN THIS, TOO.
RAAA
RAAA
RAAA
OUT OF BOUNDS!! KARASHNIKOV WINS!!
天下一武道会
MATCH 9...
RAAA
RAAA
RAAA
TRUNKS, AGE 8, VS. LAEM, AGE 15!!
YOU READY FOR THIS, MILK-BREATH?
READY FOR WHAT?

READ THIS WAY

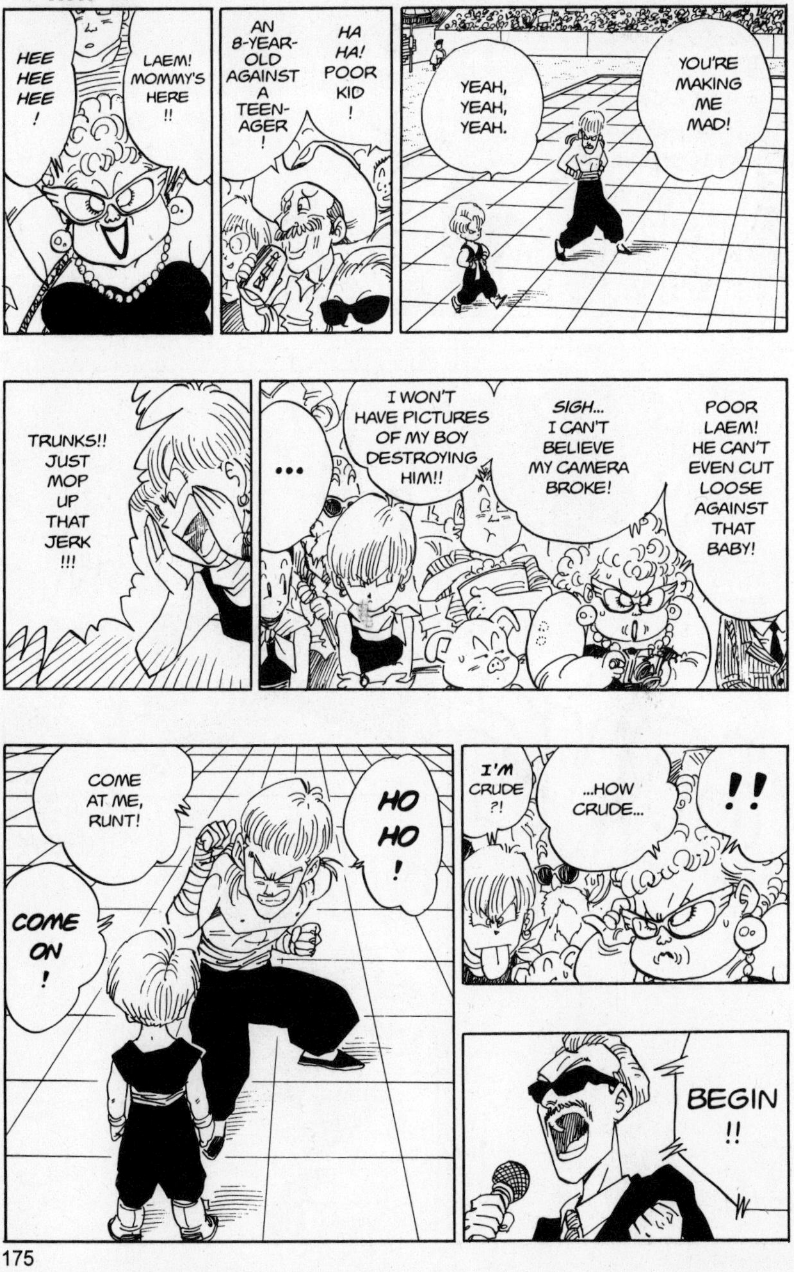
YOU'RE MAKING ME MAD!
YEAH, YEAH, YEAH.
HA HA! POOR KID!
AN 8-YEAR-OLD AGAINST A TEENAGER!
LAEM! MOMMY'S HERE!!
HEE HEE HEE!
POOR LAEM! HE CAN'T EVEN CUT LOOSE AGAINST THAT BABY!
SIGH... I CAN'T BELIEVE MY CAMERA BROKE!
I WON'T HAVE PICTURES OF MY BOY DESTROYING HIM!!
...
TRUNKS!! JUST MOP UP THAT JERK!!!
!!
...HOW CRUDE...
I'M CRUDE?!
BEGIN!!
HO HO!
COME AT ME, RUNT!
COME ON!

READ THIS WAY

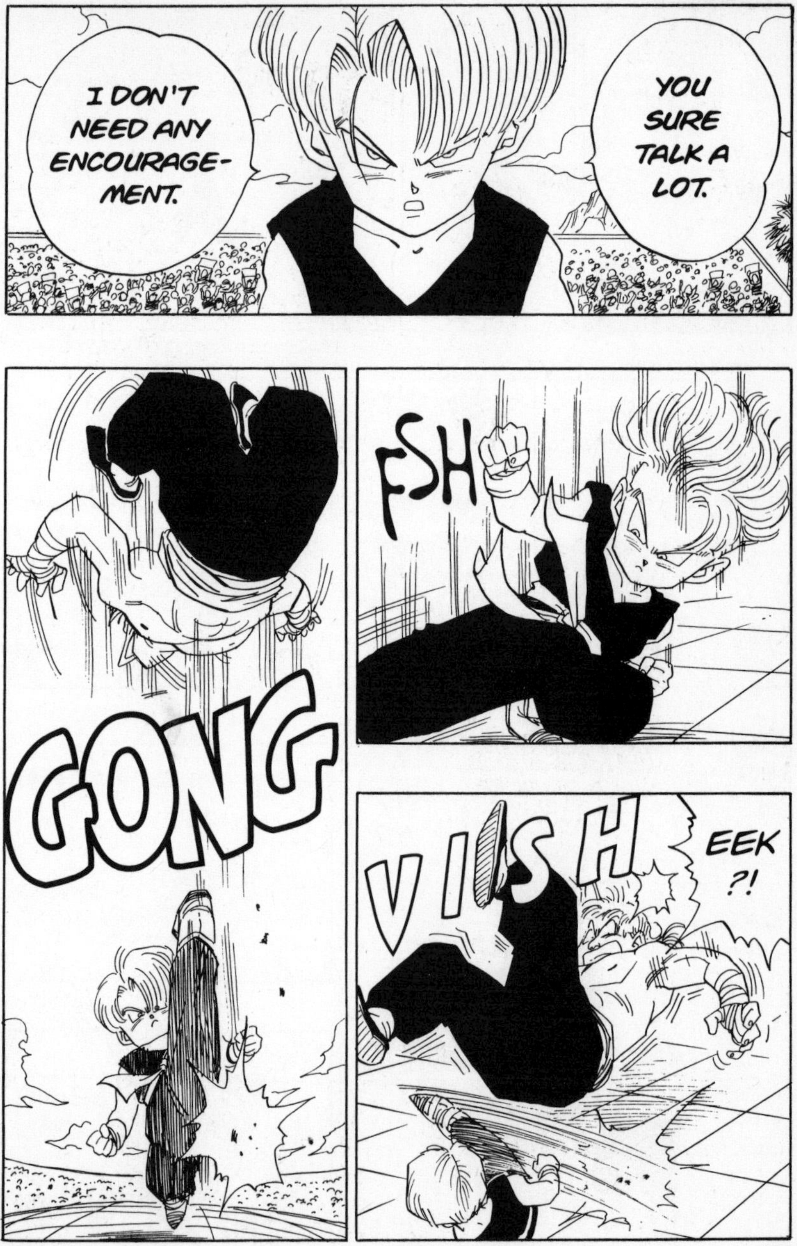
YOU SURE TALK A LOT.
I DON'T NEED ANY ENCOURAGE-MENT.
FSH
EEK ?!
VISH
GONG

READ THIS WAY

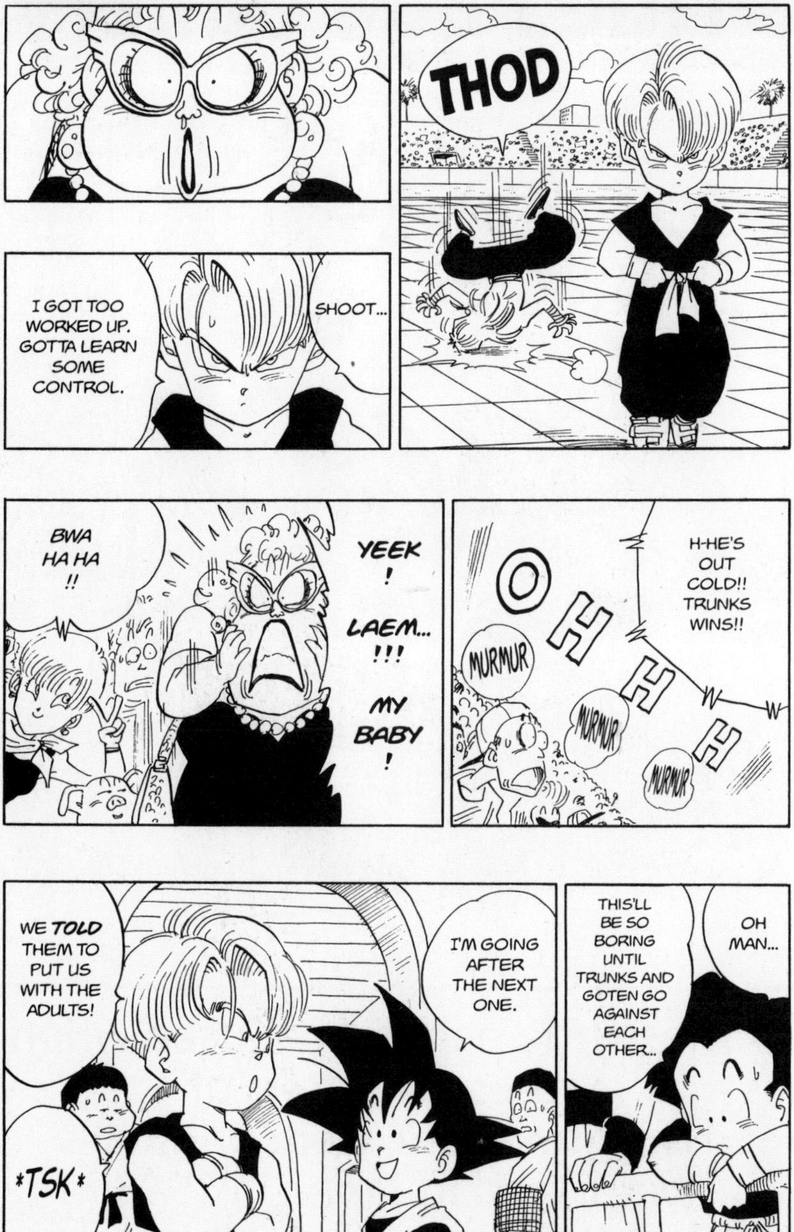
THOD
SHOOT...
I GOT TOO WORKED UP. GOTTA LEARN SOME CONTROL.
H-HE'S OUT COLD!! TRUNKS WINS!!
OHHHH
MURMUR
MURMUR
MURMUR
YEEK!
LAEM...!!!
MY BABY!
BWA HA HA!!
OH MAN...
THIS'LL BE SO BORING UNTIL TRUNKS AND GOTEN GO AGAINST EACH OTHER...
I'M GOING AFTER THE NEXT ONE.
WE TOLD THEM TO PUT US WITH THE ADULTS!
TSK

TO BE CONTINUED IN DRAGON BALL Z VOL. 21!

Title Page Gallery

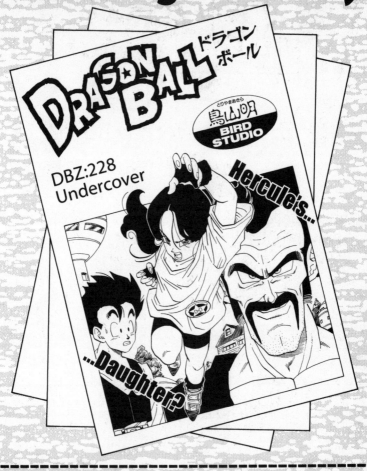

DRAGON BALL ドラゴンボール

とりやまあきら
鳥山明
BIRD STUDIO

DBZ:228
Undercover

Hercule's...

...Daughter?

These title pages were used when these chapters of **Dragon Ball Z** were originally published in Japan in 1993 in **Weekly Shonen Jump** magazine.

DRAGON BALL ドラゴンボール

DBZ:229 · A Hero is Born!

GUESS WHO?
IT'S

鳥山明
BIRD STUDIO

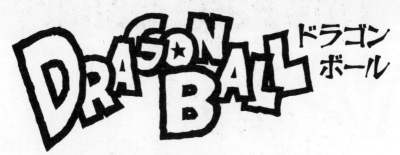

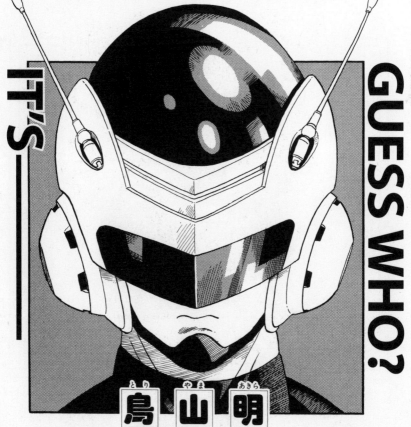

DRAGON BALL ドラゴンボール

DBZ:232 Strongest in the Heavens!

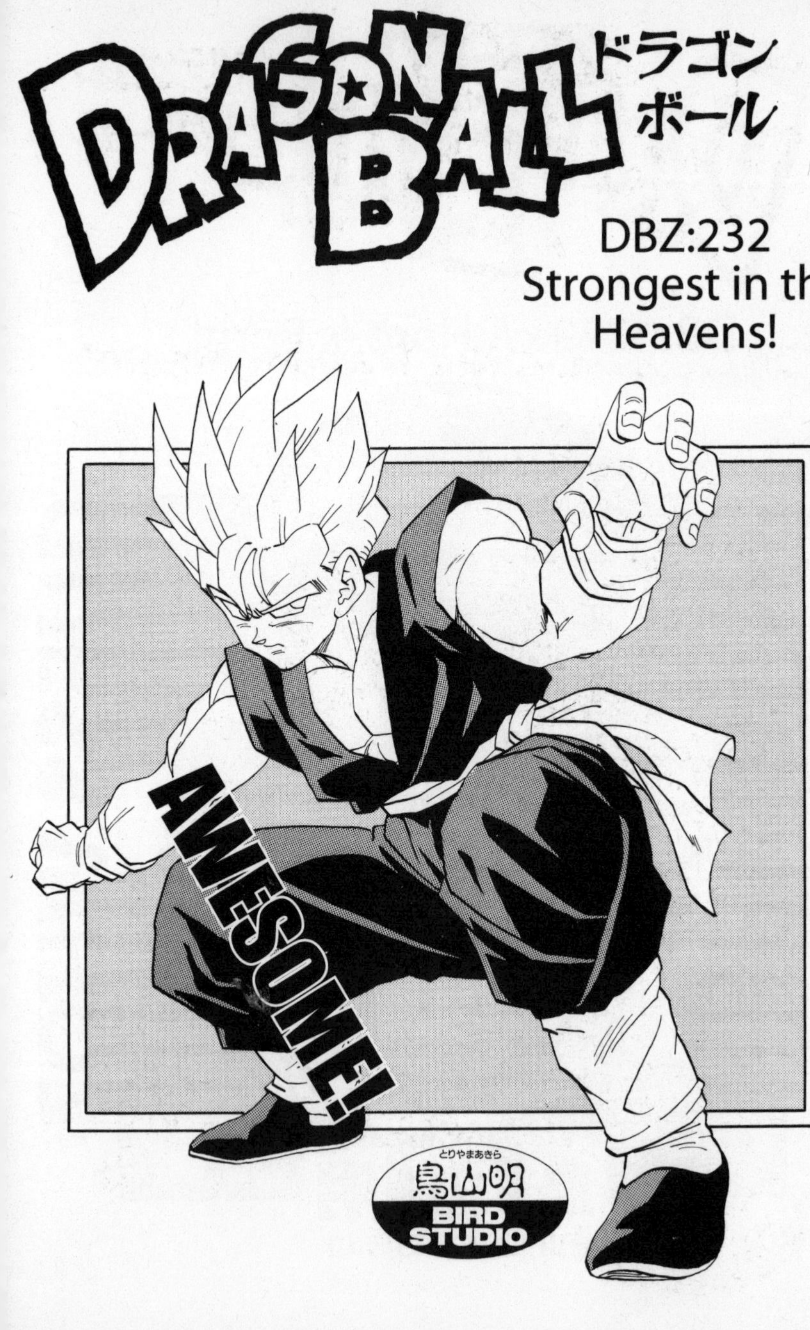
AWESOME!
とりやまあきら
鳥山明
BIRD STUDIO

DRAGON BALL ドラゴンボール

DBZ:233 • Let the Training Begin!

Let's do it!!!!

とりやまあきら
鳥山明
BIRD STUDIO

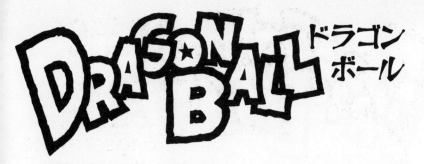

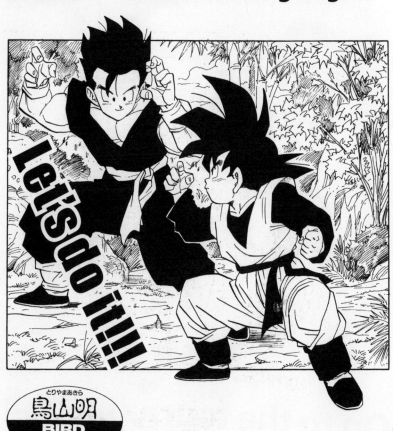

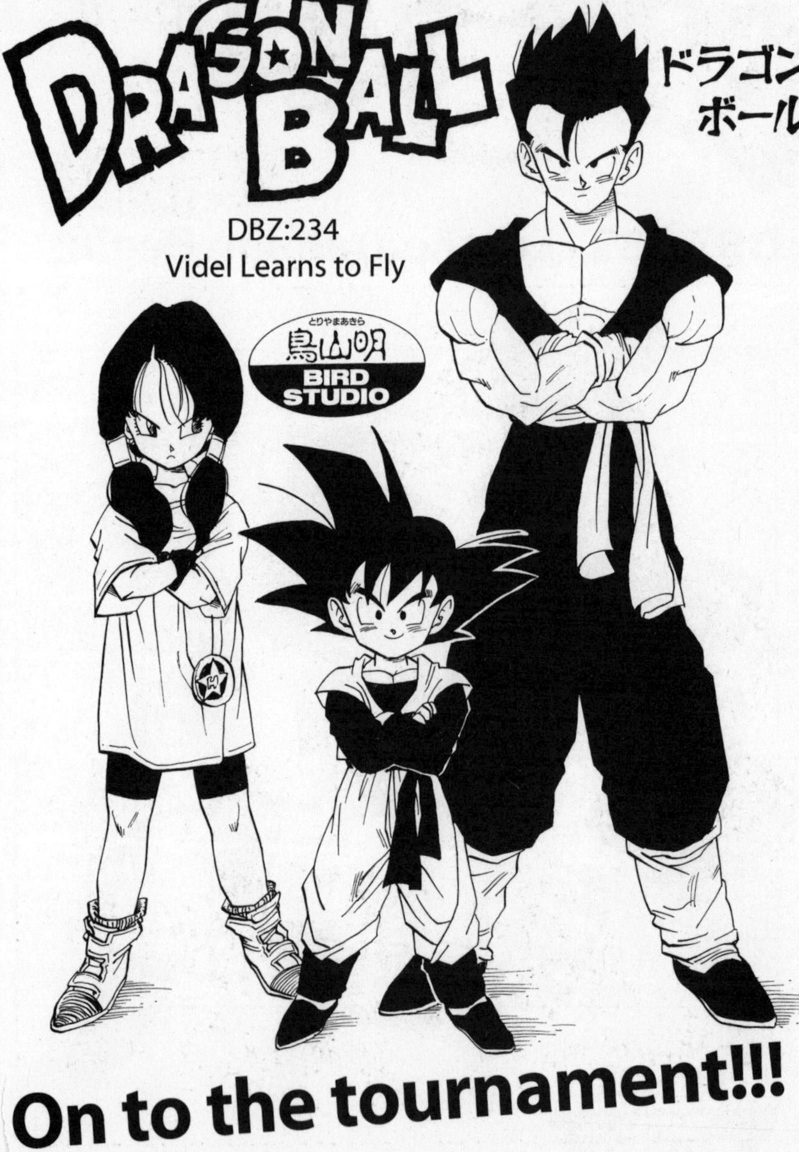
DRAGON BALL
ドラゴン
ボール
DBZ:234
Videl Learns to Fly
とりやまあきら
鳥山明
BIRD
STUDIO

On to the tournament!!!

DRAGON BALL ドラゴンボール

とりやまあきら
鳥山明
BIRD STUDIO

DBZ:236 · The Dragon Team Returns!

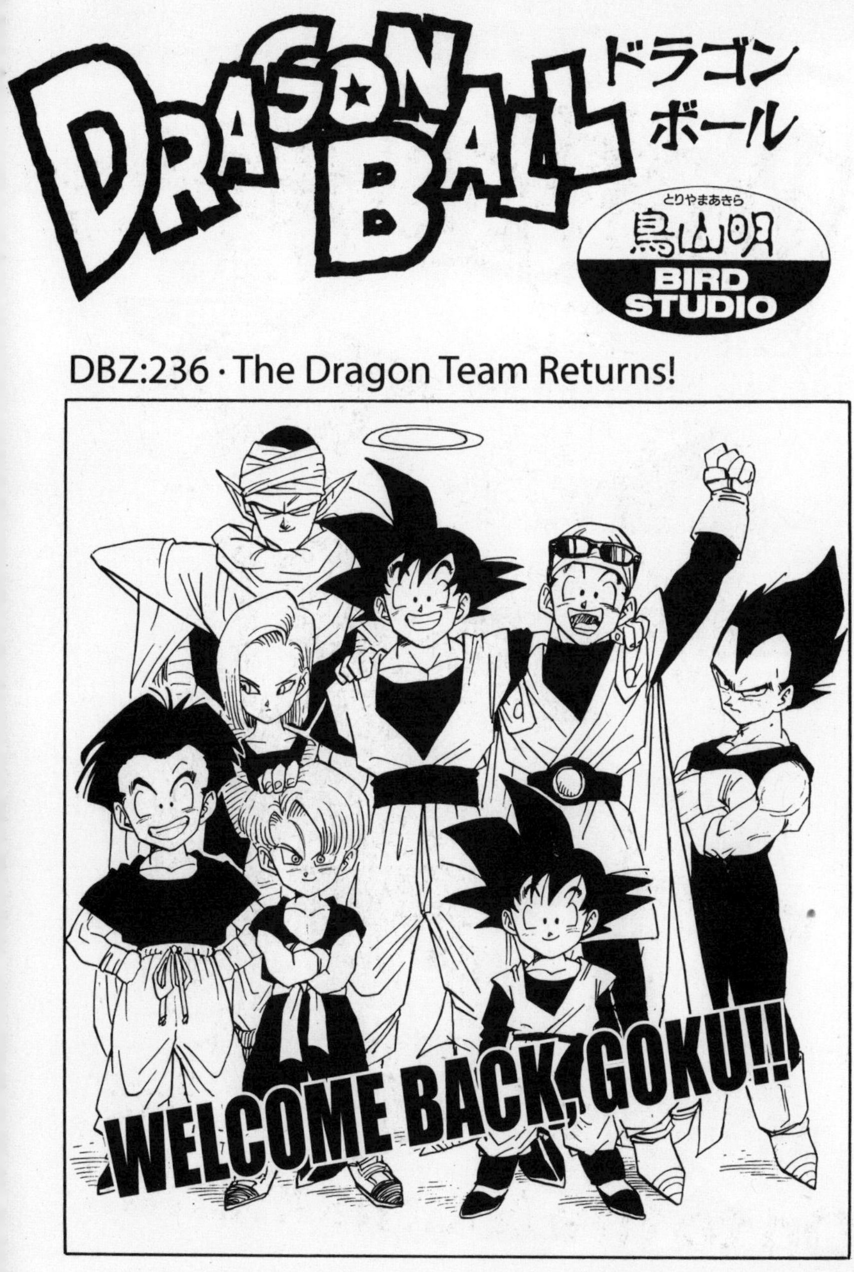
WELCOME BACK, GOKU!!

DRAGON BALL ドラゴンボール

とりやまあきら
鳥山明
BIRD STUDIO

DBZ:238
The Two Little Warriors

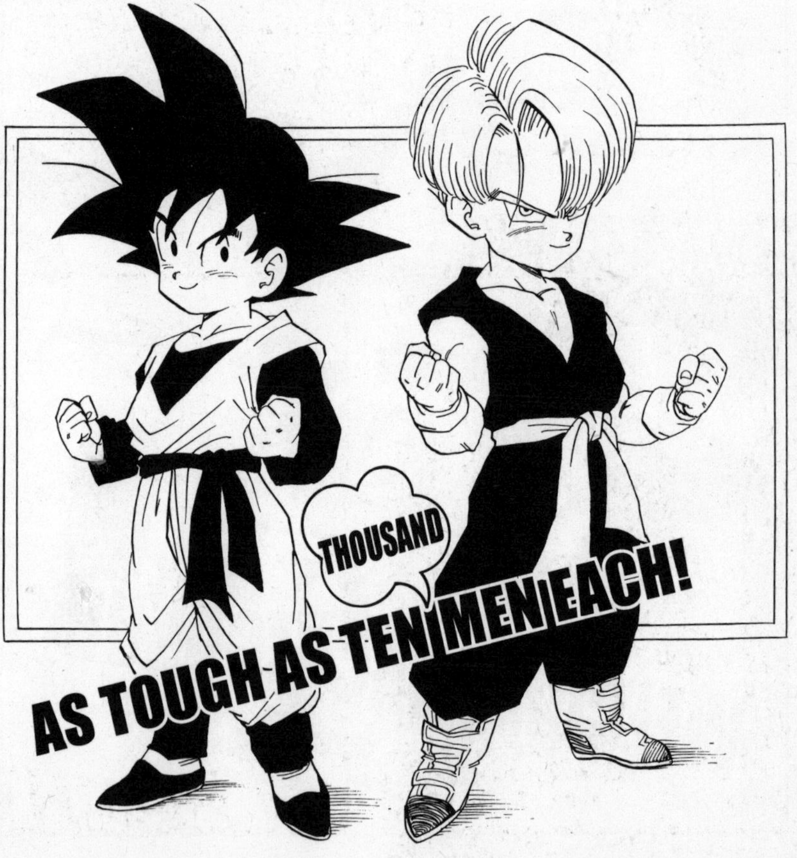
AS TOUGH AS TEN THOUSAND MEN EACH!

IN THE NEXT VOLUME...
Earth's heroes are out of retirement,
and the audience at the Tenka'ichi
Budôkai is about to see some *real*
martial arts! Trunks and Gohan have
no competition in the Junior
Division...but can the winner face the
mighty power of *Hercule?!?*
Meanwhile, Vegeta waits to settle the
score with Goku, who must return to
the afterlife in just one day. But Goku
isn't the only otherworldly visitor. Two
mysterious contestants have entered
the tournament, and they have a
special mission in this world...

AVAILABLE NOW!

HAAH

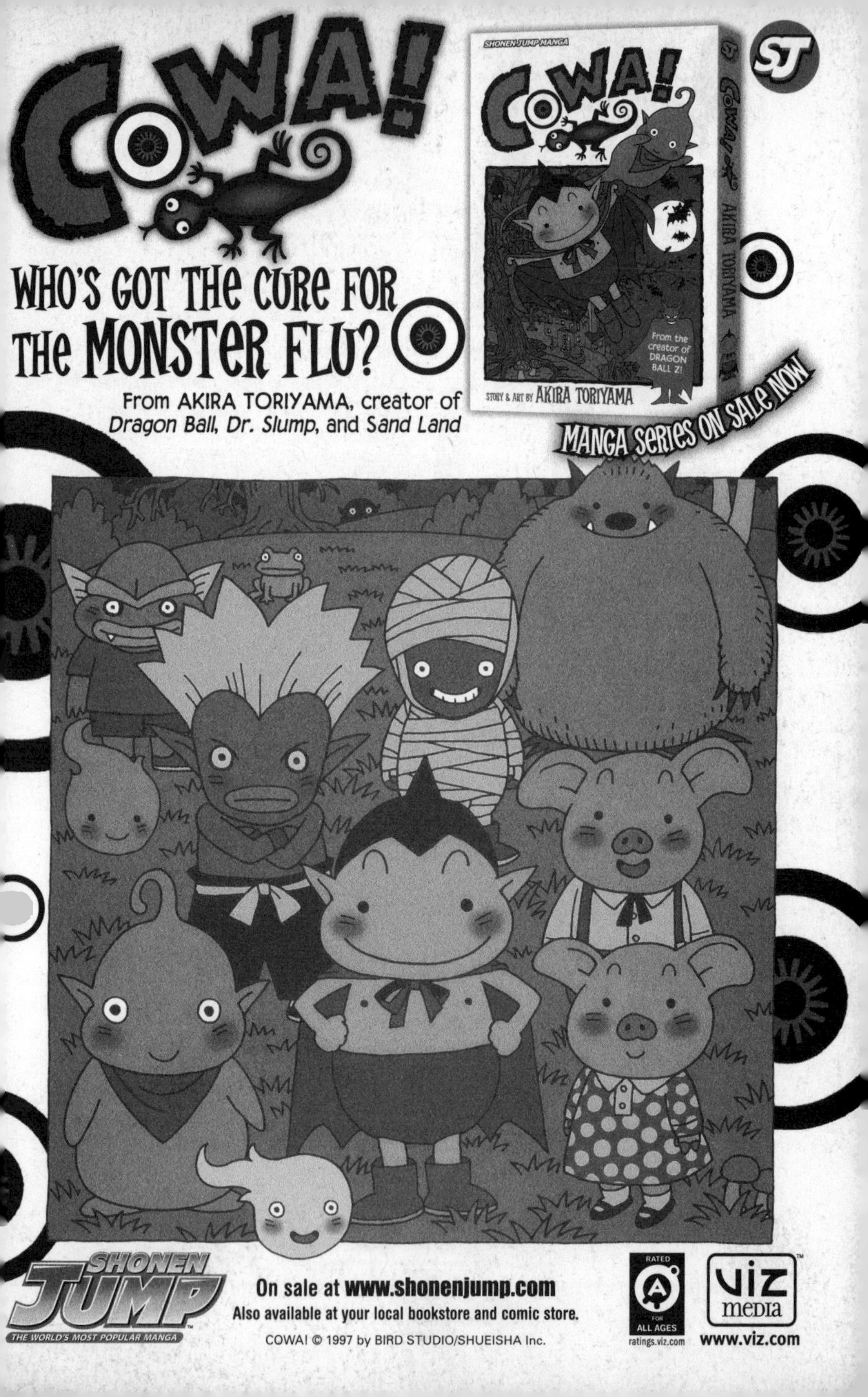
COWA!
WHO'S GOT THE CURE FOR THE MONSTER FLU?
From AKIRA TORIYAMA, creator of Dragon Ball, Dr. Slump, and Sand Land
SHONEN JUMP MANGA
COWA!
From the creator of DRAGON BALL Z!
STORY & ART BY AKIRA TORIYAMA
SJ
MANGA SERIES ON SALE NOW
SHONEN JUMP
THE WORLD'S MOST POPULAR MANGA
On sale at www.shonenjump.com
Also available at your local bookstore and comic store.
COWA! © 1997 by BIRD STUDIO/SHUEISHA Inc.
RATED A FOR ALL AGES
ratings.viz.com
viz media
www.viz.com

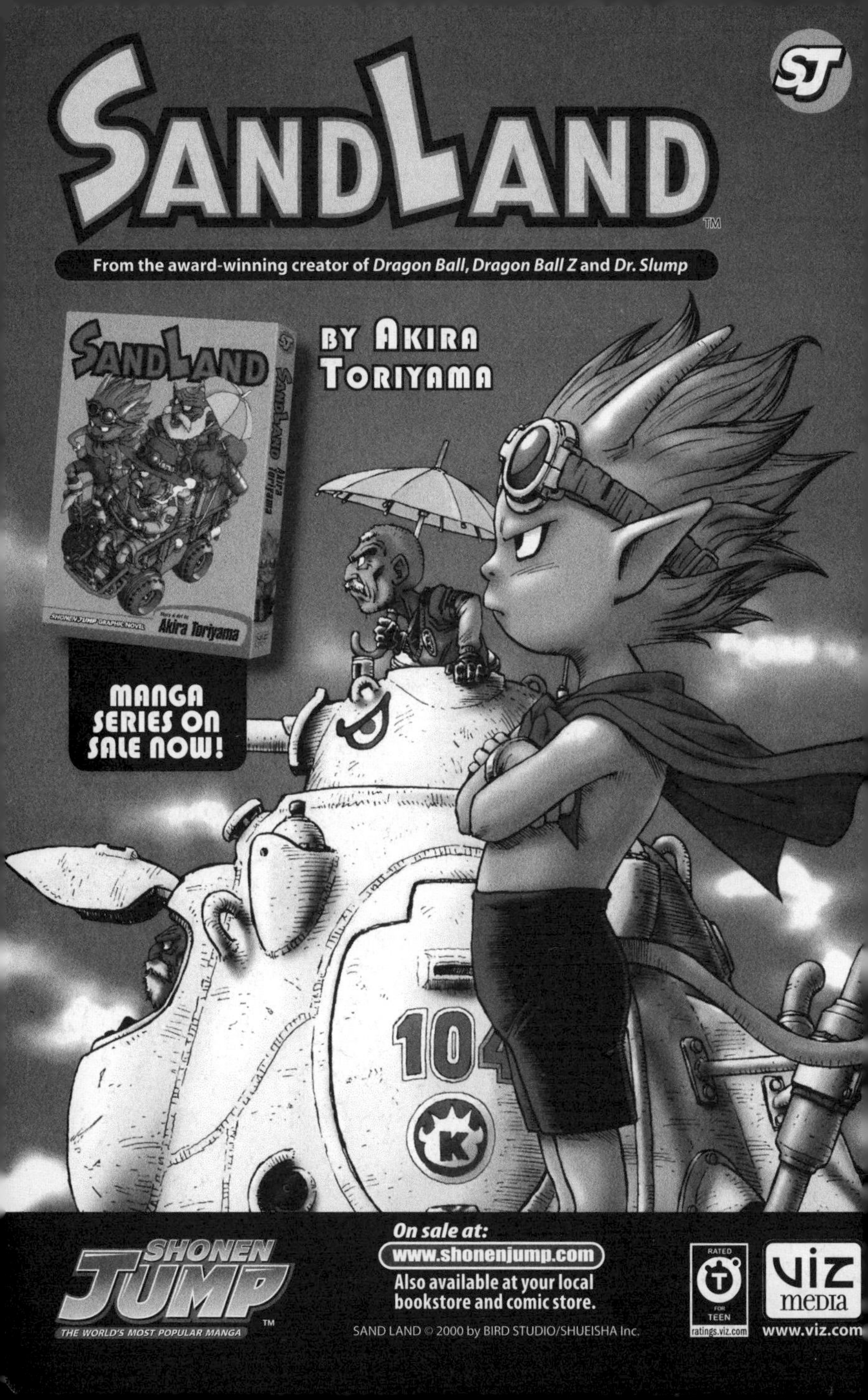

SAND LAND™
From the award-winning creator of Dragon Ball, Dragon Ball Z and Dr. Slump
BY AKIRA TORIYAMA
MANGA SERIES ON SALE NOW!
SHONEN JUMP
THE WORLD'S MOST POPULAR MANGA
On sale at:
www.shonenjump.com
Also available at your local bookstore and comic store.
SAND LAND © 2000 by BIRD STUDIO/SHUEISHA Inc.
RATED T FOR TEEN
ratings.viz.com
VIZ media
www.viz.com

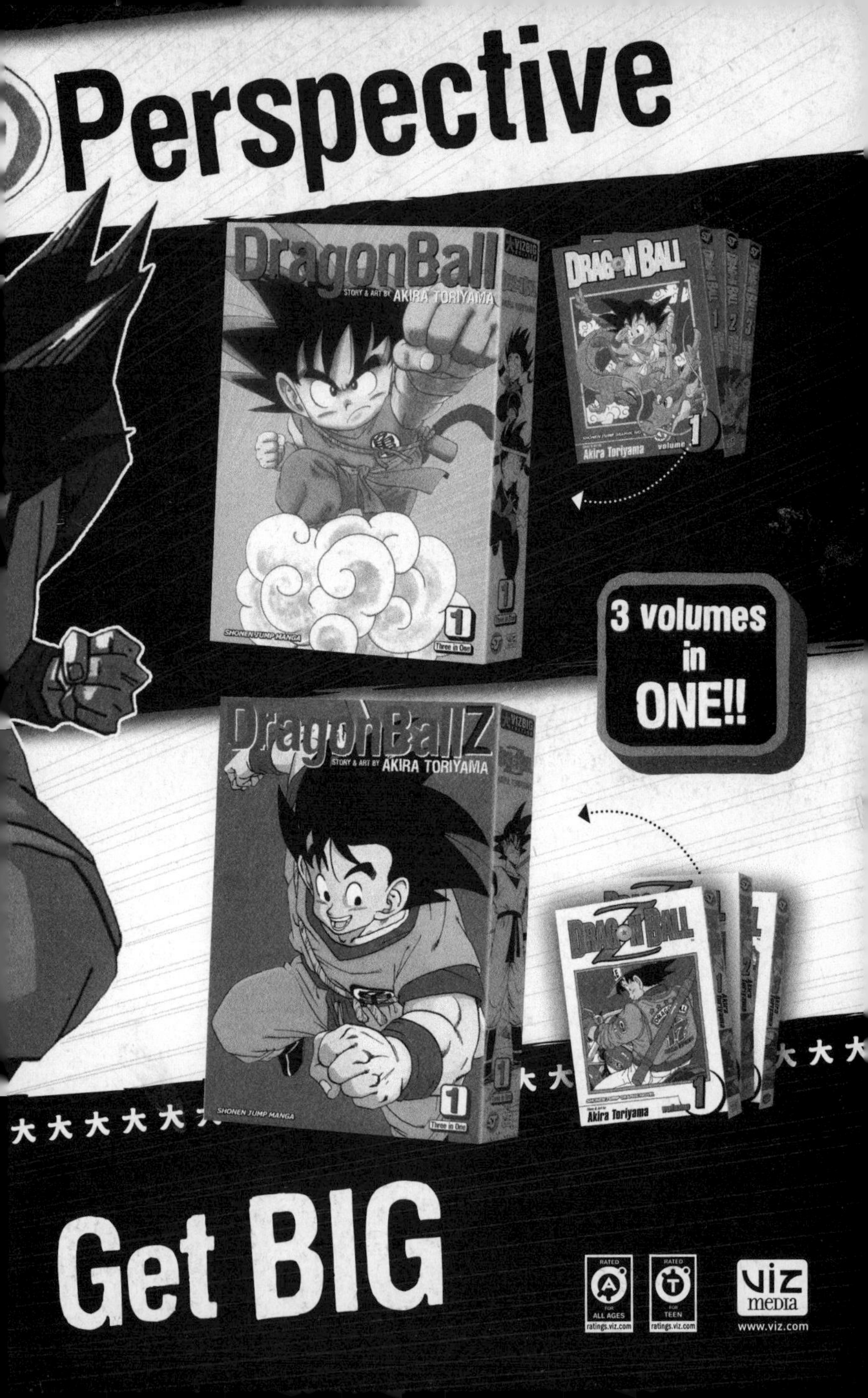
Perspective
DragonBall
STORY & ART BY AKIRA TORIYAMA
SHONEN JUMP MANGA
1
Three in One
DRAGON BALL
Akira Toriyama
volume 1
3 volumes
in
ONE!!
DragonBall Z
STORY & ART BY AKIRA TORIYAMA
SHONEN JUMP MANGA
1
Three in One
DRAGON BALL Z
Akira Toriyama
Get BIG
RATED A FOR ALL AGES ratings.viz.com
RATED T FOR TEEN ratings.viz.com
VIZ media
www.viz.com

The World's Greatest Manga
Now available on your iPad

Full of FREE previews and tons of new manga for you to explore

From legendary manga like *Dragon Ball* to *Bakuman*₀, the newest series from the creators of *Death Note*, the best manga in the world is now available on the iPad through the official VIZ Manga app.

- **Free App**
- **New content weekly**
- **Free chapter 1 previews**

 www.viz.co

You're Reading in the Wrong Direction!!

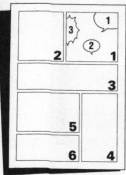

Whoops! Guess what? You're starting at the wrong end of the comic!

...It's true! In keeping with the original Japanese format, Akira Toriyama's world-famous **Dragon Ball Z** series is meant to be read from right to left, starting in the upper-right corner.

Unlike English which is read from left to right, Japanese is read from right to left, meaning that action, sound effects and word-balloon order are completely reversed... something which can make readers unfamiliar with Japanese feel pretty backwards themselves. For this reason, manga or Japanese comics published in the U.S. in English have traditionally been published "flopped"—that is, printed in exact reverse order, as though seen from the other side of a mirror.

By flopping pages, U.S. publishers can avoid confusing readers, but the compromise is not without its downside. For one thing, a character in a flopped manga series who, in the original Japanese version, wore a T-shirt emblazoned with "M A Y" (as in "the merry month of") now wears one which reads "Y A M"! Additionally, many manga creators in Japan are themselves unhappy with the process, as some feel the mirror-imaging of their art skews their original intentions.

In recognition of the importance and popularity of **Dragon Ball Z**, we are proud to bring it to you in the original unflopped format.

For now, though, turn to the other side of the book and let the adventure begin...!

—Editor